Welcome the Hour of Conflict

Welcome the Hour of Conflict

William Cowan McClellan and the 9th Alabama

EDITED BY JOHN C. CARTER

THE UNIVERSITY OF ALABAMA PRESS
Tuscaloosa

The University of Alabama Press
Tuscaloosa, Alabama 35487-0380
uapress.ua.edu

Hardcover edition published 2007.
Paperback edition published 2014.
eBook edition published 2009.

Typeface: Bembo

Manufactured in the United States of America
Cover illustration: *First Battle of Bull Run*, chromolithograph by Kurtz and Allison, 1889; courtesy of the Library of Congress
Cover design: Erin Bradley Dangar / Dangar Design

∞

The paper on which this book is printed meets the minimum requirements of American National Standard for Information Science–Permanence of Paper for Printed Library Materials, ANSI Z39.48-1984.

Paperback ISBN: 978-0-8173-5786-3
eBook ISBN: 978-0-8173-8143-1

A previous edition of this book has been catalogued by the Library of Congress as follows:
Library of Congress Cataloging-in-Publication Data
McClellan, William Cowan, 1839–1869.
Welcome the hour of conflict : William Cowan McClellan and the 9th Alabama / edited by John C. Carter.
p. cm.
Includes bibliographical references and index.
ISBN-13: 978-0-8173-1521-4 (cloth : alk. paper)
ISBN-10: 0-8173-1521-7 (alk. paper)
1. McClellan, William Cowan, 1839–1869—Correspondence. 2. Soldiers—Alabama—Correspondence. 3. Confederate States of America. Army. Alabama Infantry Regiment, 9th. 4. Alabama—History—Civil War, 1861–1865—Personal narratives. 5. Virginia—History—Civil War, 1861–1865—Personal narratives. 6. United States—History—Civil War, 1861–1865—Personal narratives, Confederate. 7. Alabama—History—Civil War, 1861–1865—Regimental histories. 8. United States—History—Civil War, 1861–1865—Regimental histories. 9. Virginia—History—Civil War, 1861–1865—Campaigns. 10. United States—History—Civil War, 1861–1865—Campaigns. I. Carter, John C. II. Title.
E551.59th .M33 2007
973.7'461092—dc22

2006017799

Contents

Illustrations

Maps

Acknowledgments and Dedication

I first heard of William Cowan McClellan while listening as a young boy to the stories my grandmother Carter told while on the front porch of her home in Pulaski, Tennessee. Nancy White Carter was not above stretching the truth a little bit about her favorite ancestor who was a veteran of Robert E. Lee's army. According to her, William was seven feet tall and was captured on the Round Tops at Gettysburg, where he was putting his size to use as a signalman. She also mentioned that he had been sent to prison and had written letters home to his family. As William had no further history presented in his behalf, I always assumed that he had died in prison. Over the years I had remembered bits and pieces of the story that would come back to mind whenever someone brought up the subject of the family in the Civil War, but I never took the time to look into it further.

Some years later, having developed an interest in the history of the early Virginia frontier and its explorers of the seventeenth century, I had attempted to figure out the exact routes that many of these explorers had taken in crossing through the Virginia Colony. After running out of seventeenth- and eighteenth-century sources, I turned to letters and journals of Civil War soldiers who served in the area hoping they might shed some light on the problem. While the effort was not productive, it did revive my interest in the Civil War, and from a new perspective of the soldier and not the battlefield. I remembered my grandmother's stories, and I wondered if the family still had the letters. About the same time, a visit to Gettysburg sent me scrambling to discover the regiment in which my ancestor had served.

A few years later at a Carter family reunion my aunt Polly Harwell Carter handed me a large shoe box tied up with a piece of string. She thought I might be interested in the contents of the box. Inside were photocopies of the Civil War letters of my great-great-grandfather

William Cowan McClellan. The letters had been saved by the McClellan family and were handed down from William's wife, Susan, to his daughter, Charlie, and then to her daughter, Nancy White Carter. Immediately I started browsing through the unorganized letters and quickly discovered that my ancestor had served in the 9th Alabama Regiment, was not captured at Gettysburg, was not in the signal corps, and had not spent the rest of the war in prison. Inside were copies of his letters dated after the battle of Gettysburg, including letters from Petersburg, Virginia, dated August 1864. This short investigation got me started on a long process of learning who this man really was, and who the McClellans were.

I had the opportunity to see the original letters at the home of my uncle and aunt, Robert and Jean Carter of Tullahoma, Tennessee, who have safeguarded them after my grandmother Carter passed away. Their sons, Robert Carter and William McClellan Carter (named after his ancestor) will carry on after them. Bob and Jean helped me search the Lincoln County, Tennessee, land records and the genealogical room at the Lincoln County Library, and they helped me find the Cane Creek section of the county where the McClellans used to live.

In Athens, Alabama, Philip Reyer of the Limestone County Archives was very helpful in going through the McClellan family files. Also in Athens, the staff at the George Smith Houston House and Library were a great help in locating information about the family. It was a delight to meet with Faye Acton Axford and Elva Bell McLin of Athens, from whom I learned more about Limestone County, Alabama. They were also very helpful in furnishing me with many leads on the McClellan family and providing copies of many original documents and letters.

Having discovered that William spent the last months of the war in Point Lookout Prison in St. Mary's County, Maryland, my wife and I set out to visit the prison site. The prison was located at the very tip of Point Lookout, where the Potomac River flows into the Chesapeake Bay. There is little left of the original prison, and the staff at the visitors' center sent us a few miles back up Route 5 to Leonardtown to look through the microfilms of the St. Mary's County Historical Society for the list of Confederate prisoners at Point Lookout. It was a rather poignant moment when, near the bottom of one of the last pages of the second reel the name "McClellan Wm C" jumped out of the page at us. We wanted more information, so we went to the National Archives in Washington, D.C., where we found his service file and some of the records of the 9th Alabama.

It was a great pleasure to meet Rear Adm. (Ret.) Thomas McClellan and his wife, Jane, who had been living in Alexandria, Virginia, and were also busy tracking down the McClellan family. We had been connected through my uncle Robert Carter, who had been given his name by Mrs. Flora Young, the daughter of Mrs. Mary White Hobbs of Fayetteville, Tennessee (whose grandmother was a sister of William Cowan McClellan). She had in her possession many of the family Bibles and letters. Through Admiral McClellan I found that Mrs. Hobbs had given some information to the Lincoln County, Tennessee, library and had donated a sizable number of family letters to the Southern Historical Collection in the Louis Round Wilson Library at the University of North Carolina at Chapel Hill. It took several trips to copy the letters in the rather extensive Buchanan-McClellan Papers, and John White and the staff there were very helpful. I was fortunate to learn more about Robert Anderson McClellan (the younger brother of William) from Thomas McClellan Ballentine, who is his great-great-grandson. Many of Robert's letters are in the Special Collections Library at Duke University in Durham, North Carolina.

Special thanks also go to the Alabama Department of Archives and History, Montgomery, Alabama (Norwood A. Kerr, Archival Reference); the late Robert Dunnavant Jr. of Athens, Alabama; the Fayetteville/Lincoln County Public Library, Fayetteville, Tennessee; the Fairfax County Archives—Circuit Court, Fairfax, Virginia; the George Mason University Library, Fairfax, Virginia; the Giles County Public Library, Pulaski, Tennessee; the Giles County Historical Society, Pulaski, Tennessee; the Historic Centreville Society, Centreville, Virginia; the Lincoln County Courthouse, Registrar's Office, Fayetteville, Tennessee; Lincoln County Historical Society, Fayetteville, Tennessee; the Loudoun County, Office of the Clerk of the Circuit Court, Leesburg, Virginia; the U.S. National Archives, Washington, D.C.; the North Carolina State Archives, Department of Cultural Resources, the Office of Archives and History, Raleigh, North Carolina; the Presbyterian Church, Department of History, Montreat, North Carolina; Rockingham County Public Library, Madison Branch, the Genealogical Room, Madison, North Carolina; the Rockingham County Court House, Wentworth, North Carolina; State Library of Pennsylvania, Harrisburg, Pennsylvania; the Thomas Balch Library, Leesburg, Virginia; the Tuscaloosa Public Library, Tuscaloosa, Alabama; and the Virginia Historical Society in Richmond, Virginia.

Special thanks to Dr. Joseph L. Harsh and Dr. Jane Turner Censer of the history department at George Mason University for reviewing the manuscript and for bringing more history to light for me at George Mason University. Thanks also to Robert K. Krick, chief historian at Fredericksburg and Spotsylvania Military Park, who read the early manuscript and encouraged me to develop it into a publishable form. Most of all I would like to thank my wife, Cathy Carter, for putting up with all of the McClellans and Carters (past and present) and for reviewing the manuscript and contributing many good ideas. She was there from the day I opened the box until the last word was written many years later.

While browsing through the shoe box at the family reunion, one more item caught my attention—it was the parole document for William Cowan McClellan, dated June 2, 1865, at Point Lookout, Maryland. It described him as having a light complexion, brown hair, and hazel eyes and said that he stood six feet five and one-half inches tall. That was close enough to seven feet. This is dedicated to the next generation of Carters, including my children Matt and Paige Carter, and to all of the Carter and McClellan women who always kept the story going.

Introduction

In June of 1861 a young Alabamian was caught up in the patriotic furor, "the rage militaire," that was sweeping Limestone County,[1] and along with many of his friends and neighbors, he rushed to join the Confederate army as a volunteer. Twenty-two-year-old William Cowan McClellan (born April 28, 1839; died December 9, 1869) was working on his father's farm along with his six brothers and sisters when Fort Sumter was attacked. Emotional ties to the old Republic quickly dissolved in Limestone County that spring, and any future plans that William had were put on hold for the duration of the war.

Many Southerners claimed to be fighting to preserve their right of self-government, which they felt the North was threatening to take away. They feared that they would also lose their American liberties, which would in turn lead to their own enslavement.[2] William was well versed in the political ideas and the current issues of his day, perhaps because of his father's political background. As one recent historian has observed, the majority of the volunteer soldiers were politically sophisticated and, as a result, they "would be more responsive to the issues in the conflict and would be convinced that they had a stake in the outcome. They would be more motivated to join up and stay the course until the issues were resolved."[3]

While that may have been true, William was more concerned at the beginning of the war simply to do his duty and perhaps to become a part of history. His was a naïve ideal that emphasized a soldier acting out a romantic concept of war that called for courage, godliness, manliness, and honor.[4] That ideal changed with the Union invasion of the Tennessee Valley in 1862, and his thoughts turned toward the safety of his family and efforts to prevent Limestone County from being enslaved by the Black Republican government—a goal that represented his own personal view of Southern liberty.

William Cowan McClellan was the first member of his family to enlist for service—an older and younger brother followed a year later. Earlier generations of McClellans had served in the militias of Tennessee and North Carolina, and his great-grandfather, William McClellan, had served as a captain of cavalry in Loudoun County, Virginia, during the American Revolution. Like William, many Confederate soldiers saw themselves as custodians of the American Revolution and believed they were fighting for the same liberty and republican values as their ancestors, as well as defending their homes and families from an invading foe.[5]

Most soldiers found it difficult to adjust to military discipline, especially the Southerners who saw it as a form of slavery.[6] William was no exception, and he found the first months of military life to be very demeaning socially and also very challenging physically. He didn't like taking orders from most of his officers, unless they were Mexican War veterans such as Cadmus M. Wilcox or Stonewall Jackson. William was forced to adjust from being a civilian to becoming a soldier, and that change formed a theme that ran throughout his letters. As the war went on, he took pride in enduring the physical hardships that he faced, as well as overcoming the lack of autonomy that most privates experienced. He also matured as a person as he took on the identity of a soldier, and the men in his company became his new world and one of the reasons he continued to fight so hard during the last year of the war.[7]

The McClellans were not native to Alabama. Like many Southerners, the family made their way into the Deep South over several generations, with each generation looking to improve its position by acquiring more land that was suitable for farming. William's great-grandfather William McClellan (II) was born about 1748, not long after his father, William (I), had come to Philadelphia, Pennsylvania, from Northern Ireland (I have added the numerical designations after each name because William Cowan McClellan's early ancestors had the same first name with no middle name). William (II) lived most of his adult life in Northern Virginia after his father moved the family from Pennsylvania and New Jersey south to Loudoun County. With the death of his parents a few years after the Revolutionary War, William (II) moved his own family to the Mayo River in Rockingham County, North Carolina, where he ran a mill on fifteen acres of land granted to him by the United States for his services during the Revolution. Seeking more available land, William's son, William (III), moved his family to Lincoln County, Tennessee, sometime after 1800. By 1813, he began farming along the banks of Cane Creek near Fayetteville. There he and his wife raised six children, including Thomas Joyce McClellan, the father of William Cowan McClellan.

Thomas McClellan worked as a surveyor, served in the Lincoln County militia, and was a respected member of the local Whig party. Thomas married Martha Fleming Beattie, who had grown up near the McClellans after her family had moved to Cane Creek from Williamson County, Tennessee. Thomas and Martha McClellan had seven children: daughters Sarah Anne (Sallie), Matilda, and Martha Catherine; and sons John, William, Robert, and Thomas. Thomas and Martha left Tennessee in 1844 for Limestone County, Alabama, where Thomas owned land that was granted to him by the United States government.

Limestone County, Alabama, is located in the Tennessee Valley, a wide and fertile valley formed by the Tennessee River where it makes a large bend in northern Alabama on its way to the Ohio River. The county lies along the Tennessee border due south of Giles County and Nashville, Tennessee, on land formerly occupied by the Creek, Cherokee, and Chickasaw Indians. The county was formed in 1818, and the county seat of Athens was confirmed in 1819, just one year before Alabama's statehood.

While not a part of Alabama's Black Belt, Limestone County still produced "a good deal of cotton," as William Cowan McClellan's brother Robert once noted, and "large sheds were built to receive and protect cotton awaiting shipment to New Orleans."[8] However, producing only about one-fourth of what Montgomery County, Alabama, produced, this was not a major cotton-producing region, but it was noted for its agriculture and large farms. The number of slaves had increased dramatically since 1820, and the 1860 Alabama census showed that Limestone County had 7,215 white residents and 8,091 black slaves.

Much of Limestone County's commerce was linked to the Tennessee River, which sent the county's cotton south to New Orleans; but it also received merchandise coming downriver from east Tennessee. The merchants of Athens were in touch with eastern markets as they traveled to Richmond, Philadelphia, and Baltimore to buy merchandise for their stores.[9] Railroad advocates such as Thomas Hubbard Hobbs and Luke Pryor worked for years to bring the railroad to Athens as part of a link between Louisville and New Orleans, and to tap into the prosperous economic opportunities that lay ahead for the developing region. The first trains ran in November 1860, one month before the secession convention.[10]

Thomas McClellan became a well-known and respected figure in Limestone County, where he served as a judge, a member of the Alabama House of Representatives, a representative to the Alabama Secession Convention, and a farmer with more than four hundred acres and eleven slaves. Politically, while Thomas had stronger ties to the tradition of the Union than many of the other Alabama planters and farmers, he included a variety of Limestone and Madison County politicians such as Gen. George S. Houston, Luke Pryor, Nicholas Davis Sr., Nicholas Davis Jr., Thomas H. Watts, Leroy Pope Walker, Thomas Hubbard Hobbs, and Lawrence Ripley Davis among his friends and political allies.

While he was a slaveholder himself, Thomas voted against immediate secession and even doubted how successful that effort would be. Along with the other northern Alabama delegates, he was outraged that a referendum had not been submitted to the people of Alabama after the vote for secession. While geography and politics contributed to northern Alabama's hesitation about secession, the background and ages of its leaders also played a role. As historian J. Mills Thornton notes, "leadership in the [secession] movement was passing to a group of younger ideologues. Many of these men came from relatively heavily populated and market-oriented communities."[11] Thomas McClellan and other rural and small-town politicians were seen more and more as conservative old fogies who were out of touch and clinging to an old-fashioned faith in the Union.

Thomas's views on secession did not make him an Alabama unionist and loyalist. Unionists tended to be open and vigorous opponents to the Confederacy, often serving as soldiers, spies, and partisan fighters.[12] Thomas actually served in the Alabama legislature during the war, and nothing in his letters indicates that he actively opposed the Confederacy. During the first year of the war, many unionists either left town or maintained a low profile—Thomas did neither. His stand against secession and his open profession of love for the old Union, however, may have caused others some concern as to his loyalty for the South. William never had this concern; whenever Union troops occupied Athens, William would write home to his father and ask him to "play" the Union man for them so the Northern soldiers would protect his property and family.

As a small planter, Thomas McClellan often spelled out his philosophy of life and business through his letters to business associates, family members, and friends. He likewise used his letters to inspire and control the behavior of his children—these tactics can be seen in many of his letters to William during the war. Thomas's stand against immediate secession, his love for the Union, and the hardships and uncertainty of the war challenged his own ideas about loyalty to the South, his social values, and his personal identity. It was difficult for him to watch three sons go off to fight in a war and for a cause that he thought was detrimental to the South. While he enjoyed seeing William grow as a man and a soldier during the war, he worried about what life would be like for him and the rest of the family after the war was over.

As the issue of secession was forced upon them, many citizens of the county, like the McClellans, faced difficult choices about their futures and the defense of their homeland. The homeland that William was sent to defend was Virginia, and not Alabama. This came as a surprise to him and many of the Alabamians who pictured themselves defending the Tennessee River Valley rather than the Potomac. William enthusiastically volunteered with the hope that he could cover himself in glory in what would be a short war. Like the other men in his company, William looked forward to testing his sense of duty and honor in battle, but he would wait nearly one year before he was able to do that on the Virginia Peninsula. Early in the second year of the war, however, many of these young men from Limestone County, Alabama, had "seen the elephant," and the romance was gone from battle. Additionally they were writing home and scouring newspapers for more information about the "Yankee" invasion of north Alabama. As the long war went on, the pull to go home and take care of their loved ones became very great.

Morale on the home front and on the battlefield was closely intertwined. The morale of the troops in the 9th Alabama was directly linked to their success on the battlefield and the safety and support of their loved ones back in Alabama. The letters William received from home helped to bolster his morale throughout most of the war, and, like many soldiers, he frequently complained of the lack of mail from home and was concerned that he was becoming the forgotten son. Many of the letters from his brothers and sisters reported on the daily life of the community and on the health of family members and friends. His brother Robert wrote of remembrances of old hunting trips with William, while his sister Matilda related scenes of current family life within the home. These letters were designed to assure William that everything at home was still about the same. His father generally wrote letters that contained advice on how William should conduct himself as a man and a soldier, and that kept him abreast of political, military, and social events and issues in Limestone County.

At the beginning of the war, people in Limestone County were willing to sacrifice many daily essentials in order to supply the soldiers with clothing and food for the battlefield. The women were expected to keep up the morale on the home front by working for the cause and maintaining a cheery disposition. They were also expected to transmit this high morale to the battlefield by writing uplifting letters to the soldiers. In addition to sending their men into battle, they convinced deserters to return to their units and encouraged bravery in battle for the soldiers at the front lines. William's sister Matilda wrote many letters of this type at the beginning of the war. In an early letter, she wrote, "I know it makes you happy to receive letters from your own beautiful home in the 'Sunny South' the whole tone of which is 'stand by your colors.'"

The McClellan family's morale depended heavily on William's well-being and on the success of the Alabama forces on the battlefields of Virginia. As the Army of Northern Virginia won victory after victory in the first half of the war, morale soared both on the battlefield and at home where these achievements helped to compensate for the Confederate losses in the west. Morale at home correspondingly dropped in response to disappointing military campaigns such as Sharpsburg and Gettysburg, and it disappeared altogether by the end of the war.

The "beautiful home" and "Sunny South" mentioned by Matilda would be threatened by a Union army that occupied Athens and Limestone County in 1862. While there was an occasional respite from occupation, this area mostly remained under Union control throughout the war, which caused great anxiety for the Limestone troops in Virginia. As the war dragged on, the sacrifices required of the women and their families became too great. Most families had experienced the death or the wounding of a loved one, and with shortages and plundering by soldiers on both sides, they were finding it difficult to make ends meet. The McClellans were lucky; only one of three sons was seriously wounded during the war, and their home was not visited by soldiers until late in the war.

As life got harder and darker for the McClellans in 1863, William's morale sagged somewhat. Although he never thought of quitting his company to go home to help his family, he was constantly concerned for their welfare and sought a transfer home to be closer to them. This request was nothing new, as William had been seeking a transfer to a cavalry company in Alabama since the beginning of the war, especially after he saw how glamorous that service was. Despite the Confederate reversals of fortune after Gettysburg, William's morale remained surprisingly good throughout the last year of the war around Petersburg. Even though the outlook was gloomy for the Confederate States, William continued to fight for Robert E. Lee and for his comrades around him, many of whom had been with the company and the regiment since the beginning of the war.

William spent the entire Civil War as a private in the 9th Alabama Regiment, serving in the Army of the Shenandoah before the First Battle of Manassas, and the Army of the Potomac and the Army of Northern Virginia from Centreville to Sayler's Creek. After being on the front lines during the Peninsula Campaign, William missed the Second Battle of Manassas and Sharpsburg due to illness. Not long afterward he was detailed to provost guard duty at Richard H. Anderson's division headquarters, where he remained for the rest of the war. Toward the end of 1864, William mentioned in a letter that the provost guard was probably going to be broken up, and when it happened, he spent the last months of the war back with Company F and the 9th Alabama Regiment.

Throughout the war William was able to observe close at hand many of the notable commanding officers of Lee's army, including Joseph E. Johnston, P. G. T. Beauregard, Thomas Jonathan (Stonewall) Jackson, James Longstreet, Cadmus M. Wilcox, Richard H. Anderson, Edmund Kirby Smith, Ambrose Powell Hill, and William Mahone. His opinion of each rose and fell during the war, generally depending upon their success on the battlefield and their military bearing that he observed while they were in the camps. His belief in a particular officer was the same as his belief in his friends: he put his trust in a man until he did something to let William or the army down—whether it was the whole army or just the 9th Alabama Regiment.

Before there was a 9th Alabama, there were Companies F and H from Limestone County. Company F, raised by its captain, Thomas Hubbard Hobbs, left Athens, Alabama, by train on June 6, 1861, and Company H, raised by Gen. George S. Houston and led by his son, David, followed a week later. With all of the companies assembled at Richmond, Virginia, the 9th Alabama Regiment was officially formed on June 26, 1861, with more than one thousand officers and men enlisting for three years or for the war. Of the ten companies that made up the 9th Alabama, eight were from the northern counties along the Tennessee River and the remaining two were from Mobile and Butler County in south Alabama.

Company Name	Company	Captain	Home County
Beauregard Rifles	Co. A	F. H. Ripley	Mobile, Alabama
Railroad Guards	Co. B	Jere Williams	Marshall County
Pope Walker Guards	Co. C	J. C. Warren	Lawrence County
Lauderdale Rifles	Co. D	J. Butler Houston	Lauderdale County
Sons of Liberty	Co. E	Horace King	Morgan County
Limestone Troopers	Co. F	Thomas Hubbard Hobbs	Limestone County
Jeff Davis Rangers	Co. G	E. Y. Hill	Butler County
Limestone Greys	Co. H	David Houston	Limestone County
Calhoun Guards	Co. I	D. W. Gillis	Lauderdale County
Marshall Boys	Co. K	James L. Sheffield	Marshall County

While William had contact with other companies in the 9th, most of his letters centered around the two Limestone County companies in which he served—first in Company H, and then in Company F. He had known many of these men since childhood, and many of them lived close enough to the McClellans to be counted as neighbors. They experienced early military life together through drilling, picket duty, skirmishing, work details, messes, and general camp life. How a man conducted himself in camp and in battle was very important for, as William found out later, someone in the company was always talking about his fellow soldiers to the people back home.

Records showed that eighty-four of the more than two hundred enlisted men and officers of the two Limestone County companies were farmers, seven were students, six were teachers, three were clerks, two were doctors, and one was a jockey. Of these men, 120 were between the ages of 18 and 21, with the oldest being 53. By the end of the war, 363 men had served in the two companies: 77 were killed or had died of various causes, 120 were wounded, 55 were captured, and 74 left the companies early (discharge, desertion, absence).[13] On September 25, 1864, William McClellan wrote home that only twenty-two men remained in Company F, and that only one man remained in Company H (and that man had elected himself the captain of the company).

The men of Companies F and H of the 9th Alabama began the war inauspiciously. After being rushed from Richmond to Winchester, Virginia, to meet the growing Union threat to the Shenandoah Valley, they saw no action. Many of the men in the regiment came down with measles either in camp or en route to Winchester, which may be why the 9th was placed at the end of the line of march from Winchester to Piedmont Station. As a result, they ended up on the last train to Manassas and missed the First Battle of Manassas by a day.

For the next nine months they drilled, went on picket duty, and built fortifications while they waited for another chance to participate in a battle. The Battle of Williamsburg in May 1862 not only gave them that chance but earned them laurels for their assault on a Union battery near the lines of Fort Magruder. The 9th's conspicuous performance was commended in reports by Gen. Ambrose Powell Hill and Gen. J. E. B. Stuart. William would be wounded at the Battle of Seven Pines, and the 9th would be heavily involved in the Seven Days Battles. One of the regiment's finest moments came at Gaines's Mill during the charge of Cadmus M. Wilcox's brigade late in the day—the charge that General Wilcox later claimed was the one that first broke the Union line. The battles that William and his comrades had longed for in 1861 were now coming on a monthly basis and would not let up until late fall.

During the Second Battle of Manassas, the 9th acted in a reserve role in supporting A. P. Hill's division. They later participated in the capture of

Harpers Ferry and took casualties in Piper's Orchard during the fighting at Sharpsburg. In 1863 they saw action in the defense of Fredericksburg, and perhaps their greatest moment of the war came during the Chancellorsville campaign in May. The day after Stonewall Jackson turned the Union right flank at Chancellorsville, the 9th was in the thick of the fighting near Fredericksburg at Salem Church, where they helped to repel the Union offensive threatening Lee's right flank. At Gettysburg, the 9th arrived on the field of battle late on the first day, July 1, and General Lee sent them into camp instead of the battle. On the second day they participated in the assault by Gen. Richard H. Anderson's division on the portion of Cemetery Ridge near the Wheatfield. They were a part of the Wilcox brigade in its abortive attempt to support Pickett's charge toward the close of that action on the third day. The 9th went on to see action later in 1863 at the Wilderness and Spotsylvania. In the summer of 1864, the regiment entered the trenches on the right flank of the Confederate line at Petersburg, Virginia, and joined Gen. William Mahone's division as they counterattacked through the Crater after the mine explosion on July 30.

With the fall of Richmond on April 2, 1865, William and the remainder of the 9th marched to Farmville with Mahone's division, only to be rushed back to Sayler's Creek to hold back the Union forces after the Confederate defeat. Several days later, the last seventy-five men from the 9th Alabama surrendered at Appomattox. William McClellan had endured the march from Richmond, but he was not one of the seventy-five who surrendered. He was captured at Sayler's Creek and spent the next two months at Point Lookout Prison in Maryland.

At the end of the war, more than 1,650 men had served in the 9th Alabama Regiment; 732 of those men were killed in battle, died from wounds or illness, were captured, were discharged, or had deserted. Hundreds of others, not in the above-mentioned 732, remained on the muster rolls at the end of the war but were not with the regiment at Appomattox.

Returning home to a land economically devastated by war and occupation, William married Susan Strong, and the couple quickly started their family with two daughters, Charlie and Willie. William resumed farming on land that he and his wife purchased just after his return, but he did not have long to live. In December 1869 he showed symptoms of what appeared to be a continuation of the back and kidney problems that had plagued him throughout the war. He died at his father's house that month.

William was an average soldier, playing no great role in the war, and he elected to remain a private throughout the conflict. He was better educated than most men and had the ability to write and report effectively on what he observed. Throughout the war he penned hundreds of letters, often writing for friends who could not write back home to their loved ones. In his own letters, William commented on his feelings toward his commanding officers, his attitude toward military discipline and camp life, his disdain for the western Confederate armies, and his hopes and fears for the future of the Confederacy. The periodic rise and fall of Confederate morale during the war is also evident in his letters. By subscribing to Virginia newspapers and reading the newspapers sent to him from home, he was able to keep up with current events on a national level and discuss the impact they had on the war. William gave vivid descriptions of camp life, sickness and disease in the army, marches, picket duty, battles, and local communities, as well as an eyewitness account of the execution of two Louisiana soldiers at Centreville in 1861. His letters were full of information on the war, but they were also full of humor and warmth. The letters between William and his family show not only the love and the strength of a family separated by war but also the personal and social values that defined a Southern planter's family.

In this book, the letters are organized chronologically and are divided by the major campaigns of the war in the east. At the beginning of each chapter, I have provided a brief look at the home front in Alabama and at the front line in Virginia. As in most collections of Civil War letters, there are more letters from 1861 than from any other year, with the volume declining each year. This is largely due to the fact that the soldiers had more time on their hands during the beginning of the war. As the amount of military action increased, they found less time for writing. During the final year of the war, soldiers also likely wrote many letters that either were never mailed or didn't survive the final battles. Sending and receiving letters became more and more difficult as communications back home were failing and fewer soldiers were moving back and forth between the battlefront and home. Beginning with the Battle of the Wilderness in May 1864, the battles became so frequent and furious that many soldiers wrote fewer letters home and included less information and descriptions of the battles.

In one of his letters early in the war, William asked his brother if he was able to read the letters since William was writing them in pencil—he was concerned that the writing might rub out. Ironically the letters that were written in pencil were among the best preserved and the easiest to read of all the letters. Considering that William often wrote on the back of his haversack or on narrow wooden boards by the dim light of a candle, it is remarkable that the letters are as legible as they are. Many of the letters are very well written; however, when William wrote "in great haste" or in unfavorable conditions, his letters were plagued with misspellings and occasionally by unconnected ideas. His writing style remained the same over time, although the subject matter changed as the war itself changed.

During the first year of the war, William's letters focused on describing his military experience to his family and assuring them that he and the members of his company were all right. He also inquired about family and friends back home and waxed eloquently about his sense of duty and how he would face the trials of the coming battle. After he experienced battle on the Virginia Peninsula in 1862, he turned mostly to reporting the military situation in Virginia and to relating the various battles in which the 9th Alabama participated. After Gettysburg, he continued to focus on the military situation intermixed with camp life. He seemed to place little value on the loss at Gettysburg, and judging by the tone of his letters, his morale remained good despite the gloomy outlook for the Confederacy. The few letters that came out of 1864 continued to present his old company and the regiment as fit and willing to fight despite the casualties and the desertions. Like most soldiers, he did not dwell on the details of the late battles; however, he went to great lengths in his coverage of the Battle of the Crater at Petersburg in July 1864.

The majority of the letters (64 percent) are from William to his father and to his brother Robert. Most of the letters sent to William from home came from his father, his brother Robert, and his sister Matilda. Surprisingly, there are no known letters from his mother. William wrote his letters to family members to let them know what was going on at the front and to impress upon them that not only was he well but he was growing as a man and a soldier. William was also looking ahead to the end of the war when he wrote home asking his family to save his letters from the front in case he wanted to have them for his memoirs.

William's father, Thomas, represents a key figure in the letters. The planter was at the center of the identity and the social values of the family, and Thomas used his letters to sustain family relationships and the bond that kept the family together, despite the distance or the circumstances of its separation. The letters to and from William formed two parts of a conversation that, as one historian put it, "became a transcript of a family's life."[14] This could be seen in the way that William wrote slightly different variations of the same letter to different family members. He tried to impress his father by proving he had grown as a soldier and a man; to his mother he would relate camp events and request items that he needed at the front; to his sisters he would report the events of the war, but not in the detail he would save for the letters to his brothers. Personal identity, social values, and gender differences dictated how William communicated information and commentary in his letters.

I have tried to identify persons and places mentioned in the letters in the endnotes, and descriptions of immediate family members will be found at the end of this introduction. Members of Companies F and H of the 9th Alabama Regiment are listed in a roster in the appendices.

I have retained the original spelling and grammar of the letters, except when clarification was essential for an understanding of the passage. I have added words in brackets when they are necessary for clarification or correction. At times William used commas instead of periods to separate sentences, and he occasionally failed to capitalize the first letter of a new sentence. To prevent confusion, I have occasionally added punctuation in brackets. Where words or sentences are illegible in the manuscript, I have inserted "[illegible]." In some of the letters William used dashes and underlines as flourishes or embellishments, which I have retained. Proper names are sometimes misspelled ("Steward" for Stuart, "Boregard" for Beauregard), and I have initially identified the proper spelling in brackets. Occasionally William refers to a young lady back home as "Miss" with a dash instead of her last name; I have so indicated with an underline.

Family and Friends Who Corresponded with William Cowan McClellan

Thomas Joyce McClellan

Thomas (born July 2, 1811, in Rockingham County, North Carolina; died October 14, 1887, in Limestone County, Alabama) was William's father. He was married on January 14, 1836, to Martha Fleming Beattie in Lincoln County, Tennessee.[15] Thomas was a farmer, a livestock dealer, a judge, a state representative, and a member of the Alabama constitutional convention. A leading Whig in Lincoln County, Tennessee, before his move to Limestone County, Alabama, in 1844, he was opposed to secession from the Union but felt he should support his home state. William was concerned that his father would be labeled a "Union man" and would be subject to retribution. Thomas was a descendant of Scotch-Irish immigrants who came to New Jersey and Pennsylvania in 1740 from Northern Ireland.

Martha Fleming Beattie McClellan

Martha (born August 19, 1808, in Williamson County, Tennessee; died June 30, 1883, in Limestone County, Alabama) was William's mother. Martha, originally from Williamson County, Tennessee, met Thomas in Lincoln

County, Tennessee, after her family moved into the Cane Creek area of the county.[16] She had several brothers still living in Tennessee who were mentioned in the letters: David M. Beattie, Josiah Beattie, William B. (Berry) Beattie, and Andrew M. Beattie.

John Beattie McClellan

John (born November 25, 1836, in Lincoln County, Tennessee; died April 21, 1917, in Limestone County, Alabama) was William's oldest brother. John joined the 26th-50th Alabama Regiment on September 17, 1861, and was promoted on July 10, 1862, to captain of Company H. He left the company after he lost an arm at the Battle of Murfreesboro, Tennessee, in 1862. In 1864, he may have been serving with a partisan ranger company in northern Alabama. Before the war he was a teacher but afterward became probate judge for Limestone County (1864–66) and a state representative (1863–65). John married Elizabeth Hussey after the war.[17]

Sarah Anne (Sallie) McClellan Davis

Sallie (born January 24, 1841, in Lincoln County, Tennessee; died July 15, 1891, in Limestone County, Alabama) was William's oldest sister. She married Lawrence Ripley Davis in 1860 and had eleven children: Sue, Etta, Williametta, Bessie, Kate, Mae, Aurora, Annie, Robert, Tommy, and Ripley Jr. Their oldest daughter was Susan Lowe Davis (1861–1939). Sue, or "Little Sue," is mentioned frequently in the letters. She was a familiar figure on Capitol Hill and was the author of *Authentic History: Ku Klux Klan, 1865–1877*.[18]

Robert Anderson (Bob) McClellan

Robert (born October 24, 1843, in Lincoln County, Tennessee; died July 27, 1898, in Athens, Alabama) was William's younger brother. He was his father's right-hand man on the farm during the first year of the war while Thomas was away in Montgomery. Before the war, Robert attended Petersburg Academy in Lincoln County, Tennessee. On September 15, 1862, he joined Company C of the 7th Alabama Cavalry (it later became the 9th) and served with distinction as a lieutenant in Company I and captain.[19] Robert returned home after the war and became an attorney. Later he served one term in the Alabama senate; became the mayor of Athens, Alabama; served as editor of the *Athens Herald,* and was a member of the Alabama constitutional convention of 1875. He married Aurora Pryor of Athens, Alabama, on February 7, 1872. His son Thomas Cowan McClellan served as an associate justice of the Alabama Supreme Court.

Matilda McClellan

Matilda (born February 5, 1845, in Limestone County, Alabama; died July 27, 1917, in Fayetteville, Tennessee) was William's middle sister and his most frequent female correspondent. During the war, Matilda helped the family on the farm. She never married and lived on the family farm until just after her father's death in 1887. She continued to reside in Athens, Alabama, until late in her life, when she went to live with her sister Martha Catherine McClellan Buchanan in Fayetteville, Tennessee. Matilda was an excellent writer and was educated at the Female Academy in Athens. She worked as a legal clerk for two of her brothers and kept their records and papers after their deaths. The care and the survival of so many McClellan family letters can be attributed to Matilda.[20]

Martha Catherine (Kittie) McClellan Buchanan

Martha Catherine (born July 19, 1848, in Limestone County, Alabama; died June 7, 1931, in Fayetteville, Tennessee) was William's youngest sister. When the war broke out, Martha Catherine was still attending school. Martha Catherine married Felix Grundy Buchanan (major of the 1st Tennessee Provisional Regiment) of Fayetteville, Tennessee, at her father's home on May 19, 1874. The Buchanans were close friends of the McClellans when they lived in Lincoln County, Tennessee.[21]

Thomas Nicholas (Tom Nick) McClellan

Thomas (born February 23, 1853, in Limestone County, Alabama; died February 10, 1906, in Limestone County, Alabama) was William's youngest brother. Thomas was too young to serve during the war. He was educated in the county schools and at Oak Hill College,[22] and was awarded his LLB in law from Cumberland University in Lebanon, Tennessee. Thomas practiced law with his brother Robert in Athens. He was registrar in the chancery of Limestone County (1874–76); a state senator (1880–83); state attorney general (1884–89); and associate justice (1889–98) and chief justice (1898–1906) of the Alabama Supreme Court. Thomas never married.

Lawrence Ripley (Rip, L. R.) Davis

Rip Davis was the son of Nicholas Davis of Walnut Grove, an early settler and leader in Limestone County, and the older brother of Nicholas Davis Jr. Rip Davis was a member of the Alabama House of Representatives in 1849–50, 1859–60, and 1861; and he served as personal secretary to Gov. George S. Houston. He edited the *Limestone News* and the *Athens Post*. He married William McClellan's sister Sarah Anne, whom he often called "Mrs. Davis" in his letters.

Nicholas Davis Jr.

Nicholas (born 1825; died 1874) was a son of Capt. Nicholas Davis and a cooperationist who represented Madison County in the Alabama Secession Convention and voted against secession. The Davis family lived near the McClellans, whom they considered close friends. Nicholas Davis attempted to raise a regiment in Huntsville in September 1861, and several companies, including the Limestone Rebels, were formed into the 2nd Alabama Battalion (later they became Davis's 5th Alabama Battalion, and eventually the 26th-50th Alabama Infantry Regiment).[23]

1

Preparing for War: Alabama to Richmond

January 14–June 20, 1861

> We have met for the last time under the government of the United States.
>
> —Thomas Joyce McClellan

Four days after South Carolina seceded from the Union on December 20, 1860, Alabama governor A. B. Moore called for the election of delegates from all the counties of the state to attend the Alabama Secession Convention in Montgomery starting on January 7. On January 6, 1861, Thomas Joyce McClellan arrived in Montgomery by train from Limestone County, along with Nicholas Davis from Madison County. Elected by the citizens of northern Alabama, they were two of the "cooperationist" delegates who were not in favor of immediate secession. Few of these delegates actually opposed secession, but the north Alabama faction was competing for power within the state Democratic party by taking a stance that opposed the south Alabamians' position on secession. Led by William Lowndes Yancey, the south Alabamians were attempting to push through the convention an ordinance of secession that would immediately take Alabama out of the Union. As one historian has observed, the cooperationists' real objective "was to raise doubts in the popular mind about the extent to which immediate secession was a carefully considered response to the threat. Yancey's opponents wished to make it appear a hasty, radical proposal, generated by emotion and replete with concealed pitfalls."[1] The delegates from the northern counties (Limestone, Madison, Jackson, Lawrence, Morgan, Marshall, and DeKalb) led a strong effort to oppose immediate secession, and they looked for ways to preserve slavery and Southern institutions while keeping Alabama from finding itself alone and out of the Union.

Attitudes toward secession may have also been shaped by both cooperationists and secessionists who attempted to determine the possibilities for securing redress of their political grievances and for guaranteeing their rights as citizens in the Union.[2] Age may also have played a factor, as "older" delegates such as Thomas McClellan found themselves in opposition to younger delegates who became the proponents of the secession movement. Rather than just being a cooperationist, Thomas McClellan was guided by a more Reconstructionist Union sentiment.

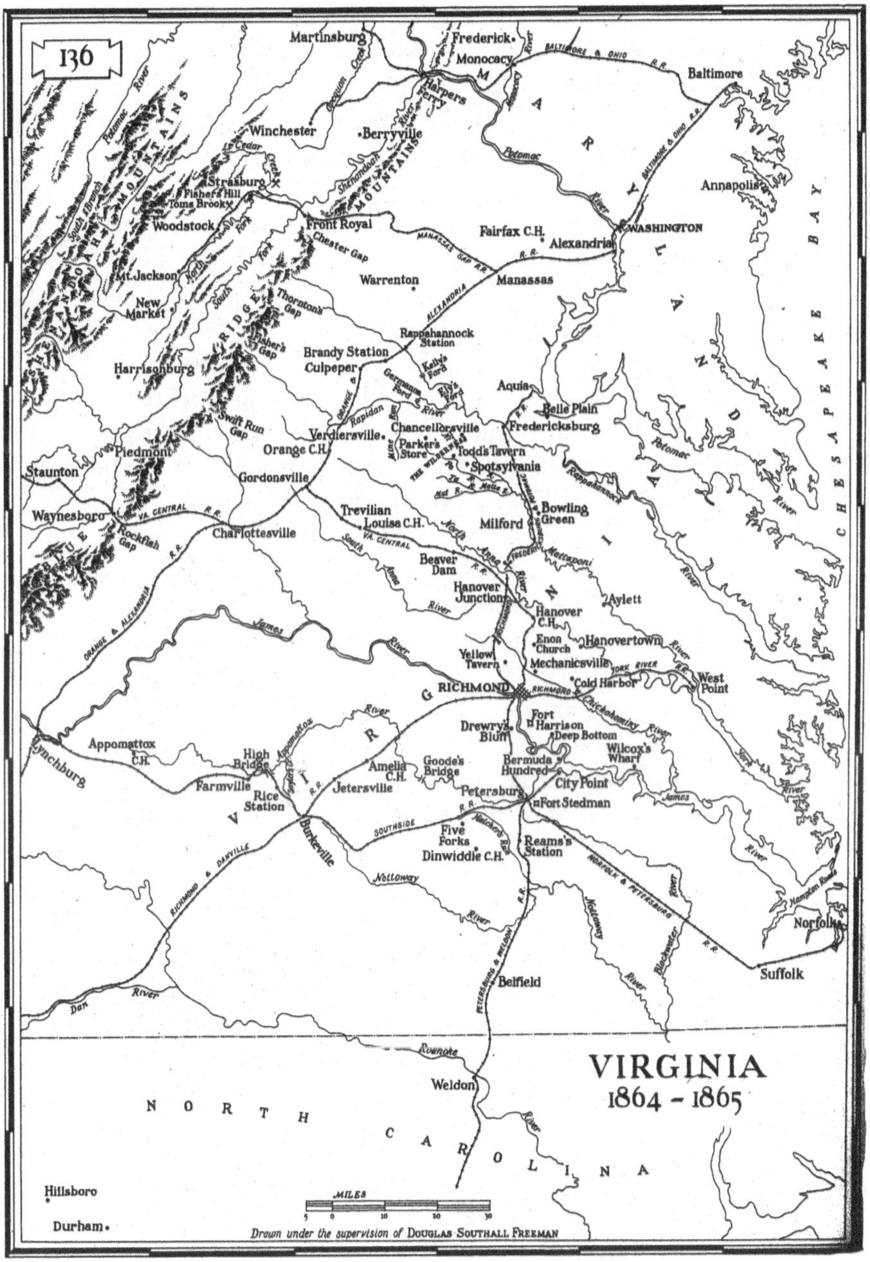

Virginia, 1864–1865

Despite the efforts of the cooperationists, on January 14, Alabama voted for secession by a vote of sixty-one to thirty-nine. Thirty-three of the dissenting delegates (including Thomas McClellan) issued an address to the people of Alabama declaring that the ordinance of secession should have been submitted to the people for their ratification or rejection.[3] The day the convention ended, Thomas McClellan wrote home to his wife, Martha:

> We have met for the last time under the government of the United States. I have no language to express my feelings when the new flag was unfurled in the Capital, to see a large crowd of both men and women transported with joy at such an event, without seeming to have no regret for the old stars and stripes . . . but it is as I conceive now, the duty of all good citizens to uphold and support the State in the action it has taken as it is the only government we have got . . . I see no other course but to submit to it, we must not do anything that would look like any willingness on our part to submit to the policy of the black republican party. You I know will feel as accutly as I do the necessity of separating from the land of our birth and the graves of our ancestors, and the only thing that makes the thought of it supportable is the hope that we may be again reunited.[4]

Thomas returned to Limestone County and found a county in complete opposition to the conclusion of the convention. A week after the convention, the people of Athens, Alabama, raised the Union flag over the courthouse and vowed to meet any traitors head-on. All efforts at harmony failed until the firing on Fort Sumter in April 1861, and then, as Capt. Thomas Hubbard Hobbs[5] stated, "never did a political sentiment die so speedily a death as that of reconstruction has died in North Alabama."[6] With the outbreak of hostilities, Union sympathizers faded into the background as a silent minority until the Union occupation of northern Alabama in 1862. Like many Southern people, Alabamians became very sensitive to Union rhetoric, and the election of Lincoln had already galvanized their criticism. The firing on Sumter spurred the South into action, and emotions ran high as former opponents to immediate secession turned toward it to oppose Northern coercion. The South, however, may have moved too quickly and was not prepared for the coming conflict. Historian Clement Eaton believes that the South did not weigh the chances of war and acted largely on a wave of resentment and an artificial sense of honor.[7]

As sentiment in north Alabama changed, regiments of volunteers were raised by local politicians such as Thomas Hubbard Hobbs and George S.

Houston,[8] who relied on the idea of glory and the prospect of a short, winnable war to recruit young men to join the Southern cause and head for battlefields far from home. The local fairground opened for the Limestone County volunteers to receive minimal military instruction before taking the trains to Virginia. As the volunteers trained, Thomas McClellan turned his attention to working for the new Confederacy when he joined the Alabama legislature. And he watched as three of his sons went off to the war.

The spring of 1861 was a time for young men to separate from their families and come to grips with the military way of life. Pvt. William McClellan hoped he would be able to go into battle and lay his life on the line so that after the war he could be proud of the part he played in Southern independence. Many soldiers and civilians viewed the coming war as a second American Revolution, and they saw themselves in the same light as their grandfathers and great-grandfathers. Trains from Alabama, Mississippi, and Tennessee were formed to deliver troops to Virginia. Lt. Col. Edmund Kirby Smith was sent by the Confederate government on May 3 to Lynchburg, Virginia, to coordinate the arrival of the troops and get them quickly on to Richmond.[9] Confederate officials were concerned about the small number of troops in Virginia as they watched the growing number of Union forces along the banks of the Potomac. The best intelligence pointed toward an invasion through Fairfax County or through the Shenandoah Valley of Virginia.

William McClellan prepared to leave for the war as a member of the Limestone Greys, a local company (Company H) commanded by Capt. David Houston,[10] the son of Gen. George S. Houston of Athens, Alabama. At the same time Thomas Hobbs organized his own company, the Limestone Troopers, which would later become Company F. On June 3, 1861, Hobbs moved his company into camp at Clem's Spring, which was about six and one-half miles northeast of Athens, and one of the finest springs in the region. They had quickly moved there from the fairgrounds, because it was located too close to Athens and the railroad line, and many of the men had been leaving camp to go home in the evenings.

While the Limestone companies drilled, George Houston was becoming concerned that the secretary of war, Leroy Pope Walker,[11] had not called for the local volunteers to be received into military service. Walker replied that he would be glad to accept the companies if they would provide their own arms; and he told Houston, when they had arms, to send the companies on to Richmond and their transportation would be paid for by the Confederacy.[12] The call for the companies to leave the Athens area came on June 4.

June 6 was the last day in Athens for Company F, as they were finally on their way to Richmond, Virginia. (Company H would leave several days later.) Captain Hobbs described June 6 as "a very sad day, and one which impressed its sadness on the most thoughtless of the company . . . For myself I feel nothing but an imperious sense of duty could justify my leaving home at this time. But, having been connected with a military company for nearly two years in time of peace, I thought it unbecoming me to play citizen in war."[13] Later, the *Athens Banner* reported the departure of Company F from Limestone County:

> The news having reached the friends of the volunteers comprising Hobbs' corps, that it would leave for Richmond by the 1 1/2 train, large numbers assembled at the depot, long before that hour, and they still continued to arrive, until the departure of the train . . . The Rev. Mr. [A. F.] Lawrence . . . stepped immediately in front of the corps, and after a spirited address, which was softened and rendered doubly affecting by an occasional tear streaming down his cheek . . . presented each member with a copy of the Holy Bible. Immediately succeeding this ceremony, the Mayor presented to each of the commissioned officers and the four sergeants, a company roll and concluded the ceremonies by a speech and an appeal for pocket change for two or three members who were known to be without it . . . The slow movement of [the] train not going beyond the speed of a footman at a walk afforded a last "fare-you-well" and one more lingering look, and grasp, of the hand of friendship.[14]

The train stopped at Decatur and Huntsville, Alabama; Chattanooga, Cleveland, and Knoxville, Tennessee; and Bristol and Lynchburg, Virginia, before arriving at Richmond. East Tennessee was still a bastion of pro-Union sentiment, and trains approaching Knoxville the week before had been fired on by Union men. The Limestone troops, however, passed through the region without incident. As the train arrived at Lynchburg, Virginia, the men were unloaded and marched across town to board another train to the north. This was necessary due to the difference in gauges of the railroad tracks of the Tennessee and Virginia Railroad and the Orange and Alexandria Railroad. First, however, the Limestone County Troopers were invited to the house of Ambrose Rucker, a Lynchburg native and friend of Captain Hobbs, who provided a warm meal for all of the men.[15] While in Lynchburg, both companies were sworn in for military service and given physicals (the entire regiment would later be sworn in at Richmond). Upon reaching Richmond, Virginia, on the morning of June 11, the Troopers marched north across the Mayo Bridge and went into camp at Camp Reservoir, near the city waterworks on the site of present-day Riverview Cemetery. Houston's company arrived after supper on June 19. They joined the 35,000 Confederate troops who had arrived in Virginia from several Southern states.[16] Eventually, nearly 30,000 Alabamians would serve in the Army of Northern Virginia during the war, and more than 9,000 would die in that service.[17]

Eight hundred miles from home, the Alabama troops stood on the brink of history anticipating the coming of the great battle—the one that would take place at Manassas on July 21. The Limestone County troops settled into the routine of camp life and began daily drilling. There was, however, time for sightseeing and visiting family and friends in Richmond, as well as writing letters to family back home.

The McClellan family members in Athens were already concerned for William's welfare, and they started their own letters to him. Along with his mother and father, William's siblings corresponded with him: his oldest brothers, Robert and John; and his sisters, Martha Catherine (Kittie), Sarah (Sallie), and Matilda. Matilda was the first to write to William in Virginia.

Matilda McClellan to William Cowan McClellan

[Athens]
June 15th 1861
My Dear Brother,
Though it is entirely uncertain whether this will reach you or not I cant refrain from writing you a few lines-I trust to fate for its safe destination. The evening you left Nick Richardson, & Lady, and Hal Malone came home with Mr. [Nick] Davis and the next day Billy R[ichardson]- and Mr Childs (Ann Childs son)[18] came out and had a gay time on the creek [Limestone Creek], fried their own fish &c Friday they all took dinner with us. I wished often during that day that you had some of our fare. You must write word how you live and give us the incidents of interest which occured by the way and indeed everything interesting connected with yourself. We are anxious to hear about what company you got into and became more so after hearing of the number who got drunk at Decatur. Pa was very grateful for the attention paid you by your friends the day you left. We havent heard one word of news since you left but probably will

to day as it is P.O. day. Mr Gilbert[19] staid here last night and wanted some of your hounds for Mr. [Alexander] Blackburn[20] but we refused to let him have any save the two you spoke of giving away- the two little dogs are growing rapidly so I imagine I recon because I feed them a good deal. We have had no rain yet. The hands have been tieing up wheat to day. Pa thinks it has more rust than he saw a while back. I mentioned going down to Athens tomorrow. Kittie's [Martha Catherine McClellan's] examination will come off Monday Tuesday or Wednesday. I havent heard from Nath Fletcher[21] since you left Sunday morning. I cant get off this morning. Uncle Andrew [22] came about two o'clock and looks better. You must be sure to write often. Troops are passing here in great numbers. Good bye your sister Matilda. We have heard that Nick Davis received his commission to raise a thousand rangers. Mr Moore[23] came in this evening and had a good time hearing Uncle Andrew talk about stealing horses for our government. I have heard that Bob Lane and Mrs Goode[24] are married.

Matilda McClellan

William Cowan McClellan to Thomas Joyce McClellan

Richmond, Va.
June 20th [1861]
Dear Father,
After a long and tiresome trip of one week we have at last, arrived in this Company in fine spirits although about one fourth of them has the diarreah. We were detained upon the road at several places, Chattanooga 8 hours, Cleavland 24 hours, Knoxville 12 hours. We were cheered all along the road with inthusiasm save about half of Tennessee- that is the portion we went through. Cleavland is about the size of Huntsville and is intensely Union. Dink Thach[25] was along, and drunk all of the time. He took down the Union flag at Cleavland. You have doubtless heard before this time of the evacuation of Harpers Ferry.[26] From what I can learn about the affair, it was evacuated purely because the Confederates could not hold it, owing to the inefficiency of the fortification about which so much has been said. A high officer told me today that 4000 defenders could not hold it against 8000 assailants. Lincoln was bringing his entire force to bare against that point. There is 50,000 troops sta-

tioned at Richmond now, and are pouring in by the thousands. When our little band reached the encampment a shout was raised like or louder than thunder. Our company is camped at a beautiful pine grove about one mile from town. We have a splendid Spring about three hundred yards off. We were sworn into the Confederate service and examined by a Surgeon at Linchburg [Virginia].[27] All but one in our company was pronounced sound and fit for service. The Surgeon complimented our Co. very highly. He said we had more muscle and breathing power than any Co. he ever examined. Capt. Hobbs Co. is encamped next to us.[28] I had a talk with him about going into his Co. He says he enrolled my name, and made no other calculation but that I should join him. I expect to decide the matter tomorrow- which Co. I will go into. [Capt. David] Houston told me I could not get a transfer unless I got a substitute. My blood boiled with rage when he told me this. I told him the arrangement was made in Athens; and that no gentleman would require more under the circumstances. Upon the whole we had a very exciting talk, but quit friends, to all appearances. He seems now to be trying to make amends for his injustice to me, by inviting me to ride with him in a hired carriage, over the city. If it was not for my mess I would not hesitate a moment about the course I should pursue. There is six besides myself as clever fellows as ever slept beneath a tent. The following is the names of the Boys: Rufus Jones, James Cain, George Hendricks, Dud Minga, William Everett, Ben. Williams who is the best cook in camp.[29] I have made many friends in our Co.- sincere friends I think. Tell John not to join any Co. as a private if he can do any better. If he and Mr. Davis raises the Co. they are contemplating I will join it. I will send you the Richmond Inquirer two or three times a week as I can get it for five cents. The above was written amid noise, bustle and confusion with nothing to write on but my bundle of cloths. After I was done a man accidentally tramped on it. Next time I will try to do better as our mess is going to get a table. Write to me as soon as this comes to hand. Give my respects to all my friends. I will write again in a day or too. Dink Thach has a Spasm on him from drinking, while I am writing. Tell Mother the bottle of Jimaca ginger proved very serviceable to me.

Your son
W.C. McClellan

2

Waiting for the Great Battle: Richmond to Manassas

June 21–July 21, 1861

> "There is . . . some horrid scenes going on in camp every day.
>
> —William Cowan McClellan

As William left for Richmond, Virginia, his brothers, John, Robert, and Thomas Nicholas, remained at home. John was attempting to raise a company with some of his friends, and Robert, having just finished school in Petersburg, Tennessee, was contemplating joining an infantry company. As William's brothers discovered, although large numbers of volunteers were still available back home, forming a regiment was not an easy task. John had originally joined Nicholas Davis Jr. in the 2nd Alabama Infantry Battalion. Unable to raise additional companies, they were placed in the 5th Alabama Infantry Battalion, which later became a part of the 26th/50th Alabama Regiment.[1] Robert would enlist in the 9th Alabama Cavalry. William's youngest brother, Thomas Nicholas, was too young for military service and remained at home with the family.

Northern Alabama enjoyed a short period of peace for the rest of 1861. Union troops, however, threatened northern Alabama in early 1862, and the Union blockade of Southern ports reached Mobile in May. William's major concern focused on the possibilities of battles in Virginia and in advancing on Washington until the fall of Forts Henry and Donelson in February 1862, and the Battle of Shiloh that April. With those Confederate defeats, the way lay open for an invasion of the Tennessee Valley and for the war to be brought to the doorsteps of the people of Limestone County. After these events, William's motivation to fight changed from the glory of participating in one great battle to keeping his homeland and family safe from invasion.

Alabama, like most of the Southern states, was not well prepared for war. Many of the soldiers from Limestone County left for Virginia with inferior weapons and a lack of basic supplies. The home front in northern Alabama was equally unprepared; there were no stockpiles of supplies and foods, and many of the essential items for home life were either disappearing or available only at exorbitant prices. In a letter to William shortly after he left home, Thomas McClellan foresees some of the coming problems and comments that money was very scarce and that the people of the county were facing economic ruin if the war went on too long.

William's second letter from Richmond to his brother Robert at home begins with his description of camp life and military discipline. The euphoria of watching thousands of military men in formation, seeing lines of tents, and hearing martial music was tempered by the rigors of military discipline and the execution of soldiers in camp. Early in the war William hoped that his two oldest brothers would join him in the company, but he would later change his mind after watching soldiers looking for their dead brothers on the battlefield at Manassas. As William matured as a person, he grew from a civilian into a soldier, and he learned to endure the rigors of camp life and military discipline. Initially, he was not used to taking orders from officers. He often clashed with his captain in Company H, whom he did not respect, and he sought a transfer to Captain Hobbs's company, as he mentions in the letter to his father in chapter 1. William wrote frequently to his father seeking his advice and asking him to intervene on his behalf through some of Thomas's influential friends, such as the Confederate secretary of war, Leroy Pope Walker.

Despite William's adjustments, the harshness of life in the infantry convinced him that a cavalry unit offered the best life, especially if it was in the cavalry back home in Alabama. His morale suffered greatly when he was sick for long periods of time, and his early letters were filled with requests for his brother Robert to temporarily take his place. William suffered from frequent backaches, a prelude to a kidney condition that plagued him for the rest of his life. Once his health returned, he dropped the idea of a substitute but continued to pursue the possibilities of a transfer.

Along with the Limestone County troops, the 4th Alabama Regiment and the 1st Tennessee (Provisional) Regiment were in camp nearby. William knew many of the men in Company F (Huntsville Guards) and Company I (the North Alabamians) from nearby Madison County, Alabama; and in Company G (the Fayetteville Guards), Company H (Shelton Creek Volunteers), and Company K (Boon's Creek Minute Men) from the 1st Tennessee of Lincoln County, Tennessee. While William developed a new identity as a soldier, the passing of time put distance between himself and his old life in Limestone County, and the soldiers in his company and in the regiments (such as the 1st Tennessee and the 4th Alabama) became his new world. When he had free time, William frequently visited with the men in these other regiments.

All of the drilling and discipline seemed pointless if there was no coming battle, and William speculated in his early letters about where the great battle would be fought. At the time, the regiment had no colonel to lead it, and speculation ran through the company about who would be appointed. Rumors also spread in late June that the army would be sent to either Manassas Junction or to Winchester, Virginia, to meet the growing threat of Union invasion. After drilling in Richmond, the 9th was sent by train to Gordonsville and Manassas to join Thomas Jonathan (Stonewall) Jackson's forces in the Shenandoah Valley, as part of Gen. Edmund Kirby Smith's brigade.[2]

William Cowan McClellan to Robert Anderson McClellan

Richmond,
June 21st-1861
Dear Bob: I am well & getting along about as well as souldiers generally do. I am still in Houston's Co., but expect to get a transfer Monday or Tuesday, although against my captains consent. We are drilling 4 hours a day. I have learned very rapidly since we have been drilling. Houston says I am as good a souldier as any in the Co. I saw today the grandest sight my eyes ever beheld[:] twenty thousand troops parading in a dark stately pine grove to the solemn sound of the drum and the pleading notes of the fife commingled with in one harmonious whole. Upon every countenance was a look of self reliance, of Stern resolve as ever marked the human face. The city is swarming with people of all classes and sexes[,] men, women and children from every quarter of the globe, except Yankeedom[.] and there is 13 of them here as prisoners. Jeff Davis is here. Some of the boys have seen him. He had been in our encampment a time or two.[3] The wise Military men are looking for an engagement at Manassas before long. In my opinion on that fight turns the destiny of the South, because both sections are going to bring all their available force to bare upon that point. There is, I am sorry to say, some horrid scenes going on in Camp every day[,] men shot down for disobedience to officers. Four have been shot since I have been at this place. To-day will be shot young Binum [Junius A. Bynum] of Courtland [Alabama], for attempting to kill

his captain.[4] My ten minutes is out- I must close. Direct your letters to Richmond Virginia.

Your Brother,
W. C. McClellan

William Cowan McClellan to his sister Matilda McClellan

Richmond
June 23rd 1861
Dear Sister:
I got your very interesting and affectionate letter this morning while standing guard. It was taken out of the office last night by McDonald[5] but I did not get it as I was half mile from our tents on duty. We have formed a Regiment composed of all North Alabamians alone. It takes four men and a corporal to form a guard. There is three reliefs during the night, and until eight oclock in the morning[.] So you see my turn will not come around again in two weeks. We stand two hours on guard and four off. We drill from four to six hours a day. I have stood the service much better than I anticipated. I still belong to Houstons Company. In a talk with Captain Hobbs I told him exactly how the case stood with me. He advised me to be silent for the present; that I would stand a better chance to be transferred after the Regiment was fully organized, expressing at the same time a strong desire to have me in his Company. Thus I have acted- whether wisely or foolishly the future can only determine. It is a hard question for me to decide. I dislike my officers; I love my mess. Though none of them has done me an unkindness but the Captain, I have a disgust for the whole of them. Houston now shows me more kindness than he does to any of his men. I had a difficulty at Linchburg, with him. It occured in this way[:] I was walking along the street and heard a noise in a Bar Room like a fight was going on. I walked off, knowing that some of our men were in there, and I did not care to mix up with them. Directly Tom Tweedy came down the street crying and said that Booth, who is a drunker scoundrel and fifer in the Company, drew back to strike him. and that he—Tweedy—drew his knife.[6] Houston cursed him and told him to go off and let the fifer alone. He was evidently on the infernal fifers side. I hunted Booth and spit in his face; and told him he was a scoundrel. He did not resist it. Houston

came up and told Tweedy damn him, he wanted him to get out of his company but he could not do it, [because] he had never joinèd it. I then said to him that I supposed that was my condition, he said it was unless I could get a Substitute. I told him I came with him as an accommodation on his part and he could not as a gentleman ask me to stay in his Co. He then remarked to me in a very boisterous way that he could resign and fight me a fair fight. The proposition I willingly agreed to. He found he had picked the wrong customer; and apologized and asked me to take a drink with him. I did not do it. Since then he has been very fond of me. Tweedy is in Hobbs Co. John Featherston[7] thanked me for my conduct towards Tweedy. Tweedy was drunk but drunk or sober he is a gentleman. You all need not be uneasy about me; I am able and know how to take care of myself. Some think our Regiment will leave Richmond in about a week or too bound for Manassas Gap, as troops are starting every day for that point. John McDonald[8] was elected 2nd Lt. at Linchburg [Lynchburg] over the best military men in the Co. Ruf Jones in place of Herbert[9] who staid home. Jones is my mess mate. We went to Richmond yesterday and bought about as many cooking vessels as Mother has in her kitchen, besides Cabbage, onions, and everything of the kind. There are seven of us in our mess, as clever fellows as ever lived. It is very hot here. If you can I wish you would send me 2 pairs of cheap pants as they asked two prices for everything in Richmond. For the present direct your letters in care of Captain Hobbs of Limestone Greys. We have beef, bacon and buiscuit to eat. Ben Williams can beat old Lucy[10] making the latter. Tell Father, John, and Bob to write and you do the same. No rain in this county in a month. Wheat crop very fine here and in East Tennessee.

Your affectionate Brother,
William McClellan

William Cowan McClellan to Nicholas Davis Jr.

Camp Davis
June 30th, 61
Near Richmond Virginia
Mr. Davis,
I am fine. As this is Sunday and I have nothing to do but sit here I will write you a letter. Though I have nothing of importance to communicate. There seems to be a building spirit pervading the

armys movement here. It seems to point to that [it] will be at Harpers Ferry. Our regiment will be ordered there in a few days. Col. Johnson[11] was appointed Col of our regiment, Gen. Oneal[12] Major. There is a great deal of dissatisfaction at the formers appointment the reason being a man about 30 years old without any field experience. There has not been any news about his appointment. I understand he is going to resign his appointment. The rest of our camp was disturbed yesterday by the appearance of Jeff Davis in our camp. He was escorted by Cavalry upon a beautiful grey horse bowing gracefully amid the deafening shouts of our soldiers. I believe he can infuse more enthusiasm in the confederate army than Napoleon ever could in the French army when in the prime of his strength and the glory of his day. I have been sick for 3 or 4 days with diarrhea a complaint that three fourths of the army is afflicted with. I am some better now[.] we had a good rain last night. The wheat crop in Virginia is very fine, corn crop not promising. I am very anxious to hear from home and whether or not you have had any rain. I understand Nick Davis is raising a company of rangers if so I want to join his co. Tell John [McClellan] not to come here as a private. I am still in Houstons co. Tell Father he need have no fears about me drinking whiskey. I have saw a nough of the effects of drinking whiskey to disgust any man on earth. I have received but one letter since I left home that from Matilda. I have written 4. There is 45,000 thousand [*sic*] troops within one and a half miles of Richmond. I have made the acquaintance of Pat Raglands Brothers.[13] They are clever gentlemen. Write as soon as this comes to hand.

Yours Truly,
W. C. McClellan, Esquire

William Cowan McClellan to Thomas Joyce McClellan

Camp Davis near Richmond, Va.
July the 4th, 1861
Dear Father,
I have looked long and anxiously for a letter from home, but have received none, save Matilda's two weeks ago. But I am going to the Post Office this evening and perhaps I will get a letter. I have gotten well at last after having the diarrhea for 5 days. I am now drilling. Ruff Jones and my self are file clerks in the company. A regiment of Frenchmen[14] left here a day or two ago for Manassas Gap,

they where the best drilled co. in the confederate army. We have rec'vd no marching orders yet but expect them daily. There is a rumor in the camp this morning that a fight took place last night on the border of Va in which the yankees lost 4 hundred men.[15] I [suppose] you have heard a great deal about the hospitality of Virginia, But since we have been here we have paid two prices for everything we have bought. Our mess had nearly all of there cooking utensils to buy. I have spent 15 dollars, most of which I spent on the road for something to eat at 50 and 75 cents a meal. One half of the camp are now without a cent. we will draw our months wages in a few days. 5 of our comp. are in the hospital with the measles. We get plenty to eat now Beef or Bacon, flower or meal. No vegetables only what we buy. We have no Colonel yet. Johnson has resigned his Col. ship. General O'Neal, I think will be appointed. J[ohn] N. Hays has been appointed assistant Surgeon of the Regi.[16] No Surgeon has yet been appointed. There was 4 spies hanged in Richmond yesterday. There is a great many a musing incidents occur in Camp. For instance there are 75 head of Milk Cows in the ground we occupy. I frequently see a man holding to a cow's tail with one hand, a milk pail with the other. You must keep my letter private as it seems all of the news written about the company home comes right back. While I write, the Booming Canon is roaring on all sides celebrating the fourth of July. I will close this uninteresting letter.

Your affectionate son
W. C. McClellan

I Have Written to Mr. Davis, twice to Ryan, once to father, once to Bob, Tell John I will write to him in a few days. Strange to say we are encamped upon Gen. Scotts Plantation.[17]

Thomas Joyce McClellan to William Cowan McClellan

Shoal Ford, Ala
July 4th 1861
Dear Will,
We have received your letters of the 20th and 23rd June, I am very sorry to hear that you are having difficulty in getting a transfer from Houston to Major Hobbs. It is very strange under the circumstances that Houston objects to it, nor would he if he has any of the

instincts of the gentleman about him, I shall feel very uneasy until I hear that you have got out of his company, but I hope you will do nothing rash to bring about the transfer. You had better be governed by the advice of Major Hobbs in reference to the whole matter. I have full confidence in his judgement and discression. I am sorry to hear of your difficulties with the man you speak of, and especially that you spit in his face. That is an indignity that I would not offer to any man, however degraded he might be. We have had several good rains in the last ten days, corn crops have greatly improved, cotton is now growing fast and so is the grass. I commenced laying by corn last friday, but will have to stop to plow over some of my cotton.[18] Jim Henry Malone, L. R. Davis, the Richardson boys[19] and John [McClellan] are trying to raise a company, but I think it doubtful whether they succeed or not, if they fail John intends going to Va. and joining Tracy's Company.[20] Nothing of much interest has transpired since you left. There are strong efforts being made in different parts of the county to bring out other candidates for the legislature. I have been strongly solicited to run myself but I have no inclination to do so. Your acquaintances here seem to take a deep interest in your welfare. They are incessant in their inquiry about you, and expect a great deal of solisitude from you. I hope you will so conduct yourself so as to merit their good opinion, and although the life of a soldier is a demoralizing one, I hope you will be able to withstand every temptation, and should it please God that you shall return home that you may look back in after life with pride and pleasure upon the present period in your history. I saw Nathan Fletcher this evening he is suffering a great deal, I think there is but little chance for his recovery. The wheat crop here is a good one, the oats is very light owing to injury from drought and rust. Money is becoming distressingly scarce here. I have been trying for the last two weeks to collect some, and have not been able to get a dollar. The best men in the county say they can't raise any unless this horrid war is brought to a close soon. I don't know what will become of the country and of this I see but little prospect. Write soon and often, say in your next letter whether your vaccination[21] took or not, and whether there is a sufficiency of arms for the troops and if they are of the improved kind. We are in great suspense here in reference to the movements of the army, we have had no war news since you left, except the evacuation of Harpers Ferry.[22]

Your father
Thos J McClellan

PS From your letter it seems that you have the power of determining whether you will remain in the Houston's Company or go to Hobbs, if this is so I would not hesitate a moment. You are at present surrounded by influences of a very corrupting character.

T.J.M

July 5th. I expect to go to Huntsville today but am almost unable to move on account of a pain in my hips, it is now 12 o'clock, showers of rain have been falling occasionally all day. The ground is too wet to do almost any thing, cotton getting very grassy and if it does not stop raining soon, it will be impossible to clean it.

T.J. McClellan

William Cowan McClellan to Thomas Joyce McClellan

Camp Davis Near Richmond
July the 6th 1861
Dear Father
As Mr Thach is going to Athens I concluded to send this letter by him. before this letter reaches you I think the big Battle will be fought. Johnson [Joseph E. Johnston][23] the commander of the confederate army and Lions of the federal army came in contact yesterday. The former repulsed the latter 3 distinct times and drove him into a little village called Winchester situated 18 miles from Manassas. Johnson had 18,000 men Lions 25,000.[24] Men who know the situation of the place say it is uterably impossible for them to make their escape from Winchester it being surrounded on all sides by the confederates. Johnson sent the women and children word to get out by to day. I suppose he will attack them today. The troops are being ordered from this place very rapidly. I think our regiment will go to Manassas Junction. There is 190 thousand troops in Va.[25] I have seen 40 thousand since I have been here. I was agreeably surprised to meet Nick Davis in Capt Hobbs tent last Friday, he went down to my tent with me and we had a good chat. he was in one of his best ways[.] you all seem to think that I am timid or backward in performing my duty. Now all I have to say no man performs his duty with more alacrity than myself or will stand firmer in the hour of trial. I was glad to hear from home that you were all well, good crops so on. Tell Mother I would like to have about 10 pounds

of her butter[.] it wont cost anything to send it to Richmond. Butter brings 50 cents per pound here. Richmond I think is almost abhorring[.] they charge a poor soldier 3 prices for everything he gets[.] the city is full of dutch and irish. you must take care of Fannie[26] and my pups. I am still in Houstons co. I intend to go to Hobbs Co as soon as the Col is appointed.

Your son,
W.C. McClellan

Mr Thach failed to get off. this is Saturday evening and we have holiday. it is raining very hard. The wheat crop is very fine, corn crop also. Tom Cartwright[27] desires mentioning to his family he is well.

William Cowan McClellan to Robert Anderson McClellan

July the 8 '61
Camp Davis
Dear Bob,
As Mr. John Johnson[28] will start to Athens to night, I have intended to write you a few lines and send by him. I also send a letter to Father. I think by next Sunday we will be on our road to the field of conflict. we have a Col. from North Carolina by the name of Anderson.[29] Thank God we did not get a Virginian. I think of all the soldiers in the Southern confederacy the Virginians are the most timid, the most cowardly. They don't seem to recognize that they are out of the old union yet. I believe they are afraid to kill a Yankee for fear the grand jury would find a true bill against them. I have no doubt the battle ground will be in Eastern Tennessee and Western Va. Mark the prediction after the battle is over. Va will receive more prais than any other state in the southern confederacy and done less fighting. You may think this strong but it is the sentiment of 3 fourths of the soldiers situated on Virginia soil. There is a disaffection in E. Tennessee and West Va. I have just heard that 12 miles of the rail road has been torn up not far from a place called Brister [Bristol] where the state line runs Va & Tenn. Lincoln is going to issue a proclamation calling on his government for 40,000 troops & tell Father I will send him the Richmond Enquirer. Send me the Athens Banner. Write to me direct your letter to Rich. it

does me no little good to get a letter from home. Tell Mr. Davis to write to John also. Give my respects to Nathan Fletcher. Tell Mr. Moore I would like to hear from him. I am well.

Your Brother
W. C. McClellan

The health of our company is now good.

Matilda McClellan to William Cowan McClellan

Ivy Bluff, Ala.
Sunday night July 21st 1861
My Dear Brother,
While writing this note my mind will be trying to peek through the rain and wind to find you at some awful encampment in all probability fondly lingering in the happy past which for years to come will be our chief delight; for you are never forgotten, especially at meal time you are thought of. It has been raining since Monday. The grass is growing finally, corn and cotton are doing well. Uncle Andrew [Beattie] came down Friday night and brought a Major Hester[30] to look at the Clark place. He likes Mr Fletchers place very much and may try to buy it. Uncle Berry [Beattie][31] has been married to Mrs Logan two weeks. They will all be here. Uncle Jo [Beattie][32] is moving from there. Tom W. Pettus[33] was here to stay with his daughter Tommie. I like her. Jim Moore also came over, he and Mr Pettus went to see Nathan Fletcher and thinks he stands a chance to recover. Clint Davis[34] was here yesterday and said he saw you in Richmond. He marched with the boys to Martinsburg [Virginia]. We have news of a battle at or near Manassas. Pa saw this morning the negro Houston left in Richmond who says he followed [you] on to Winchester and then lost your trail and came back. He told of your fuss with Goldsmith.[35] The people in Athens are complaining of that batch of officers. Old Mr French is here to night[.] His son Amos died Friday[,] was sick only a few days.[36] Mr Davis and family are here tonight

Monday July 23rd It rained this morning but finally cleared off. There will be speaking at Douglases Spring tomorrow by the candidates[37] and a picnic too. I will probably go. We were so sorry we didnt know Mr Phillips[38] was going to you all. Write whether you still need your summer pants or anything and we will mail it to you. You must write often for it is so long between the times we hear from you. Major Hester is still here and Uncle Andrew will stay five weeks perhaps. Pa is arranging some notes to speak from. He has no confidence in himself. I expect he excels the others. Be sure to write often. I don't know where to direct this to. Tell me about your washing, sleeping, and if you need any clothes besides those you wrote for. My respects to your mess. Your devoted Sister. There are about 200 men in different companies for the war.

Write, Little Matilda

23rd 1861
Father started out this evening to fill appointments over the [Tennessee] River. It will be a tight race between Donnell and Shelton. We have news of a big fight at Manassas 7,000 of ours killed & 7,000 of theirs.

William Cowan McClellan to Thomas Joyce McClellan

Piedmont Station
July 21, 1861
Dear Father
We left Richmond on the 14th and arrived at Strasburg after a night, the next day the whole Regiment having nothing to eat for 24 hours. We then made a forced march to Winchester 13 miles from the Railroad. We had scarcely got to Win. before we were drawn up in an attitude of Battle. Every body expected a fight, the enemy were in 6 miles of us, our scouts and the federal scouts came in collision but they saw proper to retreat. We had at Winchester 35,000 troops. I have seen all of my acquaintances in Col. Jones Regiment[39] they are all well and in fine spirits. The Lincoln co. troops were at Winchester.[40] I went around and saw all of them, they seemed delighted to see me. Brock Clark[41] told me that Uncle Berrie Beatty was married on last Thursday. There came a runner to Winc[hester] saying that Gen. Boregard [Beauregard][42] was about to be attacked they have overwhelming forces & we were ordered to perform a forced march to his assistance at Manassas Junction. In one hour 25,000 thousand [*sic*] soldiers were on the march to this place where we will take the cars for Manassas which is 30 miles. I

was too sick to drill before we got orders to march but I could not stand it to be left behind. it was a grand sight to see 25 thousand all moving at once. We made the thirty miles in 13 hours about as good a time as ever was made by an army of that number. We have been waiting two days to get off. Our Regiment has got a train at last, here comes the cars. I will write again when I get to the Junction. The destiny of the South will be desided at Manassas in a day or too if we whip the battle we are a victorious and free people but if not we are a subjugated people, but I think we are certain to whip the battle as the sun rises in the east. We have suffered a great deal for something to eat since we left Rich. I have had nothing to eat in the last 24 hours. Though here there is plenty to eat in the country. But it is a verry hard matter to feed 25,000 soldiers. We carry devastation and ruining before us. Burning fences, killing stock and destroying wheat.

Farewell, Your son
Wm. C. McClellan

3
Manassas to Centreville, Virginia
July 22–September 21, 1861

> The great battle has benn fought. I am sorry to inform you that I was not in it.
>
> —William Cowan McClellan

In late July, rumors and newspaper reports circulated in Limestone County of a great battle in Virginia, and everyone wondered if the 9th Alabama was involved in the action and in the other engagements that followed. Letters from William's family at home inquired about the status of friends in the regiments from Limestone County and Lincoln County, Tennessee, where the McClellans used to live. With the first units of volunteers already in Virginia, more were forming at home that would include William's brothers John and Robert. The romance of war was still in the air, as was the hope for a quick and successful war. While no significant battles or invasions had occurred in the Tennessee Valley, they were anticipated shortly, and the call was going out for more volunteers to meet this threat. Life at home for the McClellans remained relatively normal: relatives from Tennessee were coming for extended visits, marriages were taking place, school was in session for the younger McClellan children, and the crops were growing well in the fields.

The 9th Alabama was sent from Richmond to Winchester, Virginia, on July 14 to help reinforce the troops in the northern Shenandoah Valley. They took the trains from Richmond to Manassas Junction, stopping there briefly before continuing on to Strasburg in the Shenandoah Valley. While en route, Captain Hobbs noticed that a number of the men in the company were breaking out with measles; more would come down with them later when they returned to Manassas Junction. William and his company arrived at Strasburg on July 16 in time for breakfast and then had a hard march along the Valley Turnpike, where the 9th went into camp a mile and a half north of Winchester in an open wheat field. It was raining steadily, and the men were forced to use wheat stacks for shelter since they had no tents.

On July 18, after Union forces began moving from Washington, D.C., toward Manassas, Virginia, the regiment marched from Winchester, crossed the Shenandoah River, and proceeded to Piedmont Station to catch the trains for Manassas Junction. They marched over land because no direct railroad line ran from Winchester to Manassas Junction; the Manassas Gap Railroad ended at Strasburg, and the Winchester and Potomac Railroad line went from Harpers Ferry to Winchester.[1] Although the Manassas Gap Railroad ran from Manassas Junction to Strasburg, it was faster to march twenty-five miles across country to Piedmont Station (modern Delaplane) than it was to march to Strasburg and take the trains from there (they had just made the long march from Strasburg to Winchester two days before). The 9th was last in the order of march from Winchester, and on July 21, while the sounds of the First Battle of Manassas carried in the distance and the news of the Confederate victory filtered back, the 9th Alabama was on picket duty on a high hill just west of Piedmont Station.

After waiting the entire night, they took the last train to Manassas Junction and arrived around 7 a.m. on July 22. William wrote that they would have made it to the junction sooner if saboteurs hadn't torn up the railroad tracks. On more than one occasion, the movement of Confederate troops to the battlefield were delayed by sabotage, by trains that traveled at slow speeds, or by trains that stopped altogether while the crews "rested." In the event reported by William, a section of track had been torn up, halting the trains. The saboteurs were captured and dealt with on the spot. The delay probably would not have made any difference in the participation of the 9th Alabama in the battle.[2] It was raining as the train pulled into Manassas Junction early on the morning of July 22 with many of the men riding on top of the cars. They marched north from the station through the rain and mud to Young's Branch, where they went into camp without tents not far from the Stone Bridge on Bull Run.

Other Alabama regiments participated in the First Battle of Manassas. The 4th Alabama Regiment with two companies from Madison County, Alabama, included many of William's friends from home. The 4th was a part of Gen. Bernard Bee's brigade that was sent from its original position on Henry Hill to slow the Union flanking movement that came across Matthews Hill from Sudley Ford on the morning of July 21. Col. Egbert Jones and many of the 4th Alabama went to their deaths on the slopes of Matthews Hill and on Henry Hill before the Confederate forces rallied around Thomas Jonathan (Stonewall) Jackson. On July 23, as members of the 9th Alabama surveyed the field, they came to the spot where the 4th Alabama had dropped their knapsacks and bedrolls near Henry Hill as they went into battle.[3] The abandoned gear that remained on the ground belonged to the men who didn't come back—some of the same men who at that moment were being prepared for burial, or who were on the surgeons' tables at nearby Sudley Methodist Church or at the Stone House. One of those men was William's childhood friend James Bailey, who was wounded twice during the battle and died in an army hospital in Culpeper some days later. William praised Jim's bravery and his gallant death in battle, but later in the war he would say that Jim was one of the lucky ones to have died so early.

Many Confederate soldiers were upset with the decision not to follow up the victory at Manassas with a march on Washington, D.C.[4] William and the members of Company F who missed the fight hoped that they would have one more chance to face the enemy. Instead, over the next two months they faced sickness, death in camp, drilling, picket duty, and patrols. Part of the health problems that plagued all of the Confederate forces in the Manassas area arose because they set up camp directly on the battlefield. Their drinking water was contaminated with waste that had run off the fields where men and horses had fallen during battle. Only after August 12 did Confederate officials decide to move the troops away from the battle area (the 9th moved to Bristoe Station). Like many of the regiments, the 9th lost nearly one-third of its men during the first year to illness, injury, and discharges. While William avoided some of the more serious diseases, he did suffer throughout the war with yellow jaundice, mumps, camp dysentery, and severe backaches that left him confined to bed for a week at a time.

Throughout the war, the soldiers' deadliest enemies were disease, illness, injury, and accidents that took place in camp. The Union and Confederate armies were constantly plagued by sickness and disease of all types, and it was common during the first year of the war for sickness to incapacitate at least half of the men at any given time. Joseph Jones, one of the foremost authorities on Confederate medicine, estimated that on average each Southern soldier was ill or wounded six times during the war, and that cases of sickness were five times as prevalent as injuries. He further estimated that for every soldier who died as a result of battle, three perished from disease.[5]

In the face of such harsh living conditions, as well as the tough discipline they faced from their officers, William and his comrades felt the need to maintain their self-esteem as they became soldiers. The men in Company F successfully preserved their dignity by elevating the volunteer Confederate soldier over the citizen who stayed at home in Limestone County. In his letters to his family at home, William constantly berated former friends and neighbors who had not volunteered for military service, and he had no sympathy for skulkers and deserters who found ways to get out of work or military service altogether.

William Cowan McClellan to Thomas Joyce McClellan

Manassas Junction
July the 22, 61
Dear Father,

The great battle has benn fought. I am sorry to inform you that I was not in it. The battle commenced a bout day light sunday morning. it lasted nearly all day. it is said by military men to be the bloodiest Battle ever fought. There was 6,000 of us at Piedmont Station waiting for the cars to take us to the Junction. We would have reached the field of conflict had it not been for 4 yankees who tore up the rail road. The yankees were caught and suffered the penalty of there crime. We reached the field of battleground about 14 hours after it was over. There I have witnessed the most soul sickening scene ever beheld by the vision of man. the field was yet covered with the dead and dying. while a death like void rent the air. But not a tear dropped from the strong and invincible sons of the South. I am convinced that the Confederate army is composed of the bravest men on God's green earth- The North Ala troops bore the brount of the battle and nobly did they fight. Though the gallant Col. Jones and one hundred of his Regiment [4th Alabama] were killed. They were cut to pieces worse than any five Regiments put to gether. Many of my acquaintances were killed and wounded- among them James Bailey badly wounded- [Lt.] R[obert N.] Hu[gh]es killed- Peter Fletcher's little finger grazed with a ball.[6] There was about one hundred & twenty thousand federal troops engaged and about 60,000 Confederate troops- we gained a most decided Victory- our cost is between 3,000 and 5,000, that of the enemy between 10 and 16 thousand. There has been 2 fights at Manassas Jun. The first fight we killed about 900 hundred [*sic*] of the[m] our loss 50.[7] Jeff Davis reached the Battle field about the close of the fight, with about 10,000 Mississippians and said Boys I have come and charged the enemy. they run like wild horses. Twice they have attacked us, twice we have maintained the field of battle and compelled them to raise a flag of truce to bury the dead- The fight occured 5 miles from the Junc. along a stream called Bull Run. The line of battle extended from 12 to 16 miles in length. Boregard had his horse shot from under neath him. Gen. Johnson [Joseph E.

Johnston], Gen. Lee, Davis, Boregard are all here. Wilcox, of Columbia Tenn. is our Col.[8] He is a man of experience and self confidence. I think if we are not attacked, in a few days we will be marched to Washington City. Dear Father I expect to be engaged in a fight. I may fall But be assured I will fall only as the Brave fall- Striking for the liberty of our country. Give my love to Mother[.] Our army in the Battle on sunday took Sherman's battery[9] composed of 36 pieces, of artillery which is the best battery in the world- They turned it against the enemy and did great executions. Since I wrote the above I have visited the battleground again. All of our men have been buried- but there is a great number of the enemy yet unburied- Tell Bob not to join the army yet if the war continues I want him to take my place in the fall a while. I am still in Houston's company. It makes no difference here whos Co. you are in we all of us are a like. Col. Wilcox is very kind to his privates and very stringent to his men & officers. Just before we left Richmond 69 out of 74 of Houston's men petitioned him to resign his position, he said he would do so at first but finally determined to hold on to his position if possible to save him from disgrace. They would all like to have Gaines Smith for Cap. He is really the Capt. now. He is the man who will lead us into battle.[10] We have abandoned our tents to sleep in the open air, it is now Tuesday, yesterday it rained all day. we were forced marched through the rain 12 miles, we have a hard time. Tell John [McClellan] if he will join the army to come and join Col. Wilcoxs Regiment. He is a splendid commander. I am in hopes he will not join my Regiment. It is a great consolation to me when the battle is over not to look among the slain for a Brother. I would imagine that would be my greatest trial of my life- the only tears I have shed since I left home was one occurance like this. I saw a man looking for his brother, he at last found him, he embraced his lifeless Body for a moment and then raised up and in a loud voice said you have taken one of us you shall take us both. I have received no letter from home since I left Rich[mond]. Nor have I written one- we are moving about so much it is very uncertain whether or not I could get a letter though you may write to me. Only direct your letter to Manassas Junction. Tell Mother not to be uneasy about me. I am in good health. Give my respect to all inquiring friends. The Boys are all well. I did not sign the petition instructing Houston to resign his Cap'cie. I acted on the advice of Nick Davis [illegible] just before I left Rich. I am very anxious to hear if he got it. Col. Jones is not dead yet. About half of the New York Regiment was killed in the battle. This was written in great haste.

William Cowan McClellan to Thomas Joyce McClellan

Manassas Junction
July 29, 1861
Dear Father,
I am still at Manassas Junction- I am in bad health at preasant owing to the bad water I think witch is nothing more or less than a hole dug in the ground.[11] I am now able to inform you all about the Battle. Our loss is about 2,000 killed and wounded- The Enemy killed and wounded about 8,000 thousand [*sic*] or more. Our forces in the field 25,000 or 30,000 thousand [*sic*] and the enemy's 50,000 thousand [*sic*].[12] The fight lasted 6 or 7 hours. At the close of the 7th hour the enemy fled in the utmost confusion- retreating in no order whatever running over every thing that impeded their progress, like so many wild horses flying before the prarie fire. It is said that a great many ladies and Congressman came down to Alexandria to be close at hand to prepare a dinner in honor of the glorious victory they were so confident of achieving. I talked with a great many prisoners[.] they say their Capt told them that they would whip us in an hour or too and they would have nothing to do but march to Richmond. One thousand cavalry pursued them 15 miles cutting and slaying as they went. It is said they ran into the carriages of the women and they were forced to shoot down one another to keep them from running over the women and children. I have no idea that a people ever where as mutch disappointed- we have met with no disturbance since. There is a camp report that Lincoln has sent commissioners to Richmond to treat for peace. I have at last got a transfer to Capt Hobbs company. I applied to Col. Wilcox and got a transfer in about 2 minutes. By the by Col. Wilcox has been promoted to the office of Brigadier General of the forces of Lou[isian]a.[13] It was a very heavy blow to the 9 Ala Regi. Col. W[ilcox] is scarsly inferior to Boregard in point of military ability. He is an old Regular- I saw Gen. Boregard a day or too ago. There was a terable shout raised when he rode up to the lines. We belong to Gen. Johnston's division of the army. He is about sutch a looking man as Rip Davis

save he has black hair and eyes. If I do not get better I intend to get out in the country at some private residence until I get better. We live very hard here nothing but Wheat Bread and meat and not enough of that. You must write to me direct your letter to Richmond forwarded to the 9th Ala Regiment Vol. Cap-T-H-Hobbs. I now have just 50 dollars. I have been paid 21d by [the] government. Tell Bob not to Volunteer yet. I may want him to take my place by fall. Though I think peace will be maid be fore 2 months. You need not be uneasy about us at Manassas there is one hundred thousand troops here they can whip any force Lincoln can bring to oppose them. There is yet plenty of dead yankees lying about here unburried. Jim Bailey I understand is mortally wounded. I received Matildas of the 12th July the only letter I have received since I left Ric[hmond]- Tom Cart[wright] is well. Hobbs [Company F] has 100 privates only 38 able to drill- Houston [Company H] 72, 30 able to drill.[14] I learned from Matildas letter that you where a candidate for the legislature. I also saw Dr. Husie.[15] He said he heard you make a good speech at Mooresville. you must excuse this disconnected letter. I have nothing to write on but my havesack. We have just received our tents from Winchester. We all slept upon our feet or stood upon our feet 24 hours in the hardest and coldest rain I ever saw fall on Monday and Monday night after the battle. There is not a drop of whiskey nor 10 pounds of tobacco in the army. I wrote to you a few days ago. Write to me wether or not you can read my letter. I have to write all of them with a pencil- Tell Rip Davis I am more obediend to my officers ten times than his Capt But it done me good to heare Col W[ilcox] curse the Capt I saw him shake Houston and tell him Dam you to your post sir. Reckon you had better direct your letters to Manassas. Farewell

Your son,
W.C. McClellan

William Cowan McClellan to Robert Anderson McClellan

Manassas Junction
July 30th 1861
Dear Bob,

I am now able I think to give a current account of the battle of Manassas. I see the news papers make our loss killed and wounded at 4 or 5 thousand witch is about as near the truth as news papers generally do- we have heard the Col. and general say 1,500 or 2,000 thousand [*sic*] at the outside, that of the enemy is put down by our men at 8,000. the enemy themselves put down their own loss at 12 hundred. It is also stated the spoils taken by our side is worth one million of dollars. Bob you can form but a very vague idea of the horrors of war until you visit a battlefield, hear the groans of the wounded as they jostle along in a wagon and here and there lies a man who in his Death struggle griped his hands and mouth full of dirt. it is a nough to sicken the soul of the wild and untutored savage- There seams to be a calm brooding over the land at this time but nobody knows how soon this calm may be disturbed by the Booming cannon and the wratling musketry. If I knew that one more battle would deside the matter, I would welcome the hour of conflict with joy that was to decide the destiny of the South. I have written two letters before this from this place and have had no letter from home. I saw Dr. Harris and Dr. Fletcher, Dr. McDonald and Dr. Husie and others from home.[16] Dr. Ha[rris] told me he Saw Father and he was very much pestered about my transfer. Well tell him I have at last succeeded in getting a transfer to Hobbs Co. It was a very hard case, Houston working to keep me in his company, I working to get his consent to transfer. I out generald him, he offered me the position of orderly Sergeant to stay in his company witch I promptly refused. Capt David Houston has but one fault in the world. He is a fool. I want you to write to me often, direct your letter to Manassas Junction. Write me the neighbor hood news, how my filly comes on to my puppies. By the by I have got very nice day here. Write soon. We may be ordered off from here before night, no telling. We may stay here a month. The first intimation we get generally is to double quick it for 10 20 or 30 miles.

Your Brother,
W C McClellan

inclosed you will find a letter picked up by me on the battlefield, it gives an inkling of the feeling at the North about the war. [The enclosed letter was not found.]

William Cowan McClellan to Robert Anderson McClellan

Manassas Junction
August the 7th, 1861
Dear Bob
I wrote to John 2 days ago stating that I was unwell. I am a little better now. We are incamped at this miserable place yet- I have not drilled any in 10 days. Our Regiment drills 8 hours a day witch is pretty right drilling. I think the days are about as hot here as they are in Ala but cool nights. I think this war would wind to a close in a few days if the federal congressmen and the cabinet were mustered into the service in a bout a month. I believe if it was left to a vote of Both armies they would vote unanimously for peace. One company of our Regiment has just come in from burying dead Yankees. They have been out ever since we came here. They say they buried 40 in a grave. Our loss in the battle are counted to 3 hundred killed 12 hundred wounded. The enemy 35 hundred killed and a great many mortally wounded whom have died, besides a great many prisoners. I am very anxious to hear from home and all about what is going on there. Write me word how my dogs and Fannie Fern comes on. Tell sister to write to me wether or not she got my letter. If you have not volunteered yet, do not do it until fall. I want you to take my place. Every thing is so still here now that it looks favorable for peace. There is but a few Yankees left on Va soil now, there being but a few thousand at Alexandria. Gen. Boregard had his army drawn up in line of battle a few days ago. He then rode around each Regiment bowing amid the deafening shouts of a hundred thousand admiring soldiers. He looks a little like Kirk Patrick.[17] James Bailey I understand will die. William Lowe[18] it is thought will recover. They are at the culpeper courthouse 20 miles from here.[19] I have not seen Jim Bailey since he was wounded. Tell Uncle Andy to write to me. I want you to send me an indian rubercoat[20] and one pair of pants of a grey color and a yellow stripe, a good Bottle of Brandy. You know you can box them up in a little box and direct it thus[:] W. C. McClellan member of ala Vol Regi care of the Capt T. H. Hobbs Manassas Junction. But if you can see any body coming here you had better send those articles by them. Give my regards to Jim Moore and old Heartwell, Mr. J.[ohn] M.[ilton] Moore, ole nat Fletcher. Tell old Heart I am having a heap harder

time of it than he has. Bob you must write to me often, you have no idea how it helps me up to hear from home. I will send a letter to Father that I wrot at Piedmont before the Battle as it turned out to be so prophetic. I could not get an envelope at the time. Tell Matilda to write to me. How is mother & tell Tom I will bring him a Yankee cap when I come home- tell Rip D.[avis] that he can [come here] if he has a company by applying to the proper authorities [illegible] this Regiment so says Hobbs.

Your Brother,
W. C. McClellan

PS I received your letter of the 24th- 3 days ago. The whole army there thinks peace will be decided in a few days. My humble opinion is we will have another Big Battle first. I got a letter from my Sweat heart a day or 2 ago. Give my respects to Miss Mollie Pettus[21] and tell her to mind her own business and let other people a lone. When I come home if she wants to marrie all she has to do is to say so. Tell Father I would have sent him the Richmond Enquirer before I left there, but we started the day I was going to subscribe for it. If he wants all of the news he had better subscribe for it. Send me the [Athens] Banner.

W. C. McClellan

Lawrence Ripley Davis to William Cowan McClellan

Aug. 7th 1861
At home
Dear Bill
I received your kind letter several days ago and would have replied before this only we did not know where a letter would reach you. I do not know if you will receive this as you say you have not received any of the great number of letters that have been written to you by your friends. I have now but little in the way of news to write but what little I have I will send along knowing that everything from home is interesting to you. Your father was elected to the Legislature on yesterday with Old Jim Shelton[22] of Elk River. Shelton is a clever old man but I preferred Donnell[23] who was best. As yet we

have not heard full returns from the Senatorial race between Coman, Hundley & Samuel Ragland. But I fear Bill Hundley will be elected.[24] He is undoubtedly the biggest fool alive, but I see how you care little of elections and I will come to other matters. John has been busy as a hen with one chick raising a company for the war with Jim H. Malone as Captain, Nick Richardson as first & Billy as 2 Lieutenant and he as third Lt. It is a fine company of men and they meet most Saturdays to organise.[25] I was in the company but was ruled out for reasons such as the following. Capt Abercrombie[26] has just died and the interest of my children demands my attention in that section. I would have been elected either Capt or first Lt as I might wish and this would throw one of the above-named in the ranks which I did not wish to do. I have a wife & four children and am a little too old for present necessities. But I intend to come on certain if this hellish war waged against us is to continue. I have nothing in the way of neighborhood news to write as all the things are found as you left them; nobody sick that I know of and nothing talked of but war and forced determination to desist the rule of Uncle Abe forever if needs be. Sallie [Sarah Anne McClellan Davis] wrote to you a few days ago and says she will write again soon. Your father wrote too yesterday and sent the letter from Athens. He did a thing at Shoalford that has never been done at any base in this country before. He got every vote twice. Flech McKinney Sheriff, Thos. Hine Collector, Mace Gilbert assessor.[27] Higgins company[28] left Athens yesterday for Courtland to join their Regiment at that place which is now full and will soon be on the tested field. Fifty thousand can be had from this State when needed that can whip the best two hundred thousand that Old Abe has got if they will come on our ground to fight. What has become of Jim Bailey. If you know anything of him let me know when you write. I know you to be a good soldier Bill and will only say to you that you should not do imprudent things. If you get into a battle be as cautious as you can and be sure to take good aim at first as the smoke will soon get so thick that you will be compelled to fight by guess. All join in love to you and hope to see you come through safe & sound. Write often and I will do the same.

Sincerely Yours
L R Davis

Little Jan says she loves you more as you go to fight for her.

Thomas Joyce McClellan to William Cowan McClellan

[Athens]
August 8th, 1861

Dear Will,
Having an opportunity to write to you by Mr Venable who goes to Manassas, I avail myself of it, I send by him for you a box of provisions. I hear through Al McDonald[29] (Although I have not seen him) that you are in need of something to eat. I hope you have not suffered, I put a letter in the office for you written by Bob and Matilda and a line by myself day before yesterday, I suppose you have heard that I was a candidate for the Legislature, I hesitated long before I could get my consent to make the race. The other candidates have canvassed half of the county before I came out. The consequence was a good many men were pledged to the other gentlemen before I was in the field. I am elected over Maj Donnell by 9 votes and Parson Shelton over me by 12 votes. It is supposed that Sen. Coman is elected over Bill Hundley by about 3 or majority. Alex McKinney is elected sheriff, [Mace] Gilbert Tax assessor. Thos. Hine collector. We have had no rain for two weeks last Monday but on tuesday we had a shower that helped a good deal, and there is now a prospect of rain, should we get rain soon we will make fine crops of corn, cotton is tolerable promising. Your Uncle Andrew is here and has been for some weeks. I believe he thinks of remaining some time yet, he is so disturbed about Berrys marrying that I dont think he ever wishes to see cane creek again. Fannie is in moderate condition. I drove her part of the time in the canvass and the balance I rode your horse he would ride well with proper training. Bob Sloanes[30] colt is dead. I suppose it died with blind staggers. Your pups are doing well. I suppose you would say they are very noisey. Nathan Fletcher is improving, it is probable now that he will get well. Your Mother is sending you some clothes you will need for the winter. we will try to send them to you. Were all greatly rejoiced about the great battle.

Thos J. McClellan

William Cowan McClellan to Sarah Anne McClellan Davis

Manassas Junction
August the 12th 1861
Dear Sister
I am happy to inform you that we have removed 12 miles from Bull Run [near Bristoe] and got a healthy place with two or 3 great springs within our lines. This is quite a romantic looking place. The cedars are so thick I think the yankees would have a hard time finding us. In my last letter I was complaining of being sick. I have about gained my strength and health in general. I had fever for 4 days and a slight touch of palpitation. In yours of the 28th you wanted to know how I get along in camp life. Well the boys say I am a good cook but the first meal of flour I attempted to make up I got the do[ugh] completely stuck to my hands. I worked away on it until I was tied up in it completely. I tell you I did not know what to do. a gentleman of experience came along and told me to put more flour into the bowl. Tell Mother it parted me verry quickly. I have done but little washing. I am hiring out a negro to do it for me at five cents a garment. at night roll is called every man spreads his rug down in tent blankets on my end and goes to sleep. roll is called again at daybreak and again at Evening. if a man is missing as soon as he walks in he is mustered off to the guard House a prisoner. I got into Capt Hobbs company. I have benn getting along very smoothly. Capt Hobbs wife is living in two miles of our camp. he stays with her about half of his time. The boys say they are going to stop him from going to see his wife. But he always asked permission of his company to get to see her. There has been a great deal of sickness in our Regiment. I have frequently at the dead hour of night heard the solem salute fired over the graves of poor soldiers. we have lost 15 or 18 men since we left Richmond. At Richmond Capt Hobbs has bested Houston twice. it is reported that poor George Hendrix is dead. we left him sick at Winchester with the measles. He got better and left there. no one knows where he went. I think it intirely probable he is in Richmond. Say nothing about this to Mr. Vaughan.[31] as soon as I can learn something definite about him I will write to Vaughan. To day is Monday yesterday I went to see my acquaintances in the 4 Regi ala. They were all glad to see me and gave me a good dinner. Tell Mrs Moore I saw all

of her kin[,] all well. Les Moore[32] was not wounded in the Battle neither was Peter Fletcher. But Peter did faint several times during the fight.[33] I expected to meet Jim Moore and John [McClellan] there. The 4th is incamped a mile and a half from here. Jeff Davis opposed the course of Gen Johns[t]on on the day of battle more than he did Gen Boregard I have heard men say in the hottest of the Battle Gen Johns[t]on in a torrent of bullets had praid aloud to the almighty god to spare the lives of his men and give them victory. I am very anxious to hear how the election went in Limestone, I hear Billy Day[34] was elected income tax collector. Tell John that Gracey has been promoted to Major.[35] Tell Bob if he wants to do a smart thing not to volunteer yet. I am very popular with the Boys in this company. they all call me Old Bill. I think if the Boys could vote Father would get two thirds of the Votes in the company. There is two of Mr Sheltons sons here very clever fellows.[36] Tom Cart [wright] is as fat as a hog. My hair is about an inch long. My Whiskers about 3 inches long. Hard indeed is a soldiers life. Tell Bob I am not looking about wanting him to take my place in the fall. There is one hundred and forty thousand troops in two hours march of Manassas Junction. Prince Napoleon has been to Manassas some of our Boys saw him.[37] I wrote a letter or too home in which I stated the killed and wounded on both sides it appears you failed to receive it. I will state the confirmation of the facts in the case. Our loss killed 250 to 300. Enemy 3500 our wounded 12 hundred Enemy still larger in proportion. Prisoners 600 so says Gen Johns[t]on. Tell Mrs Cartwright that I have just heard from Jim Bailey he is mending and thought to be intirely out of danger. This letter will be taken to Athens by a gentleman who has a discharge by the name of Strange[38] a member of Houstons company. I wrote to you to send me a pair of pants and india rubber coat, a bottle of Brandy which I want to drink for my health. You must all Write. give my respects to Mr Davis[39] and Jane, Pax and to the one Liz in fact all of them.

Direct your letter to Mr W.C. McClellan Manassas Junction Va Care of Capt TH Hobbs company F 9th Regi ala Va.

William Cowan McClellan to Robert Anderson McClellan

Manassas Junction
August 13, 61
Dear Bob.
Your kind letter of the 6th is at hand. I was glad to hear of Father's election to the Legislature- I got the letter last night, the officers and the men of the company gave a shout for old Limestone. I also received at the hands of Mr. John Carter[40] the bundle you sent me which was very acceptable. I can use everything advantageously except the cravat. If I was to put it on the Boys would laugh at me. The box of provisions I suppose is with the 4th [Alabama] Regt. by this time. We get enough to eat now; but the time has been when I would have given five dollars for a piece of meat and bread. That is when I remembered the oft repeated saying of Mothers that I ought to be thankful if I always had as much to eat as I get home. I have 45 dollars on hand yet. I have been paid 20 dollars since I have been in the service. Nearly everybody is out of money- officers and privates.

I think we will have a battle in a short time. Capt. Hobbs was up at the junction yesterday and saw a man who has deserted the Northern army who says the enemy is advancing towards Alexandria to which point our army is also advancing. There are 80,000[41] to move before we do. You must have no fears about our ability to whip them for the moment our army is ordered to march there will be raised a shout that will cause the earth to tremble. In my opinion if there is a fight at Alexandria Washington City will fall I don't think Jeff Davis wants Washington, but such will be the impetuosity of our troops that nothing on earth can prevent them from marching madly on to the Capitol. As an evidence of it, Beauregard puts the rear guard in front of the troops now moving on that way. Col. Wilcox was once the bosom friend of Gen. [George Brinton] McClellan- they both were Capts of companies in the Mexican war. Col. Wilcox waited on McClellan when he was married. He says Mc is a very fine man. I have no pistols yet. I am allowed to carry it any where I please, though if I was at home I would not start with one, it is a good deal of trouble to carry it. My health is some better than it has been. David Houston still drinking whiskey. He seems determined to disgrace himself at home and abroad. Soldiers can send letters free of charge now. My coat is as good as ever

I have worn it much, pants also. Tell Uncle Andrew to write to me. I am in hopes Malones Company will get in this Regt. Take good care of Fanny Fern. Tell Father to talk with Mr. Johnson who is going home on furlough. He is a member of Houstons Company- and he will be about Pecks having been a taylor for Peck.[42] He is a sensible man and a good friend of mine. I would like to have the india rubber overcoat I wrote for if it can be sent in any way. Stay at home Bob until I tell you to volunteer. Tell Mr. Davis to write to me. Give my respects to R. C. Davis.

Your brother
W.C. McClellan.

And tell him too the Lincoln County boys are well.

William Cowan McClellan to Matilda McClellan

Manassas Junction,
August 18th 1861
Dear Matilda,
I am glad to inform you that I am well and able to drill 8 hours a day. I received the Davis kind letter yesterday. I was glad to hear that John got an office in the Malone Company. I am in hopes that company will come to Va. I have received the box of provisions you sent me. I was over to see my friends in the 4th [Alabama] yesterday. They are all well. Poor Jim Bailey died a few days ago. He like many others sealed his devotion to his country with his lifes blood. Jim Bailey was the first boy I ever [k]new[.] with him is associated many of the most pleasant memories of my youth. But it is some consolation to know Jim sold his life dearly. I have benn told by men who saw him that he fought desperatley until he fell wounded upon the field. When down weltering in his own blood he was observed to [have] raised him self in a sitting position while he waived his hat to his comrades around him and told the[m] to stand by there country's flag. Jim died at culpeper court house on the Richmond and Manassas R. R. about 30 miles from here. I would have gone to see him had I not been surrounded by Bristling Bayonets. Tell Mrs. Cartwright I console deeply with her in her bereavement, and if it pleases god to let me live through this war I will bring the remains of her idolised son home to his native state. The health of our Regt is a great deal better than it was some days ago.

Troops are still moveing on to Alexandria every day- We have news of a battle in Missouri and Death of Gen. Lions[.] we were victorious.[43] Troops continue to pour in from Texas, Louisiana. The combined world cannot whip the army here, they are invincible. No fear exist in the army[.] they could march againced twice their number without the trimbling of a nerve. A Brigade of Louisiana Tigers[44] got here to day. They are the most desperate men on earth. On the day of battle there were some of them in the fight who had no Bayonets on their guns. The Yankees found it out and determined to charge Bayonets on them[.] they did so. The Tigers drew some large knives with strings to them witch they threw at the Yankees scarcely ever missing their aim. The Yankees soon ran like Rats from a Burning Barn.

Your brother, W.C. McClellan

August 20th
It has been raining about 4 or 5 days[.] the mud is about as deep as you ever see it in the house, but in our encampment. Tell Bob to drill every chance he gets[.] Nothing is [illegible] to a soldier than to be well drilled. I am the best drilled man in Capt. Hobb's companie and Col. Wilcox says Hobbs companie is the best drilled co. in the Regiment.

Yours,
W. C. McClellan August the 20

William Cowan McClellan to Robert Anderson McClellan

Manassas Junction
[mid-August, no date]
I have But Little system in Writing Letters, the first thing I think of is the first thing I write down, up one side of a sheat of paper and down the other. take care of Fannie, dont give her much corn to eat, it might caus her to go Blind. I will send my Watch home by Mr Phillips. Tell uncle Andy to Write me. Send me Jim Baileys Obituary by R. A. M. [Robert Anderson McClellan] I have seen the one signed W. T. S. Dr. Sanders I presume.[45] Tell Jim Moore, Al Martin to come on with Floyd[46] and join Capt Hobbs co, But you must not come Robin, tell John that the improved musket is a hundred percent Better gun than the Rifles he is getting. Give my compliments

to all of the girls in the country. tell them when I get Back I dont expect one of them can get Within 50 yards of me. I hear cannon towards Fairfax fireing about as fast as the Beating of your puls[e]. tell R. L. D. [Lawrence Ripley Davis] to Write to me. We were not in the fight he spoke of, direct your Letters to Manassas.

Your Brother,
W. C McClellan

P.S. Mr Pickett[47] tells me Malones co is still at Huntsville- Capt Hobbs says if the proper steps were taken Malones com[pany] could be annexed to this Regiment, which is one of the finest Regiments in the confederate service. I suppose Capt Hobbs has consulted with the Col or some one about it. It is nothing uncommon for a Regi to have Eleven companies in it- tell John I could give him some useful information about camp life, also about double column at half distance, about close in Mass deploy column on the 4 divisions, Wright and left into line Wheels, form square, reduce square, on the leading division, take Wheeling distance, March & Col. W[ilcox] has been curseing this Regi all the while untill the other day- he told us we had drilled remarkably well and that he was going to quit drilling be fore long.[48] Bob if I ever get home I wont mind double quickening it to Athens, no more than I would to Bill Vaughans,- Give my respects to Dr J. R. F. [John R. Fletcher],[49] Mr. J. M. M. [James M. Moore], Mr. B. S. [Dr. W. T. Sanders?] and J. H. M [James Henry Malone]. W. T. V. [William T. Vaughan] and I reckon old Hartwell.[50] I am in good order my flesh is as hard as a mules and I am about as tough. you spoke of Miss Mide Edmundson[51] paying a visit to your house, if she comes, why, give her my respects and tell her I'm a high private in the front rank.

Matilda McClellan to William Cowan McClellan

[Athens]
Thursday evening August 22nd 1861
My dear Brother,
We received your's of the 7th provismo yesterday, the only one we have gotten since the one you wrote the 29th July. I was glad you sent the old letter penned while at Richmond- as it contained the first intimation we have had of you meeting with the Tenn[essee]

boys. I was sorry to read of your sufferings. A box of provisions will start from Athens, Saturday, but I know of nothing to send but butter and dried fruit; which we will do when we hear whether you got the box Pa sent you or not. I expect you boys divide with each other; if so you can get some justice out of this box. The ladies everywhere are making clothing for the soldiers.[52] Mother will make you a grey suit and trim in yellow; also two pair of Linsey drawers, & two flannel shirts, which she wants you to put-on as soon as compatible with comfort. She will send you all you need. Your shoes I expect are wearing out. We have had a tremendous rain this evening. It is nearly dark now and has quit raining though cloudy yet. Mother went to the Davis's this morning, and Bob rode over after her. Pa is suffering intinsly from a pain in the back of the neck; and is unwell generally. I hear Jim Moore has quit Malones company[53] and will go on to Virginia. He and all the family are disturbed at the death of Jim Bailey, very much. I hope Malone's company will get-in the 9th Reg't, John wishes to. We commenced pulling fodder yesterday, but it rains so much they wont make much speed at it. The army worm is destroying, partially, crops in the neighborhood. I hope they will not be seriously injured. Bob saw Bill Day, a few days ago. He inquired particularly after you. Clint Davis helped him more than anybody on the day of the election. D[ay] got more votes than all of the other candidates together. Your little dogs are half grown; and promise to resemble all their kindred in all respects. Fannie Fern is looking well <u>and much esteemed by all who know her.</u> Sister received and responded to your letter long ago; but not knowing to which Regi you belonged. I suppose you will never get it. She intends writing again. We have written one or two letters every week since you left, it must be owing to the irregularity of the mails that you don't get them. By the by, you must write as often as circumstances will admit. Heart and lady are very anxious to inform you of their continued affection. Willie and Payne[54] send many messages and say they intend writing you. Uncle Andrew got a letter from Matthew Buchanan[55] who says the rain washed fences and a good deal of small grain. He said he had not seen Uncle B[errie] nor any body else here, we think but little about them. I have heard that Mr. David Blackburn[56] is very ill. I send you the election returns. Dr. Coman was 109 ahead of his competitors. Nath. Fletcher is improving. We got our funeral ticket to the funeral of Jo Todd.[57] I send you a piece of paper Bob scribbled on, but on the wrong sheet. This is Friday, and Pa has recovered and gone to the woods to get boards today to cover the French crib which they are hauling today. You must write nice letters to your sweet-heart. Little Sue[58] writes every body and is very good looking indeed. Write often for we are always anxious to hear from you.

Your devoted sister,
Matilda McClellan.

William Cowan McClellan to Robert Anderson McClellan

Manassas Junction
August 24the, 1861
Dear Bob,
I have written 3 or 4 letters home recently but owing to the uncertainity of the mails I fear they have not been received. I will send this one by Mr. Irie Hobbs.[59] I sent a letter to Athens about a week ago by Mr. Strange who had a discharge. We are encamped at the same place we moved to 3 weeks ago. The health of our Regiment is better than it has been. But I can hear every day the solemn salute fired over the tombless grave of a poor soldier. The Eleventh ala Regi is just by us. Also 4th, 10th, 12th, 17th ala Regiments. I was standing guard yesterday upon an eminance which over looks the valley of Manassas. As far as the eye can reach you can see nothing but tents and men. Where ever there is a spring you will find as many men as it will afford Water enough for. The army seems to be in a perfect lull at this time, but nobody knows how soon it may be changed to the impetuosity of a storm. The country around here is very thickly settled. Land poor the corn is just beginning to ripen. You have no idea of the difference in the climate here and in Ala. At night I sleep under two heavy blankets an scarcley keep warm at that. The following is a list of our dayley rations: 3 quarters of a pound of pickeled pork, a pint and a half of flour, a half pint of coffee, a little sugar occasionally- One candle equally divided betwean five messes. When we draw Pork or Beef we get a pound per day.[60] We drill from six to eight hours per day. I often think of what Rip Davis said about Hobbs and Houston when they were with there companies in Athens that they knew nothing about Military tactics- I have heard Col. Wilcox curse David Houston and others, one hundred times about drilling. Capt. Hobbs comp. is now a very fine

drilled co. The best in the Regi. We have quit the regular companie drill and got to drilling in what is called Skirmishing drill, it is the prettiest drill I ever saw. You ought to see us falling down behind a stump, a pile of brush, a fence, a gully, any thing firing all the time at will. Then you ought to see us when Capt Hobbs pokes his head out from a pile of brush and gives the command Skirmishers rally to Reserve. Every fellow breaks like a quarter horse for the Reserve which is a bout 200 hundred [*sic*] yards in the rear of the Skirmishers.[61] Your humble servant as always about the first that gets there too. N.J. Floyd is a fine Lieutenant. I am verry anxious to learn Where the Malone comp[any] will be ordered to. Tell John that he has got the only office I would have in a companie. A third Lieu-[tenant] has an easier time than anybody in a com[pany]. Say to mother I have not lost a thing but a pocket handkerchief since I left home. You must write me more whether or not you can read my letters, they are all written with a pencil. They may rub out before they reach you. My health is now good, and if it pleases almighty God to continue me in that Blessing I never will relax my grasp upon my musket until my country is Liberated or I am layed in my grave. Though I want to pay a visit home between this a[nd] Christmas.

I will close this letter as I had nothing to write on the out set. You must all write to me at least twice a week. Give my respects to Mr. Moore. Write to Mr. Will[62] and tell him to write to me. Treat Fannie Fern well. Tom Cart[wright] is well. William D. Pettus has just returned from a Hospital where he has been for 6 weeks he is well.[63] George Hendrix has not been heard of yet. Mrs Hobbs has been in camp several times lately. We send our letters free now.

Your Brother,
W. C. McClellan

Broad Run is the name of our camp companie F 9 Regiment ala Vol

William Cowan McClellan to Robert Anderson McClellan

Manassas Junction
Aug. the 30th. 1861
Dear Bob,

I expect to send this letter by Tom Bass who has gone to the Junction to day to be examined by the Medical board for the purpose of getting a discharge. I have no doubt he will get a discharge. He has been prostrate after 10 days not able to turn him self over without assistance with the Rheumatism. Tom is good game he never applied for a discharge, Capt. Hobbs did it for him. We received orders on deep parade yesterday evening to cook 3 days provisions[64] and hold ourselves in rediness to March at a moments notice. I don't think there is any likelihood of another attack from the enemy at this point. But I do think Boregard intends to take possession of the Arlington Heights, so say other military men of high standing. Old Abe has sent us word if one of us crosses the Potomac he will make that noted stream run red with Blood. It is the general opinion here if Kentucky would declare them self out of the union with the disaffection in Maryland, Ohio, and southern Illinois peace would be made in less than a month. Poor David Houston has been ordered under arrest by Col. Wilcox for getting drunk while he was officer of the day. he has been under arrest for a week. he will be tried to day at the Junction. I guess he will be deposed as Col W is one of the courtmartialmen. You may look for him home before long covered with disgrace. I am sorry for Houston although he treated me wrong once. Upon the whole he has done me many little kindnesses. more than all the other officers I have had anything to do with put together. So you see if I had accepted the position of orderly Sargeant witch he offered me I would now be 3 Lieutenant. the only position in a company I would have, and a position I think I am fully qualified to fill. I heard that Nick Davis is raising a Regiment. I would like to belong to his Regi Not that I am dissatisfied here but I would stand a better chance for promotion in Nick's Regi. There are 108 men in Hobb's company, 96 of them are appointees for office. So you see I will have a bad chance. Tell Mr. Rip [Davis] he or Mr. Nick [Davis] can fix any way for me to get another transfer I would take it as a favor. I would like to be in that Reg because John is in it, because Nick Davis is Col of it. At the same time I have no objection to Capt. Hobbs com[pany] either officers or privats. I tell you Bob a soldiers life is very hard indeed. But I stand up to my post without a murmur. Last night I stood guard in the hardest and coldest rain I ever saw fall at this season of the year. You say Mother wants to know who my mess is. Tom Bass, John, Rawlings, Tom Sandifer of Mooresville, Mc Rogers of Madison co. ala, R. R. agent above Huntsville.[65] Rogers is one of the cleverest men I ever new. he is now lieng just to my left with a burning fever while Tom Bass is on my right grunting with the Rheumatism. I have received yours of the 17th. You say you have not heard from the south West or from the South east. The Devil of it is I have heard from Boath places. You must all Write to me at least once a weak. Tell John I think he has treated me verry badly. I have written to him two letters I have received none from him. if he has never written to me and Will excuse me for writeing those two I will write no more, I hope before long to address you from Arlington Heights. Tell Mr. Moore to write to me. Tell Father I would like to hear his views about this war at present.

Your Brother,
W.C. McClellan

9 Regi ala Vol. coF care of Capt. Hobbs

William Cowan McClellan to Matilda McClellan

Broad Run.
Aug. 31, 1861
Dear Sister,
As Mr. [Tom] Bass did not get off yesterday I will write you a few lines to send by him tomorrow. I will send the bundle you sent me home by Mr. Bass as the weather has got too cool to wear them. I need a thicker pair of pants. Tell Father the next time he goes to Athens to get me a pair, it does not make much difference what color they are so they have a yellow stripe down the leg. [If] I had some rather they where grey. I have worn my Houston pants all the time they are very good pants yet, my coat is verry good also. Tell Peck to get me a good long India rubber over coat. it is of more service to a soldier than all the rest of his apparel. put them in a box and stuff the crevices with envelopes and paper, a pound of smoking tobacco. I have got plenty of money- Tell all the gals howdy for me and tell them God bless them for I have not thought about one of them since I have been in the army. The truth is I have had no time to think about anything- Col Wilcox says he was all through the Mexican War. he says he never saw as hard times on soldiers as we had in our March from Winchester to the R Road and our March from the Junction over to the battle ground and over it 3 or 4 hours in mud up to our knees raining millstones and pitchforks all the time and we in a double quick. Sleeping upon the

ground at night when we had to stick our knives in the ground to sink the water from our sides, it has carried many a man to his grave and will carry many more.[66] I was very sick when we started from Winchester but I performed every inch of the march. I am now in good health. I have written this Letter as well as many others. I write in great haste Never having time to read them over. You must all Write-

Your Brother
W. C. McClellan

Manassas Junction 9th Reg, ala Vol. care of Capt. Hobbs Co F

Matilda McClellan to William Cowan McClellan

[Athens]
Saturday August 31st 1861
My Dear Brother,
Bob sends off a letter to you this evening but as it was written a day or two ago I will write you a few lines to night. This has been the second clear day we have had in two weeks: cotton I suppose will be too big. Pa, Mr. Davis, Bob, and Tommy started to the depot [went instead] to a barbecue at Providence, but found nothing there but one live pig; then they went to the depot where they left Uncle Andrew to take the cars for east Tenn (Cleveland) sometime soon. He will return week after next. He says he will write you. As soon as he is able he will join the army. Pa rode today in a bran new buggy he got from Gill,[67] in recognition of his indebtedness to Pa. He gave his old buggy; and this one some time back would have sold for 250 dollars. New harness with it. I know you are crazy for news. Everything I believe has the same appearance about the place they had when you left- such as our golden harvest which has done as well as it promised, but betokens the advent of cooler days; I hope you will pardon me for telling you we have a <u>new garden gate.</u> I know you often think of the old things and places. it is now ten o'clock and John has come bringing three letters from you. I will stop now and read them. Yes three long letters this evening which gave us a great deal of pleasure and when you contrast the tone of one letter with the one you sent from the Northern girl[68] I know it makes you happy to receive letters from your own beautiful home in the "Sunny South" the whole tone of which is "stand by your colors"[69] Last week we got a late and old letter you sent at

Richmond of which I wrote you. Johns letter came to hand this evening. We get all your letters and read them very easily, though some of them are late. Your letters by Mr Strange were also at hand. We all had heard repeatedly of Jim Bailey's death but Mr. Strange almost convinced us to hope he still lived to reap the rewards of his gallantry so justly merited. Mrs Cartwright has named her babe Effie Bailey the latter for Jim. Pa, met Capt Francis.[70] He's going to the depot to get with a Regt from Texas of which he is chaplain. He has been up about three days, I understand Miss Sophy has an interest in Mr Firester of the 4th Ala Regi.[71] Burk Johnson[72] has sold out at the depot and intends to overseer again. John says they have about eighty men (80) and they intend going in camp here awhile. They can go for twelve months as they furnish their own guns. I am a fraid you cant read my letter, Mr Davis has been reading a long letter aloud by an irishman who is on our side. They said it was a good thing, I think he lived North, here the children together have confused me so I can scarcely write a connected sentence. I heard to day Billie Lowe[73] [Pvt. William Manning Lowe] had come home. Mrs Sue Davis has been with him several weeks. Mol is out here, Mrs Moore has been in Athens a week and Mr M. was caught on this side of the creek. I expect she has had twenty coniption fits. I am going to Athens tomorrow [to] Mount Zion for a big meeting; and will after finishing this letter until I take one of those trips. I may see some of your friends at Mount Zion. There has been a great change in the people in one respect as they are working for our soldiers. We are afraid they will have to winter in the old climate they are in and we must do all we can to forebear their suffering. When we send your flannel drawers and shirts you must wear them next [to] your skin. Dr Hearns[74] bought some for Tom just like yours. Mother will have hers woven this week.

Sunday Sepr 1st 1861
I went to church to day; and told Mrs Pettus of Willis Ps [William D. Pettus's] good health. She was very glad indeed to hear of it. Tell him they were all at church to day. Hal, Aunt Lucie, children showed in; and anxious to hear from him. Tom Cartwrights people are all well. Give my kindest regards to the Soldiers. I know as they send some messages when they write home. We had a very large congregation and fine sermon. Your friends inquired particularly of your whereabouts especially Billy Day. I havent been to this church since I went with you. Lizzie Douglas[75] will commence teaching

school at their Spring tomorrow. Mr Davis's children will go [illegible], I suppose Alice Moore[76] came up this morning to start to school in Athens North F. about the same [time]. I will send you the brandy for medicine. Mother has some excellent blackberry wine which will be of great service to you, Pa is creeping in but I was visiting in his room and tells me he cant get an india rubber overcoat in this part of the county. We will get one if possible. The little banner[77] has come out this week for the last time. I will write to Billie McClellan now and send Uncle Will word to write to you. Uncle A. [Andrew Beattie] will go up there when he gets back from east Tenn. You must write often for you dont know how glad we are to receive letters from you. The negroes send their half dozen messages round. I will write Bob one in a day or two if anything new transpires. We discussed your character this evening. I contended that your leading characteristic was that you were a good judge of human nature. Some of the family thought you was a jovial prince of a boy who trusted everybody until they did something to deceive you. I expect you would have liked to have heard us. Mr Davis is here.

Your Sister
Matilda McClellan

William Cowan McClellan to Robert Anderson McClellan

[Broad Run]
Sep the 6 1861
Dear Bob, I received your kind letter of the 31 Aug. You seem to want to take my place in the army. When I wrote to you asking you to take my place, my health was Bad and I did not think I could stand it- But I have been in good health for some time and if I continue to enjoy that blessing I will stay here until about the middle of December then if you will take my place I will come home. Two of us is enough to fight at a time. I think I know how you feel. you feel that you ought to be fighting for your country As did I. But 3 months service has completely cooled my patriotism. I have heard a many a man cursing the southern confederacy saying he would not care a darn if it was sunk. At the same time if called upon to fight he would fight like a devil. I would advise you to stay at home for the present. I may call upon you sooner to take my place. I expect you all think I am a sort of a grumbler But I grumble less

at the duties I have to perform than almost any man in Capt. Hobbs companie. Oh how I would like to take a coon hunt on old Limestone with you. Sweet are the pleasant recollections associated with that lovely stream. it has more charms for me than the rockey James, or the muddy Shanandore [Shenandoah], or the Potomac whose waters divides two Mighty Nations from [illegible]. It is now raining verry hard. Give my respects to old Hartwell[.] To all of the gals, Tom Cartwright is well give my respects to Bill Vaughn, tell old Brunswood[78] I have passed through Brun[swick] county [Virginia].

Your Brother
WC McClellan

William Cowan McClellan to Thomas Joyce McClellan

Manassas Junction
Sept 6, 1861
Dear Father,
We as I stated in my last letter are expecting marching orders every moment. Our troops are now in 8 hundred yards of the enemy with a continual skirmishing going on between the parties so you see a general engagement is un or voidable before a great while. The Federal troops seem backward in wanting to bring on the fight. Our troops have gained several hills that commands a full view of Arlington heights clost enough to be reached by our cannon. It is said by military men here that the taking of the heights amounts to the possession of Washington City.[79] Our best cannon can throw a Bomb or a Ball in any part of the city, and be perfectly secure from the fire of the enemy. Well may each party be backward or tardy in their movements when they do come together it will be the bloodiest day the world ever saw. It is said here that 20 thousand of our men have crossed the Potomac for the purpose of making an attack from the Maryland heights while the attack is cannonaded from this side. But it is extremely doubtful as the enemy have batteries planted all along the river. But there is one thing certain the troops are all gone from around here, but our Brigade and we may have to march before night. Our Brigade has been reposted unfit for service upon account of sickness. Our Regiment is in better health than it has been for some time. Our Regiment is said to be the best drilled regiment from Alabama.

I have just received Bob's letter of the 31st August. I was very glad to hear from home that you all are well also glad to hear of the doubt of Jim Bailey's death. Though his friends in the 4 all say there is no doubt about him being dead. Ever Body that visits our soldiers say they have undergone a great change, they have changed the light gleeful expression for a hard stern rigid look which marks the circumstances of all. This I suppose is attributed to so much sickness in camp. more than any thing else. Our Col. [Wilcox] I am afraid is going to be promoted to Brigadier General. He is one of the best military men in the south. He was Capt of a company in Mexico. He was the first man that ever waved the united States flag upon the dome of the capitol city of Mexico. He has been a Regular in the United States service ever since, until last Spring- He is frequently sent for, to go to Head quarters for the last 4 days. Gen. Johns[t]on has had him with him at Winchester[.] he is a man 35 years old. Tell Mother I will be very much obliged to her for the suit of clothes she spoke of sending me. I suppose before this reaches you will have received the letter I wrote by Mr. [Tom] Bass nameing some things I wanted such as writing paper, smoking tobacco, india rubber cape. I have quit chewing tobacco[.]it does not hurt me to smoke.

We have two men in our regiment that are going to stand before a courtmartial for going to sleep upon their post. I have one dozen peaches this season, for which I paid a quarter, one water mellon for which I paid 50 cents. You must all write to me once, twice a week.

Your Son,
W. C. McClellan
Care of Capt. Hobbs The 9th Regi. Ala. Vol.
Camp of Capt T. H. Hobbs. Company F

You must excuse my writing so bad This is very mean paper this is the first letter I have written with a pen since I left home.

Sarah Anne McClellan Davis to William Cowan McClellan

Athens
Sept the 9th 1861
My Dear Brother
I have waited a long time for a reply to my letter to you but have come to the conclusion that it never reached you as your move-

ments are so frequent and sudden, you have been so prompt to write home that I feel such that you could not forget me. I have a very bad chance to write having so many responsibilities acting upon me and I am so inexperienced too; that it takes all of my time to discharge them. Things are going on about as they were when you left, every body is working for the Soldiers all of the time, you will believe this when I tell you that Kittie is *hard* at work *knitting socks* (I did not think anything could induce her to work) she has knit more than any one lady in the neighborhood except Matilda. She is very much mistified that you do not say something about her in your letters. Mr David Blackburn died a few days after he got home from Virginia. Uncle Andrew has just returned from East Tenn, he says all of the sensible people are on the side of the South.[80] He is gone to Fayetteville now but will return in a few days to spend the winter with us. I hope he would be a great deal of company at the same time a great advantage while Pa is at Montgomery. Mollie Bronaugh[81] had a congestive chill last week and has been very ill ever since but is a little better to day. Miss Mollie P[ettus] is pursuing her same old course. I [have] not seen her since I received your letter. Mrs Bibb[82] comes to the neighborhood very frequent, but I have not seen her since she has bourn that name and never expect to; at least never intend to associate with her again. Matilda saw Mr Tom Allen[83] in Athens the other day, he said he had just got a letter from you. I was somewhat astonished at this, what was the nature of the epistle? Col Jones' remains arrived at Huntsville Thursday night. Mr Davis was there when they came, he said he never saw a large a crowd in H__ before. Willie Lowe is at home[.] His recovery is thought doubtful. Capt Malone is making every effort to get his company into confederate service but he will find it hard to do. Pa says he would be very glad to have you write to him. Mr Davis says you must write to him, he has written two or three. Mother says you must write her word what you need and she will try to send it. Fannie Fern is doing finely and looks splendid in the new buggy, your dogs also are doing well they are very mischevious but well treated especially by Tommy who pets them on buddie Willie's acount. Paxy, Jane, Mol & Sue all send their love to you. Mol talks often about the man who has gone to fight for her. Write often to me. More anon

Good bye, Your affect. sister,
Sallie, D.

Sepr 9th 1861
I came over yesterday to stay with Sister to day while Mr. Davis and John go to Athens to day. I received a letter from cousin Andy Wright who wants to get a letter from you. I also got one from Puss Davis[84] who says all are anxious to hear from you. I sent Uncle Will [McClellan] word to write you. We are all listening to hear of another battle. every thing is so still. The last letter we got from you was of the 24th of August. We know you have written since. Bart Lowe[85] says Jim Baily requested to be brought home to die, and when that couldnt be done he wanted to be intered in his native land He was told later that couldnt be done this time of year. He then said he had fought like a man and would die like a man; and made no more requests. Leslie Moore arrives in Richmond this week. A good many of the 4th Ala Regt are at home[.][86] Bob Lowe has Typhoid Fever, Peter Fisher is at home on furlough. Write very soon to your sister Matilda. Hobbs company will soon have good warm cloths sent them.

John Beattie McClellan and Matilda McClellan to William Cowan McClellan

Sept. 10 1861 [the first section is written by John]
Dear Will
I received a letter from you two or three days ago which was the only one that I have received. I suppose the other never arrived. My neglecting to write to you has not been because I did not feel a duty [illegible] in your [illegible]. I enjoy hearing from you every day or two by one means or the other but as you know I am generally an indifferent correspondent, but I will try to make an effort in the future. Nick Davis is not raising a regiment as you seem to have ben informed. Our company together with Higgins & Gilberts of this County will go into camp at Huntsville in the course of a week, there to be organized into a regiment under I know not whom. I do not think there is any probability of our being ordered to Virginia. The recent movements in Kentucky seem to indicate that we will go in that direction, at any rate I hope to get into active service soon somewhere, I regret very much to learn that by leaving Houston's Company at the time you did you failed to get

office, I hope there can be some arrangement made by [illegible] so you can get into our Company as I think that at this time there will be little chance of our being in the same field of operations. Uncle Andy is now staying at our home but is now gone to Fayetteville whence he will return in a day or two. He is greatly improved in health and spirits. Peck says it is almost impossible to get an overcoat of the kind you want but the other things will be sent on shortly and the coat too if it can be obtained. Charley Sale[87] who returned from Va. a few days since has died. We have just heard of the fight at [illegible] Hill but do not yet know whether your regiment was engaged. There is considerably much anxiety about it. I dont know of any news in the county. I shall write to you soon after our company gets to Huntsville. Write to me often.

Your brother,
JB McClellan

Tuesday night Sepr 10th [the following section is written by Matilda] Sister and I wrote to you yesterday but as John has written half of a sheet- I will try to fill this page. I see in this letter Bob has sent-up to night for me to send off a proposal to take your place immediately. I think you know better not [to] be hasty on your movements, as you know it takes Pa sometime to think as his children do. He is affraid to think Bob will not return when you rejoin your company. Can he take your place awhile. I never heard only from you. It is late I have been up long since Mr D. [Davis] Pa and the rest retired[,] fixing Johns things to go into camp tomorrow which will be the day you will have been gone 14 weeks. It appears like an age since that bright morning you started. There is great commotion here with regard to Kentucky. Arms are passing up there daily. Zollicofer[88] is stationed at Frankfort- (the Captital of that state) and has a large force. Leslie Moore will be buried day after tomorrow. We got the letters you sent by Tom Bass yesterday. Dont be disturbed about your clothes, for the whole company will have new clothes soon. I would write better but am tired and it is late. Write often, Pa will write soon. We looked for Uncle A. [Andrew Beattie] back to tonight; I will write if he brings any news. Good night, your sister, Matilda. We will send you some thing for medicine if Mr Phillips will carry it. Pa says be kind to the Griffis boy.[89]

William Cowan McClellan to Robert Anderson McClellan

Manassas Junction
Sept 13 61
Dear Bob.

Lieutenant Floyd will start to Limestone to morrow to get recruits for our Regiment. I will send this note by him. I hope you will not be one of his recruits. My health is very Bad now I have the yellow Janders [jaundice] my skin is as yellow as a pumpkin, my eyes are also very yellow. Our Sergean [surgeon] says it will take me 3 or 4 weaks to get over it. I am confined to my tent. I am going to get Lieut Floyd to see the Col for me this evening to see if you can take my place a while but I fear the only way the swap can be brought about is direct communication with Gen. [Leroy Pope] Walker. If I possessed good health I would never release my strong hold on my musket until my country was liberated or filled a soldiers grave. The Janders are a lingering disease though not a fatal one. I will wait until Floyd comes back from the junction[.] he went to see Gen Johns[t]on about going to Limestone. He may not go. Lieut. Floyd has got Back[.] he does not know when he will get off to Limestone- our regiment has been joined to another Brigade, it is the only Regiment in our old Brigade that is fit for service.

Our Regiment I think will leave for Fair fax courthouse to morrow. I will wait until dress parade our orders will then be read out. I suppose our troops are going to attack Arlington heights in a day or two. I would give my years wages to march with the Boys to Fair fax but I am not able to walk. I suppose we will be left here in a little hospital. I will send this letter by Mr Beckum[90] who has been discharged from Houstons old com[pany] which Gaines Smith has manage of now. Old Gen Houston has been here for several days trying to get his son restored to his position. Old Billy Robertson has arrived here a few days since he found his son verry low he had him moved to a house. I suppose he is improving slowly.[91] Tell Father not to get uneasy about me and comeing here. Less Moore died of fever in Richmond a few days ago. J. E. Fletcher[92] is out in the country. A little Lick you must send me the cordial you spoke of sending. If I knew Nick Davis was in Richmond, I would write to him and get him to see [Leroy Pope] Walker for me. I will write again in a few days.

Wm. C. McClellan

William Cowan McClellan to Thomas Joyce McClellan

Manassas Junction.
[mid to late] September 1861
This was written upon a Board a foot long 6 inches wide
Dear Father.
I received a letter from Sister the 15th dated the 9th Sept informing me of the health of you all. We have heard here that the health of North Alabama was verry Bad. I wrote a letter a few days ago in which I stated I had the Yellow Jaundace verry bad. I am some better. I have been sick about half of the time since I have been in the army mainly dierhea, the yellow jaundice is caused by a foul stomack. The Surgeon says I have got a good condition although I have been sick so much. I cannot eat pickle pork or Beaf without derangeing my bowels. We are at the same place we moved to a Month and a half ago. Broad Run. I now hear the Boom of canon towards Alexandria it is verry constant and verry heavy.[93] To day I think will be a Bloodier day than the ever memorable 21st. We will be apt to learn in a few hours what is to pay. I will then inform you. I wrote to Bob. I wanted him to take my place a while but if it does not meet withe the entire approbation of you and the rest of our family I do not want him to do it. if my health was good I would never think of such a thing as quitting the army. I think if I was at home I would get well in a month. I suppose I could get a furlough if I was to apply for it though it is getting very difficult to get a furlough upon account of so many applications. Tell Bob to consider well before he agrees to take my place. plowing is a mere matter of Moon Shine compared to a Soldiers life- drilling from 5 to 7 hours a day at a double quick step, toat your wood a half mile- sometimes on your shoulder to get your supper, rubbing your gun an hour or so, wash your cloathes and several other little things too tedious to mention, is your daily occupation. All of which I have performed cheerfully when I was well. Gen. Houston called upon me in my tent last night. He and his son Both seem verry kindly disposed towards me. The old gen. is doing his best to have his son replaced to his position as capt. but it seems he has not met with but little success.[94] N J Floyd has been appointed recruiting officer of our Regiment. He started for Limestone a day or two ago. Floyd will get more recruits than any other man in the Reg[iment] could get.[95] I was sorry to see him leave, he is the best officer our com-

pany had. He was my officer in the company the favorite of all the Boys. John Featherstone will be appointed quarter Master of the Regi I suppose. I have talked with Captain Hobbs about getting Bob to take my place. He says I cannot get a substitute under any circumstance. I think my health will be Better as soon as cool Wether sets in. I am a good deal better of the Jaundice this morning. Tell Bob to stay at home and attend to matters this year by christmas I think I can fix it so he can take my place. 250 of our men whipped 3,000 of the enemy and run them from Halls Hill[96] where they were intrenched a few days ago, the fireing we heard yesterday must have been an artillery drill as we have heard nothing of a fight yet. Dan Coleman[97] who is one of Gen Cocks aid decamps paid us a visit a day or two ago, he says he has seen 3 Balloons go up a day for the last week from the Enemys intrenchments upon Arlington Heights.[98] Our Brigade is now composed entirely of alabamians, I understand we will be stationed 8 miles below Washington city to defend a battery we have placed there in a fine thicket at the mouth of a little creek. Just opposite on the other side of the Potomac is Mount Vernon. You must write as soon as this comes to hand.

Your son
W C McClellan

Father 3 months service has been worth more to me in the way of makeing a man of me than the last five years of my life. It has learned me to be self reliant and independent of the favors of men, it has learned me to do my own thinking, to attend to my own business, and provide for my own wants. Some men this war will ruin forever, some it will be a blessing to. If it please god to crown the southern army with success and return me and my comrades to our peaceful home after a year or two [of] strife, I will consider that I have spent my time gloriously. My pants are about worn out. I will Patch them in a day or so so they will do to weare some time yet. I suppose our uniforms will be here in a few days. Tell Mother to send me the home spun suit she spoke of sending.[99] I have got a pair of new shoes. I have got 2 peaces of the Bacon you sent me yet, did it come from home. Send me a bottle of Brandy and some of Mothers cordial. I will not drink too much, When do you go to Montgomery. I have written to Uncle Will [McClellan]. I told him he and Uncle [Andy] Wright and John might send me a

Box of provisions. I am not neading it at present. I will let you know when I need anything. My love to all tell Sis I will Write to her in a day or two.

Robert Anderson McClellan to William Cowan McClellan

North Alabama
September 16, 1861
Dear Will,
We have received no letter from you since those you sent by Tom Bass. Tom is improving some since he returned. I talked with him in Athens yesterday. He says you are fearful that we would have killed all of your hounds. they are all still living but the big old spotted one and Lex. They have long passed through the dark valley of the shadow of death on their way to eternity. Their clarion long call are heard no more upon the trail of the wild deer or the long track of the wily hair. I went to Athens yesterday to see if Malones Company had left. They are still there but expecting orders to leave today or tomorrow. John was not there. He had gone to Nashville to see someone about some cooking utensils. he got back, I suppose last night. They will go to Huntsville. Higgins company has gone to Memphis. Perhaps Malones company will go the same way from Huntsville. Nick Davis is not raising a regiment now, although he may be elected or appointed Col. of one of them collecting at Huntsville. He did set out to get up a Regt when he got back from Richmond but Humphreys and Clint were trying to form a Brigade and he quit. Clint is now raising a cavalry company, but I do not know how many men he had got. Uncle Andy got back from Lincoln last Thursday evening. He brings but little news from there. He staid all night at Willey Buchannans as he went up. His gal was solicitious of your welfare but more so of mine. I think I shall take her in before long. Puss Davis, two preachers, and Uncle John [McClellan] and Uncle Will [McClellan] will be down in a day or two. The preachers are on their way to Mooresville to a big meeting. The others are coming on a visit. Miss Mide Edmondson will be here during the conference which begins the first of October at Athens. If she is good looking I will hop around here considerably while she is down. In fact I have concluded to get married anyhow, I have a notion to go down to see Andy W[right]. I think I can

come in over the concentrated powers of all the enemy especially as they have gone to the war. At least I will try it. We will get done pulling fodder this evening. Some was lost but there will be about thirty stacks. The fields in sight look as dry as they generally do in December; though the country still retains its beautiful green color. But on all hands are to be seen indications of the departing summer days, while the touching wind from Yankeedom tell tales of coming winter. Since I wrote the above Rip Davis came in. He brings news that there was a battle at Leesburg[100] a few days ago in which we killed 600, wounded 1500, and took 4000 prisoners. he says that your regiment was in the fight, our loss very slight. I suppose it is uncertain yet. I will find out before I send this letter, so I can direct it right. Rip says Clint has his corps about full. He got 40 or 50 horses in Huntsville yesterday. Alfred Martin and Jim Moore are neither going with Malone. Jim Moore was defeated for office and will not go. Martin is a coward and will not go. I wrote an obituary of James Bailey. I spoke of what you wrote in your letter that he had acted nobly after he had fallen. I put it in the Independent. John Blackburn[101] got back some days since. I saw also Jack Bridgeforth[102] who has returned from Hobbs Company. Leslie Moore was buried in Huntsville the other day. I am still eager willing and anxious to take your place. I suppose you could get a transportation ticket as did Pete Fletcher and it will cost you nothing to come home. I can get a ticket from Clements.[103] I will write no more on this letter until tomorrow.

17th Billie Vaughan passed here just now on his way up to Rip Davises to help him put silt under his house. This is one of the most beautiful mornings that ever dawned upon the earth since I have been knocking about these diggins. The winds seem to sleep among the trees, now and then lifting the leaves just enough to be seen. A few clouds set along the heavens like the distant dome of some majestic temple while the sun rides gracefully along her silvery course. I caught a coon and a "possum" last night- the coon made no fight- I shot him. Rush is now the best coon dog in the county. He takes them in every time I go. He has had some masterly fights but has always come out victorious with Jack- Gen Johns[t]on to help him. Father will take this letter to Athens tomorrow. Rip will go down with him. I expect to get a letter from you this Evening at the office. Write soon and often. As soon as possible we will get the coat. RAMc

William Cowan McClellan to Robert Anderson McClellan

Manassas Junction
Sept 19, 61
Dear Bob
I received yours of the 6th, Johns also. I wrote a letter a day or two ago in which I stated that it was almost impossible to get a substitute for any length of time so you see you cannot take my place.[104] I do not know that I would give up my place now any how as my health is almost restored. I am almost well of the Jaundice although I am considerably reduced. All I ask is health. when a man gets sick here Bob there is but little attention paid to him every man is for him self and him self only. For that reason I would like to be in Malones comp. for me and John would be of mutual benefit to each other. The Richardsons I suppose would also be verry happy that you volunteered. I think you will have a shoving time enough. you may have to use that strong arm of yours at that little gate that stands by the tree. Show this letter to Father and ask his advice about it. We are still at Broad Run not far from the Junction but expecting orders every day. I am not quite able to March yet. 6 or 8 of our men are in the same fix. We will be left or hauled.

Your Brother,
W.C. McClellan

I will write again in a day or two. Tell Rip Davis to Write to me John, Matilda you all must write.

William Cowan McClellan to Thomas Joyce McClellan

Manassas Junction
Sept. 21. 1861
Dear Father
We have at last got marching orders. to Morrow morning at 6 o'clock we take up our line of march to Senterville [Centreville]

distance 18 miles.[105] 18 miles nearer the goal of contention of the capitol of the united states. In a week that beautiful city, the home of George Washington and once the pride of every heart upon the continent may be reduced to a blackened mass. On the other hand that city may stand. its present occupants maintain their positions. and upon the sloap of Arlington may lay the inanimate Bodys of thousands of the Brave Confederates. I may fall in that glorious struggle struck for liberty. But be assured of one thing. I will fall facing the enemys guns. I do not think it will excite me any more to go into Battle than I have ben a many a time when I walked into the garden to kill a Beaf. Our Regiment has been drawn up into a line of Battle twice. I saw but few men who was not as firm as the rock of ages. I do not know of cours that we are going to attack Arlington, it is mere conjecture with me, but the intire force of Manassas except enough to man the batteries are moving on that way. My health is now very good. The Jaundice have almost left me. I expect to perform this March in a wagon not being quite stout enough to March. Pleas send me a pair of heavy Blankets, it is almost impossible to get Blankets here and when we do find one we have to give from 6 to 10 dollars for it. We were paid 21 dollars for our uniforms at Richmond is all the Government money we have received since we have ben in the service. I have now 41 dollars. I have the (20) dollar gold piece you gave me yet. My old black hat is as good as ever except that it has some Yankee Buttons stuck about on it. I wrote to Bob a day or two ago to stay put at home for the preasant. I think it is folly for us all to leave home at once. I also wrote to Bob that I would like to get into Malones co. for reasons I have already named[.] if you think it could be done I would like for you to make the effort, perhaps some of your friends in Huntsville could get me a transfer. Gen. Clemens [Newton Nash Clements] for instance. Since writing the above our Surgeon informs me that I cannot march or even go on with the Regiment for a few days. My self with several others of our co. will be left here in the Hospital. I expect to send this letter by Gen. Houston, who is going to start Home to morrow morning- Capt David Houston has been restored to his position or office. There is a great deal of anxiety here about the cours Kentucky will be forced to take- some say Gen. Polk ought to remove his forces from her soil- Others say that they would hold Columbus let come what might. Those of the former opinion say it will be decidedly to our advantage for her to occupy a neutral position & then we would have 800 miles less border to defend- I think the way things are moving on Kentucky will be delluged in Blood simply becaus She is trying to maintain a poisition of armed Nutrality.[106] I get a Richmond paper nearly every day. Sorry to learn that Gen. Walker has resigned.[107] Tom, Kelly, and Willie's letters will be left here with me. they have ben sick for some time though not dangerous. Also my mess mate McRogers, who is just recovering from the typhoid fever. you must all write to me directing your letters to Manassas- give my respects to Bill Vaughn.

Your son,
William Cowan McClellan

4
Camp at Centreville, Virginia
September 27–December 31, 1861

> We are still encamped quietly at this place awaiting impatiently an attack from a cowardly foe . . .
>
> —William Cowan McClellan

Thomas McClellan wrote to William that not only was paper money too scarce for the wealthiest men to pay their taxes, but terrible price inflation was setting in with no end in sight. This season had also been one of the worst for gathering crops, and Thomas despaired about the suffering and sadness caused by the war. William's brother Robert joined a cavalry regiment that currently was in Alabama, while his brother John was still trying to raise a company of volunteers. Unlike William, the brothers had volunteered for service only after northern Alabama was threatened by possible invasion. State authorities in both Tennessee and Alabama were calling for more volunteers for a twelve-month period.

On September 22, the 9th Alabama moved from the area of Manassas to the village of Centreville, where the Confederate forces were concentrating. The 9th joined the 10th and 11th Alabama regiments along with the 38th Virginia, the 19th Mississippi, and the Thomas Artillery to form a brigade in Gen. Edmund Kirby Smith's Second Division (the Virginia and Mississippi regiments would later be replaced by the 8th and 12th Alabama regiments). At the same time, Gen. Joseph E. Johnston positioned the army around the Fairfax Court House with outposts overlooking Washington, D.C., at Munson's Hill and Mason Hill, which were commanded by Gen. J. E. B. Stuart. In support of those operations, the 9th Alabama went on picket duty and patrols that took them to Mount Vernon, Falls Church, and Fairfax (other patrols took them west along Braddock Road past Centreville toward Leesburg). At the same time, the Union army occupied a position along the heights on the Virginia side of the Potomac River, extending from Georgetown to Alexandria. By October, Johnston became concerned that the strength and efficiency of the Union army were making the Confederates' advanced positions in Northern Virginia hazardous, and he pulled the army back toward Centreville and Dumfries.[1]

In October, much to the dismay of the men in the 9th Alabama, Cadmus M. Wilcox was promoted from colonel of the 9th to brigadier general, and he took charge of the brigade. Morale sagged as no colonel was immediately appointed for the regiment, and the men grumbled about the possible candidates. Filling the position of colonel would create a constant morale problem for the regiment—one that would eventually lead to increased desertions by 1864.

While not directly involved in the action, William Cowan McClellan and Company F cheered the Confederate victory at Ball's Bluff and watched as Union prisoners were marched through Centreville on their way to Richmond. The battle, the only significant one in Northern Virginia that fall, began on October 21 when a Union reconnaissance in force along the Potomac River east of Leesburg, Virginia (in preparation for a possible flanking movement to force the Confederates out of Leesburg and probably to force the evacuation of Centreville) had escalated from a skirmish into a small battle at Ball's Bluff, which proved a disaster for the Federals. Afterward, the fall and winter of 1861 saw only minor raids and many rumors of an impending final battle for Washington.[2]

When not out on picket duty, the 9th set up camp in tents just west of Cub Run and on the north side of the Warrenton Turnpike. Confederate soldiers and free blacks began work on the extensive fortifications at Centreville, and they turned the village into an impregnable fortress. Later, their efforts focused on constructing a military railroad between Manassas Junction and the fort at Centreville. By Christmas, the regiment was building winter cabins near the Lewis House, about one mile south of the Stone House on the Manassas battlefield.[3]

Captain Thomas Hubbard Hobbs described the work on the Centreville fortifications in his journal: "I was in charge of a party at work on the breastworks. Centreville is now surrounded by a cordon of entrenchments which frown from every hill. We are on the hill next to Rock Run [Big Rocky Run]."[4] Construction on Artillery Hill began before the First Battle of Manassas, and work on the remainder of the fortifications began in October 1861. Company F was one of many companies that provided men for the work details each day to build the redoubts and breastworks. Drilling was cancelled to keep their work on schedule. Later, the men began constructing their winter quarters: log houses with six to twelve men in each cabin. With fifty thousand men in and around Centreville cutting wood, the surrounding countryside became a virtual desert. Trees were cut down farther east along Braddock Road to improve the field of vision from the fortifications atop the ridge at Centreville, and cannons positioned in the redoubts commanded the countryside for miles in every direction. According to one local historian, the five-mile-long fortifications at Centreville began

> on the left at the valley of Cub Run . . . crossed Rocky Run about 1,000 yards north of the Warrenton Turnpike and ran . . . along the crest of the plateau above Rocky Run a distance of two miles, to a hill northeast of Centreville which overlooks the valleys of both Rocky Run and Little Rocky Run. Here they turned at a right angle and extended south for another three miles along the plateau commanding the valley of Little Rocky Run to its confluence with Bull Run . . . The works, with perfect fields of fire down the long slopes descending to the two streams, consisted of 13 battery positions containing embrasures for 71 field guns, connected with one another by infantry trenches. The salient angle near Centreville was defended by a massive bastion pierced with embrasures for seven guns and flanked by skillfully sited outworks.[5]

The formidable fortifications at Centreville probably could not have been taken in battle. The war, however, was focusing on the cities of Richmond and Washington, and not Centreville. An army could easily bypass this position on its way to Richmond, which is exactly what Gen. George McClellan would do when he launched his Union invasion of the Virginia Peninsula in 1862.

Through the fall and winter of 1861, William still hoped for an assault on Washington, D.C., but he saw that possibility become less likely as the weeks went by. What he did not realize was that in a September 31 meeting with Beauregard and Johnston, President Davis informed them that the men and materials needed for an assault on Washington were not available. Most of the original volunteers in Company F were waiting on their friends from home to finally enlist and were becoming angrier with the men who kept finding excuses not to join them. Lt. Nicholas Floyd was sent back to Limestone County to raise troops for the company to replace the ones who had been lost to sickness and injury. Without being in a single battle, the 9th had already taken significant casualties through sickness and disease. William wrote home that in addition to those who had died, fifteen men in the company had already been discharged and twenty-five more were not in camp for various reasons. For the next three months, William would have to be content with picket duty, patrols, and building military fortifications.

William Cowan McClellan to Matilda McClellan

Centreville.
Sept. 27, 1861
Dear Sister,
My health is now better than it has been since I left home. I stayed at Broad Run about 4 or 5 days after the Regiment moved to this place. Yesterday I came on to the Regi. We are now incamped precisely where the Yankees were incamped before the Bull Run Battle drinking out of the same spring and using the same ditches around our tents. Centreville is situated upon a high hill commanding a view of the country around for miles. I stopped and cast my eyes around as far as the eye could see there was tents soldiers wagons and horses. from that vast assembly of soldiers there went up some of the most interesting music I ever heard. Brass Bands comengling with the harmonious notes of the drum and fife. by the by we will have a Band in a few days. A Brigade left here last night in the direction of Washington city. There is no troops here this morning but our Brigade and it is said that we have Marching orders now, we have been ordered to cook three days provisions. As you can see we are the rear of the army. We have a powerful army between here and Wash. Lincoln a more powerful one. Matilda thease armys [are] the most powerful ever assembled on earth. We must meet before long, it promises to be the Bloodiest Battle by far ever fought by men. it is currently Reported that Lincolns Artillery was crossing Main Bridge all day yesterday. Our Regiment has the advantage of almost any Regi in the army. we have the Best Col. by a long way in our Brigade. it is said that Gen Johns[t]on says Col Wilcox is the Best officer almost in his division of the army and he shall be in the next fight to show what he is. I have received no letters since the 11th of September. I am extremely anxious to hear from home. I sent a letter by Gen Houston- one a few days previous to that, by a Mr David Goldsmith who belonged to Houstons co & deserted a few days ago. is he in Limestone or is he in the North his wife is in Athens, his Mother and Father are in the North. I saw the Louisiana tigers drill yesterday they went at double quick charge Bayonets. they yell like a pack of hounds making the most friteful noise I ever heard. I am in fine spirits and eager for a fight. Tell Rip Davis when we have a fight and take Washington city he had better come up, it will be a glorious time. I would like to see him up here any

way. I am now twelve hundred miles from home, 20 miles from Washington city, 7 miles from Manassas Junction. You must continue to direct your letters to Manassas Junc. I heard nothing of the 4th ala Regi but I have no doubt we will hear from her when the smoke clears up from the Battlefield. I heare the Booming of Cannon in the direction of Washington city. Artillery drilling perhaps or they may be fighting. you would be astonished to see how little attention the soldiers pay in sutch things occasionally you will hear a man say if they dont quit this foolishness some body will get hurt. I hope the next letter I write will be headed, Washington City, October 4, 5, or 6 th- Give my respects to every Body. What has become of Malones co and John. I hope Bob is at home yet. Tell Father to Write to me tell Mother I will soon need her Warm Drawers and Shirts. Tell Mother I would rather see her than any Body on Earth. I will write again in a day or two. It is raining very hard. You all must write. your Brother

Wm C. McClellan
Manassas Va

Tom Cartwright is well and in fine spirits. Tom Kelly is better, so is William Pettus. Tell Mr [Jim] Moore if he was here he would soon grow so he would not be as afraid of thunder.

W.C. McClellan

Robert Anderson McClellan to William Cowan McClellan

Limestone Creek
September 28th 1861
Dear Will,

The last letters we got from you were those you sent by Nick Floid. Though Houston has returned and we understand he has a letter from you. If you desire it the proper steps will be taken to get you a transfer to Malones Company, Although L. P. Walker has been resigned I suppose his influence could get you one. I was in Huntsville today. John could not come out on account of having to go to Decatur this evening to get a few more men in the company. The boys are all in fine spirits and are living fine. They are camped in the grove where [William Lowndes] Yancy spoke last summer. I learned from Col. Zeb Davis[6] that he is a candidate for Congress.

He will give the other candidates Jones & Foster all they can toat on the stump and beat them to death on the ground. Without knowing anything I think he will clear the field. Nick Davis is to be the Col of the Regt at Huntsville. Clint Davis has a cavalry co. about made up. He will join Pope Walker's legion forming at Huntsville[7] I would advise you to wait until malones Co is gonne into a fight. Then perhaps they will come on to the Potomac. If they do then you would have no trouble getting in it. I have abandoned the notion of going to the war, if I ever had any other idea. Though I will take your place anytime. You seem to be uneasy about your dogs. They are all doing well. I offered to let Gabe Hilliard take Nimrod & the speckled puppy- not one of the young ones- to run fast with awhile. He promises to take good care of them. he will train them by the time you get back by running them with his older dogs. Besides he is coming to go with me over in the swamp towards Vaughans. I will have all the dogs taken good care of. You need not be uneasy about them. As these lines are very dim and I will have no time in the morning to finish this letter before I go to the depot after John as he comes back from Decatur I will close for tonight and go up to the house where Rip Davis, Andy Beatie & Tom McClellan are discussing the events of the war. So good night; have to go.

Sunday
Again the skies are clear. The big heavens sends down its fervid glory of dazzling silver while the earth throws back its glittering scintilations of responding beauty more splendid than the sun light that flashed its blazing glory athwart the golden plains of Eden in the days of yore. But you doubtless have as beautiful weather as grand scenery on the rolling Potomac as we have here. It might be a beautiful sight to see the spires of Washington city lifting their gilded summits gracefully up against the distant mountains or piercing the far off smoky sky, while away back to the west rises in solemn grandeur the dark towering blue Ridge. But to one surrounded by such stern realities as you are this is stale uninteresting stuff. So I will quit. We have some good clothes to send you by the first chance. Warren Phillips is going on before long with Captain Hobbs Co[mpany's] clothes but I reckon we will send you yours before he goes. Venable[8] starts in a few days for the Alabama volunteers on the Potomac. You will be certain to get your clothes soon. James Moore

went up to Huntsville some days ago but they gave him leave to come back a few days as he left his business in a bad condition. He will return in a day or so. We are picking cotton in the Barret field. Getting about one hundred to the pound. The cotton will be short this year- very. Old Heart [a McClellan slave] is in unusually good health at this time. Your puppies are beginning to run the trail like regulars. I have not been so successful hunting since I wrote last- not having caught but one oppossum. I have tried several times but I was not quite smart enough for him. In fact, Rush was barking up the creek last night while I was writing but I did not go to him. The neighbors are all stirring about as usual. Uncle Andy [Beattie] is still here. He & father are going up into Williamson Co Tenn near Nashville to see some kinfolks before long

R A McClellan

William Cowan McClellan to Robert Anderson McClellan

P.S. direct your Letters to Manassas
Centreville.
September .30. 1861
Dear Bob
I received your kind Letter of the 19th yesterday. it was very acceptable as I have not heard from home since the 15th. Your letters generally wreach me in .5. 6 or 8 days after they are written. My letters are not neare so prompt in wreaching you from the fact that there is so many Letters mailed at Manassas. Our Brigade is still incamped at Centreville. we drill an hour and a half company drill before Breakfast. We drill two hours Brigade drill commencing at 9.o.c ending at 11.o.cl. We drill 2 hours Battalion or Regimental drill com. at .4.oc quitting a 6 o.c. p.m. so you see we drill 5½ hours a day performing pretty nearly all of the evolutions at a double quick step. I witnessed a very exciting occurance yesterday on Battalion drill. Two men fell out as they frequently do in ranks about shoveing one another. they struck a lick or two and when parted Col Wilcox told them to step out of ranks. he asked them what they fell out about. the smallest one of the two told him the Big one was always shoving him out of line and he could whip him in a minute. The Col told him he was too small to fight the other man but says he I will sadisfy you. He formed a square made them give up their muskets and put them in it

and says dam you go at it. They fought along time the little man got a terrible thrashing. Col asked him if he was satisfied he told him yes that he hollowed a long time before they pulled the Big one off. But the entire Regiment was making so much fuss that he could not be heard- all of this occured in less than five minutes. Well thers plenty of this stuff. The country here resembles Tennessee very much, Hilly and rocky, oak and fine growth mainly but in places nothing but pine. We now have on hand 3 days provisions cooked and hourly expecting Marching orders to Fairfax. It is reported here that our troops have given Back to Fairfax Evacuating those Hills we had possession of. There was an Artillery company left here last night. We have 6 peaces of artillery attached to our Brigade.[9] Fairfax is only 5 miles from us. a fight is expected every day. Lincoln is getting reinforcements every day. and so are we. I have bought a fine pattent Leather double cased silver watch. I know Father will say I have acted foolishly. But tell him to hold on until I clear my self. I bought the watch from Tom Tweedy who was slap out of money besides he had borrowed some from me. I give him the 20 dollar gold peace I had and the five dollars he owed me for his Watch. it is a brand new watch. Mr Tweedy gave just 40 dollars for it before he left home. It keeps splendid time. I had but little use for the money and more use here for the watch. Tell Father I intend to send it to him by the first one passing to Huntsville or Athens. it will suit him exactly. Tell him to ware it until I come home or if I never come to ware it on. The watch is worth all of 40 dollars. I have now 16 dollars. Jeff Davis owes me 33 dollars which he will pay me in a few days. But as a Wag remarked the other day, he is a hard old case he said Jeff was the hardest man he ever worked for he would not pay him off or let him quit- my health is verry good. I have ben drilling a weak since I had the Jaundice.

October 1, 1861

President Davis passed by here yesterday evening in rout for Fairfax.[10] great deal of enthusiasm among the men as he passed they called upon him to make a speech. He declined to speak. But said men the time has come for Blows, words can affect nothing. a shout went up and on went Jefferson Davis to take his stand at the head of an admiring and confideing army. orders have been issued to our Brigade to send all of our sick back to Broad run. I think the plan will be to get the Northern army to chase us to Bull run. everybody is expecting a big battle daily. I was disagreeably surprised to heare of Mrs Robinson & Graves[11] visit to our house if they repeat the offence let me know and I will Write the old Ladies a Letter. The North wind begins to sigh through the morning pines. The leaves begin to drop from the fading oak. The meadows are turning to a golden hue all unmistakable signs of approaching winter. I may send this letter by a Mr Davis of Morgan county who has or is about to get a discharge. I would send my Watch by him ife he was going to Athens and I knew he was reliable.

Your Brother,
W.C. McClellan

William Cowan McClellan to Thomas Joyce McClellan

Centerville
October, th3, 1861
Dear Father,
We are still at Centerville expecting orders to move on to Fairfax. I wrote to you some time ago stating that David Houston had been restored to his position. I suppose I was mistaken. he just took charge of his company without the sanction of any body. He found out that he would be cashiered. he sent up his resignation and it was accepted. Gains. Smith has ben Elected Capt. my friend R.[ufus] C. Jones beat Tom McDonald for first Lieutenant- It was the best thing that has happened since we have ben in the army. The McDonald boys talk about resigning and going home and joining a Calvary companie. They are unpopular with the men.[12] I have just ben paid 22 dollars for two months service- the government owes us 11 more. If I had Johns position I would soon make a fortune. I am a great lover of Money. I have now on hand 40 dollars in money and a 25 dollar Watch. I spoke of wanting to get into Malones companie some time ago. I would still like to make an arrangement of that kind. you must not under stand by this that I am in the least dissatisfied with my company, far from it we have got the biggest and best co. in the Brigade and the best company officers. is the thunder of it. they seem to have ben well chosen at the start- so you see I stand but little chance to get an office but by the death or resignation of some of our officers. But I am perfectly happy to serve my country in the capacity of a private for a while longer. I leave this matter with you. I am willing to do as you say whether I stay in

this co. or try to get a transfer to Malones company. We have orders to eat up our 3 days provisions. The prospect for a fight is not so great now. It is reported and believed by such men as Capt. Hobbs that 30,000 of our troops have crossed over into Maryland.[13] You must all write to me you have no idea how much good it does me to get a Letter from home. Tell L. R. Davis to write to me. you must all direct your letters to Manassas Junction. Our wagon Master gets the mail from there every day. How is Lieutenant Floyd getting recruits. Tell Al Martin if he does not come with Floyd I intend to Brush him when I come home. This is Thursday morning, clear but foggy.

Your son,
W. C. McClellan

Robert Anderson McClellan to William Cowan McClellan

Glengary Alabama
Oct 5th [1861]
Dear Will,
I will fill out this sheet in the way of a letter to you this calm, gentle Friday evening. We have got no letter from you since I wrote but hear that Houston has one from you, which father will get to day in Athens as he has gone there. Uncle Andy went over to Rips [Lawrence Ripley Davis's] this morning. They will start for Nashville Monday. Perhaps Rip will go with them. Uncle Andy will probably leave here entirely when they get back. He has been here three months. I will miss him considerably. He has cursed me and kicked me about a good deal but I do not mind that. We have news of a big fight in mosouri [Missouri] which resulted in our taking the victory with 5000 prisoners besides $20,000 dollars.[14] Many such victories will certainly bring peace after while. If it does not we will get sick before the war closes. there is very little news afloat in the county generally. The Limestone Rebels have moved from Huntsville five miles in the county, to the Blue Springs. None of us have ben there since they moved. John came up from the depot last Sunday evening and staid all night. The fifteen companies Humphreys[15] had at Decatur, for the purpose of forming a brigade, have all left for their homes. We are doing tolerable good cotton picking up on the French land. The best hands get 160 to 180 pounds per day. The field will make from seven to nine hundred to the acre. The bal-

lance will be mean. We have just begun to gather corn today, over the Creek; for the hogs. The canvass for Congress in the District promises to be pretty lively. Four are now in the field- Foster, Jones, Linsey, and Davis.[16] With this crowd Zeb Davis will be elected very easy: but it is feared that a seccessionist will be a candidate who would beat the field, as all of the men now are of the same party. Zeb has been speaking down in Lawrence County this evening. They say he is a good talker. I think Rip was hurt at Zebs running- he wanted to run him self. Nick will be Col. of the Regt. now forming at Huntsville. Clint was out a day too since. He has his cavalry co. about made up. It will belong to Pope Walkers brigade under Colonel James Clanton of Montgomery.[17] Nick F[loyd] sent a buggy up after Alfred Martin but it was no go. I saw Robert Mills[18] not so very long ago. He looks as usual out of his eyes. Hon. J. M. Moore was here the other evening. He has not changed very much since you left. He still toats that big stick, wares that old snuff colored hat and looks as sly as a swamp fox. Well as the hour of three has dropped from times great old wheel I must begin to think about going to the field, not of battle or carnage but of cotton, where the sable sons of Alsisa are gathering the white harvest of the South into the wooden baskets from the forest's white oak. So, in five minutes I will be leisurely walking along up the banks of Limestone Creek, thinking of the many times in years past you & I have splashed in its turbid waters together.

Your Brother,
R. McClellan

William Cowan McClellan to Robert Anderson McClellan

Centerville,
October 6th, 1861
Dear Bob,
I have received but one letter from home in a month. I have Written 6 or 7 in that length of time. I cannot immagine the caus of your silence unless it is the fault of the mail. We are still at Centerville drilling 5 hours a day. I made a calculation the other day in drilling 5 hours a day we travel 18 miles, we have been here 4 months, the first two months we drilled 8 hours per day. you can make a calculation of it and tell how many miles the Limestone Troopers have Travelled, 100 miles forced marching. All of this we

have done and Killed no yankees. Bob I tell you what we are doing, we are running this so called Southern confederacy so near into debt that she will not be able to pay out in 20 years. I suppose President Davis says Lincoln has to come out from his entrenchments to fight or not fight at all if that be the case I think we are Stationed here for the next 12 months to come. Though it may be one of old Jeffs tricks to induce Lincoln to with draw part of his force from Arlington and then take it. I tell you Bob Lincolns army never will travel the centerville pike again. They have too great a horror of masque Batteries of which commodity we have in abundance. We have a Battery situated upon a hill in the suberbs of Centerville that would murder the yankees for miles up the pike. The Battery is situated precisely where the Blackrepublican Congressman and young Ladys stood and listened to the thunders of Bull Run.[19] Our Brigade is composed of the 9.10.11. ala Regi. 38 Va. and 19. Missisipi Regiments. Col. Wilcox is a long shot the best officer in the Brigade. Gen. Forney[20] not excepted. When Gen. F makes a mistake Col. W commands: Battalion study, or in other words stand fast. They have had several arguments the Col. always succeeds in convincing the Gen. of his error. I predict if Col. Wilcox ever has a chance to display his Milatary Skill He will be second only to Boregard and Johnston in this division of the army. A Lieutenant in the 10 ala Regi was shot directly through the head just now from the firing of a salute over the grave of a Soldier a quarter of a mile off. The Liet was lieing on a cot in his tent sleeping. I saw White Buchanan[21] the other day, all of the Lincoln (not Abe Linc.) Boys are Well.

October th.7.1861
Bob since writing the above the Whole Nature of affairs have chainged. All of our Camp equipage and sick men have been ordered to Manassas preparartory I suppose to a double quick retreat or advance. We have it from good authority that the federal forces are advancing. We also have the news that Gen. Boreguard had .12. thousand yankees surrounded With no possible chance of escape,[22] I hope they Will come on if We can get them out of the Hills and hollows we will give them thunder. I think this fight Will deside the matter. If We get Whipped it will prolong the War perhaps for years- If we Whip them We Will have possession of Washington city and Liberate old Maryland. We can then stand a side and let the outraged Marylanders do the Work they say they can Whip Pennsyl-

vania with Rocks if they had them. I tell you Bob, We have to contend with an army by no means as cowerdly as they are represented. another thing the Northern troops have a good gen. to lead them, that man, McClellan. I suppose I have ben asked a thousand times if I was any akin to Gen. McClellan. I tell them yes in the event that I am taken prisoner I am a Nephew. I am the only McClellan in our Regiment or perhaps in the Brigade or in the southern army. John [McClellan], Where is John, at Huntsville or in Miss. or in Va. Step[toe] Picket has just arrived here. I will go and see him I suppose he can tell me. Mr. Pickett has been appointed our Quarter master. This month so far has been Warmer than last month, though We had a big white frost a night or too ago- I am not needing any thing at presant. Tom Cartwright is in my mess now he is well. Billy Pettus has gone to Manassas his health is verry bad. I think he will get a discharge.[23] Tom Kellys health is also verry bad.[24] I will have to get another sheat of paper.
[The letter ends here.]

Thomas Joyce McClellan to William Cowan McClellan

ShoalFord Ala.
October 10th 1861
Dear Will,
I was in Huntsville yesterday for the purpose of starting your cloths to you, They consist in two under shirts two blouses one blue cotton shirt two pairs of gloves one large home made blanket one pair of dark striped jeans pants, the blanket is died purple, a pocket handkerchief, one bottle cordial and one of home made wine and two huge looking pipes a present from poor old Hartwell, and I have been thus particular so that you may know what to look for upon their arrival, the box in which your things are packed is rather too frail I fear to carry them safely being the one in which the caster was brought from the North, perhaps you remember it. Mr. Venable is to start for Virginia tomorrow, I saw Clint Davis yesterday he says he is very anxious for you to be in his cavalry company and that if you desire it he can have you transferred through Gen. Walkers influence, I think it likely that he is mistaken about his ability to effect your transfer, as I understand it is very difficult to get an exchange for any cause, I also saw Nick Richardson he told me he

had a conversation with Floyd about getting you transferred to Malones Company, Floyd told him it could not be done without the consent of the Capt. and that Hobbs would not consent to it, The cavalry service I suppose is quite as hard as the infantry, though it pays better, but I don't know that it makes much difference about the pay of a soldier, as they seem to spend all they get, be it much or little. Clint's Company is to be an independent one, attached to Gen. Walkers Brigade, Nick Davis as well as Clint. says they will use all their influence to have you transferred either to Malones or the cavalry company, I am at a loss to know what is best in the case, You are now in a good Company officered by gentlemen, and as a general thing it is bad policy to make frequent changes, You have been in the army long enough to know that a soldier cannot get in any position that is free from hardships and toil, I wrote you a long letter a few days ago which renders it unnecessary to deal in particulars in this one, write to me on recpt of this and let me know what you wish done in reference to changing places in the army. We have secured your letter of 3rd inst, I am rejoiced to hear that you have regained your health, Little Sue [Davis] is better, thought to be now out of danger, Give my respects to Maj. Hobbs, Lt. Floyd I understand has gone to Mobile & don't know what success he has met with recruiting, Your Uncle Andrew left here on tuesday for Nashville, The candidates for Congress speak in Athens tomorrow.

Your father,
Thos J McClellan

Matilda McClellan to William Cowan McClellan

[Athens]
Tuesday night-Oct 11th 1861
My dear Brother,
We have written so many letters recently. I feel at some loss what to say. the most important thing that has occured since Pa wrote last night was Bobs [McClellan's] going to Mr. Vaughn's and having his hair trimmed. You know this is quite an event here, Mother is going to send twelve pair of yarn socks and six pair of linsey drawers in the box of uniforms to be distributed by Capt. Hobbs among the men and for fear your box will not arrive you had better speak for a surplus of each, if they get there before your box. Your things are

made nicer than those. Mother got you a double blanket- but it came to pieces when she dyed it. If you want another blanket- write for it. Col. Davis is rather sick of speaking, Pa says he is as tired of it as he (Pa) was after his first speech, We have had no frost here yet, it will make a great havoc when it does come as the trees and grass retain their verdue to a great extent. Indeed the yard looks at least as fresh as it did when you left- Lieutenant Floyd speaks in flattering terms of you. He says if your health was commensurate with your will, you would be a number one patriot solder. In fact we hear good reports of you from others of their company, This is as it should be for nothing could be more gratifying to us. Write frequently and particularly I wonder if Tom Cartwright ever writes home about you, they never tell if he does. If anything transpires I will be sure you know.

Your Sister
Matilda.

Robert Anderson McClellan and Thomas Joyce McClellan to William Cowan McClellan

[Athens]
October 17th 1861
Dear Will,
As father has failed to fill out these two pages I will do so myself as it has been about two weeks since I wrote. But I have but little to write that is not written already in this letter. Today has been a long rainy, sunless, cheerless one fit for nothing but sitting by the fire roasting chestnuts or some other indoor occupation. I went out this morning hog hunting. After rambling over the hills so familiar to you beyond the French place. I started away out towards the Isom houses.[25] A short time after I passed the Fielding field[26] Jack, Nimrod, Rush and the blue puppy- not Jeff of Abe- came by me like lightening after a fox which they started while with Mike over on the creek. The last I heard of them they were flying with an eager vim on the trail far away towards the pine slash. The dying accents of their musical voices fell sweetly upon my ear as they floated swiftly along up on the misty air of Indian summer. I have all your hounds yet and intend to keep them. I would like to pass an eulogy on the character and services of each one of them but I have not

the space to do so now. The flying fox or the bounding deer is the only encormisims that are necessary. The life and deeds of Rush are too familiar to the whole county to require a single word from the pen of the hunter. He has erected for himself a monument of fame that can be seen from all parts of the nation around. Upon that fame I am willing to let him repose undisturbed by the historians pen or the painters pencil. If the lumbering elk or the falling tree furnishes no evidence of his gallant exploits nothing I could say would do it. With the request that you write often I will close for the present as it is growing late in the night, as almost any body would say. Indeed the night rolls so easily away with me situated as I am alone in the office. How long I will remain alone in it or how long it will be before I too shall desert it I cannot say.

Your brother, Bob

[Part of the enclosed letter from Thomas Joyce McClellan:]
. . . meetings which is the second Monday in Nov. The call session meets on the 28th inst. I have but a few more days to stay at home. I feel very reluctant to leave home, more so I believe than on any former occasion. I was at old man Newby's[27] sale on Tuesday last, hogs sold higher than I ever saw them in my life. I understand 127 cts is being offered in Athens for pork and same to be had at Hunts[ville]. God only knows where meat is to be had to feed the south, citizens soldiers, or negroes. I think if the confederate government knew how great the deficiency is in this respect, the authorities would soon make an effort to invade the north. I believe it must be done or the greatest suffering will be enacted in the South that was ever known in any country. There is not meat enough to half supply the demand, and the people have nothing to buy it with if there was.[28] You can have no idea of the scarcity of money here. The best men in the country are not able to raise money to pay their taxes, much less any thing else. The heavy rains continue, it is now about 12 o'clock and it has been raining all day. It has been the worst fall for gathering crops I ever saw. Kitty and little Tom[29] are going to school to Miss Liza Douglas. Tom talks a great deal about his buddy Willie. Oh this horrid war what ties it sunders, how much suffering it causes, how many sad hearts it makes. Write to me at Montgomery. I shall be there until about the 15th of December.

Your father
Thos. J. McClellan,

Robert Anderson McClellan to William Cowan McClellan

Camp Bradshaw near Huntsville ala
Oct 18th/61
Dear Brother,
I have written two letters to you since I have heard from you and feel almost as much incensed at your failure to reply to them as you professed to feel at my tardiness in replying to yours sometime since, especially considering the labor it cost on account of the scarcity of anything of interest to you to get this letter. There are now three thousand men here and we are daily expecting three thousand more. The whole so given to Gen. L. P. Walkers brigade. This army composed as it is will be exclusively of Alabamians bound together by State pride as well as national patriotism, will be sure to make itself known and felt if ever brought into active service. Our Company is now in a Batallion,[30] whether we can get four more companies the requisite number to form a regiment I do not know. Our company has born off the honor as the finest among the 25 or 30 here & is the favorite with the ladies a great many of whom visit us daily. Gilbert's Co. is with us and is also a very fine one.[31] We have had a good deal of sickness such as measles, but nothing of a more serious nature. Bob Johnson, J. H. Moore, & John Goodman are just getting well as also Lem Hide, George McKinney, Billy Peck[32] and other of your acquaintances. We have been making inquiries as to the proper method of proceeding to affect the transfer of yourself. Col. Malone and Wm Holcomb,[33] Nick Davis has promised to do everything in his power to that end. If we can enlist Gen. Walker on our side I think it may be done easily if not it will be difficult. In the meantime make inquiries your self as to the best way to proceed and write to me soon. It is unnecessary for me to aprise you that there is nothing which I so much desire [than] to have you in the same company. Write me. I hear from John there is a hot contest going on for 3rd Lt. D Richardson will be appointed Surgeon by which I will become second Lt. Direct your letters to Huntsville Ala.

Affectionately Your Brother
RA McClellan

William Cowan McClellan to Thomas Joyce McClellan

Centerville, Va,
Oct. 22, 1861
Dear Father-

I received 2 Letters from you yesterday I have replyed to Mr D[avis] Letter you can send over and get the Let[ter] of Rip it contains a rough description of the incidence that occurred during the time We were on picket guard also a description of our retreat Back to Centerville. you say Clint Davis desires me in his cavalry company. tell Clint I am more than willing to make the change provided it causes him or any one else But little Trouble. so far as Capt Hobbs is concerned he would not hesitate a moment about giving his consent to my transfer. I desire to make the change for these reasons I have ben in the infantry service for nearly 5 months my health has ben Bad about half the time, perhaps Cavalry service would agree with me Better. I have done my duty in every respect since I have ben in the service. I am not hunting a soft or easy place in the army I have long since ben convinced that a soldier is taxed to the utmost of his capacity in whatever manner he serves his country. I know exactly what a cavilry soldier has to do, He has to feed and rub his horse his stirrip his pistols always keeping them in order, do his cooking. Sometimes- he has to sit perfectly still for 24 hours on picket without ever moveing or allowing his horse to move, again they have to ride at full speed all day. Our Regi has raised a shout they say there is 500 hundred [*sic*] yankee prisoners passing a long the pike taken at Leesburg yesterday.[34] I will defer until I learn more. Too thirds of the army of the Potomac are encamped a round Centerville.[35] Brass Bands, drums by the thousand are the first thing I hear in the morning the last thing at night, you advise me to be regular in my sleeping hours I have but little taste for camp carousels as soon as role is called I lay down to rest, We have role call at 8,oclock. In day time I generally stay about my tent attending to my own Business. I think I have a great many friends in our company They frequently get into an argument and call old Mc to settle the matter of dispute. I Broke down coming in from picket the other day, and stopped in the Bushes, in a few minutes 4 of the Boys came Back to look for me though the trooth of the Business was they were Broke down themselves. Tell, Clint. Davis to get me transferred if he can. I have always ben wanting to be in a company of Horsemen, get me the papers and express them too me I will get them signed by Hobbs, Wilcox, and Gen Johnston if necessary. I suppose it will be some time be fore I get my Box as there has ben an imbargo layed upon the transportation of such articals here for the presant. I suppose our commanders are anticipating a retreat or a thrashing & they do not want the Yankees to get such Things. They will be stopped in Richmond. I think, Father, We will have a general fight here in less than 2 Weeks if We have it at all. If we have one fight in that time I think a great many of our troops will be ordered to other points, Mobile [&] Kentucky. I think though we will have it in a few days. I have a very bad cough cold and & I will go out and learn the particulars of the Leasburg fight. Well John Fetheston has just returned from stone house near Rock Bridge, he says he saw 516 prisoners 19 commissioned officers 2 colors a mong the number comeing on this Way. The 38 Virginia Regi will guard them to night- the fight took place Below Leesburg upon the Potomac yesterday. We had 2,500 men, the Enemy ten thousand, our forces were commanded by Gen. Evans, the Enemy by Gen Bacon[36] So says the men Who were in the fight. Our loss is said to be between 200 to 250. The loss of the enemy very heavy. Our men drove them into the River and then planted their cannon upon the Bank and slaughtered them like hogs. The Enemy were attempting to cross the River in small boats, our cannon knocked them plum out of the water every last crew and all, a glorious victory. This is perfectly reliable[.] Featherston as well as a great many of our officers saw Gen Evans. Write as soon as this comes to hand. Direct your letters to Manassas. We captured a vessel near Dumfries and the Potomac with 70,000 overcoats. No danger of freezing.

W.C. McClellan C.S. American

William Cowan McClellan to John Beattie McClellan

Centerville, Va. Near danger
October 26/61
Dear Brother,

I received your kind Letter of the 18 inst last night as this is Saturday and I have Nothing to do But Wash my cloths and prepare for inspection. I write you a letter, Though I have nothing of much importance to communicate- Save two of the most powerful and hostile armys ever assembled upon the soil of America are standing here almost face to face, ready at any moment upon the commission of a Blunder on one side to pitch upon them from the other. you have doubtless heard of the Brillant Victory of Gen. Evans Near Leesburg on the Potomac. He there defeated drove Back killed drowned compleately routed a federal force of 10 thousand. While He had but 25 hundred men. Gen. Evans had 3 Mississippi Regi under his command which accounts for his victory, they are the Best fighting men in the service, Alabamians next. you would be astonished at the boldness and fearlessness of our army here. When an order is issued to go on picket or advance towards the enemy line there is a terrible shout raised. When ordered back every man is down in the mouth. By the by the 9th ala Regiment has received an irrepareable loss, Col. Wilcox has ben promoted to Brigadier Gen. of our Brigade.[37] In Col. Wilcox we have lost the ablest Col in the southern confederacy- Here comes Gen. Boreguard & Johnston and their guard consisting of 20 mounted men right by my tent to salute Gen. Wilcox- Every man in our Regi has ben proud to say I belong to the 9th ala Regi. But how is it now. We are all ready to desert- I suppose [Archibald] Gracy of Florence ala will be appointed Col of our Regiment. Old Boreguard & Johnston are as fat as pigs- I under stand Booregard says he is now prepared to do Battle and can Whip any force that can be Brought against him. if you could see our fortifications at Centerville you would think so. There is 9 distinct fortifications spacious a nough to contain 12 peaces of Artillery. I have helped to Work upon some of them my self. We have one hundred-20 free Negroes at Work all of the time upon fortifications. The health of our Regi is very good at presant. We can start 650 fighting men- I have concluded if I can get a transfer to join Clint D[avis's] Cavalry co, as the Infantry service does not agree with me. if Clint does not get into the service upon account of not haveing the requisite a mount of men, I will Join your company. I wrote Clint Davis a letter upon the subject a day or two ago- you had better see Nick Davis he can do more in the matter than any body else- William Holcomb is very anxious to be transferred to malones co. Billy is a clever sensible fellow. I hope If I get into that arm of the service he will too. I know a transfer can be obtained, a young man in a Mississippi Regi applied a few days ago and obtained one to a Cavelry company. He told me so himself- Our

Regi was called upon on the 15th to perform Picket duty. We marched 14 miles and arrived upon the banks of a little stream called Acquitine 6 miles from Mount Vernon[38] -our company was detailed to go on first and I was detailed with 7 others to take the most advance outpost- I could distinctly hear the enemy order arms, and I have heard the like of drums on earth. They began then beating the long role. We were ordered off that night in double quick time- that was the Night our intire army started back to Centerville- We did not arrive at Centerville until next evening- there I saw assembled 80 thousand men, it was a grand sight. Send this letter out home. I will have to get another sheat. If you see Nick Davis in the mean time I will make inquiries as to the mode and means of getting a transfer- I have not received my Box sent by Mr. Venable yet. There has ben an embargo layed upon the transportation of goods for the soldiers, perhaps this is the reason I have not received them. I understand it will be lifted to day. We have all suffered some With cold- a great many of our Boys are verry ragged, occasionally cursing old Phillips, George Peck, and the ballance of the county[39] -you may all look out for a Big Battle here be fore long, in my humble opinion this Battle will deside the matter if We are victorious. They will be willing to make peace- My health is just tolerable I have a bad cough- direct your letters to Manassas Junction. We get most of our supplies from there, our quarter Master gets our mail there daily- Write to me soon. Brother-

William Cowan McClellan

William Cowan McClellan to Robert Anderson McClellan

Centerville_Va_
October th31 18/61
Dear Bob-
I received your verry kind Letter Monday connected with one from Father I was very sorry to hear of the scarcity of pork hogs in North ala and elsewhere, tell him he need not be uneasy There is Beaf cattle enough in the valley of Va to supply this division of the army for the next 12 months to come- I suppose Kentucky can supply our army upon her soil with Beef. Tennessee can supply our troops on the Southern coast- While Texas Missouri Arkansaw our army of the West. I have come to the conclusion That Beef is a great

deal Better for soldiers than Bacon at least I have it best, you may think this strange as I never eat much Beef at home, but I have been forced to eat it so long I have got to be fond of it, I was sorry to learn that I stood but little chance to get a transfer to Clint Davises Cavelry .co. as I think that mode of warfare would suit me better Than upon foot, Though I was not All disappointed, I have learned since I have become a soldier to take every thing fast and easy. Col. Wilcox has been promoted to Brigadier Gen of our Brigade, in him the 9th Regi ala has lost the best Col in the confederate service- had he remained in the united states service he would now occupy a place second only to McClellan- He has gone where he justly deserves to be, he will do honor to the position, But it is a terrible Blow to the 9, Regi, ala, Vol, Wilcox superceded Gen. Forney, We have no Col but I suppose Gracy of Florence ala Will be appointed Col. Capt. Hobbs I think will be promoted to Major, I would like to be with you this morning over in the Barrens with Nimrod, The Blue pup, Jack and the ballance of the Dogs fox hunting. Oh how I would like to move at Will once more. With no pointed Bayonet to obstruct my progress no guard to say halt No foe to watch,- often I think of theas thing When standing upon my cold and lonely post at the dead hours of Midnight, When the Busy camp is hushed in slumber, When the cold chilly frost of Heaven falls Merciless upon the poor Centrie [sentry], as their foot step are heard tramp tramp tramp upon the cold grounds, But in doing this I am conscious of occupying One of the most responsible positions it is possible for man to occupy Watching over The lives of thousands. You have heard before this time of the Brilliant Victory of Gen. Evans. We Whip Them every time We fight. I hope and trust it wont be long before We Will have a general engagement here, Let them come- Gen Boureguard says he can whip any force That can be brought against him at this point. I have not received my cloths By Venable yet I am needing Them Verry much, We are looking for him every day, When We retreated a week or so ago our Baggage was all sent to the Junction. I lost all of my Shirts save the one I had on, We have had ice here a half of an inch thick, several Big White frosts, We get some chesnuts to eat by giveing 30 cents a quart for them, We also get some verry fine apples By giving 30 cents per dozen, I do not eat many at them prices, We go on Picket duty to morrow again We Will be on 4 or 5 days.

Wm McClellan

Direct your letters to Manassas Jun. You must take good care of Fannie and not spoil her gaits. I expect to make her a very fast nag. When I get back, tell John M. Moore to take good care of his Sheep They will be worth 5 dollars a peace when the War is ended You do the same, Wool will Bring almost any price before 12 months- I have ben corresponding with Miss _______ over East for some time past, She writes a good letter- Give My respects to old Hartwell tell him I Will Let him know how his pipe smokes as soon as I get them, I am very much obliged to him for them, I will write to Father at Montgomery in a few days, tell L,R, Davis to write to me, all of you write Me

Your Brother
W,C, McClellan Manassas Va

William Cowan McClellan to Martha Beattie McClellan

Centerville, Va. On cub Run[40]
Nov. 3, 61
Dear Mother-
I have just received my Box, I am under many obligations to you for the many valuable things you have sent me. The socks came just in Time as I had Worn out the last paire I had, The shirts also came just in time as I had lost the last ones some days ago when they were sent to the Junction to keep the Yankees from getting them, But some one of our own men was kind enough to steal them for me. My green shirts are very much admired by the boys. I am wareing now the Jeanes pants. I left home with Brown jeanes you recollect, I am very proud of the home made Blanket it is just the sort of one I needed, The Cordial and Wine was also very good. I need nothing now to complete my Winter clothing, Save a good pair of heavy Boots, to wade the snow and mud in, I am told the snow is frequently 2 feet deep here. Tell Bob to see Brittle[41] in Athens and get him to make me a pair of No, 9 long legs. Mr. Brittle will know What sort to make. You can send them by some one passing, this is Sunday I have nothing to do But sun my cloaths, comb my head, and read my Bible, yesterday it rained all day. The wind blew very hard as it always does here rainy days. I have seen but one Woman in the 2 months Mother, until yesterday morning I walked out to a neighbors house about a mile from camps, There I found an old fassioned Lady sitting by the fire. She says come in soldier, are

you cold? take a seat by the fire. thank you madam. We had a long talk a bout war a bout peace a bout the country and peoples, She Told me extravagance corruption and sin had Braught this Nation to what it is at, She told me I looked like a good soldier, in fact I had a good time of it, I more than once thought about the old fire-side at home- Tell Rip Davis to Write to me of the transfer matter, tell Sis to Write, I was very glad to hear that Little Sue was better.

your affectionate Son,
W.C. McClellan Esq
direct your letters to Manasas Va.

William Cowan McClellan to Robert Anderson McClellan

Centerville Va. Cub Run
Camp Washington pike,
Nov. 9/61
Dear Bob
We are still encamped quietly at this place awaiting impatiently an attack from a cowardly foe, I fear we will have to wait a long time, the Enemy seam to be beating back to wards Washington city, our pickets have not seen a yankee in several days, Report says the yankees are freezing to death for the want of wood, provisions for their horses not being able to procure hay, our Blockade Below Washington being effectual it is said they are cutting all of the shade trees about Alexandria. I am not satisfied at this, if you could see the woods our Regi has been getting wood from, you would come to the conclusion that it is almost impossible to supply an army of a hundred thousand men in wood, we have cut all of the timber off over 12 or 15 acres, our Brigade will have to move in a few days to Where we can get wood, The promotion of Col Wilcox has litterly ruined our Regi, Col Henry[42] has been appointed Col, he is a man of but little military capacity consequently a great many of the officers in the Regi are resigning among the number Hal Bibb,[43] We poor privats have to stick it out, I suppose I would give 500 dollars to be in Clint Davises Cavalry company, I dont want to be lead into Battle by an ignoramus, Col. Henry is fit for nothing higher than the cultivation of corn. Maj O'Neal has been appointed Lt, Col, he is annother old granny he is a clever man but is not qualified for Lt Col- Capt, Hobbs, and Capt, Williams[44] ran for Major, Capt Hobbs seemed somewhat mortified it being the 2, time he has run

for this office, Major-O'Neal beat him at Richmond- some say Gen Wilcox will have Capt Hobbs appointed Major yet Capt H being a favorite With him, some one of our Regi has just received a letter from our old quarter Master Dr Berlerson of Decatur[45] stating that 10 thousand hessians[46] have made their way into East Tennessee if this be so,- all I have to say they are a doomed peoples. They Will fall before our impetuous Boys like Weeds before the reapers hook,- We Whip them every time We meet, no matter how great their numbers, or how few ours- The infernal scoundrels cant stand the Bayonet- they scamper like a herd of cattle,- All I ask in Battle is to die with my hands clutched upon ones throat. When we get after them they leap over Bluffs Jump into Broad rivers any thing .oh. God, to get away from the Rebels. I worked day before yesterday upon the Breast works near Centerville, We are erecting fortifications upon every hill in 2 miles of Center[ville] the one I worked on is in the yard of that infernal preacher that piloted the yankees to Bull Run you recalled- he was taken prisoner, is now in the guard house at Richmond.[47] I paid his wife_50_cents for my dinner. I thought of you all as I drove my spade into the sandy soil of old Virginia. We Boys sometimes get up a little fun- but most generally we glide along very quietly, young Redus[48] of our co was Burried yesterday he was a very clever young man. He was also a very healthy man he had typhoid pneumonea- & he makes the 4th man that has died in our company, many a Brave southerners bones repose beneath the sod of Fairfax county- I received your letter of the 2 Nov last night, the obituary, of Jim Bailey is very good, I showed it to several of my friends they all said it was a very good obit, maybe I will send it in [illegible] my next letter, I wrote Mother a letter a day or two ago thanking her for the many good cloaths she sent me by Venable, Mr. Phillip has not reached here yet, I need nothing now save a pair of heavy Boots No 9-get Brittle to make them if I can get them by the Middle of next month I will be satisfied William Holecomb, Hal Malone[49] and my self are very anxious to be transferred to Malones, Clint. Davis companys- I prefer Cavalry Tell Rip Davis to find out what can be done in the matter there if they do not succeed. let me know I will then write to the Secretary of War my self.

your Brother
W.C. McClellan Esq
Manassas, Junction, Va

William Cowan McClellan to Martha Beattie McClellan

Camp Centerville.
Nov. 9 61
Dear Mother,
Mr Phillips. arrived here safe and sound this evening with our goods and chattels-[50] I received my Box with several valuable articals their in contained- The tin Bucket of Butter was very acceptible, the Bucket its self will be quite an acquisition to my cooking vessels. I am now writing by one of the candles you sent me also with paper and pencil just received. The sugar you sent me came just in time. I have had none to go in my coffee for 10 days. I understand Lt. Floyd will be here in a few days with 18 recruits for our company. our co will then be the largest in the Brigade wich will favor my chances for a transfer to Clint. Davises co. Tell Bob to copy off all of my Letters Written with pencil. If I ever go home I will want to see them,-tell Tom Nick [McClellan] I will now crack a few of his chestnuts picked up by him no doubt by him under the old chestnut trees on the Bluff- William Phelan[51] is a mess mate of mine. he sends you all his regards- Phelan is one of the best soldiers in our company. he attends to his own business and goes strait along- Tom Cartwright is in my mess also. he is well- I have formed quite an attachment for Tommy he is a very shifty Boy and holds his own very well With the World. Nothing more at presant,- Mother

your affectionate Son
Wm.C. McClellan
Manassas Junction Va

William Cowan McClellan to Robert Anderson McClellan

Camp Near Centerville, Va
Nov 14th /61
Dear Bob
I am now at work on the redoubts as a friend has pen and paper, I will pen you a few lines during the hours I have to rest I wrote you a letter last night and said to state in conclusion that my yarn about my getting tight was all stuff But too men out of our company drank too freely of king Alcohol. We work about every 3 days upon the Breast Works laboring 6 hours per day standing guard, going on

picket, working on roads, cutting and hauling Wood 1 ½ miles, cooking. This imploys me from day light until 9 oclock at night- all of this I do cheerfully When in good health and I am happy to state to you that my health is now splendid. I way 190 pounds 5 pound heavier than you ever saw me, I look as hard as flint All I ask a continuation or perpetuation of the Blessing. come Weal or come woe I Will be found at my post. 12 or 15 of our company have been discharged 25 are in all now absent from our comp[any].[52] We that are left are all stout looking men. In writing These Letters Bob I take But little pains My object being to inform you where I am and what I am doing. I will write to Father at Montgomery to Night. I intend to put him up a good letter of about 6 pages in length. I am afraid Lincolns grand armada will take him prisoner Way down south in Dixie Land. I will send my watch and letters Back by Mr. Phillip deposit at Willie Allens.[53] You speak of paying your addresses to Miss Maggie Lipscomb. ah old fell I have got you on the dead you just ought to see the Letters I have received from her, She is all right on the goos- Miss Maggie writes like a Book, If the sun will ever shine out Brightly a gain upon the southern confederacy you may look out I will launch my Bark upon the Waters of Indian creek * * * * you speak of Fannie Being sleek and gailey, glad to hear that she is prospering, like to take a ride With Miss M., Miss _______ and her _______. Give my respects to Nathan Fletcher. Tell him When I get my leg Broak I intend to go home and lie down by him on a pallet, I have not seen Jim E. Fletcher in 6 weeks he is a way down on Aquia creek. Tell Rip Davis to pay us a visit it shall not cost him any thing, it will pay any man to see this army, the locality, fortifications & Tell Bill Day to answer the letter I wrote him, an old coon _______ My Regards to all inquiring Friends, Old Hartwell and The dogs.

Your Brother
W C McClellan Manassas Ju. Va.

P.S. my hour is about out I Will now lay down this good gold pen and take up the spade.

William Cowan McClellan to Thomas Joyce McClellan

Camp Centreville
Nov 16 1861
Dear Father, I take my seat by a dimly burning candle at the hour of 9 to write you a short letter. We have never been so widely divided.

It is with the consciousness that we have never been so widely sepparated that I bid you howdy. almost the intire length of the Beloved South whose interest you and I are so faithful to want to promulgate now divids us. The earnest wish of my heart is to meet you at our peaceful home in peace once more- My health is now very good I am fleshier now than you ever saw me. We have been at work every day on the Redoubts and Roads or I would have written to you be fore this Time. Our fortifications are said to be impregnable. I have worked very hard upon them- some say we will have a fight here, others say not. I am of the latter opinion though I hope I may be mistaken about it, I would go into a fight to morrow with a smile upon my countenance Willing to fight until the last man in our army expires. I think I speak the centiment of our hole army here. It seams we are attack[ed] at many points Boath by land and by sea. We have heard of the success of the enemy fleat at Port Royal dismantling our guns and takeing possession of the Fort, it created but little excitement[54] here. Mr Phillip arrived here safely about a weak ago with our cloaths, he returned a day or two ago Home or started at least, I sent some Letters home by him, The last letter I receiv[ed] from him was dated Nov 5 from Bob all Well, Tom C[artwright] got a letter from home dated the 8 stating that Malones co had been ordered to Pensacola and would start next day the 9th Nov. I must close I am getting verry cold Besides sleaping having done a hard days work. This is sunday. We have to start out on picket in a few minutes. It is very cold here now- some say we Will Winter it here. you must excuse this letter it has ben Written in great haste- I Will Write in about 5 days again as we come off picket at that time-

your effectionate Son
W.C. McClellan

William Cowan McClellan to Thomas Joyce McClellan

Camp Centerville_Va
Nov_21_1861
Dear Father-
We have just returned from picket duty- I saw no yankees. While out though I went several miles beyond our lines upon a scouting expedition. Nothing of any importance has transpired here recently save our Cavalry chased a forageing party of Yankees Within 5 miles of Alexandria and took them prisoners. 32 men, 4 waggons, loaded with corn.[55] some of our co saw Them as they came through Centerville it seams We are always cutting them off from their main Body and takeing them prisoners. Our army here has taken very near one thousand prisoners in the last month including Gen. Evans's 650 taken at Leesburg near here. Our men attach but little importance to the takeing of Port Royal [South Carolina] by the federals our Military men say We can take it Back When We choose. Some say the next Blow that is struck upon the coast by Lincolns grand armada Will be at Mobile. It is said Gen Beaureguard sent a messenger to South Carolina asking them if they needed any more force to defend their coast. They Thanked him very kindly for his offer to assist them But replyed that they had plenty of men to Whip every Yankee that would invade Their Soil & he had better watch his own points. Father I have heard in times past a great deal of abuce heaped on the South Carolinians about their impetuousity & hotheadedness indiscrestness in affairs of State, all of this may be true, it is equally true that a Braver people never lived upon the face of the Earth, I have mixed a good deal with South Carolina troops in order to learn the natures of these Rebelious people I have heard Beardless youths say they had rather see the hearts Blood of their Mothers and Fathers poured out upon their Hearth stones than consent to a Reconstrucktion of the Union upon our own terms[56] There is a reciprocity of hatred existing between the Northern troops and South Carolina troops equaled only by the heathen natives of old, There is a post on our picket line where 4 S. C. have ben shot, a S.C. told me that 12 yankees had repented in Blood and groans there cruelly. We are in possession of the sad news of the capture of our Ministers to England Slidell & Mason at sea- such men as Col. O'Neal. Capt. Hobbs, say it will kick up a fuss with or bet-

wean The united States and England-that Old Abe Will say the Capt of the Steamer who took Slidell & Mason acted Without authority, Old Lincoln will then give this disobedient Capt 50,000 dollars to undergo a disgrace and swear a lie, He will then deliver up Slidell & Mason to the British Government.[57] We are expecting an attack here every day, The Enemy have advanced a little in the last few days, Gen. Johnston says he is ready, and it is said when he says he is ready to fight, the Victory is ours, always haveing his plan cut and dried before he strikes,- Gen, Johnston is not so popular With The Volunteers as gen. Beaureguard, The former being two slow in his movements. President Davis, is not near so popular with The Volunteers as he was before the Battle of Bull Run. They say he kept Beaureguard from pushing on and taking Washington City and perhaps putting a final to the War proberbly.[58] Our men here have great confidence in our commanders I Think they aught to have, this army has been successful in every single ingagement great or small we have Whipped them badly every time we have met them at Bull Run, at Bethel, C[hurch],[59] at Falls Church, at Leesburg and in several other Battles of less importance, untill now the combined displeasure of the Lincoln Government cant drive there Best gen McClellan with their Best army against Us. The last letter I received from home was dated Nov 5 from Bob, all well they had not heard from you since you left. I got a Letter from Bill Day, dated Nov. 9 Stating that L. P. Walker's Brigade was ordered to Pensacola, and would start about the eleventh of Nov 11. My Letters from home will be very much delayed upon the Road on account of the R. R. Bridge across Holsten River being burned down. Mr Phillips left here about 5 days ago for home, I sent nearly all of My Letters received from home Back by him. My clothes all fit I have plenty for the Winter, The Weather is very cold here now ice a half inch thick, Wind always Blowing very hard- a young man by the name of Redus died in our company a few days ago, his Father reached here 4 days after he was burried, tell Mr, Shelton his sons are Both Well. I am popular with Both men and officers in our company. Lieu Bibby [Hal Bibb]has resigned 7 other commissioned officers on account of Wilcox Being promoted to Brigadier Gen They cant stand Col Henry he is no military man, I dont Blame them I would Resign to if I could.

your son, WC McClellan. Manassas

P.S. Nov. 22.1861

Old Abe is changeing his policy very much in regard to our prisoners. He turned loos some days ago .33. prisoners on parole of honor, Belonging to The, 6th. Alabama Regi, They Were landed at fortress Monroe. They came amediately to their Col, 25 of them proved faithless to their Oaths,[60] They say they will fight Old Abe The 6th time and wont forsake him the 7th. The Ballance of them said they would pay there friends a visit at home, they would then return to the confederate army,- That is the kind of men the army of the Potomac is composed of. They where taken most of them on the 18th of July. They say they have had nothing to eat But Bread and Water and it appears that old Abe cant feed our prisoners, what few he has,- a young man of our company talked with one of them. Father I wish you could pay us a visit you would see one of the Best organised armys in the world Situated upon ground simerly to a Basen, you can see our intire army from the Hill our Brigade occupyes, Save 12,000 who are down at Dumfries on the Potomac sustaining our Blockadeing Battery.[61] It is a grand site at night to see the camp fires of 60 thousand soldiers, We have every kind of Music calculated to inspire man with pride, and courage- a great many Brass Bands, The 9th ala Regiment has a Band, My health is now very good, I way 187 pounds, upon the whole a fine looking Soldier haire short Beard long. We have quit drilling and gone to Work on Breast Works, We have fortifications extending 8 miles in length We have staked out a R Road leading from Manassas to Centerville 7 miles distance commence Work on it in a day or two Soon finish it with 50,000 thousand [*sic*] hands.[62] Wilcox appointmnt to Brigadier Gen has damaged our Regi considerably We all swere we would have no other Col for a while, But they crammed old Henry on us, Gen Wilcox is now our, gen, our Regi is said to be the Best drilled Regi in our Brigade you must direct your Letters to Manassas instead of Centerville. Good Bye

Your effectionate Son
Wm C McClellan Manassas, Va, Warrior

William Cowan McClellan to Matilda McClellan

Centerville,
November,22,1861
Dear Sister Matilda McClellan
I have ben sitting most of the day on the pike near the slaughter pen looking at our men kill Beef, There is one continuel stream of people, horses, Waggon, stock of all discriptions passing here at all hours. It is just as common for me to see a string of Waggons as long as from our house to Mr. Fletchers, as it is for you to see Henry[63] drive by the Wood pile. Just cast your eyes up towards Centerville 2 miles, to one who had never seen but few tents it would present the appearance of a snow Clad Hill. Here comes an officer under Whip and spur going to head quarters,- these things I scarsly ever notice- Here comes a Sutlery Waggon[.] I give him (75) cents for (2) chickens. Yonder stands old Governor Letcher making a speech to the 38, Va, Regi. Well I will go to camp and Clean my chickens, Mess mate what did you give for them chickens, Bill, 75 cents, right Big price, yes, poor as the Devil at that ain't they-yes, put on that Camp kettle Phillip and les have them for supper[,] Bill I hope you are not going to eat them feathers and all, no of course not, Well slosh her in, Bill dam if this aint an old setting hen, all right we will eat her any how. The sun is now about a half an hour high, the drums are Beating for dress parade, I hear a thousand drums commingling with the keen notes of the fifes, here comes our Brass Band I can hear a dozen more. They make the Welkin[64] sing in fact the hole valley sends forth a strane of music. Dress Parade is over silence again reigns in camp. The Boys are all eating supper. Well Tom I will give the old hen a whack, supper is over the Boys are all sitting a round their fires talking up on various subjects. half after 8 oclock has come the drums are again heard,- fall in says the orderly Sergeant to role call, every man that does not answer to his name is put upon double duty- every man then spreads his pallet and goes to sleep role is called next morning just at Break of day These are some of the things that day by transpire around me, you would suppose With so much of life so much of men so much of music that I enjoyed myself, But far from it underlining all is a deep solicitude for my country, No man thinks more about the troubles of our country than my self, I some times come to the conclusion that we are bound to triumph, again I come to the conclusion that We have

great odds to contend against and it may take us years of Bloodshead and strife to gain our independence. All of this the Brave Sons of the South Will cheerfully undergo be fore subjugation, I understand My Box is at the Junction. I will get it to morrow perhaps[.] Tell Bob if it is not too much trouble to coppy off my Letters If I should get home I should like to see them, they would serve in place of a diary to denote times and places and incidents. My health is now tolerablely good, tell Tom Nick I think a great deal about him perhaps he may have to toat a musket before We gain our independence. Tell Kitt to Write to me. Tom Cartwright is Well. William Pettus has ben discharged.

Your effectionate Brother,
W.C. McClellan
Manassas Junction, Va.

William Cowan McClellan to Matilda McClellan

Give my respects to old Heart and Clanady
Camp, Centerville, Va,
Nov 23. 61
Dear Sister,
I have just returned from off our picket duty, I saw no yankees While out Though I was several miles beyond our advanced lines. Nothing of importance has transpired since I wrote by Mr Phillips save our Cavalry took 32 yankees prisoners and 4 Waggons & Teams load With corn a few days ago.[65] The Yankees were out on a foreaging expedition. Some Thing is going to happen here before long that will make old earth tremble once more. We had orders this evening to send all of our goods we could not toat on our Backs to the Junction and hold our selves in readiness to march in 30 minutes notice. We may advance on Washington city or We may Beat another retreat The couriers are flying about more lively than usual, A Cavalry company of ours was fired into a night or so ago on the Fairfax Road by some Yankees- Killing one man and the Capts. horse. The Cap. gave the order to dismount and charge on them Which they did takeing .9. prisoners. The fight occured in a dense pine thicket. I received a long letter from my sweet heart last night giving me the general News in her neighborhood also informing me if I ever returned from war to have me in spite of the laws of

man. She writes me some very interesting letters informing me that She and all of her relations are true Southern people and hopes the Confederate army will be victorious & Well. We are all getting along pretty Well generally. getting plenty to eat Working on a R. Road. We are building from Manassas to Centerville 6 miles in length. We will soon finish it. We have 50,000 hands at work on it, I got a letter from Billy Day, dated Nov 12 informing me that L. P. Walkers Brigade had been ordered to Pensacola, I was glad to hear it If they had come here They would all have frozen to death This Winter The Sleet is falling very fast at this moment grounds frozen an inch and a half deep, Capt. Hobbs and all of his company are in good health at this time. Old Irie [Ira] Hobbs is here yet you say Dave Houston is in Athens That is a mistake he is in Richmond with his Shirt Tail out and no money one of his old company saw him there and gave him 5 dollars, poor David thou hast fallen. I received Sallies Letter of Nov 1 about 3 days ago, also yours and Bobs of Nov 5 5 days ago. I am in good health at present,

your Brother,
William Cowan McClellan

Write as soon as this gets into hands. Tom Cartwright is well, Bill Fields [William Eppa Fielding] is complaining a little.

William Cowan McClellan to Robert Anderson McClellan

Camp Centreville. Va
Nov 25, 61
Dear Bob,
Our guns are now stacked in line of Battle- The report is The enemy are advancing. I hope it is so, a cheerful smile rest on the face of all The Boys generaly- Let the Yankees come. I heard on all sides it is a grand sight to see 50 thous. troops turn out- Cavalry Artillery firing on all sides. Old Gen. Wilcox is riding around us careless as usual. Beauregard & Johnston and Smith all passed by our Regi looking like they were ready for the fray. This place is very strongly fortified. I think we could Whip Lincolns Whole army combined, if they Will attack us here. our line of Breast Works extends about 10 miles in length. Every quarter of a mile we have a strong Battery. Bob I fear this report that is very often heard of in

camp and believed by many of the advance of Yankees Will turn out to be a general Review of the Army. We had a considerable snow last night, had the ground been dry it would have been 2 inches deep. The Blue Ridge presents an un broken chain of Whitetops that will stare us in the face the Balance of this Winter. We will have a pretty tight time of it here this Winter in old rotten tents. Wood to haul 2 miles and But one load a day allowed at that. for a company. Tell Henry about this and tell him not to haul but one load a week for you all. I have written Father 2 letters in the last week one two pages the other 6 pages long. Bill Day a long letter. Bud Cartwright a long letter, Bill McClellan a long letter after finishing this scattering affair. I will write to Miss ________. Well as my hands are getting very cold I will want to close, in closed you will find Jim Baileys Obituary. Give My Respects to all inquiring Friends, Old Heart included. I sometimes think about going home but this thought is generally associated with Things far in the future, It has been nearly 6 months since I left home. in that time I have seen many strange sights. a Boy who had never been 30 miles from home. I tell you Bob I am almost as well acquainted with Fairfax county as I am with old Limestone having travelled nearly every Road in the county. The Boys say that Noah's Ark landed on the Blue Ridge and its inmates Settled in this county. it looks so old, though there is some Beautiful country in Fairfax and Prince William counties. carry me Back from old Virginia Shore is the wish of your humble servant. Write often.

your Brother, caution
Wm C. McClellan Esq— Manassas Jun. Va

William Cowan McClellan to Robert Anderson McClellan

Camp. Centreville. Va.
December 6th 61
Dear Bob,
We have just returned from Picket duty. Nothing of a startling nature happened while out. We took one yankee prisoner. Our company went on duty Monday night it was so cold that Cub Run, a little stream upon which we were stationed which is a very swift stream was frozen over at .10. oclock,- we were not allowed a spark of fire on post,- We had fire at our reserve a half mile in our

rear,- My squad of 6 men stood for 5 hours after that we were relieved every 2 hours and allowed to go to the reserve and warm. Liet. Floyd who had command of our company sent some men about 2 miles off and got some Whiskey. which helped considerably to repel the cold. Some of the Boys got a little happy but I assure you I did not drink enough to effect me in the least. nor do I ever intend to especially in the army, a man that drinks Whiskey here is always in trouble. We stand picket 4 miles from camp. about a mile from our picket line Capt. Hobbs wife Boards. She and her little Boy came out to see our Regi pass. Mrs. Hobbs must be a woman of courage to take up Board in a mile of our extreme line. Our Brigade has a certain part of our line to guard. each Regi stands .3. days which brings our Regi on every ,15, days. Since writeing .4. days ago our army has taken .40. more prisoners. Night before last one of our Cavalry companys went a way down about .12. miles from Centreville on a scouting expedition on aquitine [Accotink] creek not far from where We first went on picket. They crossed the enemys line, The Yankees stretched a rope a cross The road. They knew our Cavalry were to retreat in. They then sent a heavy body of infantry to run them through placing on each side of the road where they tied the rope a squad of men. Our Cavalry came dashing down the road and ran up against the yankee obstacle jamming up in great confusion while the Yanks were fireing from all sides into them. Our men soon cut the rope with their sabers. 6 are missing. Two of our men killed, two yankees, and were down stripping them of their Boots when taken prisoner.[66] This is the last rope trick they will play on our Cavalry. Everyday something of a dareing nature turns up between our scouts and those of the enemy. We are expecting a fight every day, it is my opinion the Big fight will be down at Evans Point Battery, that Battery is giveing the yankees more trouble than anything else, our men down there have got so proficient they can sink a Boat at a single Shot. We have 12 thousand men there. The 4th Alabama and first Tennessee Regiments are there. By the by Jim Ned Fletcher was up here a few days ago. He's looking very well and in good spirits,- he told me poor Pettus, Fletcher and little Tommy Harris[67] had been discharged, poor fellows I am sorry they have such delicate constitutions. I received last night .3. letters one from Father dated Nov 24 one from Uncle Will dated Nov. 24 all Well, one from you dated Nov 23, Father complains of me not writing. I wrote as soon as I heard he had gone to

Montgomery in fact I have written him 2 letters since he has been at Montgomery. I suppose he is at home now as he wrote me that he would be there in two weeks. Since writing the above We have had dress parade. We took 7 prisoners yesterday 2 Cavalry men missing. Tell Kittie I did not loose my buttons and thread. they have been very useful to me. Tell her and Tom to learn all they can at school. I now see the folly of my idly spent school Boy days. I find in my intercourse with men that I am more than an average man among men, had I applied myself in those precious days I might have made something of my self. Reflections, like these have troubled me upon many restive pillows, I have got a great many friends in our company. They are frequently in my tent and very often invite me into theirs, always asking me advice and my opinion about matters generally. among my strongest friends are George Gilbert, Charles Trimble of Franklin Co ala whose Father has been judge of that county for 20 years.[68] David Phillips[69] & I have had but one difficulty in the co, that was with a big fellow by the name of Steward. I caught him in the collar and drew Back to strike him he then acknowledged he had lied and turned him loose. he is now a good Friend of mine, Some of the Boys was disposed to run over Tom Cartwright. as soon as I got well I took him in my tent and told them they had to stop it or they had to whip me. They chose to do the former. I will write a gain in a few days. This is a very mean pen I am writing with. I am detailed to work on the Breast Works to morrow. Give my respects to W. B. Vaughn and the Sly the misterious J. M. Moore.

Your Brother
W.C. McClellan Manassas, Va

William Cowan McClellan to Matilda McClellan

Army of the Potomac
Camp Centreville. Va.
Dec 10th 1861
Dear Sister
I have just returned from one of the most heart rending scenes ever witnessed by man. I saw two men tied to a post and shot dead.[70] They were of the far famed Tigers. Men who fought Bravely upon the plains of Manassas on the ever memorable .21. of July. The of-

fence for which they were punished was chargeing bayonets on a Lieut[enant]. They inflicted upon him two mortal wounds. They were drunk when they committed the crime. They were tried by a regular courtmartial and doomed to be shot. They were dressed in striped pants and red shirts with little red caps on their heads. All of the Tigers wore a similar dress. They were marched up in the presence of fifteen thousand men as boldly as a Tiger ever walked among a flock of sheep. They were then ordered to kneel down by the post they were tied to. The priest then prayed one of the most powerful prayers I ever heard. He pressed the cross to their lips and imprinted a kiss upon them. 12 of their own company were ordered to shoot them. When they had taken their places 10 paces in front of them, the caps were drawn over their eyes, one of them pulled it off, and said I will die looking in the muzzles of those rifles. The command was given, ready, aim, fire. Neither of them flinched until the balls had pierced their Bodys. The Priest then made a very brief and appropriate talk to the Soldiers- telling them that drinking caused the death of those men and Putting an enemy in their mouths to steal their brains away. It will have a good effect upon our army. Nothing of any importance has transpired since writeing a few days ago, some are disposed to think that the enemy have retreated to the Potomac. I believe all idea of an attack at this point has subsided. Quietness again reigns in Camp save now and then a report that is started in Camp that gains admittance into the minds of the credulous. We soldiers all rest satisfied that Beauregard and Johnston couldn't be outgeneraled by the Feds and we can do the fighting. Gaines Smith is one of the finest looking men I ever saw every step he takes is that of a Military man every look and gesture. Smith is about 6 feet 2 inches high strait as an arrow, Gen. Johnston is also a fine looking man. Gen B. [Beauregard] has nothing very striking in his appearance save his eyes. They flash and sparkle like lightening all the time- searching to penetrate each wink upon which they rest. I frequently get invitations from these gentlemen to visit them at their head quarters. I have always declined doing so upon the plea that I am a private. I suppose the caus of their partiality towards me is the close relationship I have existing between Gen. McClellan and my self. My health is tolerably good at this time. I am just getting over a very bad cold and cough. The health of our company is very good at present. Capt Smiths company are as ragged as Beauregards. The weather is very mild here at this time. I am making arrangements to get a swap to Capt Malones co, it will probably be a month or so before I can effect the change. The last letter I received from home was dated Nov. 24, except one tonight. Write soon.

Your Brother,
William C. McClellan Manassas Virginia

William Cowan McClellan to Thomas Joyce McClellan

Camp. Centreville. Va.
Dec. 18th/61
Dear Father.
Young Hal Malone and myself by the advice of Capt. Hobbs will telegraph tomorrow to Capt Malone at Huntsville to summon the .2. men who wanted to swap places with us. All parties here are willing to the exchange. I also wrote John a letter also directing it to Huntsville. If Capt M. co. has gone to Mobile please go up and forward Bothe the dispatch and letter to them at Mobile. Since writing the above I have telegraphed to Capt Malone at Huntsville. I understand by a letter a day or two ago that Nick Davis' Battalion had gone to Corrinth Mississippi there to remain until they could procure arms. Bobs letter of to day is a confirmation of the fact. I was surprised to hear that there is a likelyhood of North ala being invaded by the yanks by way of Collumbus Kentucky.[71] There is one thing certain they will never invade her by way of Richmond. We have been planting the confederate flag in their faces here for 4 months trying to get them to fight us, but it is no go. They always retreat the day before the Battle is to be fought. The Generals call it Staggered movements, but to a common man it is nothing but old fashioned craw fishing. I heard an old man of .70. say this was the best disciplined best drilled best fighting army that has ever ben organised under the sun. This old man sports a fine carriage and horses a body guard and is frequently seen rideing around Centreville, he lives in Hardaman county Va. I was glad to hear of your safe return home. The dog law you passed at Montgomery I think is a very good one, you are at liberty to Kill all of my Dogs.[72] We have about 20 dogs in our Regi. Tell Bob I have got a dog that can tree opossoms faster than 2 men can Shake them out. When we go out on picket duty he generally trees several. All quiet here at pres-

ent, no talk of a fight. We have good fortifications and good Generals, good fighting, let them come. Tell Matilda I had my ambertype[73] taken yesterday at Centreville. I have undergone a very great change in .6. months. We had an election this morning for .3. Lt. George Gilbert, 2nd Sergeant, orderly Sergeant W. L. Wayland, Sergeant Crenshaw.[74] Where the candidates I was a strong Gilbert man. Wayland beat Gilbert .5. votes. Hal Bibb has resigned. The company are all glad of his resignation. Al Martin has not got here yet. Write to me as soon as this comes to hand. Nothing of importance to write.

Your affectionate Son
W.C. McClellan
Manasas Jun
Fairfax county Va

William Cowan McClellan to Thomas Joyce McClellan

Camp, Centerville, Va.
Dec. 20th 61.
Dear Father,
I am now in fine health and good spirits, hopeing this will find you enjoying the same blessing, as the word goes. Events are transpiring every day to stir our Blood and actuate us to deeds of daring, day before yesterday some of our troops had a fight near fairfax courthouse.[75] it is said for the first time that our side got a little worsted. This morning a forraging party of one hundred and fifty wagons 2 hundred cavalry, and fifteen hundred infantry left here. They are going after corn which they expect to get not far from Alexandria. I expect about night They will come in at a double quick step, and waggins gone. Several men went from our Regim but I assure you that I did not, The long role was beat in several Regiments last night, 2 Regi in our Brigade left here about 3.oclock this morning for the Purpose I suppose of renewing the skirmish at Fairfax. I think it is the object of general Johnston to force them into a fight and then fall back to our intrenchments here at Centerville. but I have no idea The yankees will ever get here, I dont think our troops can be restrained until they would get within 3 miles of our fortifications. On yesterday a crowd of men came from Richmond on the cars yelling and waveing there hats and said a man high in

authority in Rich had received or dispatched direct from England in which he was appraised of the fact that England had made an unconditional demand of Slidell and Mason upon the Lincoln government. Also that he had to open the Blockade within .30. days, a great many here believe it to be true. if it be so this horrible war will soon close. or the yankees will be the worst whipped people on earth, If they have the Bravery to refuse to give up Slidell & Mason old England will push her out upon the Sea Board while we will withdraw our troops from the coast and give them a taste of the bitter fruits of invasion. I hope to God this news is so and old Abe will refuse promptly to give up our Ministers the Ball will then be opened . . . I Think we can thrash them after a while our selves but With Englands Navy we could do it so much quicker. This news is published in todays Dispatch, Richmond Inquirer and other papers. We get the Richmond papers here the day after they are published. by the by I am pretty well Booked relative to what is going on in the country. I think our prospects are brightening a little, but there seems to be no outlet yet, Capt. Hobbs is trying and will probably succeed in getting his company accepted as a cavalry com. Gen. Wilcox tells him he thinks it can be done[.] I have not heard anything of Capt Malone since his son, and my self telegraphed to him to send on those men that desired a swap with us. The weather is very warm here now for the season of the year, We will go into Winter quarters in 2 or 3 days about 12 miles from the Strawsburg [Strasburg] R. Road at a little place called Gainesville . . . my respect to all my papers has given so I will close for the present. your son.

W. C. McClellan Manassas Junction, Va

The fight I spoke of just now has turned out to be a sham fight betwean the yankees. So Capt. Hobbs tells me, I have just had a long talk with Capt H he has ben very low spirited for some time past but seams greatly helped up since the last european news, he says he can see a little light hole for the first time in 4 months, I was glad to hear that. Dr. Sanders was likely to get an appointment as seargeant of This Regi, since Dr. Anderson resigned we have ben without any. you may say Dr. John Hays is here it is true but the Regi would be a great deal better off without him, I have heard him cursed more than any Body save Abraham Lincoln, The Boys call him that dam Dog faced Hays, Hays an myself have always gotten along very well. Bob speaks of the cecessionists abusing the old union men when this war is over if it pleases God to return me safely home and a cecessionist speaks in disparity of the old Union men then We Will fight. thease are the centiments of the entire army Witch is composed principally of Union men. Since writing the above I have ben under arms for 8 hours expecting every moment to march. The expedition I spoke of yesterday composed of 4 Regi marching in front of our waggons had a very Bloody fight about 12 miles from here on a creek call flat lick, one South Carolinan R. a Kentucky Regi, The 10 ala Regi commanded by Col. Forney, Col. F[orney] got his arm Broke. his Lt. Col was killed.[76] Step Pickett heard the role call of Forneys Regi[.] 80 were missing, including killed and wounded, a Lt Col was killed in the Kentucky Regi, our loss is very heavy. Col Forney and his regiment has just arrived from the Battlefield killed wounded and missing 80. Col. F's Regiment belongs to our Brigade Gen Stewart [J. E. B. Stuart] was commanding during the fight, the way it happened that Stewart was in command there was 4 Brigades sent out a regi each to quarter our Waggons. some of our waggons had loaded when the fight commenced all of our wagons got back safe to Centerville. our troops had the yankees in a trot when they received reinforcements, Forney Broke the yankees line twice before the reinforcements of the enemy came. his men fought desperately Col F. arm was broaken early in the engagement but kept his saddle and gave commands. The Enemy had at least 10 thousand men in the fight, our force was 35 hundred with this odds we had them thrashed had it not ben for there reinforcements, Gen Wilcox told Capt. Hobbs or said to him by God sir Gen. S[tuart] has no wright to lead my people into Battle if they have to be cut to pieces I want to see it done myself, it is reported that Gen. Johnston has gone on to the Battlefield with 8 Brigades and says he will have possession of it before sun down when we got the news here that Forney was in a fight our regi raised a Shout to forward to his assistance, had it not ben for Wilcox we would have gone any how. you will heare all about this Battle before this letter reaches you, I expect we will be into a general fight before long, at least I hope so, it has in the last 4 hours turned very cold, my hands are so numb I cannot write.

Your son,
W. C. McClellan

Walk in lemons and get squeezed. I now hear heavy cannonading in the direction of the enemy lines.

William Cowan McClellan to Matilda McClellan

Camp Centerville. Va.
Dec [25] 1861
Dear Sister,
I received your very kind letter yesterday dated the 15th Dec. As we go into Winter quarters to morrow I will write you a few lines. Every thing is perfectly quiet here now save occasionally you see a drunk man going to the guard house. This is Christmas day the familiar word Christmas gift is frequently spoken by the Soldiers but it does not sound like that house hold word did at home, here it is spoken by the lips of rough War worn men. there it was lisped by the gleeful Voices of Children. I imagined this morning that I could see Tommy [McClellan], running all about the house and kitchen saluting every one he met with this word. I often think of the pleasant associations of the past and wonder why I ever became discontented and dissatisfied with little things, When at home and at peace with mankind, 6 months Soldiering has done wonders for me it has cooled my impetuous nature and left me a man of Patients and forbearance. I will send by Mr. Ezell[77] this letter. Also my ambrotype is not a good one by any means, I had it taken at Centerville When there was 30 men in the room telling the Artist if he did not make haste they would tear down or run off with his gallery, there is too much of my Body taken in the picture, makeing my head look too small for the Size of the picture. Tom Cartwright and my self will send our letters to Madison Station by Mr. Ezell who has been discharged from our Company upon account of inability to perform service, I expect you have heard something [about] a letter I wrote to Miss Mollie P[ettus]. I wrote her a short letter just for the fun of the thing more than any thing else. tidings came to me away up here on the Potomac that Miss Moll and myself had a secret understanding that letter was my first and last. but Matilda I tell you I have got a shore nuff Sweetheart in Madison county ala.[78] While out on Picket I formed the acquaintance of a Miss Jinney Miller[79] who is worth 50 thousand dollars. a lady of fine sence and education. several of the Boys always went with me but I was always her

favorite. We had to Skip off from our co. and cross our line of Pickets and go two miles beyond our lines to see Miss Jinnie. She lives in a fine house surrounded by a fine plantation and innumerable slaves and hates the Yankees very much. Dr. Tweedy[80] arrived here this morning. He has just spent an hour in my tent, he told me a great deal about Limestone and the people there of. he seamed very much surprised at the amount of flesh I have gained since he saw me at home. T. T. Tweedy is off at a hospital some where in Va, Bill Fielding[81] is as fat as a hog. he has found out a great many of his kinfolks since he came to Virginia he has cousins liveing 10 miles from here, Bill, or, Eppy is a mess mate of mine. by the by he is a man of good sense but a very singular fellow I have a great deal of fun out of him, I had a fight with an Irish man 3 days ago. he got drunk and came into my tent about the time I was going to Pallet, and commenced cutting up and said he was going to sleep with me I bore with him for an hour and ordered him out of my tent. he caught me by the hair pulled it little the next thing he knew he was out side of my tent flat of his back. he attempted to come back I downed him again this time pouring a camp kettle of water on him as he got up and said now is the winter of my discontent and left. you must excuse this disconnected letter I write down the first thing that occurs to me. that Irishman is the only man I ever thrashed, save, Bob and John, give my respects to all inquiring Friends,

Your affectionate Brother,
W. C. McClellan

William Cowan McClellan to Thomas Joyce McClellan

Bull Run, Camp near Manassas
[December 31, 1861][82]
Dear Father,
Christmas has passed very quietly by, it has ben to us Soldiers nothing more than every other week, since writing home we have moved one mile south of Stone Bridge, Here we are building cabins for Winter quarters, company F has 5 dozens built. it will take ten for our company it will be 2 weeks be fore we can go into them, Board timber is very scarse, rock more so for Backs for our chimneys. to morrow we go on Picket. We now go on every 30 days, half

Regi goes at a time the left Wing of our Regi went on Picket duty 3 days . . . I understand We have Cabbins on our post out there,[83] We have a Report in camp of a fight at Annandale,[84] the report is that we whipped the yankees very Badly,- one of our men went there they had been one hundred waggons sent down there for Captured Baggage I have heard very heavy cannonading in that direction, though I doubt the above report of so heavy an engagement. The general opinion is that the campaign is over until spring. Alfred Martin arrived here 4 days ago he says if he had of known Camp life was so disagreeable he would have staid at home. just such sentiments you might expect to come from such a man, such a Soldier adds but little to Southern independence, Al is in my mess he has told me a great many yarns about Alabama, it is now 9 o'clock taps have been beat on hours, the candle is very dim, I must close, below you will find a drawing of our cabins.

your Son,
W, C McClellan

5
The Road to the Peninsula
January 8–March 24, 1862

> We whip them every time we meet.
>
> —WCM

At the beginning of 1862, William and the 9th Alabama remained encamped in the Centreville area. Hopes for a quick invasion of Washington, D.C., and an early end to the war had faded. With increased Union activity in Washington, Confederate leaders were trying to figure out the Union army's next move now that it was under the command of Gen. George Brinton McClellan. By January 1862 there were 98,050 men in the Department of Northern Virginia,[1] and Confederate forces, in their winter quarters at Centreville, continued their work constructing fortifications and building a military railroad between Centreville and Manassas. Joseph Johnston's army defended a line from the Potomac River below Mount Vernon north to the Potomac River near Leesburg, Virginia. All of the approaches to Richmond were thus covered, except for a possible flanking movement far around their right flank via the Potomac River.

Gen. Joseph E. Johnston moved the Confederate army from Centreville toward the Virginia Peninsula on March 8, in anticipation of General McClellan's movement to attack Richmond. McClellan wanted to avoid a frontal assault on the fortified positions at Centreville while marching on Richmond, and he moved around them by attacking up the Virginia Peninsula. He planned to reach West Point on the York River and to use the Richmond and York Railroad to support his drive on Richmond, while cutting off and capturing the Confederate defenders on the peninsula by advancing from the Rappahannock River to the York River. With Johnston getting the jump on him, McClellan modified his plans of attacking Richmond by landing at Fort Monroe on the very end of the Virginia Peninsula.

As they evacuated Manassas, the Confederates left behind 3,240,000 pounds of subsistence stores and 2,000,000 pounds of bacon and salted meat at their meat-cutting plant, located at Chapman's Mill in Thoroughfare Gap at the Prince William County and Fauquier County line.[2] The retreating Confederate forces burned all the stores and supplies they could not carry

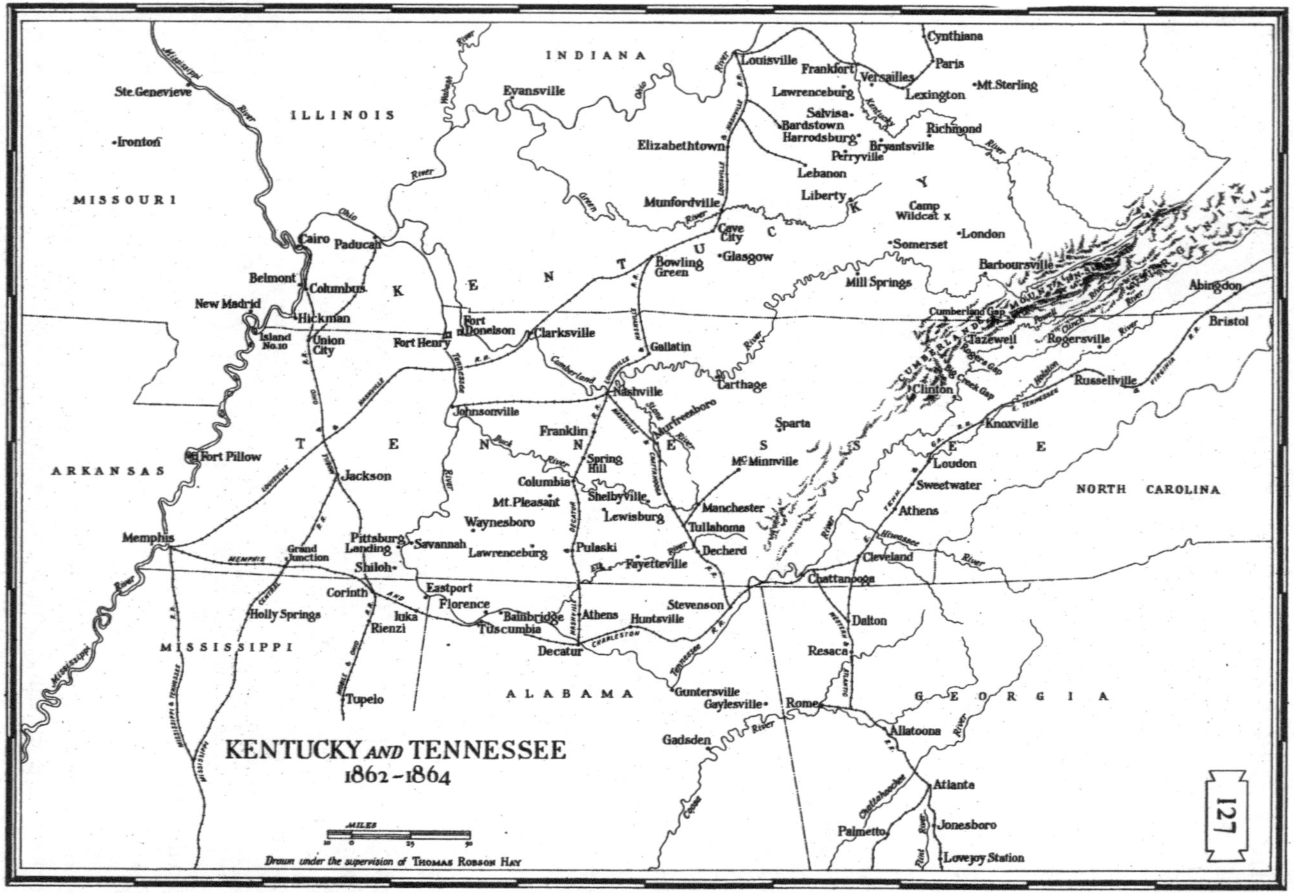

Kentucky and Tennessee, 1862–1864

and then burned their winter cabins. They remained near Culpeper for two weeks before crossing over the Rapidan River and going into camp near Gordonsville, where they remained until their removal to the Virginia Peninsula in April.

Meanwhile, closer to William's home, the fall of Forts Henry and Donelson in February 1862 left the Tennessee River Valley open to invasion by Union forces. Adm. Andrew Hull Foote led a squadron of Union gunboats down the Tennessee River to Florence, Alabama, in February, where they were met by Union loyalists who hailed them as deliverers from the Confederates who had taken over the state. After Confederate forces were defeated at Shiloh, Tennessee, on April 7, Gen. Don Carlos Buell's army captured Huntsville on April 11 and soon occupied the Tennessee River Valley in northern Alabama, including the towns of Decatur, Athens, and Florence. More importantly, he severed the Memphis and Charleston Railroad and captured locomotives and rolling stock.[3]

Throughout 1862, William and his comrades wondered why the Confederate armies in the west could not achieve victories like those of the Army of Northern Virginia. The citizens at home in Limestone County agreed as they watched Union forces move with ease through the Tennessee Valley. Facing this reality, the local population had to make a decision whether to stay home and take their chances with the invading army or to flee the immediate area. According to one historian, most of the ardent supporters of secession disappeared from northern Alabama in a matter of days, leaving mainly a mixture of Unionists and Southern citizens who felt deserted and betrayed by the retreating Confederate forces.[4] The McClellans decided to stay at home.

William Cowan McClellan to Thomas Joyce McClellan

Cedar Grove Winter quarters
January 8 1862
Dear Father,
I have neglected to write to you for several days simply be cause I have been too busily engaged at work upon our cabbins to Write. We have been getting along very slowly for the want of tools to work with. We will have by to morrow night 5 cabins ready to move into. We have the other 5 in a forward state of building. We find it very cold work [to] have to dig a foot in the ground to get through the frozen earth. and then heat Water to make up the mor-

tar with. you would laugh if you could see the roof We have on our huts. We started on Picket New Years day. one night while we were out it sleeted all night, I stood 4 hours without a spark of fire. We had some fun skating on a mill pond that was close by. Nothing of a startling nature occurred save of Frank Cook[5] halted a hog supposing him to be a yankee, the hog did not halt of course. Cook banged loose at him but unfortunately for We poor hungry Devils he missed him- night before last We had a snow about an inch deep. Virginians say this has been a very mild Winter so far for this country. Capt. Hobbs is now acting judge advocate of the courtmartial which is quite an honor paid him by Gen. Smith consequently he has nothing to do with his company for a month, the Boys are all very glad of it as they have had a few more liberties by the transaction. Nick Floyd has had command of the troopers the Boys all love Floyd. he is one of the cleverest men I ever knew He takes great interest in the company, always kind and agreeable in his deportment towards those men under him, But let a man do him a wrong and he is as stern in retaliation as he is agreeably to those he likes. I received Bobs letter of December 30 yesterday. I hope the dispatch had gone on to Capt M[alone]. when you went to Huntsville. Hal Malone got a letter from his Father last night stating that those men were still anxious to swap, If I effect the swap I will come by home and stay a few days, this would be the greatest pleasure of my life to spend a few days among the familiar scenes of my boy hood in times like these. Did you send my boots by Smiths. uniforms. they have not arrived yet[,] boots or uniforms. I may get them in a day or so. have you got the letters sent by Mr. Ezell and Ambrotype also, some say old Abe and England are bound to fight, I have just read the Richmond Dispatch, I think our prospects are brightening a little, in great hast your affectionate son

W. C. McClellan
Manassas Junct

Matilda[,] There is one Maryland Regi at Centreville consisting of 8 hundred men, I saw them the other day going out on Picket. They were well clad and in good spirits. Tell the preacher to lay down the Book of Life and take up the instrument of death,- and join his Brave Countrymen.

W. C. McClellan
Manassas Junct.

My boots & comfort have come at last, the boots fit me very well.

William Cowan McClellan to Matilda McClellan

Virginia, Junction, Manassas
January 10th, 1862
Dear Sister,
I wrote a letter to father two days ago, but failing to get it off, I will send both of them by a Mr Wetherford[6] who has been discharged from our company. He makes the 17th man discharged out of our company, We have 84 men rank and file. Every thing is driving along about as usual, we will get into our winter quarters in a day or two. I consulted Capt. Hobbs again last night about my swap he says all that is required to complete the swap is for these men to come on here, or on the other hand, get the consent of Gen. Johnston to let us meet those men at Mobile- The former I would much prefer, because I would then go by home- I have not heard a word from John since he left Huntsville. well Matilda for the first time during the war I am out of soup, I have written this evening no less 5, letters. I have several to Sweet hearts that I frequently Write to, I find I am very popular with the women folks 12 hundred miles from home. My honest convictions are now I never will marry. I have learned to do my own cooking and sewing I can make up my own bed. Well I must close it is so dark I cannot see the lines, so goodly. Write soon tell Sallie to Write.

By your Bro.
W. C. McClellan in respect to all Friends.

William Cowan McClellan to John Beattie McClellan

Camp Near Louis house.
January 14, 1862
Dear Brother,
I have almost come to the unmistakable conclusion that you never intend to reply to the innumerable letters I have written to you. It is true that they contain but little news or information. It is equally true that your letters would prove very interesting to me. We have completed our Winter quarters at last after a month hard labor. I moved into my cabbin yesterday. Last night we had a snow 2 inches deep, in fact we have had snow upon the ground for 3 weaks. The Virginians say this has been the mildest Winter they ever saw here. I have not suffered with any more than I usually do at home. I got a

letter from Father a few days ago in which there was an extract from one of your letters giving an account of the sickness and disease prevalent among the troops at Mobile. You all seem to think it a very distressing amount of sickness, so it is but from your statement of the men able for duty and those on the sick list, it is not as much sickness as we have. The first two months we were in the service at Richmond. Houston had 19 men out of 80 for duty. At Bull Run Capt. Hobbs had 40 for duty 50 on sick list. Diarrhea & intestinal fever were the principal diseases. Boath of which I had very often. Capt Hobbs drew up papers for a swap for Hal Malone and myself. It was signed by Capt Hobbs, Col [Samuel] Henry, Col. Wilcox. It was then sent up to Gaines Smith who signed it but put upon it disapproved instead of approved which played the devil with my and Hals swap. I am assured by Col. Henry & Capt Hobbs that it will be no difficulty what ever to affect the exchange if you will send those men on here. Wilcox and Henry will fix it up immediately. Capt Hobbs will write to Capt M. [Malone] upon the subject to day. He will inclose the request we presented herewith and will answer there if those men come by changeing names. Write or start these men immediately and let Hal and myself know what to depend upon. I telegraphed to Capt .M. a month ago to start those men but suppose he has not received it. My health is very good at present, I way [*sic*] 200 hundred pounds.

In great haste your Brother,
Wm. C. McClellan

Write soon as this comes to hand without fail, no talk of a fight here soon. dont Shoot an English vessel if one should happen to come to Mobile, We are on good terms with England up here. some think she is going to help us out of the scrap.

Wm. C. McClellan C.S.A

William Cowan McClellan to Thomas Joyce McClellan

Camp near Louis house
January 15, 1862
Dear Father, your very kind letter was handed to me day before yesterday . . . [Here William again discusses his attempt to transfer to Malone's Company; it will not be repeated here.] I had no idea

I had so many friends until by some hook or crook it got out that I was going to leave[.] every man in Hobbs com. seemed to be very sorry I was going to leave many of them told me that they had rather see any man in the company leave than me. Some of the Boys say I am the most popular man in the com- among my strongest Friends are George Gilbert 2, Sergeant, David Phillip. I also have some good friends in the other companys, Lt. William Couch of Athens is a good friend of mine[.] so is our Adjutant. May,[7] a friend of mine. This I mention not in a boasting way, but merely to show you that I have conducted myself properly since I enlisted in the army[.] from the tenor of your letter you had rather I would stay here, to going South- you address some very good reasons for so thinking, but I think you are mistaken as to my chances of health on the coast. I think I would stand camp life much better on the coast than those who have just gone down there. The amount of men on the sick list John speaks of is very distressing[.] it is true but even that is not as bad as it has been with us at Richmond. Houston had 84 men I recollect at one time[;] he had but 20 men for duty. At Bull Run Capt. Hobbs had 40 men for duty[,] 55 on the sick list. When we left Broad Run our Surgeon reported the Regi. in good order. We had 16 men left unable for duty. When Capt. H[obbs] left Richmond, he had 108 men, he now has 80 men some few off at Hospitals. Our company has had as little sickness as most companys because Capt. H[obbs] makes the men keep clean. At Richmond our Regi. numbered 980 men, now we have 575 men. The question naturally comes up What is the cause of all this falling off [of] men. In my humble opinion the only answer to the question is Manassas is a sickly country. there is not a man in our company but what will gladly exchange to the coast if they could. as it has not rained but little here in two months and still you can dig a hole and get Water, at best it is a low marshy place about Manassas. In the summer season the Water is Warm and filthy. You probably think I am fickle, not satisfied any where. But I pledge now my Word I would not be disconnected intirely from the army While I enjoy my preasant health for no earthly consideration While this war continues. As you have left it to me Whether or not Provided I get an exchange to Malone's co. I will go if those two men come here.

In haste, your affectionate Son,
W. C. McClellan

William Cowan McClellan to Matilda McClellan

Camp near Louis house Va
January 17, 1862
Dear Sister,
My health is very good except a bad cold caused by a change from sleeping upon the ground to a bunk to use a camp expression, a bunk is made by driving forks in the ground, put some poles on them, plank upon the poles. Blankets on the planks and we have a very snug sleeping place. To day the tall pines and cedars that stand very thick around our cabbins are bending and cracking beneath the heavy weight of icicles Which is hanging from every limb and leaf, it is one of the most fearful scenes I ever looked upon, the snow is two inches deep, tramp, tramp, goes the foot Soldiers out to cut wood or Bring a bucket of Water or chase rabbits which are very plenty about here, Strange to say When 25 or 30 men get after one, they always pick him up, they either turn his left or right flank, or form a hollow square or take him by a simultaneous charge, on one occasion I was commander of a division, I outflanked every Rabbit that showed his Tail on my squad caught seven, I have been at 5 different places spoken of in the story in the paper Bob sent me. Old Fort Loudon at Winchester where Washington carried dispatches to Braddock is an old dilapidated structure. Berries Ferry just above where We waded the Shanandore [Shenandoah] on the 18th of July is on the Ashby Gap Road. It is the finest country along that road I ever saw I have also been at Long green[8] not far from Faire fax court house, The Louis house now the Head quarters of Gen Johnston is where Washington once had a hunting camp[.] this is a very fine building though a little old this house stands in the heart of the Battle ground of the 21 July, It was the Head quarters of our generals on day of Battle and who ever lives to read the history of the war will see and hear a great deal about the Louis house which stand on a half mile of our cabbins[9] We have ben pretty near all over Prince William to Fairfax county. We have ben in five miles of Mount Vernon, 12, miles of Washington. There is some talk of a fight here in the coarse of two weeks, a general assault upon our lines from North Carolina to Missouri. I believe this is all stuff. The Yankees wont come.

William Cowan McClellan to Robert Anderson McClellan

Camp near Louis house,
January 17, 1862
Dear Bob,
Your kind favor of Jan. 10th is at hand. I was glad to learn that Father has made plenty to eat both the hog and the homony. Tell Rip Davis and J M Moore I congratulate them on the hog question. I am very sorry that my letter to John was so long getting to him. We are expecting a fight here in a few days. ammunition has been examined thoroughly to night perhaps We are going out to hunt some more hay. You all seem to be in low spirits about the future prosperity of the Southern confederacy. We are all in fine spirits up here. There is one Thing certain England is determined to pick a fuss with the United States if possible. I noticed in a Richmond paper to day that they are still hammering on old Abe for an apology to the British flag. Capt. Hobbs has presented a petition to have our company changed to a cavalry, co, Floyd just told me Col. Henry & Gen. Wilcox had signed it and had been forwarded to Johnston. I hope it will succeed but I doubt very much whether or not it will succeed.

Yours with great respect.
Wm C McClellan

Tell Sister Sallie Davis I will Write to her Soon. Tell her to Write to me. Bob I feel remarkably well to night I way 200 pounds. well here comes [William Eppa] Fielding he was the Colonels orderly to day- orders come from Head quarters asking old [Samuel] Henry if he needed a Surgeon. Danger a head. Burnside expedition landed I expect.[10] Good,

WC McClellan
Miss M[ollie] E. T. [Tretting] is all setting up.

William Cowan McClellan to Thomas Joyce McClellan

Camp Near Louis House
January 19, 1862
Dear Father,
As it is raining to day and I have nothing to do I will write you a

letter, everything is very dull here at present though some effect to believe that we will have storing times before long. I believe our generals have ben expecting a fight for some time, but it is all knocked in the head since this Big snow and rain fell the Enemy cant effect anything With their Artillery. so [Gen. George] McClellan will have to wait until it dries off some, We have the news here that England has expressed her determination to open a direct rout to Norfolk, The excuse for so doing is to have communication With her consuls at New Orleans, Charleston and Richmond, this will be a recognition of the Southern confederacy de facto defining and can but amount to a full recognition. now is the time for old Abe to hit a powerful Blow and he knows it. Nothin but a very Brilliant victory can retrieve his broken fortune, or turn the sympathys of England which day by day are growing in favor of the South. Well I will change the subject I have not stood guard for 6 Weeks, the cause is this we have 30 guards every day, guard mountain at ,8, o'clock. there is 2 orderlies selected from the guard who have the cleanest guns and present the most Soldierly appearance. one of the orderlies waits on the Col. the other reports to The Adjutant. I am almost certain to be one of the orderlies. I have nothing to do but sit by old [Col. Samuel] Henrys fire and chat [with] him during the day and make one trip to Wilcoxs head quarters a half mile off to carry up the daily report. The Boys all say it is not worth while to show guns against me, that I will be dead certain to be orderly, Well We draw beef 6 days out of the week Sundays we draw canvass hams, flour all The time nothing else save coffee without sugar once a week, My mess has sent to Linchburg for a keg of Molasses. we will have a good time when it comes. Capt. Hobbs petition to have his company changed to a Cavalry co has ben sent back disapproved by Gen Smith about as I expected. My object in writing is to inform you all that I am well so you must excuse my disconnected and Badly written Letters. Write soon nothing more at preseant.

Your effectionate Son,
W C McClellan
Manassas Junction Virginia

William Cowan McClellan to Robert Anderson McClellan

Camp near Louis house
January 22, 1862
Dear Bob,
Mr. Tweedys substitute Tobe Gray[11] arrived her to day- as Mr. T starts home to morrow I will pencil you a few lines although it is now after role call. Nothing has happened recently worthy of attention, we have not had a clear day for two weeks or more having snowed or rained all the time, the mud in our streets is about 8 inches deep. . . . there seems to be but little sickness in camp at present but I fear this will not be the case long if it does not dry up pretty quick, the mud seems to be twice as Bad here as in ala, our cabbins are in a thick pine Slash out by the Home place, around us is some high country but the reason Gen. Smith preferred the low land was to shun the Wind and have protection of the pines- The most distressing thing now is the suffering of the poor unstabled horses, last night 4 of them passed off the toilsom stage of action among the things that were, those that remain look very poor and emaciated. When these poor horses get so poor that they cannot perform service they are taken off and sold at, 75, or ,80, cents per head, We then buy fresh horses at ,100, to, 125 dol[lars] a piece, some of the boys say that these 80 cent horses are picked up and sent back to us to eat labeled pickled Beef. I have often thought if transportation did not cost so much Father could buy these frames and fatten them up and make a fortune on them. We have ,80, head of horses in our Regi. Poor Tobe Gray has a hard road to travel before he becomes a soldier, He looks as ugly as ever, the Boys will have a great deal of fun out of him, they have carried Al Martin through the poles since he came here, I hear the Boys hollowing now where is our new recruit and asking Gray if he can eat cow. yes says Tobe all hands commence bellowing, Martin has been complaining every sense he has been here, until a day or two ago. he regained his usual health, you must go down to see Tom Tweedy if he is sober he will tell you some very interesting stories, He is a good man a very great pity he drinks, Tom and myself have been great friends from first to last, He tells me he is going to quit drinking I hope he will for his wifes sake if nothing els, Tom has read some of her letters to me She writes as fine letters as I have ever read from a lady. I have heard nothing from John or Capt Malone since the 28 of Decem-

ber. Capt H[obbs] wrote to Hal those men were still anxious to exchange. Hal, Capt, H, and I, have all written to them to send them on but can hear nothing from them. Bill Fielding is still in my mess he has a very good violin gives us some very fine music. There he sits now playing the old folks at Home. Capt Hobbs & Lt Floyd with their flutes and Fielding with his fiddle or fidle make fine music by the by We Boys are talking of putting up a Ball room to do our dancing in. Well it is Bunk time. Tell Father to go down someday and see T. T. Tweedy, Write as soon as this is received my respects to all true Southerners and old heartwell. Mr Tweedy has a letter to Sallie Davis. good night. give us Dixie, Fielding

your Brother
Bill McClellan

William Cowan McClellan to Robert Anderson McClellan

Camp near Louis house
January 25 [1862]
Dear Bob,
Your lengthy letter of Jan 17 came to hand yesterday. I was extreamly sorry to hear that Mother was complaining, hope by this time she has recovered. We have the news here of the defeat of our forces in Kentucky under Critenden, also of the death the brave Zollicoffer[12] who was one of the ablest statesmen, but from all accounts unfit for a commander- upon account of his inexperience in Military affairs, Probably this victory achieved by superior numbers will encourage the yankees to attack us at this place. I hope to God it may. I desire above all things on earth to drive a bayonet to the hearts Blood of some of the Hell bound invaders of the North. They resort to every mean trick that can be conceived of to Whip us such as hoisting our colors, concentrating their forces upon us where we are weakest, Generals Johnston & B. [Beauregard] & W. [Wilcox] told a Capt in our Regi that that fight would take place in Ken[tucky] this combined attack on our forces was to defeat us at that point and draw off a part of our force here, so they could walk us back from their capitol which gives us character abroad. They say over in England that it does not look much like subjugation when the confederate flag floats from every hill in 30 miles of Washington, This is the important point to be gained to

stop Englands favoritism toward us, I visited the Battle field again to day nearly every grave has ben dug up and the bleaching bones of its remnants scattered all over the ground. I saw one poor yankee that had ben prised out of his shallow grave with a rail- His leg from his knee down was still sticking in his boot, some of the boys were a little backward about pulling off his boot- but a negro and I pulled it off—his foot looked as natural as ever, there being flesh from the ankle down[.] nearly all of the Enemys graves have been disturbed. over half of the Yankees killed at Bull run were buried in great haste[,] shallow graves[,] consequently their skeletons can be found all over the Battle field. $60,000.[13] I received a long letter from my sweetheart last night. She writes me some very interesting letters, I write a great many love letters for the Boys. I will write one for A. Martin as soon as possible as I finish This Badly Written babbled document, Allen is in love with Miss Trudy French.[14] He says nothing but a very patriotic letter will save his bacon or win her affection. My health continues good.

yours Truly, W. C. McClellan
9 ala Regi Volunteers,
Fielding says he will write to you soon, Matilda.

Camp near Louis House
January 27
Bob, failing to get my letter off I will add afew words[.] all is still quiet, some char about a fuss brewing between the South and United States- some say hostilities have actually began- it will be bad if we do have to dig our hands in fraternal blood, peaceable secession is the idea. Well I heard to night by good authority that Gen. Beauregard had been ordered to Ky, he will wake them up when he gets there from under the thumb of the old grannies Johnston & Smith & Davis[.][15] Gen. B. is the man that would as he said eat supper in Washington city on the 22nd of July last had he ben let a lone. He will be a bright light in the aremy to which he goes.

Yours, W.C. McClellan

The above is the shape of our cabbins, double cabbins with five corner chimney in each end of the double huts.

Write Soon
William Cowan McClellan Manassas, Va.

William Cowan McClellan to Matilda McClellan

Camp Near Louis House
Jan 31th 1862
Dear Sister,
I have not received a letter from you in so long I have concluded you have forgotten me, but as I never count letters with you all I will not wait for a reply. The mud is about 6 inches deep here and raining everyday. The weather has been very warm for two or three weeks probably it seems warmer to us because we have moved into our huts, or Winter quarters. Just as you please to call it. There is a gooddeal of Sickness in our company Though there is but one man very ill, Roden our .co. commis[sary] says he has pneumonia.[16] Well we go on Picket to morrow. we will have a very disagreeable time of it. it is 8 miles out there and a very muddy road to boot. Lt Col O'Neal returned yesterday from ala. He says he saw a quarter master at Knoxville belonging to Gen Zollicoffers Brigade who had run all the way from the wild cat Battle ground.[17] He says the orders were every man take care of him self, and he presumed they did it- from all accounts it was a complete stampeed upon our side. They needed the Manassas Boys to put the Yanks Through [illegible]. But There is one consolation we were whipped by Kentuckians and Tennesseans. Prinsipally Beauregard has gone over There. He will wake the invaders up a little. I have not heard a word from John or Malone in two Months save through your letters, Tell Father to buy the Clark place if he can, land is going to be very high in the South as soon as we win our independence. Old Cadmus Wilcox says 8 months more will wind up The Ball. I had as soon have his opinion as any mans in The C.S.A. This has been a rainy day. I must close as I have written 4 or 5 letters in fact. I do the love letter writing for about ,20, men in our company, I wrote a letter to day for Al Martin to Miss Trudy French. I will enclose it to any body except home folks, I have engaged 3 young men of our .co. in the last months. I get to read all of the guards letters of course. They furnish pen ink paper. You must write soon as convenient, I have received Sallies letter of Jan 17, I will write her when I come off Picket. Well I have nothing to write.

yours with great respect.
WC McClellan
Manassas Junction Virginia

William Cowan McClellan to Robert Anderson McClellan

Camp, Near, Louis, House
February 4th, 62
Dear Bob,
Since writing home I have ben on Picket. we started on the last day of January that night we had the most tremendous snow storm I ever saw, in hours the snow fell 2 inches deep. it fell to my lot to stand those two hours. I thought a many a time during those lonely moments how terrible will be the curse inflicted upon the man or men who were instruments in bringing this infernal war upon the country, Just to think in our company There was 20 youths who had never cast a vote or had any hand in the affairs of the nation being compelled to stand out in a snow storm with out a spark of fire or a house top or anything of the kind to Shelter us, The next night we had another two inches, Feb 2 we had another one inch deep so yesterday we came home 8 miles in a five inch Snow- This was hard on men that never saw a snow over 3 inches in depth- but I stood it remarkably well, to day I have ben on a detail to go to the Slaughter pen after Beef- being the fourth day I have been exposed to the cold and snow. But I forgot to tell you about an adventure I had while on Picket duty. I was on my post alone about 12 o'clock snow coming down like fury, I was standing in a corn field there being but one tree near me, I heard some thing cracking the stalks about 50 yards off, I listened very attentively for a while, I heard another stalk pop I turned around and looked towards the tree and saw some thing white. Says I[:] halt, Signal, 3 times, I then pulled down on old Betsy. She failed to fire. I wasted 3 caps on her, I then turned her up and poured a pint of Water out of her, in the mean time the man That relieved me came a round. I took his gun and turned her loose at the white object. She went like a 32 pounder I tell you. Robin I never heard such Bellowing on Earth[.] Bah Bah Bah[.] I went back to the out post reserve. In 10 minutes here comes Lt Floyd of the company reserve, and the Adjutant from the regimental Reserve. The Col told me I am a sight. I have received Matildas letter of the 25th informing me that John is at home on a Sick furlough, I am sorry to hear his health is bad but it is nothing more than all men have to go through before They become Soldiers, I have been all along there, Hal Malone is still writing to his Father about our swap. If those men are still willing to come Why dont

they draw up the request present it to their Col, to Gen. Walker and if approved come along. If they are not willing to come let me and Hal know it, Theo David,[18] who has a Brother in our company want[s] to come to this region so David here tells me, Tell John to let me know what to depend on. Send on your Sausage meat and butter any thing I dont care what, Capt Hobbs is going to Ala on a recruiting expedition. he takes a noncommissioned officer and a private with him. I would have been one of the Privates had it not ben for the Swaping arrangement. I am pretty certain. Nothing more at present. As ever, W. C. McClellan. excuse This hastly Written Letter By a dimley burning candle. I am very tired and sleepy will send you Beauregards report of The Battle of Manassas in a day or too.

Yours, W. C. McClellan

William Cowan McClellan to Robert Anderson McClellan

Camp Near Louis House
Feb 7th 62
Dear Bob,

As I have an opportunity to send you a letter I will write you a few lines, T. [Thomas] B. Kelly has got a discharge from our company, Tom is a good friend of mine- he has promised me to go and see you all in a few days after he gets home. poor fellow he has the consumption, The Dr has been trying to get him to except a discharge for two months he has at last when unable to stand camp life any longer reluctantly agreed to go home. Tom is a little slow in conversation but he is a well informed sensible man and as much of a gentleman as you ever saw, there is not another man in our co afflicted as Kelly has been but what would have ben at home 2 months ago, He will be down to see you. he is a mess mate of mine. he can tell you a greatdeal about matters up here, if you desire to know or anything els. try and get him to stay all night when he comes and make him sleep in my bed. I will send you a Bullet by him that killed a yankee, I will send Father a Walking stick that I cut near Where Shermans Batteries was taken By the Henry House. My mess takes the Richmond Dispatch. We get it the same day it is daily, every thing looks favorable in England. We pay one dollar for every 12 papers we receive. I am looking everyday for those men from Mobile. It is still raining The ground is very marshy. We have a hard time getting wood enough to burn. Send on your provisions, have you got any Sweet potatoes Buter sausage & meat, I got a letter from my dearly beloved yesterday. She is quite interesting now upon the cowardice of the Yankees- and the Bravery of the Dixie Boys. Tell John to Write to Me Also L. R. Davis. my health is tolerable good at preasant though not as good as it has been. give my respect to all inquiring friends- tell old Heartwell his pipes burned up some time ago, I have quit chewing tobacco, I smoke a gooddeal.

your Brother with great respect.
Wm. C. McClellan
Manassas Junct Va

How is Miss Cissy C. getting along who goes to see her now. write soon give me all the news.

William Cowan McClellan to Thomas Joyce McClellan

Head Quarters Army of the Potomac
camp near Louis House
Feb 9th, 1862
Dear Father- I wrote a letter 2 days ago in trusted in care of Mr. [Tom] Kelly of our company who has a discharge, Since that time I have ben taken sick, I have had a high fever for two days until this evening it has abated. my discharges are composed of Black bile. I think I will be up in a few days again the sole cause of my illness was 6 days exposure in Snow 5 inches deep which could have been prevented by our company officers if they had seen proper. I am more anxious to swap than ever. This is Sunday Capt Hobbs, starts home to Limestone tuesday recruiting. I will write more to morrow, we have news here of the capture of Fort Henry by The yankees,[19] distruction of the R.R. Bridge, & , lookout for Decatur the crisis is fast approaching, the darkest hour of the night is just before day.

Feb. 10 Capt Hobbs requests me to write Thomas a letter to induce him if possible to join his comp, I will do my best to get him. Capt H. will pay you a visit while canvassing the county, He is going to move heaven and earth to fill up The ranks of his company. Col. Thinks you can do him some good over in the Sanderson and Knox neighborhood. The recruits will be paid 50 dollars down, which will be a considerable inducement for a great many to enlist you hardly ever see more than two out of a family in the army. Look at the Fletchers but two of that name in the Service of their country out of 7. strong young men. Probably this year some time if I live and Bob wants to try his hand in War I will let him take my place for a while, Tell John if those men of his will swap with Malones and my self when he goes back to Mobile They will have a good opportunity to come free With Lt Murphy[20] of our Regi who is Recruiting down there for Capt Ripleys co. I have written so much about this swap I have got so I can sing it. I am a good-deal Better This morning no fever, Tell Nat, F[letcher], There will be no fighting on account of Breaking up the Union foot [by] foot [by] foot, ask him if he ever Snorts fire now a days.

Yours with respect,
W.C. McClellan

William Cowan McClellan to Matilda McClellan

Head quarters A. of Potomac
Feb. 10th 1862
Dear Sister:
Your very interesting letter of 25 came rapidly to hand a few days ago. I will now answer it or rather an appology as I have nothing to write of any importance at preasant. I am very much obliged to you for the pains you take in writeing me all of the particulars of the neighborhood all of which are very agreeable to me to know, A thousand times I have called to mind some familiar spot about home even counting the limbs on those familiar trees that stands in the yard or looking into every pannel of fence from the Big gate to the house. I often in my sleep hear Mother tell Candice to bring in the supper, or Tom Nick fussing about somebody bringing his boots or Bob stepping into the dairy stealing cream . Jim always tells on him. "Mistice, Mr Bob ben in de dairy stealing your cream an how say you no Jim cause I seed him ." Thease slowly spoken words are as true as the gospel at supper. Bob gets no cream for coffee unless by slight of hand, Jim is standing close by, he cannot speak for fear Bob thrashes him, but he grins until the old Lady finds out what is to pay. Well as I am settled here for life perhaps, I want you to send the best looking ambrotype you have on hand of your self to Me by Capt. Hobbs when he returns to camp. Has L. R. Davis died or

does he still live. I will write to Sallie next. Tell Milton the poet to send me a good pipe and some goobers, and I will fight harder for him. Tell Dr. J. R. F[letcher] that Gen Johns[t]on says he would like the best in the world to see him up here. You must all write me often. I will do the Same. What has become of Cliffy, Miss Coe, and Bobs gal. Tell them not to fret them selves away. I will be at home after awhile with many scars of honor, and a White head to comfort one of them in her latter days. I have been looking and thinking a great deal recently. I dont think this war can possibly last more than .40. years longer. Excuse this Brillant Epistle.

yours with great respect
W.C. McClellan, Manassas Junction

Robert Anderson McClellan to William Cowan McClellan

Shoal Ford Ala.
Feb. 15th '62
Dear Will:
This letter will be handed to you by Robert Ryan, who belongs to a Maryland Regiment, but is now here on a furlough. He is a brother-in law of William Walker[21] of Athens. He is a very sensible, but quiet boy, and I would ask for kind treatment at your hands for him. I do not know that I have anything of importance to add. The Federal excursion up the Tennessee River resulted about as I stated in a former letter. Our company is still drilling as I said. We are going into camp at the Wilson place Thursday to drill three or four days in succession. We have news here now of a fight that is going on at Fort Donelson. It is said Pillow has repulsed them three times.[22] We will hear the final result tomorrow I suppose. A very deep snow fell last night for this climate[.] it is about 3 inches deep. The weather is very cold now & has been for some days. Mr. Smith can not live but a few hours at furthest, a few days. He can eat nothing. John starts back to Mobile with Nick Richardson Tuesday night. He has gotten about well now. He is now 1st Lieut, Captain Malone having been elected Major to fill Chadick's place who is now Colonel. Billy Richardson is now Captain of the Company, but he is very sick in the Mobile hospital. John Milton Moore belongs to our–or the "Sanders Rebels"–Company. He held on as long as he could, but when he heard the wild blast from the northern bugle amid our own native vollies he sprang forth among the defend-

ers of our Country. John Fletcher joined our Company but he went up to Nashville the next day, and got an assistants place in the hospital. Sue Davis, Jimmie Harris,[23] Annie Richardson, and Bob Ryan are all over at Rip Davis'. They go home tomorrow. Ryan starts for Virginia Monday. Enclosed you will find some love letters on which I have been practicing- send them off for some of the boys.

Your Brother,
Robert

William Cowan McClellan to Thomas Joyce McClellan

Head qtr Army of the Potomac
Camp Near Lewis House
Feb 15th 1862
Dear Father

I have not received a letter from home since the 25th of January 20 days ago. I have concluded that something has gone wrong at home or probably the fault is the mail. I am now sitting up in my chimney corner with my jaws about as large as Clem Johnson[24] with the Mumps. I have had them 3 days, for two days I have not ben able to eat a bite, this morning I tried to eat so. rice, but I could not come to it[.] it made me dance a jig for a few moments. by being prudent I think I will soon get well, the Mumps has ben in our Regi for 6 months it has gradually worked its way along until it has got about half through the Regi. I am rubbing my jaws with heartshome. I suppose there is a gooddeal of excitement in North ala about the yankees coming up to Florence.[25] we heard of it the next day after the yankees left Florence our Regi was on its head to go down to Flo[rence] and clean out the yanks to use a camp expression. It seems the yankees have whipped us all around. The hardest blow they have hit us yet was the taking of Roanoke Island, from all accounts that was one of the Bloodiest Battles of the war.[26] Our men drove the Federals to their necks in the water two or three times but we were over powered by numbers and forced to yield not before however Killing about one thousand of the scamps. The Richmond papers represented our loss at 8 hundred Killed and wounded but have gradually narrowed down until now they say we had but 40 killed 1,000 prisoners. There is quite a contrast between our troops in Va and those in Ky. The former fight desperately regardless of the number of the Enemy, The latter run from equal numbers

I think the main cause of this is the troops in Kentucky are not half drilled and disciplined we cant expect to Whip the best drilled Soldiers in the world unless we too are well drilled. If we have any advantage over our Enemy it consists in cause and courage. Last night the ground froze very hard this morning it commenced snowing at 7, oclock. It is now about 2 .oc. Still coming down in torrents now 3 inches deep. probability is it will be a foot deep by morning I have suffered less with cold this winter Than usual. David Phillips has landed safely in Limestone, I sent a letter by Tom Kelly who left here 7 days ago, Also a walking stick cut on the Battle field of Manassas. Dan Hundley[27] was up here a day or two ago to visit the Battle field. He has been in Ky until recently he has been assigned the command of a Battalion at Knoxville Tenn. I made his Acquaintance. He is a very nice man he asked me about my fuss with Houston, I didnt know how this matter became so public unless by men of the co. writing back, I am in hopes none of my letters have ever been read by any body except the family. Send on your box of eatibles. The mail has come in from the Junction but I get no letter yet. I write to you all, certainly you can spell one another and rite to me.

your Son,
W. C. McClellan

a fight is expected here in a few days.

William Cowan McClellan to Matilda McClellan

Camp Near Lewis House
Feb 20th 186[2]
Dear Sister,
I have waited in vain for a letter from home for 3 weeks but still none comes, I have at last concluded that something more than the appearance of the yankees at Florrence has happened. never before have I failed to get one or two letters a week. By letter received in our camp I learn that about 3 thousand Malitia had collected at Decatur to defend the Bridge if the yankees had made their appearance. what scattering there would have been. one drilled Reg could have whipped out the whole concern. It seems the Enemy have ben very successful in the last month they have whipped us in every engagement save Fort Donalson, and news came here last night that the enemy has taken Fort Don. [Donelson] after 3 or 4 days hard

fighting. Our prospects in the future looks very gloomy indeed but in the end we are bound to triumph. The North must remember they have at least eight hundred thousand good fighting men to whip before we are subjugated- the little defeats we have suffered will stimulate our men to enlist to repell the invaders. The North ought to remember that when we are subjugated She will also be exhausted in men and money but they dont care for the lives of their own men. one of the Fed. generals at Washington was sent word that they had won a great victory after losing a thousand men. he said he did not care a dam how many men they lost so they gained the victory at Roen [Roanoke] Island. I am now confined to my house by the mumps I am near well of them[.] We have nothing here but rain, snow and mud, it is now raining- Several of the Tennessee Regiments have ben ordered back to Tenn among them the First, Ten Regi.[28] take good care of my old fine cloths I expect to get Married in them when I come home. Has Tom Kelly been over yet with my letter, Stick and Bullet. Tell Rip Davis & Sallie to write to me did J.M.M. [John Milton Moore] go to meet the yanks. Tell father not to fret him self about the country, Whistle sing and be merry is the best plan . . . I have just received your letter of 9th Feb. Bobs of the 31 of January. I am in hope the disasters to our arms will induce those little white livered cowardly Brainless foppish fortune hunting slackers to join the army and fight for their country. Such men will have to give me a wide berth when I return home. I suppose if Malone and my self swap with those men it will be immediately or not at all, such is my desire as well as Malones,- Beat Milt Moore for Esquire if possible. Capt Hobbs is stirring them up in Limestone by this time. you must write to me often if possible.

Your Brother
Wm.C. McClellan

William Cowan McClellan to Thomas Joyce McClellan

Head qtr. Army of Potomac.
Febu 27th, 1862
Dear Father
I take my seat to write you a letter amid a thousand rumors of a distressing character. One is that the Enemy have possession of Nash-

ville, another is that they have cut off our communication on the M. and C . . . [Memphis and Chattanooga] R. R. between Knoxville & Chattanooga. The former report we believe as old Johns[t]on sent them while at Fort Donelson that they might have Nashville if they would respect private property. Nashville is of a great deal more important to the confederacy than Richmond to my notions. Annother report is that Buckner and 12,000 thousand [*sic*] of our men surrendered to the enemy.[29] This is believed to be so here. There was treachery some where I dont think our men are cowardly enough to give them selves up 12,000 thousand [*sic*] in number no matter how great the strength of the Enemy. admitting they had ,80, thousand men and had our men in a hollow square they could have concentrated on a point and gone out, I dont think you will ever hear of more than 20 men of the army of the Potomac surrendering at a time. Our Pickets on the write [right] wing of our lines have ben driven in. We are expecting a fight here every day. The Boys are all spoiling for a fight you would suppose the recent disasters our troops have met with at various points would have a tendency to dishearten or intimidate our troops here[.] far from it they will fight 50 percent better now than they did on the 21th of July. Some Yankee may get hold of this letter before it gets to its destination if so all I have to say is I can whip the hind legs off him before he can say god with his mouth open. We heard yesterday the yankees had undisputed possession of Athens Ala[30] and Press Tanner[31] had given them a big dinner, I [have] no idea it is so, but if the Enemy were there no doubt Press would give them the write hand of fellowship, If you have not paid him for my Pistol yet, don't do it, turn him over to me, tell him I will pay him as soon as peace is made. If he wont fight for his country he ought to arm those that will, I understand when the yanks came to Florence there was but five men who did not go to meet them in Athens Press was one of the number. L. P., G. S. H. two more of the Brave Lads.[32] I am in hopes if the Enemy ever invades North ala and we have no drilled and well armed troop there to meet them the maliatia will not oppose them. it would only result in the slaughter of the undrilled unarmed citizens. I have entirely recovered from the Mumps, My health is fine. I way full 200 pounds and considered the best man in ,co, F. We have a game or play a game called Bull pen.[33] in our Regi We play it from morning until night from 25 to 50 on a side every Body seems to enjoy them selves- it is fine exercise. Lt John McDonald[34] has just begun to get me to play on his Side. I have not received a letter from home in 2 or 3 weaks, not since the Florence raid. I think of Home very often frequently I waik up in the night thinking I am at home with my musket in hand, But I only have to cast my eyes up to my low Board roof to convince my self that I am still in old Virginia. Write often effectionately

Your Son,
W. C. McClellan
My respects to all

William Cowan McClellan to Robert Anderson McClellan

Tom Cartwright is well
Camp Wilcox
March 4th, 1862
Dear Bob,
As I am left alone in my cabbin I will write you a short letter. Our company went out on Picket yesterday the cause of my not going was I had a very severe attack of Diarhear brought on by overexertion of which I am better this morning. I weighed 3 days ago ,205, pounds. When I am passing about out of our Regi, I am often saluted as Lt., Capt and would be called Gen. I have no doubt if I had a Horse to ride. We are expecting every day to hear of the Enemy having possession of Nashville and Savannah Ga. We have ben expecting an attack here for several days. we were ordered to send back all Baggage we could not toat yesterday but the order has ben countermanded in consequence I suppose of a 3 inch snow which renders an attack impracticable at present. There has been a great deal of talk here recently about evacuating Manassas and falling back to Gordonsville 60 miles from here on the R. R. leading to Richmond. Stone wall Jacksons Pickets have ben driven in at Winchester and it is supposed the enemy intends coming down the Ashby gap road and attack Manassas in the rear. In that event our forces will fall back to Gor. where we can get reinforcements from Richmond if necessary. It would be a pity to give up Manassas and Centreville after so much work in preparing the redoubts, and all of our Winterquarters. I was at Manassas yesterday for the first time since I landed there on the 20th of July last, then there was but few shantees scattered about here and there now there is ,25, acres of

land compleately packed with Houses, of all sorts nearly every state has a large Depot. then a general Depot Book stores, dry goods Stores. Eating Houses goober peas-Shanties- Black Smith shops, 16 pounders gazeing at you on all sides these buildings are generally constructed of plank and post. I have not received a letter from home since the 9th of Feb I thought for sometime it was on account of the slides on the R. R. but some of our company have ben getting letters 5 days after date all the time- if you are going to quit writing let me know and I will do like wise. If you see Capt Hobbs before he starts back here tell him not to come we are getting along very well with out him. Floyd is acting 1,2,3, Lt and Captain Also. and we had a full compliment of officers, Lt Wayland has been temporarily promoted to the quarter[master]ship of the Regi and I hope he will be confirmed to the position or permanently be consigned to it as you please to call it. You must excuse I need ink when I commenced writing I could not find this consequently I had to cut my finger to get Blood to write with. Give my respects to LR Davis and any other man you see sooner. Write Write Write Write

I am very anxious to hear If you beat John M Moore for Esquire in the Shoal ford beat. Has the Fletchers gone to war yet. Tell Dr. J R [Fletcher] that old Gen Johns[t]on is still being anxious to see him. He asked me the other day what he was doing. I told he was fortune Hunting. the old gen shook his head and said here is the place to win a fortune.

Effectionately, your Brother
Willie C. McClellan Esq

William Cowan McClellan to Thomas Joyce McClellan

Gordonsville, Va.
March 20th, 62
Dear Father,

We or our army left Manassas on the 8 of this month. Our retreat was one of deliberation and order haveing no fears of the Enemy whatever. The effect of this retreat I suppose is to Shorten our Picket line and if necessary concentrate our forces. We Marched every foot of the way 8–9 miles, I marched to Culpeper courthouse 45 miles from Manassas. We strewd tents here and stayed 3 days, I was left with the Baggage in co. with 15 others of our Regi with orders to remain until the Tents were removed which was not done till night the day the regi left. I applyed at Culpeper for transportation on the cars to this place which was granted me. I am now sitting in an old Box car writing this note. Our Brigade if it is lucky will reach here to night, our whole army I understand is moving on to this point. The Winchester & Leesburg and Dumfries forces. We crossed the Rhapahannock and Rapidan Rivers the latter is 12 miles back. The general opinion is we will make a stand at this place. This is where the Linchburg & Charlottesville R. Road intersect.[35] I saw Jim Baileys grave at Culpeper he was interred with five hundred other Soldiers in a nice plank fence grave yard & all of them have nice toomb stones, on Jim's I found this inscription

J. H. Bailey
4 Ala Reg Vol
died August 12, 61

Write soon, your effectinate son,
W C McClellan

My health is very good at presant. I must unload my Baggage

William Cowan McClellan to Robert Anderson McClellan

Gordonsville, VA
March 21, 1862
Dear Bob
I wrote to Father day before yesterday for fear it does not reach him. I will write you a few lines, we commenced our retreat on the 8 of this month from Manassas giving up all our breast works & shanties the latter were all burned. The first day we marched one mile, 2 day 5 miles, 3 days to Warrenton. It is one of the most beautiful places I ever saw, it stands on the north bank of the Rahapanhock River, next day we crossed the river march 12 miles and crossed what is called the southern prong of the Rhapahanik. This country is very hilly resembling very much Tennessee. The army as it went pressed into service horses, cattle & hogs & corn Hay. 12 miles of the road we traveled was cut out by our Pioneers.[36] We ar-

rived at Culpeper Courthouse on the 14th. This is a beautiful town about the size of Athens. Warrenton 14 miles south of Centreville has 3 thousand inhabitants all of whom moved off as the army passed by. We camped 3 days at Culpeper. I was detailed to guard the Brigade tents which were to be put upon the cars for Gordonsville[37] I applied for transportation to this place which was granted us. We have been here four days. The boys chose me for orderly Sergeant as we had no officer in the squadron. I have made requisitions for provisions for my men drawing ham, flour, coffee, sugar, suciss rice & beans. We stretched 2 large Belle tents in a wind blowing like fighting cocks, but we have orders to load our tents on the cars and to rejoin our Regi at Orange Courthouse going back. We are loading up now. There is a world of government stores there and think our army will move here before 3 days. Well I must go down and get a transportation ticket back to the Regi from the commandant of this post. it is rumored here that we have had a Big fight on the Tenn. line and won a glorious victory. What has become of our recruiting officers. Thousands of recruits are coming in dayly; one thousand were moved here yesterday. I saw yesterday 80 union prisoners on the way to Richmond taken near Winchester. They had 80 thousand dollars in gold, Last of which was paid them by Lincoln, go[vernment] to reinlist to fight against their state. Jeff Davis gets the whole of this yellow stuff and storres beside. They were a guilty looking set of scoundrels. Bob if you dont quit your union talk old Jeff will get you into his jail at Rich[mond], My health is very good at presant, I have no letter from home of a better date 15 of last month, excuse this hasty letter. direct your letter to Gordonsville.

Your Brother
WC McClellan.
Gordonsville, Va

William Cowan McClellan to Robert Anderson McClellan

Camp near Orange Courthouse
March 24, 1862
Dear Bob,
I returned from the Gordonsville to the Regiment day before yesterday. Yesterday I visited James Madison's old residence and grave.[38] It is by far the most beautiful place I ever saw. It is situated upon

an eminance commanding a fine view of the Blue Ridge about 10 miles distant. There is 20 acres of land in the yard thickly set in shrubery of all kinds while over them waive the tall white walnut trees under whose branches the old statesman of a better age reposes. His monument is about 30 feet high composed of fine granite. A gentleman by the name of Carson now lives there, a brother of whom lives in Baltimore of some eminance. I will inclose you an evergreen that I filched from Madison's grave. Well we are packed up with tents struck. Horses and wagons turned over to the divisional quartermaster with orders to reform at Richmond to morrow at 10 o'clock. I don't know whether or not we will go to Alabama. I understand General Wilcox says we will go to Wilmington, North Carolina. I hope we will go to Ala. The 38 Virginia Regiment has been taken out of our brigade which seems to indicate we are going south. Some other Alabama regiment will be put in its place. the 19th or 4th probably. We will then have 4 Alabama Regiments and the 19 Mississippi Regiment in the Brigade. If they will send Old Wilcox to Alabama with his brigades he will soon drive the Yankees from his native state. With a little aid your letter of 12 March is at hand. it is indeed very disturbing to be visited even by a friendly army. Bob, you speak too harshly of our government & our country and people. All occupying high places. I think are doing their duty; you think [hard] of the army pressing provender and forage for its use. This the army is bound to do sometimes. I have seen a great deal of pressing into service since I have been in the army. When this reaches you I may be close at hand- or I may be in North Carolina . . . no telling where. Old Johns[t]on keeps his own secrets, the day I left Gordonsville I saw Jeff Davis & Johns[t]on meet there and had a long confab. I told the Boys something was going to happen. I will write you again at Richmond, if not address your letters to Richmond.

Farewell, your brother
Wm McClellan
Orange, Courthouse, Va

Here comes Gen. W. and staff. we are off for Dixie land.

6

The Peninsula Campaign and the Seven Days Battles

March 25–July 27, 1862

> . . . as long as there is a Soldier left on Southern Soil let him strike for freedom in the face of death . . .
>
> —William Cowan McClellan

Athens, Alabama, was sacked by Col. John Basil Turchin's Eighth Brigade on May 2, 1862, with many households and buildings being burnt or plundered. The Union troops under his command were allowed to pillage the town for two hours, possibly in retaliation for recent attacks by citizens and guerrilla units on Union troops and trains. (By the end of July 1862, both Colonel Turchin and his commanding officer, Brig. Gen. Ormsby MacKnight Mitchel, faced court-martial charges for the actions of their troops in Athens.) Although other war-related incidents took place in Athens and Huntsville both before and after Turchin's raid and the region experienced Union raids and occupation throughout the rest of the war, this one event greatly angered the Limestone County troops away in Northern Virginia. Despite the Confederate victories in Virginia, the invasion of their homeland caused anxiety and a loss of morale among the Limestone County troops. William longed to go back to Alabama to deal with the invasion himself, although the McClellan home went unscathed, possibly because it was located several miles outside of Athens.

Along with Gen. Joseph E. Johnston's army, the 9th Alabama moved to the Virginia Peninsula in April, and Companies F and D went on picket duty along the Warwick River. While on picket duty at Warwick, William Cowan McClellan would come under fire for the first time, with bullets piercing his clothing. He would see action again during the Battle of Seven Pines at the close of the Peninsula Campaign in May, and later during the Seven Days Battles in June and July, when the 9th would be in the thick of the fighting at Gaines's Mill and Frayser's Farm. William had waited eight months for his first taste of battle, but soon he began to wonder if the war would ever end.

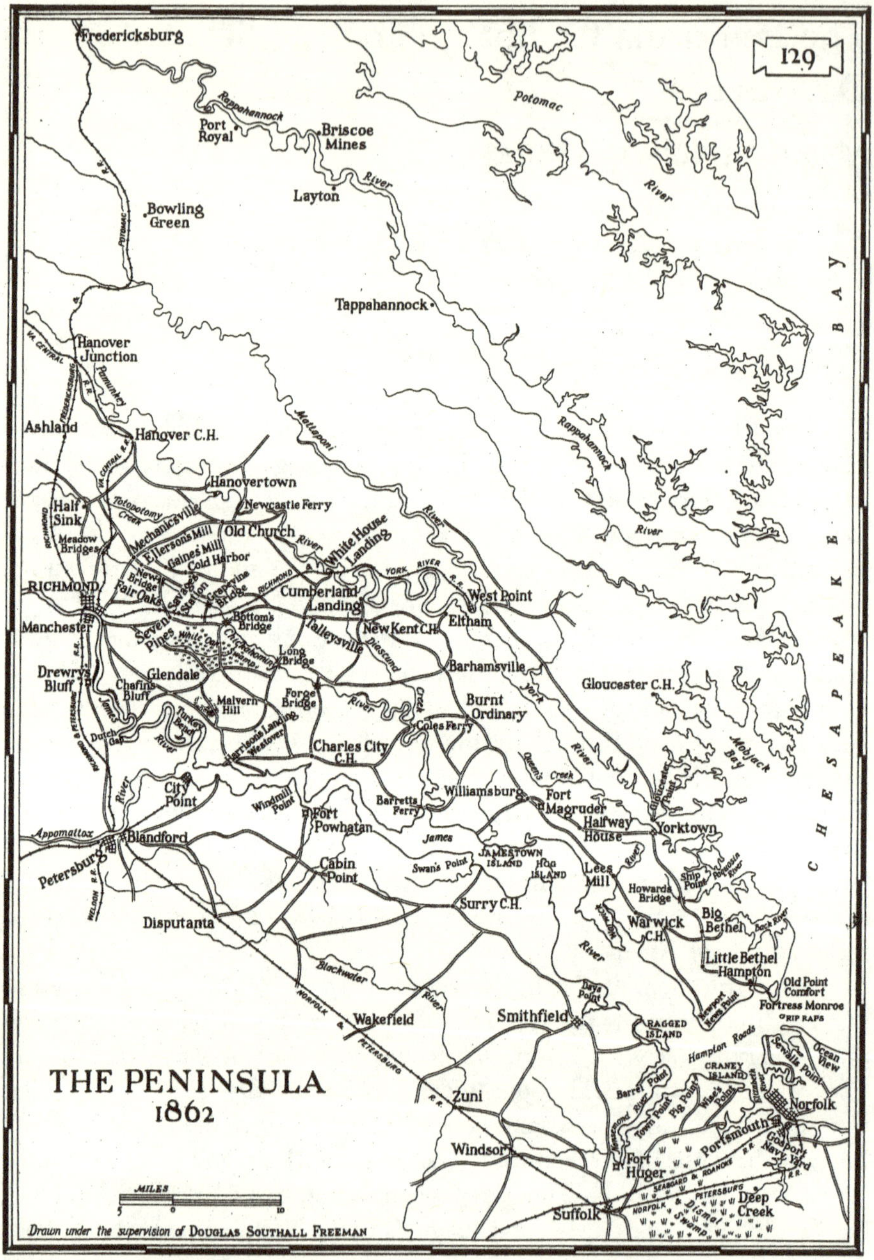

The Peninsula, 1862

To meet the advance of Gen. George McClellan's 100,000-man army which was moving toward Richmond, in March Gen. John Bankhead Magruder's heavily outnumbered Confederate forces entrenched along the Warwick River, where they had dammed the river and its tributaries to flood the line and to make McClellan's advance more difficult. The 9th Alabama, after a long trip from Northern Virginia, was sent into the line along the Warwick River near Grovestown Wharf, below the great bend of the James River and to the south of Williamsburg. The regiment had marched ten miles during the night of April 1 in the rain to Warwick River, and it went into position to the right and rear of the Confederate forces that were defending the peninsula. Maj. Archibald Gracie Jr., commander of the 11th Alabama Regiment, was put in charge of a special battalion consisting of five companies from Wilcox's Brigade. This included Companies F and D from the 9th Alabama; and Lieutenant John C. Featherston, adjutant of the 9th, was ordered to report to Major Gracie with his detail of Company F, commanded by Capt. Thomas Hubbard Hobbs.[1]

This battalion was posted on the Warwick River near its confluence with the James River, close to Balthrops. As Gracie later noted, these companies were selected randomly and not due to their early training or qualifications as sharpshooters. Despite being armed principally with old smoothbore muskets, the soldiers were brought to a high degree of proficiency by frequent drills and target practice.[2] While the opposing picket lines enjoyed some humorous bantering back and forth, this was deadly serious business. Advanced picket line duty called for vigilance and care for a man to avoid becoming a target to enemy sharpshooters.[3]

The rest of the 9th Alabama participated in the Battle of Lee's Mill (Wynn's Mill) on April 16.[4] When Gen. George McClellan finally positioned his large siege guns to be used against the Confederate position, Gen. Joseph E. Johnston quickly removed his troops in May from the line they occupied along the Warwick River at Lee's and Wynn's Mills, and they moved up the peninsula. Johnston's plan called for the Confederate army to fight a rearguard action as the army left the Yorktown–Warwick River line on May 3 and withdrew toward Richmond.

The 9th Alabama (minus Companies F and D) left Green's Landing at nightfall on May 3 and joined Brig. Gen. Joseph Brevard Kershaw's brigade near Lebanon Church for a night march to the redoubts outside of Williamsburg. They reached the town on the evening of May 4 but were ordered to countermarch (along with the rest of Wilcox's brigade) to the redoubts about sunrise on May 5.[5] Fortified by engineers, Williamsburg included trenches that stretched for four miles and a bastion fort at Fort Magruder. On May 5 the Union army under Maj. Gen. Joseph Hooker and Brig. Gen. Philip Kearny moved on Williamsburg, defended by parts of Maj. Gen. D. H. Hill's and Maj. Gen. James Longstreet's divisions.[6] A Union artillery bombardment preceded an infantry assault in front of Fort Magruder. The 9th Alabama was in the fourth brigade of Longstreet's Second Division[7] and were posted in a ravine just to the right and rear of the redoubts at Fort Magruder. They were involved in some of the fiercest fighting and were credited with capturing the guns of the 5th New Jersey Regiment.[8] Although by the end of the day the Union army was successful in driving the Confederate army from Williamsburg, Johnston was also successful in buying time to allow his trapped army to escape to Richmond. In total, in the Battle of Williamsburg, about 31,000 Confederates had faced 41,000 Union soldiers, and casualties were 1,570 and 1,866 respectively.[9] (Wilcox's brigade reported 231 casualties,[10] and the 9th suffered 55 casualties during the Battle of Williamsburg.[11])

Late on the evening of May 5, the 9th Alabama left Williamsburg and started west toward Richmond. On May 7, Gracie's battalion (including Company F of the 9th Alabama) was deployed as skirmishers to cover the rear of the entire army. That evening they came to New Kent Court House where they remained through May 9.[12]

On May 14 Gracie's battalion of "sharpshooters" returned to their original regiments in Wilcox's brigade,[13] which included the 10th Alabama and the 19th Mississippi regiments; the brigade was assigned to the 2nd Division under General Longstreet. Although Wilcox's brigade was in Longstreet's division, he had released the brigade to Brig. Gen. Richard H. Anderson during the Battle of Williamsburg.[14] During this portion of the withdrawal to Richmond, the 9th Alabama was leading the brigade toward Drewry's Bluff, with the Union army not far behind. On May 15, Union gunboats (including the *Monitor*) moved up the James River toward Richmond and were driven off by fire from Confederate artillery posted at Drewry's Bluff.[15]

By May 20, Gen. Joseph E. Johnston had 60,000 Confederates in line five miles east of Richmond facing 100,000 Federals.[16] On May 31, the two wings of McClellan's army were split by the Chickahominy River near Mechanicsville, and with the river up due to heavy rains, an opportunity arose for the Confederates to attack the two Union corps to the south of the river. Johnston attacked the corps of Erasmus Keyes and S. P. Heintzleman at Seven Pines, just to the east of Richmond.[17] The 9th Alabama was one of four regiments in Wilcox's brigade (including the 10th and 11th Alabama regiments and the 19th Mississippi), and they formed a part of Longstreet's division on the right wing. As General Longstreet marched and countermarched his brigades, only two of Wilcox's regiments made it into the Battle of Seven Pines on the first day. After being driven off the field of battle on May 31, the Federals moved against the 11th and 9th Alabama regiments at 8 a.m. on June 1. A dozen men in the company, including William Cowan McClellan, were wounded before Gen. D. H. Hill ordered Wilcox to withdraw his forces. By the end of the second day of the battle, both sides were back in their original positions. During the Battle of Seven Pines, the Confederates, with 42,000 men on the field, suffered heavy casualties: 980 killed, 4,479 wounded, and 405 missing; with 42,000 men, Union losses were 790 killed, 3,594 wounded, and 647 missing for the battle.[18] Gen. Joseph E. Johnston was seriously wounded in this battle, and Gen. Robert E. Lee took command of the Confederate forces, which from that point were known as the Army of Northern Virginia. Lee launched an attack on June 26 at Mechanicsville, beginning the Seven Days Battles, during which he attempted to drive McClellan away from Richmond and to strike a fatal blow against the Union army.

On Friday, June 27, 1862, Gen. Fitz John Porter's 5th Corps of the Union army occupied a strong defensive position along a plateau overlooking Boatswain's Swamp near the gristmill of Dr. William Gaines. The mill would give its name to the Battle of Gaines's Mill. Porter's mission was to cover the Chickahominy River bridges and to stop Maj. Gen. Thomas Jonathan (Stonewall) Jackson's forces from crossing the river until the artillery and supply trains had started on their retreat to the James River. Lee saw an opportunity to destroy a significant part of the Union army and sent Jackson (who had just returned from the Shenandoah Valley), supported by Gen. Ambrose Powell Hill,[19] on a turning movement around the Union right flank. General Longstreet's and General Hill's forces would attack the enemy head-on and drive the Union forces into Jackson's guns. After two hours of unsupported attacks against the fortified Union position, Hill's forces had made no measurable progress. Longstreet was now ordered to move against the Union left flank, even if just to make a demonstration. The Wilcox Brigade—which now included the 8th as well as the 9th, 10th, and 11th Alabama regiments—participated in this attack. The 8th and 9th Alabama formed behind the 10th and 11th Alabama regiments and supported them on the assault on the left of the entrenched Union position. The regiments were exposed to enfilading fire from Union batteries along the ridge and a destructive infantry fire from the breastworks in front of them. As the

10th and 11th regiments wilted under the intense fire, the 8th and 9th Alabama advanced through their line and maintained pressure on the Union left.

Many Confederate units claimed responsibility for being the first to break the Union line that day, in what was then considered the toughest day of the war.[20] The Wilcox Brigade and the 9th Alabama put in their claim as well. A monument to their accomplishment stands on the battlefield today. The Wilcox Brigade suffered 584 casualties out of the 1,850 men present for duty at the Battle of Gaines's Mill. The 9th Alabama suffered 134 casualties, including Capt. E. Y. Hill of Company H and Capt. Thomas Hubbard Hobbs of Company F (who was mortally wounded).[21]

On Monday June 30, 1862, after the Battle of Gaines's Mill, the Wilcox Brigade moved down Darbytown Road and went into line of battle around 2 p.m. just west of Western Run and Glendale Crossroads. The Battle of Frayser's Farm (also called Glendale) began as Lee was attempting to cut off McClellan's retreat by sending a brigade under Maj. Gen. Theophilus Hunter Holmes down Quaker Road to intercept the enemy, while Longstreet, A. P. Hill, and Jackson struck the rear of the retreating forces around Glendale. Longstreet's assault began at 6 p.m. with the brigades of Micah Jenkins, Roger A. Pryor, and James L. Kemper out in front, supported by George Edward Pickett's and Winfield Scott Featherston's brigades. Gen. Richard H. Anderson then ordered Wilcox's Brigade forward to support the other brigades where needed. The 9th and 10th Alabama regiments came to the relief of Jenkins's brigade, charging across Western Run and into a withering fire of artillery and musketry. They recaptured Cooper's Battery B of the 1st Pennsylvania Light Artillery, which had just been recaptured by Union troops from Jenkins's men.[22] The 8th and 11th Alabama regiments took heavy losses on the left of the other two Alabama regiments. Both were eventually forced to withdraw from their forward positions, and the four regiments of Wilcox's brigade shared a pine grove in the middle of the battlefield until relieved. The brigade suffered 471 casualties and the 9th Alabama 130 of those.[23] In addition, the commanding officer of the 9th, Maj. J. Horace King, was severely wounded. For the combined battles of Gaines's Mill and Frayser's Farm, the 9th Alabama had suffered 264 casualties,[24] one of their highest totals of the war.

The 9th would not participate in the final battle of the Seven Days Battles on July 1 at Malvern Hill. Although the Confederates were defeated at Malvern Hill, the Union army continued its retreat to Harrison's Landing despite protests from several Union generals to counterattack a badly damaged Confederate army.[25] With the constant fighting and the heavy casualties on the peninsula and in front of Richmond, the nature of the war changed from something almost romantic to a hell of savage killing.

Despite being slightly wounded and seeing seven members of his company killed in battle, William's enthusiasm remained high. He seemed to have accepted the deaths of men in battle as readily as he did the deaths of men in camp due to sickness. Yet the death in battle of his company captain, Captain Hobbs, was keenly felt. William was fighting alongside brave men, and he once wrote, "the ragged Alabamians go steadily on, they are unmovable." He remained more concerned that his family back home find a place of security to avoid the Union forces occupying Limestone County.

Beginning with the battles on the peninsula at Yorktown and Williamsburg, and culminating with the seven days of battle outside of Richmond, the Army of Northern Virginia was successful in slowing and then stopping McClellan's offensive up the Virginia Peninsula. Not only did the Confederate army save Richmond, but Robert E. Lee was able to seize the initiative and take the war away from Richmond's door toward Northern Virginia and Washington, D.C. Along with the rest of Lee's army, the 9th Alabama would head north to Manassas in August.

William Cowan McClellan to Matilda McClellan

Richmond Va
March 25, 1862
Dear Sister,
We are now encamped or rather in barracks only 3 hundred yards from where we were 9 months ago. little did I think of ever seeing this encampment again When we left it last July- but after many hard ships privations and trials We are Where we started never having fired a gun at the Enemy. I wrote to Bob yesterday from camp near Orange .C. House While in the act of starting to this place, We arrived here at one oclock This eavening. It is generally thought that We will resume our march to morrow to some unknown point but I am strongly of the opinion that We will be ordered to North, ala, or eastern Mississippi. There was a gooddeal of talk yesterday of our going to North Carolina but I learned that from a soldier.[26] We travelled all night morning found us at Weldon, N. Carolina on the Rhen oak [Roanoke] River, with orders to countermarch Back to City

Point amediately on the 28th. We arrived at Petersburg here. We understood the enemy were advancing on, gen. Magruder 75 thousand strong, our Regi was put up on a Scooner. We shoved off and floated down the Appomattucks River to City Point on the James. We stayed here severall hours We then got aboard a Scooner, a sail Boat, and a steamboat all lashed to gether and set out for Yorktown down the Broad James. The River gradually got Wider, 30 miles below City Point it varies from 3 to 4 miles wide. As we sailed by the far famed Jamestown I thought of the many little stories I have read at school of this Indian village.

York Town April 1, 1862
Since writing the above I have had many ups and downs, We reached Richmond on the 20th on Board a steam Boat called the North Hampton, the 19th Mississippi was also on Board, We had a very pleasant trip down the James River to City Point 50 miles from Richmond. We made it in 4 1/2 hours. at City Point we took the R. R. to Peters Burg Va 9 miles distant. We arrive at Petersburg about 8, o'clock at night, tramped round until 10, oc, We could not get cars to go any further, We were quartered in a large commercial House in the city With 2 other Regi of our Brigade they came by R. Road from Richmond. We remained in Petersburg until 4, oc next day. We took the Southern Branch R R for North Carolina. I also thought of the first Boat load of the african race that landed upon our soil 4. miles below Jamestown. We landed at What is called Grovestown Wharf, Here the River is 6 miles in width. We disembarked just at night rain falling in torrents. We had 10 miles to march and a Bad Road. We started in a few minutes it was so dark We could not see our hands before us and then I would fall into a mud hole up to my knees. I lugged on about five miles the Regi being scattered all over the country, I proposed to my companions John Morris & Dan Thompson[27] to go to a light We saw some distance from the Road they agreed to it and We found a good clever fellow, hot supper on tables. We dryed our clothes & blankets spread down the carpet & had a glorious nights rest. Next morning We paid $1.00 a peace and left for the regiment 5 miles farther on, When we reached it was composed of the Col, drummer, and 10 privats, We are now in 3 miles of Yorktown in a thick, large, rich, fine woods, expecting a fight every day, I have a very violent

cold some fever. Write soon direct your letters to Richmond, Va for the present.

your Brother
W C McClellan
Yorktown Va Peninsula

William Cowan McClellan to Robert Anderson McClellan

Greens Landing[28]
Warwick River Peninsula, Va
April 13, 62
Dear Bob, Fort Sumpter
When I wrote last I was at Lebanon church,[29] one week ago We Beat the long role and started out to meet the advancing Enemy. We in camped at night in 2 1/2 mile of the enemy, every one expected to have hot Work on the following day, early next morning our camp was detailed for Picket duty. We arrived at this place at 12, oclock and took our positions at Greens Landing on the Warwick River, before night the yankees appeared in great numbers on the opposite side of the River our companies opened fire upon them which they returned promptly after John Morris called them dam cowardly scamps. We had a hard time of it sharp shooting. the River is from 2 to 4 hundred yards Wide, We had 6 minny muskets[30] and a Sharps Rifle, one of the minny Muskets I manned all the time for 2 days. We as well as the Enemy Were concealed by trees, a young man in our camp by the name of Crews was wounded through the thigh. We saw two yankees carried off on the other side Both appeared to be dead. Two balls passed in less than a foot of my body. Last night our company was on Picket again. We had a very interesting conversation a cross the River the yankees ask us how much we can get for our slaves. Now I replied 2,000 dollars, We asking them how much they would give for cotton[;] they replied 40 cents. As I had a strong voice I was chosen spokes man of our crowd. They inquired for old Jeff they said they were going on to Richmond after him. I told them they tried that the 21 of July last[.] they then comenced cursing With a vengance, in fact We soon agreed to quit shooting at each other. our company has been sepperated from the Regi 9 days, had but little to eat. Capt Hobbs arrived

10 days ago With 40 recruits. our company now numbers 124 men, We are expecting a fight every hour, We have 65 thousand troops here, more arriving every day.[31] We have news of a great victory achieved by Johnson & Beaureguard at or near Corrinth Mississippi.[32] the Death of Gen Buell and compleate rout of the federal army. I do not believe it. direct your letters to Yorktown

Write soon
your Brother
W C McClellan

William Cowan McClellan to Thomas Joyce McClellan

Lebanon Church,
April 15 [1862]
Dear Father
Lt Floyd and my self came back to our old camp this morning to get sum clean cloths, tell Mother those Shirts and socks came just at the right time. I have just washed and put on one of them- all was quiet down at Greens landing this morning When I left except occasionally a minne Ball or a Rifle cannon Shot would fall in our midsts. Only about half of our recruits have arms yet. Some of my old acquaintances refused to take guns When we started out to meet the Enemy there being about 15 unmanned guns in our company, H.J.C [Hezekiah John (Bud) Cartwright]. Lt. Wayland offered him one but he refused upon the plea that he was not drilled Well enough and another recruit took his gun. Say nothing about this to any body I like him and do not wish to do him an injury, But White eyes wont do. By the by Matilda Writes me word some body has ben abusing me by letter, I would like to know who it is. I did not believe I had an enemy in our company if I have he has kept it to him self very close, But there is one poor sneak in the company despised by every body in it Who is a relative of the Robertson family mean enough to do such a thing. This man professes to be a friend of mine but he is so deceitful I no not whether he be friend or foe, tell Matilda to Write me Word who it was in her next letter so I may be on my guard. We are expecting a fight every day, We have 65 thousand troops. Reinforcements are arriving dayly from Richmond. Longstreats division I understand Will arrive here to morrow there is now 2 or 3 hundred thousand men on this battle

marred Peninsula a great many more than there was in the days of the first revolution when Corn Wallace gave up his sword to Washington,[33] if our army is defeated at Yorktown our company will be cut off and taken prisoners, Major Gracy of Florence ala has command of our companies comprising 4 of the Best in the Brigade. This is quite an honor to our co as Gen Magruders called for men of the best morrel courage to hold greens landing at all hazzards to keep the yankees from outflanking our army at Yorktown. Well the sun is about down and Floyd and I have 5 miles to Walk, excuse my haste and a bad Pen.

your effectionate son
W. C. McClellan,
YORKtown Va.

Write as soon as This comes to hand, We have it from good authority that Beaureguard Repelled Buells army and killed Buell him self. I got Matildas Miniature. in haste

W C McClellan

William Cowan McClellan to Matilda McClellan

Greens Landing
April 16,1862
Dear Sister,
I wrote Father a Short letter yesterday, but as I have few leisure moments I will write you a short one this beautiful day. The birds are singing on every bow while the air is fragrant with the rich perfume of the bursting Buds and flowers all unmistakable omens of approaching Spring. While nature glides on in all of its beauty and lovelyness Man the wickedest of all Earths inhabitants are arrayed in the most Savage diabolical inhuman war ever recorded in the history of the World. Here we are on this noted spot the Peninsula rangeing from 4 to 8 miles wide by tens of thousand ready to rush upon each other at any moment in deadly conflict. What ever may have ben the causes of this division in our government. I am fully conscious that I or the party to which I belonged contributed nothing towards it, it is now too late to talk of the past, I now hear the Boom of cannon at Yorktown the Ball Will soon be apassen I expect to fight as bravely as any one. The army conceives that Victory

can only be won by desperate fighting. McClellan and his army are here to meet us, the Manassas army coupled with that of Magruder are here for the express purpose of meeting Them. The Enemy can be seen all along our line, our Batteries and those of the Enemy are three quarters of a mile past. our Brass Bands play Dixie those of the Enemy play Yankee Doodle. at this moment our Batteries 200 yards off is casting Brasse shells a cross the River among the Yankees. We have 4 companies here to guard this landing[.] our co. Stands every 4th day. Sharp Shooting is going on all the time, Yesterday a Lt in a South Carolina comp[any] was wounded in the thigh in consequence of Which he had to have his leg amputated, this makes the third man wounded on our post, a young man in our company By the name of Crews[34] received a wound in the leg I came in a few inches of being Shot two or three times, they have some very long range guns & a Shot fired at us killed a Horse 4 hundred yards in our rear passing straight through his Body. Since writing the above day be fore yesterday We have had an engagement with the Enemy at dam No. 2 or Winds Mills [Wynn's Mill] 2 ½ miles from here it was from all accounts the most desperate fight that has occured in this war.[35] At dam No. 2 the Warwick River is a mear branch but cannot be crossed owing to high banks save at a narrow pass. At 9 oclock on the 16th the Enemy commenced forageing over the River in great numbers. Our Battery on this side opened on them, the Enemy responded with 6 Rifled cannons. The fire was incessant for 2 or 3 hours, We had from 2 to five Regi engaged as the front of Battle about 4 O.C. P. M. our men gave back until the Enemy gained possession of one of our Batteries, about this time the 2d Louisiana Regi was ordered forward from the rear, the yankees thinking they had us on the dead hoisted a Black flag, the Louisiannians maid charge on them driveing them back across the River cutting off 3 companys all of whoom they Killed Save 5 men. Some say the yankees never hoisted a black flag that the Louisiannans told they did so to justify them in Showing no quarter. Our loss on the 16th was about 90 men 20 or 30 killed dead, the Enemys loss is a great deal heavier. We lossed a Col of a South Carolina Regi. the 9th and 10th Ala Regiments Were in the fight With Brigadier Cadmus M. Wilcox at their head, Wilcox has command of that point I do not know the loss of our Regi, you must remember that our company is on picket on the extreme right of our line a mile and a half of James River the far famed Tigers are the only troop between us and James River. We are now on duty I can just raise my head and see Yankees by the dozzen on the opposite side of the River. Bud Cartwright and 15 others of our recruits are With the Regi- for the purpose of guarding the Surgeon in time of Battle, They have no arms all has ben quite for 2 days Boath Sides preparing for a Big fight no doubt. This is April 18th, 12, oclock. Write soon We get no letters now.

Your Brother Wm. C. McClellan, Yorktown, Va.

give my respects to Boeaureguard. I am very anxious to hear from John and, Co, tell Sallie I have never seen her friend Ryan. Capt Warren of our Regi handed me those Letters, given him some where on the Road. Good night

W. C. McClellan

my respects to the gals I left behind me.

William Cowan McClellan to Thomas Joyce McClellan

Richmond
May 26th, 62
Dear Father,
Five days ago I heard that I had a letter in E. F. Ragland co & care,[36] they sent me an envelope to camp upon which was written Guntersville, ala Paid ten cents Ragland & co. Richmond Va. I inferred by this that you were in Gun[tersville]. I With a greatdeal of difficulty obtained permission to go and see about it . . . Ragland told me he had mailed my letter to me in care of Gen. Wilcox this is probably the last I will ever heare of this Letter, I earnestly hope you and family are at some place of security Where you will not be molested or insulted by the enemy. I would give a great deal to know the extent of their atrocities and destruction of property in our Neighborhood I fear they have destroyed all you left at home. It is heard that men who opposed secession as bitterly as you did should be driven from home and the property you have gained by honest toil destroyed and scattered to the fore Winds of heaven. When will this war end is upon every tongue, But it must not end in our defeat, no never as long as there is a Soldier left on Southern Soil let him strike for freedom in the face of death, death is a sweet Word, compared to subjugation, our army is now in line of Battle around Richmond in sight. Our Brigade is in LongStreats division.

We occupy the Post of honor North of Richmond. you would suppose that this army had become discouraged after retreating so much from it, the prevalent Sentiment through out our army is that We will give the yankees the worst Whipping When They under take to take Richmond an army ever got. They are in 7 miles of Richmond now on the Pamunkey River under cover of their gun Boats. I think they have given up the notion of attacking R[ichmond] by Way of James River since their signal repulse at Drury Bluff They acknowledge our shots tore through their Boats With fearful effect, Well may they dread the James it is lined With one hundred pounders for 6 miles below R[ichmond]. We have had 3 Battles With the enemy in the last 3 Weeks driving them Back every time. I will send this letter home or go to G[untersville] by Ben Williams If you are from home, Father you could come up and see me, this Battle Will be sure to come off under a Week. My health is tolerably good at preasant, Our Regi Won laurels as Bright if not Brighter than the 4th Ala at the Battle of Williamsburg, We took a Batterie consisting of 9 guns at the point of the Bayonet. Ala and Mississippians are doing the Best fighting in this army it is almost impossible to whip them however great are the numbers opposing them, and, it seams they are but forward and front in every Battle. H J C[artwright], D. T. C[oleman] are Well, [Elias] Tobe Gray is dead, also Thad Gray[37] of Moorsville recruit. Capt Gillice of our Regi Who was wounded in the arm at Wmsb is dead.[38] Dont give down under the depressing weight of Misfortune Father is all I ask. I hope We will meet again at home.

your Son
W.C.M.

William Cowan McClellan to Thomas Joyce McClellan

Camp Near Richmond
June 16th [1862]
Dear Father,
I have looked long and anxiously for a letter from you But nun has yet come to hand. I know too well the cause of this, I have been in two Battles[:] Williamsburg on the 5th of last month, Seven Pines on the 31st of last month and first of this, thank god I come out with but a Scratch at the latter place. I was Slightly Wounded in the

hip it is just about Well now. I have stayed with the Regiment all the time. I assure you that We were decidedly in Both of the engagements, the Battle of the Seven Pines is said to have been the hardest fought Battle of the War, Alabamians and Mississippians as usual did the hardest fighting- the only charge the yankees made at 7 Pines was at the 9th Va regi Which gave way, the 3 ala Reg was ordered up at them, They went charge, Alabamians charge was the command. the yankees threw down their arms and disappeared through the Swamps. I would Write you a long letter but Sterling McDonald[39] starts in 15 minutes for ala By whoom I will send this. Our guns are now in line of Battle. We are expecting every moment to be ordered off to fight, We are all ready and Willing for the conflict. I have an Infield Rifle taken from a yankee at 7 Pines, Our loss at 7 Pines in killed Wounded and Míssing is 2,300 the enemy admits 8 thousand, We took 8 hundred prisoners, only one hundred and fifty of our men Were killed on the field, We hear through the newspapers that old Mitchell has left Huntsville for Chattanooga perhaps you can all breathe freer since he and his bunch left. Oh if Wilcox Brigade could just get hold of him for an hour an a half They Would Whip him so badly his Nigger Wife would not know him. Well Father I must come to a close. My health is tolerably good at this time. I think of you often from home fretting your self to death about the country, Bud Cartwright is writing to his father. Give my respects to all hope this will find you all well. Good By, in haste.

your effectionate Son
W. C. McClellan Richmond Va

William Cowan McClellan to Thomas Joyce McClellan

Camp, Near, Richmond Va
July 6th, 1862
Dear Father
I understand by a letter from Bill Calvin to Bud Cartwright that this letter can reach you directed to him at Somerville, ala. Calvin kindly proffers to carry all letters directed in his care to their destination. Poor Bud was not there to receive his letter. he is a prisoner in Washington city, We have ben fighting here for 8 days we have driven McClellan 25 miles down James River, captured 10 thousand

prisoners, our loss is very great between 15 and 20 thousand. The Enemy at least 40 thousand, We fought them under great disadvantages haveing to charge them from Breast Works hills and labouring under all of the disadvantages of an attacking party has to under go in a Broken country. But we drove them Steadily on taking every Battery that dared to open fire upon us. Longstreets division bore the Brunt of Battle [Battle of Gaines's Mill], Wilcox, Pryor, & Fetherstones Brigades lost half of their commands. Our Regi Went into the fight with 425 men. We fought 2 days and now have but 90 men for duty, We lost 70 killed on the field I do not know how many wounded, our company was very lucky compared to others in the Regiment, we had 7 killed on the field. L. C. Roden, John Morris, John McDonald, David Bridgefourth, Sam Cruse, Pady Slone, Mark Shelton, Sagt. D. L. Phillips and Albert Brooks mortally wounded.[40] 18 or 20 others wounded, thank god I escaped unhurt. I was slightly wounded in the Battle of 7 Pines, Capt Hobbs was wounded in the first volley first day. So was Lt Wayland, the former Severely in knee the latter in thigh. They mowed us down in the charge But we layed down two to one When they retreated. Longstreat says Wilcox has got the best Brigade in his division and Wilcox Says the 9th ala is worth any other two regi he has got. I will give you a Wicked expression of a yankee prisoner we took, met and captured a Batterie from at Williamsburg where he made good his escape but we got him the other day. The yankee said the 9th ala Regi would charge Hell with Barlow knives. I am now at camps near Brook town.[41] Gen Lee has the yankees surrounded in a Swamp on James River some few have got off on transports but a large portion of them will be Starved out and taken prisoners. we took 4 thousand Sick prisoners in addition to the 10 thousand well ones, they got very few prisoners of ours. The way Bud Cartwright was taken we charged a Batterie and took it and were unable to hold on account of overpowering numbers. Bud was at the Battery busily shooting and the Regi was ordered to fall back. he as well as several others did not hear the order and was taken prisoner. our reinforcements came up and retook the Batterie and drove the yankees on. Several of our wounded taken at the Batterie were recaptured again, Lt Couch[42] of Athens for one. Father we have gained a glorious but dearly Bought victory, This is by far the greatest Battle ever fought on the continent if not equal to Napoleons great Massacres. There will yet be a faint struggle and McClellans grand army

Will be no more. God Speed the day, I suppose the yankees have tormented you a great deal in old Limestone but have not injured your property much. Bare with them a little while longer the day of reckoning is at hand When the noble army of the Potomac drop up on them like a clap of thunder from a cloudless sky. Alabamans have fought with a desparation never equaled before in this Battle, you may exterminate them but they can never be Whiped. Father I often think of you and family these dark and trying hours of Peril. I frequently implore the god of mercy to protect you while at the mercy of an unprincipaled foe. Write to me at Richmond.

your effectionate Son
W. C. McClellan

[I] was wounded in the finger, Capt Buchanan[43] flesh wound in leg. Tom Grimes Killed.[44]

William Cowan McClellan to Robert Anderson McClellan

[inserted above the letter] Mr. William Calvin, Sir read this if you choos, and please convey it to Bob or Father. The boys are all very glad you have volunteered to convey letters to their anxious parents I send you a letter to Mr. Phillips conveying the news of his son Davids wound. Please forward it to him. Write to me soon. Your friend, W. C. McClellan

Richmond
July 8th 1862

Dear Bob,
I seat myself after 8 days hard fighting to Write you a letter. We have driven McClellan 17 miles from his fortifications on the Chickahominy down James River under cover of his gun boats. Our forces have completely surrounded him but he has a strong position backed on two sides by his gun Boats, had he had no gun boats to fall back on we would have captured his entire army. Our cost is very heavy, the enemy's a great deal heavier. our loss can't be less than 15 thousand men, the enemy's 25 thousand besides 10 thousand prisoners. We had 7 men killed dead in our command 30 wounded. Capt. Hobbs was wounded in the knee the first days fight. The following are the names of those killed on our field, T.C. Roden, John Morris, John McDonald, David Bridgeforth, Sam

Crews, Pady Slone, Mark Shelton, badly wounded David Phillips, Albert Brooks, Brackean, Asy Moore.[45] Slightly wounded A[lbert] Martin in leg, Bud Cartwright taken prisoner while bravely challenging a battery in company with 3 others of our mess. Bob I have heard a great deal of the cruel oppression of the foe in old Limestone. I hope it is not as bad as represented. Write and let me know. I received a letter from John dated 15 June he has had a bad time of it.

Yoür effectionate Brother
W.C. McClellan 9th Reg, ala. vol.

Our Brigade fought desperately on Friday and Monday. Gen. Longstreet said Wilcox had the best Brigade in the confederate States. The 9th Ala has ben in 3 hard battles each time She has taken a batterie. 2 weeks ago we had 425 men now we have but one hundred able for duty. Gen. Wilcox has put all of his Regiments together in one regiment[.] they make a very small one at that. I have been in 3 battles by the will of God I have come out alive having received but a slight wound at Seven Pines. Nobly has Alabamamans fought in these last desisive Battles for Independence. Many of her brave sons have sealed their devotion to their country by their hearts Blood. Many a Southern fireside has been desolated by the craven messenger of Northern cruelty and oppression. Although nearly half of them are laid in their shallow graves on the Battle field. The remainder will march to the cannons mouth and stab the Yankee gunners to the heart unawed by the superior numbers or the display of burnished weapons and dazzling uniforms the ragged Alabamians go steadily on, they are unmovable. By Her Side stands Mississipi and Tennessee.

William Cowan McClellan to Thomas Joyce McClellan

Camp Near Richmond, Va.
July 27, 1862
Dear Father
Young Brundidge[46] whom was wounded in the late Battle near Rich. Will start to his home near Decatur, Ala in a few days by him I will send this letter hoping and trusting that you will get it, Nothing of any importance has occurred in the last two or 3 weeks to

disturb the quietness of camp. The enemy seems content to cower under cover of their gun boats although we have given them several opportunities to come out and sun themselves. A Skirmish took place yesterday at Malvern Hill. Stewarts cavalry charged the yanks and they maid for the swamps, our loss one man killed several wounded. We are slowly fortifying near Drewry Bluff,[47] I will give you a short description of the fortifications around Richmond. Our fortifications that is the first line of fortifications commences at James River about one mile and a half from the city. They consist of very powerful Batterys containing from 12 to 20 guns they extend all around Richmond the distance between them being so short that musketry would deal death and distruction to the enemy in passing between them. The second line is some 4 or 5 miles from Richmond commencing at Druries Bluff and running North to the write Wing of our position before McClellan defeat here[.] the line of works twice intersect almost every body is of the opinion that we will never get an opportunity to fight behind them as the Yankees have never charged a Single Breast work until Old Jo's [Joseph E. Johnston's] Boys had left them. While Old Jo's Boys have charged their fortifications repeatedly and always taken them. The truth is when ever the Yankees throw a few bombs into our ranks the Rebels go in double quick time and takes the big cannons away from them. I have heard of the horrid brutalities of the federal army in Athens, alas I suppose they plundered the town of every thing valuable in the way of goods- money, horses, Negroes and not being content with this insulted and outraged the fair Ladies of Athens,[48] Tis heard indeed that we shouldn't be kept here listening to these horrid crimes of the enemy without a chance for vengeance. Oh that we could be there for one day- yes one hour not a single hell hound would be left to tell the tale. I hope these outrages have not extended over the country, If I knew they had I would leave in one hour for home to avenge these horrible crimes and to die in so doing would be glorious indeed. I hope you have acted prudently and there by saved your property from distruction. We hear that Dr. McDonald & G. S. Houston have taken the oath of allegiance if they did so it is to save their property for which I do not blame them, I think there is no harm in taking an oath by compulsion. It is with pain that I announce to you the death of Capt. Hobbs. A Braver man, nobler Christian, never lived in my opinion. He was wounded on the 27 day of June just as we got into the fight, one of the boys that was lying clost to him when he was wounded spoke to him and asked him if he was much hurt. He replyed as cooly as if he had ben at home no not much don't say any thing about it to the Boys, he says let them go on in the charge. Labreer[49] kept his word and the company went through the fight with out knowing but what Capt Hobbs was along. This was bravery Patriotism and self devotion to country unsurpassed by any body- He was wounded in the Knee Ball stopping in a soft bone in his knee. He died a day or to ago at Linchburg in the presance of his Wife and Friends. We have lost the best Captain in the entire confederate States, If he had lived 3 weeks longer he would have ben Col. of our Regiment. This morning a tear stands in every troopers eye. No more will we hear his familiar voice, no more on inspections will his kean eye detect a dirty shirt. When he would say Tom Cartwright a little soap and water would add greatly to your looks, and I think your feelings also. He made his men keep clean and he supplyed or procured every thing that could be had to add to the comfort of his company. The loss of Capt Hobbs is a very heavy blow to Limestone County. Our side of the county always disagreed with him upon the actions of county and state politics. I am now convinced that what he advocated he was honest in. We have lost 10 men killed in our company 33 wounded. David Phillips to the astonishment of all is getting well, he was shot through the bowels. Father it strikes me that there is a brighter day a coming When our homes shall be freed from the foot of the invaders. We are now victorious at every point, a Strong feeling pervades our army. Old Stone Wall [Jackson] has returned to the battle. Now is the time for Braggs[50] army to strike a blow. My respects to all.

Your affectionate son.
W.C. McClellan, Rich, Va

William Cowan McClellan to Robert Anderson McClellan

Camp Near Richmond Va
July the 27th-62
Dear Brother,
I sat myself down this memorable day to write you a few lines. Twelve months ago to day the booming cannons thundered over the Plains of Manassas. We were victorious, it was herrald fourth to the

world as the greatest Battle ever fought on the continent. so it was at the time, but what has happened since, a few days ago the same old Army of the Potomac [the old name for the Army of Northern Virginia] fought 8 long days each day being a greater Battle than the Battle of Manassas. Why Manassas occurred to me at this time is I hear the Boom of cannon at Richmond in commemoration of that great day. One year ago to day poor Jim Bailey sealed his devotion to his country by his lifes Blood. poor fellow he may be the first man I ever knew, Hard things occur in this cruel war, in one of the last Battles I had friends to fall. by my side to the right and left no time to stop and help them farewell. Roll on We must take that blazing battery and we did take it- manning the 3rd Battery for the gallant 9th. Then I will take occasion to say that Our Regi. Stands among the first in the confederate States, in point of courage & prowess as an evidence of it was ordered to drive at the enemy and remain in the Battle with 595 men in the Tuesdays fight we had 310 man killed and wounded. Well might Gen. Wilcox who looks as thin as a rock of ages, shed tears as he looked at the mangled forms of his old Regiment next day. the fight was renewed. Wilcox formed his Brigade consisting of 90 men to impact any weak point in our line but fortunately none occurred. But if Wilcox had given them an order to charge a Battery every man would have cheered him and Bounded like Bucks in the very Jaws of death after haveing lost over half of their number in the previous fights. All is now quiet down the James River, McClellan is burrowing in the earth I suppose his object in this so as is in the event he is repulsed again in his onward to Richmond he will give the command rats to your holes. Stone wall Jackson has left here for parts unknown. The Yankees are looking for him too maybe thus appearing before long in the rear of Washington. Gen. Magruder has gone South some where, Knoxville probably. he did not like the command with him, Old Jo. Johnston the Fox has almost recovered from his wound. [Maj. Gen. Benjamin] Huger, the man that failed to take his position between McClellan and his Gun Boats is under arrest had he performed his part of the work there is not a shadow of a doubt that McClellan and his grand army would have all ben taken prisoners. Old Bob Lee is here chief cook & and Bottle washer, the spirit of the Rebel Army. During the fight old Jeff could be seen streaking around on a Blood Bay horse tipping his hat occasionally when the rebels send forth cheer after cheer for Jeff Davis. Our Brigade in company with

Pryors and Pickets Brigade of Longstreats division Brought on the attack allowing relief of Micah Jenkin's position. as usual the order was given to charge. on we went through an open field under fire of 50 guns charged to the musle with canister to grape and shell coming line profusely with minie balls by the barrell. Our line seamed to be gradually melting away Regiments on our right and left wavered a little and laid down, the 9th ala a little in advance of any other Regi drawing most of the fire of the enemy also remained a little [illegible]. Gen. Wilcox who always stayed clost to the 9th came up and waived his sword over his head and said a rise 9 ala and charge the invaders of our homes. Just a glance at this brave gen dispelled every fear, that voice was familiar one shout from the 9th on to the Battery they went. the whole line hearing Wilcoxs strong voice was electryfying and they rushed to the charge the 9th Ala Planted her flag in front of the Battery. 4 of company F fell dead on this charge, In all we have lost 9 killed, 33 wounded. I have just read a Northern account of the arrest of Gen. Mitchell summons to Washington for trial for the Savage conduct of his Brute Soldiery upon the people of Athens ala. The Northern account says the commander of the federals at Athens told his men he would shut his eyes for two hours and turn them loose to gratify their beastly passions on the fair Women of Athens, rape plunder and destruction ruled the hours.[51] Oh when will we be permitted to meet these Savages in human form excuse this badly written and spelled letter. Write to me if possible My health is not very good at preasant.

your affectionate Brother
W. C. McClellan Rich Va

7
The Second Battle of Manassas to Fredericksburg, Virginia
August 9–November 18, 1862

> The Boys are all Sick and tired of Maryland . . .
>
> —William Cowan McClellan

On July 26, Thomas Joyce McClellan had left Athens for Richmond, Virginia, on business, which included visiting William during the first week of August. The visit from his father was a surprise and a morale booster for a young man who had found it difficult to get a furlough to return home. The family of Capt. Thomas Hubbard Hobbs,[1] who had died on July 22 from wounds inflicted at Gaines's Mill, waited in Athens, Alabama, for confirmation of his death.

By the end of August, the Union army had pulled out of Huntsville (though it would return in July 1863). Behind them they left stripped and devastated homes and plantations. As the Union army left the area, 1,500 slaves in Madison County left with them.[2] In addition, the Union occupation had set the local population against each other as Unionists had come out in support of the occupation. Now those people faced the wrath of the Confederate guerillas and the Confederate supporters in town.

The harsh reality of war had come to northern Alabama, and the war was now a part of their daily lives. While prospects remained good for Confederate success, individual spirits fell with every Federal intrusion into Limestone County. Union troops continued to march through Limestone County on their way to other battlefields, so the area experienced random burning of stores, looting of homes, destruction of crops, and killing of livestock. Confederate cavalry and infantry also passed through Athens in route to raids and battles in other parts of Alabama and Tennessee, but they were unable to provide much protection for the local citizens.

When the Union army moved out of Athens and Limestone County in August, the morale of the loyal Southern citizen had risen, and many of the openly professed Union sympathizers left town. Most Union sympathizers, however, maintained a quiet allegiance to the Union and were under suspi-

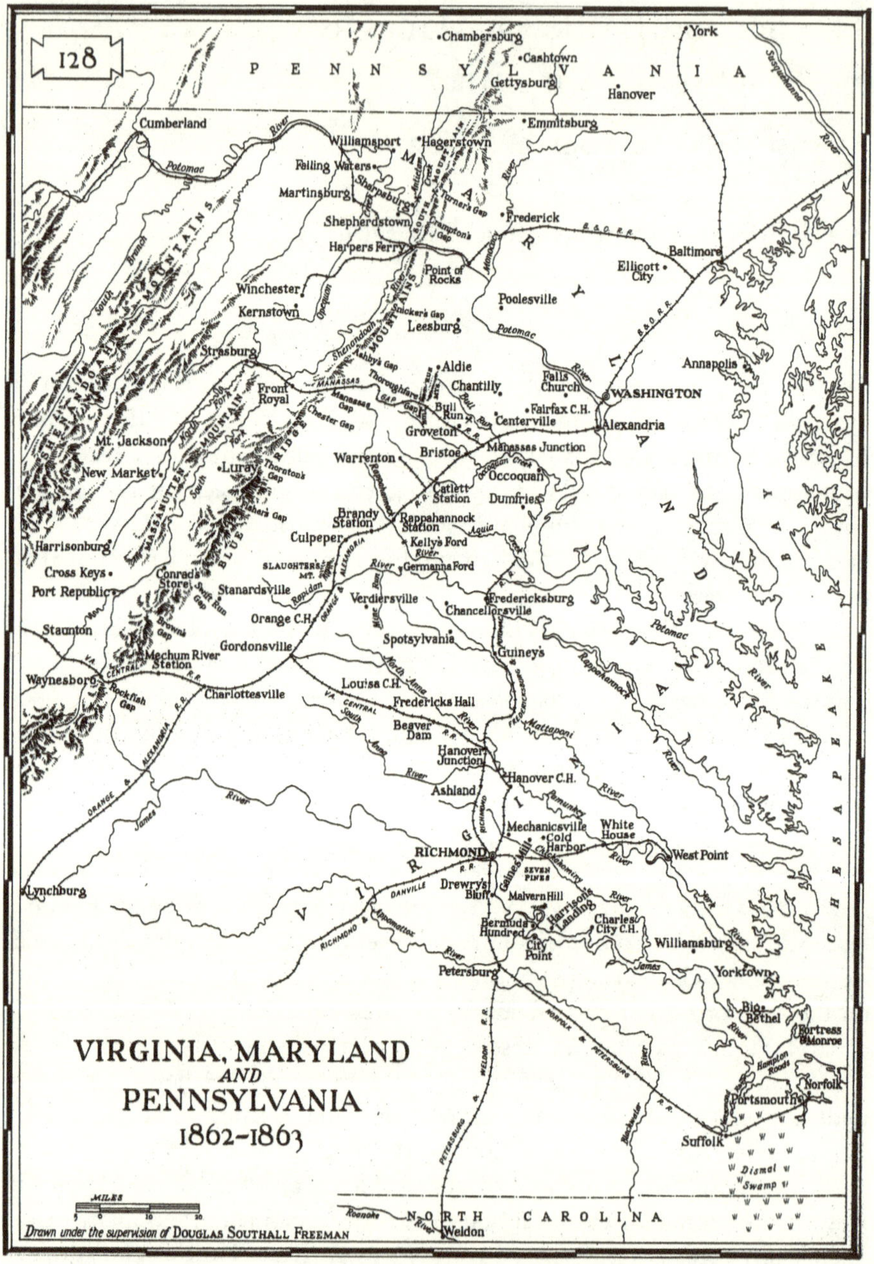

Virginia, Maryland, and Pennsylvania, 1862–1863

cion by those openly loyal to the Confederacy. It was a situation that had existed since the earliest days of secession. Morale in Limestone County constantly went up and down depending on Confederate victories on the battlefield and on the occupation of the county by Union troops. Initially many Athens citizens such as Mary Fielding had projected a brave front: "As for giving up! I wouldn't do it while there is a [Confederate] soldier left in the south . . . maybe when all the men are killed you'll [Federal soldiers] have the glory of conquering women and children but we won't give up before."[3] By the summer of 1862, however, some of these same Southerners in the occupied regions were undergoing a crisis of faith. Mary Fielding found one of her cousins "entirely subdued, ready to do anything they say for peace."[4]

On the battlefront, the tide of the war appeared to be turning toward the Confederates' favor. Combined with Robert E. Lee's advances in Virginia in the summer and fall of 1862, Gen. Braxton Bragg and Gen. Edmund Kirby Smith were advancing their forces northward from Tennessee into Kentucky and toward the Ohio River in September. After the Seven Days Battles, Lee had been faced with both an opportunity and a dilemma. With the massive army of Gen. George McClellan still sitting in their strong position at Harrison's Landing on the James River, another large army was forming in Northern Virginia under Gen. John Pope. Lee's failure to destroy McClellan's army on the peninsula left him in a precarious situation of watching and waiting for McClellan's next move. McClellan's position on the James threatened Richmond and kept Lee tied to its defense, thus seizing back the initiative that Lee had won in battle on the peninsula. Despite his success against McClellan, Lee's victories had not changed the picture in the east.[5]

While initially ignoring Pope's growing army to the north, Lee realized that, unless he attacked first, he might be crushed between two armies that could amount to as many as 200,000 men. After Pope moved south to occupy Culpeper Court House, Lee risked abandoning Richmond and moved to meet the new threat. Stonewall Jackson and A. P. Hill were sent to strike the enemy's right, and they first came into contact with the Federals at Cedar Mountain on August 9. In a poorly managed battle during which they forced the Federals from the field, the Confederate forces suffered 1,338 casualties to the Union's 2,353.[6] The Battle of Cedar Mountain revealed that Pope was probably in the process of launching a major offensive southward. Regardless of the outcome of this battle, Lee planned an offensive that would break the stalemate in Virginia by turning the Union position, destroying Pope's army, and letting the Confederates move into Maryland

and Pennsylvania. This offensive would culminate in the Second Battle of Manassas.

Without waiting to be sure that McClellan was withdrawing from the Virginia Peninsula, Lee speculated that McClellan was attempting to join Pope's forces and move south on Richmond. After failing in his attempt to smash Pope's army at Cedar Mountain, Lee concentrated his forces on the Rapidan River in front of Pope while he sent Jackson ahead and to the west to turn Pope's right. On August 28, 1862, Lee and James Longstreet followed behind Jackson, and as Lee approached Manassas, Lee ordered Cadmus M. Wilcox to take his three brigades (including the 9th Alabama) through Hopewell Gap to flank the Union defenders at Thoroughfare Gap. After the Confederate forces were through the gap, Wilcox was directed to place his division at Brawner's Farm on the right rear of Longstreet's forces to act as their reserves. Wilcox's division would suffer no casualties during the coming battle.

After several days of heavy fighting during the Second Battle of Manassas, the combined forces of Jackson, Lee, and Longstreet threatened to encircle Pope's forces and destroy them in detail. Yet Pope was able to fall back and make an effective retreat back to Centreville. The Confederates suffered 9,197 casualties against 16,054 for the Union forces.[7] Lee's victory at Manassas prevented any Union attack on Richmond for the foreseeable future.

The Army of Northern Virginia was in good spirits, if not in the best of health. The constant fighting and movement of the army in the summer of 1862 had put a strain on the men and the supplies required to sustain them. Straggling and illness in the army became major problems even before the army moved north. Just prior to the Battle of Second Manassas, Lee's army had numbered about 50,000 men; however, only a little more than 30,000 would participate in the battle.[8] While the Army of Northern Virginia marched north to try and trap Gen. John Pope at Manassas, William Cowan McClellan was recuperating from a camp illness in a private home at Gordonsville, Virginia, along with other members of the 9th Alabama. Although he tried to rejoin his regiment after the Second Battle of Manassas, he made it only as far as Winchester before he was turned back due to the presence of Union troops between himself and Lee's forces.

After Second Manassas, Lee decided to continue the initiative that his forces had built up since the Seven Days Battles and to mount an attack into Maryland—something he had discussed with President Davis earlier in May. Historian Joseph L. Harsh has argued that Lee had developed a new strategy after the Battle of Cedar Mountain, one that would allow him to maneuver on the offensive and to break the stalemate in the eastern theater.[9] The movement into Maryland would allow the Confederates to obtain much-needed provisions (and hopefully new recruits), but even more importantly, the Maryland campaign would take the war from the doorsteps of Richmond and into Union territory for the first time. The longer the Confederates could remain north of the Potomac, the more relief they would bring to war-torn Virginia. Lee reasoned that the demoralized Union forces could be held at bay during an offensive and that they could continually be forced back by the use of turning movements.[10]

On September 4, Lee's army crossed into Maryland at the fords along the Potomac near Leesburg, Virginia, and headed toward Hagerstown, Maryland. Lee sent Jackson to eliminate the Union garrison at Harpers Ferry, Virginia, which lay across his main line of retreat. The 9th Alabama was in Wilcox's brigade, which was in Maj. Gen. Richard H. Anderson's division, and most of the regiment went to Harpers Ferry to help occupy Maryland Heights (several companies had gotten separated from the regiment and ended up going to Hagerstown with Longstreet). After the garrison's surrender in Harpers Ferry, they marched to Sharpsburg and arrived around 10:30 a.m. on September 17. The movement to Hagerstown may indicate that Lee's objective was to move into Pennsylvania. As events unfolded, however, his plans would change.

By discovering a lost copy of Lee's orders for the coming campaign, McClellan was able to force Lee into a defensive position west of South Mountain near the village of Sharpsburg, Maryland. Jackson had subdued Harpers Ferry in time to rejoin Lee, and on September 17, the Confederate army fought a spirited defensive battle against a force twice its size along Antietam Creek. While the Battle of Sharpsburg (or Antietam Creek) was a stalemate, it was viewed as a Union victory since Lee was forced back across the Potomac River. The South suffered 13,724 casualties to the North's 12,469 in some of the bloodiest fighting of the war.[11]

During the last hours of the battle, the 9th Alabama had been placed in reserve behind the Confederate line near the Sunken Road at Piper's Orchard. There they suffered twelve killed and forty-two wounded.[12] After repelling several halfhearted attempts by cavalry and infantry to engage the rear of their lines, Lee's army and the 9th Alabama went into camp at Bunker Hill near Winchester, Virginia.

Within weeks Generals Bragg and Smith had been driven from Kentucky and Tennessee, while Robert E. Lee had retreated back into Virginia.

What had started as a promising fall now looked like dual disasters for the Confederacy. While Lee had been successful at Manassas and had held against all odds at Sharpsburg, he had failed to destroy any portion of the Union army and he was unable to remain north of the Potomac for an extended period of time.

William McClellan saw the Battle of Sharpsburg as something less than a victory, but certainly not a defeat. Like the Confederate army, he needed time to rest, recover, and resupply. And, like many Confederate soldiers during the Maryland campaign, he was still barefooted. In responding to a military opportunity, Lee had pushed an army plagued by shortages of clothing and food, sickness and exhaustion, and a relentless string of battles into a battle that it was not prepared to fight. The ragged, barefooted Confederate soldier became a symbol of the fighting spirit of the South.

In Virginia, even after the Maryland campaign, things still looked promising, and William believed that the prospects for Southern victory were improving and that independence might not be that far away. On a personal level, people were changing (both at home and on the battlefield) as a result of the war. Matilda McClellan wrote to William and told him how the war had changed her, and William replied in November that the war had made a great change in him as well, as it had in all of the boys in his company. The tragedy of the war and the loss of friends had made him more serious and focused as a soldier, and less of a gleeful boy. He had become a soldier and had grown as a person as well.

William Cowan McClellan to Martha Beattie McClellan

Richmond, Va
August 9th [1862]
Dear Mother,
I am glad to hear that you are well, you must not distress yourself about me. I am getting along very well. Words are inadequate to express my feelings of surprise and pleasure when I met Father. I hope it will not be long until the enemy will be forced to leave our country. I have been staying with Father in Richmond for three days, it grieves me to tell him good bye. he will start home in a day or too.[13] If you can by any means whatever to get me transferred to a cavalry co. in North ala I wish you would do it. Have me elected

to some office, get a fool man to take my place or through influential friends get the Lee of war to transfer me. This is the only way I will ever get to press ala soil again. In my opinion there will be no furloughs granted this winter. There is not an Alabamian in this army that would not give almost anything for such a change. I cannot imagine why I do not get a Letter from home. It has been almost too months Since the enemy left there [Athens, Alabama], they must have gone back on you once again. The health of our company is very good at preseant. The Cartwrights are well. [John C.] Featherston is acting Adjutant General. [Nicholas J.] Floyd is off sick as usual. [Lt. George A.] Gilbert in command of the company. Baugh elected 3rd Lieutenant. Capt. King in command of the regiment.[14]

Your son,
W.C. McClellan
Winchester, Va.

I would write more but Father can tell you things better than I can.

Your son
W.C. McClellan

William Cowan McClellan to Robert Anderson McClellan

Gordonsville, Va.
August 20th 1862
Dear Bob,
I am now at a private House 4 miles South of Go[rdonsville] . . . Sick with backache and Diarhea which taken together makes a Bitter Pill, I am better to day than I was yesterday, The army is up at the Rapidan River fronting old Pope or McClellan.[15] A Battle is expected dayly. All of our forces are here and I presume McClellan and co, also McClellan has changed his Base from 6 miles of R[ichmond] to 75 miles from it. Bully for him, one more move will send him home. I think if we can Whip the yanks one more time at this place the war wont last more than 5 years longer. Father told me you were going to gain a Cavalry company when he got back. my advice to you is to stay at home as long as possible but when you do go, go on Cavalry, infantry will break down the stoutest constitution it is possible for man to possess. To day I am at a beautiful resi-

dence all quiet, no rattle of canteens. no hum of voices- no rumbling of waggons, and above all no roleing drum or the Shrill notes of that detestable fife. You will appreciate my feelings when you have ben in the army 14 months Starved to death marched to death nagged to death & dirty & sick.

Your Brother
W. C. McClellan

August 26th 62
Dear Bob, since writing the above I have improved greatly in looks & health. I will be able in two or 3 days to go to my Regiment which is now beyond the Rappahannoc River 45 miles from here and about 20 from Manassas. the yankee army has been retreating for a week our men overtaking every day or so and giving their rear guard some good foot races. Our army has taken several hundred prisoners, and compelled them to burn up 3 miles of their waggon train to keep them from falling into the hands of the Rebels, Where they intend to make a stand no one knows but it is supposed they will stop at Warrenton Station or Manassas, The Brave Mississippi Cavalier Steward[16] has ben crowned in the rear of the federal army[.] part of his men have visited our old stomping ground Manassas, Night before last Steward and his men surprised Pope Where he was sleeping in a House near his army,[17] they got his horse, Bridle and Sadle, and also got his uniforms, Boot and hat[.] I have just seen a man that says he saw Popes horse & Saddle, He maide his escape in his Shirttail and drawers. Bully for Pope in his Shirttails. I am now staying at the house of a Mr. W. Michie a clever old bachelor, he has a cousin name Henry Michie Staying with him whoo taught school at Mooresville 20 years ago. he says Bill Wallis & Luke Pryor the Blackwells[18] and a good many others went to school to him. He also says he visited Capt Davis & Maj Ragland frequently. Capt. D. & Maj. Ragland and old Billy Fielding went from this neighborhood, from this place I can see old Nat Raglands House or the house he lived in. It is called the Green Springs settlement[.] ask Rip Davis something about it, this is called Louesa county or Lewesia county [Louisa County]. I am getting plenty of every thing to eat now and mending very fast. I get a honey dram each morning, the people here are very hospitable and kind, they live like fighting cocks.[19] I should direct this letter N Gunterville ala in care of Dr Davis.

August 28, 1862
John Rawlings who is staying in the Neighborhood was at Gordonsville yesterday, saw 350 prisoners just taken this makes near one thousand taken since Father left here including 45 officers all of whoom have ben put in irons until a few days ago Old Pope took back all of them infamous orders how quick the old Devils changed his tune. When Robert Lee told him he was putting all of his officers taken from his command in irons how do you suppose Brigadier Gen Pope Stood this change. Pope tells Lee he was jokeing about hanging the citizens of Va.[20] John Rawlings has ben very sick but he is up now going about. he is boarding in a mile of me, I see a card in the Richmond papers Signed T. J. Foster of the Hall of the house of Repre. inquireing for J. E. Bailes.[21] who was wounded at the Battle of Richmond, Bailes was in our company he was wounded at Malvern Hill on monday in Boath Legs, He was taken to Chimborasso Hospital in Richmond where he died two weeks after receiving his wounds, he was a brave boy. He was the son of Jeff Bailes of our county, if possible let him know the fate of his Brave Son, I suppose he has got Mr. Foster to hunt him up or find out what has become of him. I will drop Mr. Foster a few lines on the subject. The news has just arrived that Longstreat was between McClellan and Pope and Manassas. Pope is making for Harpers Ferry. By this it seems MCC [Gen. George McClellan] has failed to form a junction with Pope, one report is that McClellan is at Fredericksburg another is that he has gone to Washington by Water. Our last division of 12 thousand troops arrived from Richmond to gordonsville a day or two ago in route for the Potomac. Suppose old Mc was to sail about on his Boats untill our troops get up at Manassas. he could then Sail up James River and take Rich. before our forces could get half way back. The consequences would be we could swap Capitols with the yankees. our army is now 75 miles North of Gordonsville, The cars only run to Orange courthouse 9 miles North of Gord[onsville]. Direct your letters to Gordonsville, Lewisa county Va.

August 30th 1862
This is Saturday. to morrow John Rawlings and my self will take up our line of March to the army, we will have to march 65 miles as the yankees have Busted up the R. R. all North of [here]. This is the meanest Pen, Ink and Paper you ever saw.

Orange Court House. I hope and trust the yankees have left our county, Nothing pains me so much as the unavoidable silence of those at home, a Soldier has a nough to torment him to death when he knows all is well at home But when all communications is cut off and am unable to hear a word from home or Whether or not that home has not ben reduced to ashes it is indeed trying to a mans soul. I would give five hundred dollars if I could get in a Cavalry company to opperate in Southern Tenessee and Northern ala. There would be some yankees less or no Bill McClellan. Such a life would suit me a great deal Better than the one I am leading, well I must close I may be in Washington city or Maryland.- or I may fall as thousands have fallen in freedoms cause-

your effectionate Brother
W. C. McClellan

William Cowan McClellan to Robert Anderson McClellan

Winchester, Va
Sep 24, 1862
Dear Bob,
After three different attempts to get to the army I am still at this place, I started last Tuesday and was turned back because the yankees were between here and the army, but all obstructions are now removed. I will start again to morrow in company with 200 hundred [*sic*] men-[22] on last Wednesday our forces and the enemy had a desperate fight in Maryland Which resulted in a stand off fight- our troops fought With a heroism never equaled on the continent but the enemy five times our number gave way but little, but When our Boys would go at them with the Bayonet they all ways gave way- our Brigade was put in to the fight 3 different times during the day. Afterwards Wilson & Capt Raburn [James Rayburn] of our Regi was killed.[23] Tom Smith of our company was killed[24] 5 others wounded, Thursday our men were in line of Battle all day the enemy showing no disposition to fight that night Jackson & Longstreat fell back this side of the Potomac. next day one division of the yankees crossed over, Jackson fell upon them like a thunder bolt driving them Pele Mel into the Potomac with great Slaughter. On Saturday Jackson & Longstreat again crossed into Maryland, 15 thousand prisoners have surrendered to Jackson and Longstreat in the last 2 weeks 14,000 at

Harpers Ferry. The enemy are reinforcing rapidly our army is almost broken down barefooted and ragged but they will fight as long as there is a pea in the dish. Floyd and Fetherstone where neither in the fight. I am looking for letters from home every day. Tell Mother to make a suit of cloths as soon as possible. I am needing them very bad 2 shirts, 2 pair drawers, jacket & Pants. No undershirts[;] Body Lice are too bad This is all I need. Some body Will have the kindness to Bring cloths to the poor Boys of Limestone especially Mr. Phillips.

your Brother
W C McClellan

William Cowan McClellan to Robert Anderson McClellan

Camp On Bunkers Hill[25]
October 2nd 1862
Dear Bob,
We are quietly incamped 8 miles North of Winchester I suppose for the purpose of recruiting our much wearied army. the Boys are all in good spirits in anticipation of news from home; I joined the Regi[ment] 5 days ago, you doubtless have heard many flattering reports about the reception our army met with in Maryland. The Boys say they met about as many union men in Maryland as Southern men. The cold Shoulder and Sneer almost as often as the welcome smile. we got but few Volunteers while there. But you must remember this was in the pan handle of Maryland that joins Pennsylvania down below Baltimore. I suppose we have more friends. The Boys are all Sick and tired of Maryland;[26] they tell a good thing that happened as our Regit filed passed a union Ladys house. She Says there goes the ragged barefooted Rebels, Why don't you all ware better cloaths. one of the 9th ala quietly remarked madame We dont put on our best cloaths When we come Hog Killing. She felt Bad I guess. Bob you must write to me as soon as you get this and let me know what the yankees have done in our county. Have you joined a Cavalry company yet- Bob I would give five thousand dollars if I had it to be in Cavalry with you, two young men in our Regt have just left here for North ala, Their father applied for their release which was readily granted. N.J. Floyd and my self stayed in Winchester 10 days. We got acquainted with some beautiful women

one of whom I intend to live with when this war is ended if I am alive. She is as pretty as a spotted dog and performs splendidly on the piano. Rich as a [illegible]. We lost one man in the last fight. Tom Smith son of Gid Smith had his head blown off by a cannon ball, five others wounded: C[ecrops] Malone, George Steward, J E Johnson, Jim Tucker, Tom Davison.[27] Bud Cartwright sends you his best Love, he was not in the last fight. What the next move of our army will be you know as well as I.

Your Brother
W C McClellan Winchester Va

William Cowan McClellan to Matilda McClellan

Camp On Bunkers Hill, Va.
October 3rd, 62
Dear Sister,
Again the glorious privelage of writing to you all is alloud me which has ben denied for five months. This robs war of half its horrors horrible as it is. Since then I have under gone many hardships and trials but thank god I am yet alive. As I have written several times I was taken sick about 10 days after Father left me I stayed at a private house 6 miles below gordonsville 3 weeks consequently I was not in the last fight at Manassas and Maryland. I joined the Regit 6 days ago at this place 7 or 8 miles north of Winchester. We are now incamped I suppose for the purpose of recruiting our Wearried army. The Enemy seam to be more than willing to this as he has not dared to place his foot on Virginia soil since old Stonewall run them head long over the Bluff at Botellers Mills.[28] This is said to be a worse Slaughter than at Balls Bluff, the Potomac looked perfectly Blue With their dead bodyes, while many hung dead from the crags and snaggs of the awful precipice. it is sayed that no one could look upon this horrible sight with out a Shudder. It seams that from the number of Battles the amount of Bloodshed that this war ought to be brought to a close- but no it seams it has just begun. I see in to days paper that Lincoln in his message says that if every Southern State is not in the union by the first days of January the Slaves there in are free. what a poor blustering fool he is,- after his armys have ben whipped and driven from our soil in disgrace- he has the imprudence to free the Negroes of the South at a word.[29] I think

this message of his will cause the North West to With draw her armys from the field eventually and then uncle Abraham is gone up the spout for 90 days. If to the contrary the North West sticks to Abe and is in favor of the Abolitions of Slavery let them come. We can Whip them combined though it will take us years to do it. This country the Valley of Northern Virginia is a perfect desert & Beautiful farms fenceless cropless and barren all that meets your eyes. But still the people are the most hospitable in the world, They are a different people from those about Richmond. I am anxious to learn how much the yankees have damaged North ala. I hear so many reports about the burning of Athens and the destruction of the entire county. Write and let me know all about it, has Bob joined a cavalry company yet, If there is any earthly chance I want to get a transfer to the same cavalry com. he joins, it is the only branch of the service that I can stand or that suits my presant position. Our Regt now numbers 165 men we lost a good many in the fight at Sharpsburg Maryland, they where not in the Battle of Manassas, though several were wounded by [word omitted] Burns Wolley[30] of company F lost a finger- Capt Fetherstone was in neither of the last fights, Gilbert commanded our company at Ma[nassas], Baugh at Sharpsburg. No more of War. How does the old place look. Is it as far to the big gate as ever, or to the Stables- how does the horses come on, many chestnuts, have you any thing to eat. Any Body dead Any Body Married. How does L R Davis come on. The papers say Nick Davis is considered True [to the Confederacy], George Lane left With his Friends, Clemens remained but Boarded yankee officers during their Stay at Huntsville.[31] What is the News in Limestone. Give my respects to all Friends[.] Write as soon as this comes to hand Matilda, and ancer the above questions. excuse Bad spelling Writing[.] I am as ever

your affectionate Brother

W. C. McClellan

William Cowan McClellan to Thomas Joyce McClellan

Winchester Va

Oct. 21, 1862

Dear Father,

My anxiety about home has be come much greater of late than it was while the enemy were there. It has now been 50 days since they left and I have not heard a word from home, I have understood that there was a mail rout on horse back or by hack from Huntsville to Winchester but Still no letter comes for me. I will write you a long letter. We have heard of our defeat at corinth and of Braggs Victory in Ky.[32] I hope the accounts we get of the latter are so, it is high time our Western army is gaining a Victory as this one in Kentucky is the first one. They have bin whipped in the fights in the ballance just able to hold their own or hardly so much, In Va we have never ben Whipped, The last fight was complete [illegible] fall. Our forces lay in line of Battle 24 hours-in sight of the enemy. but they did not choos to advance. just before daylight gen Lee crossed the Potomac unmolested. The enemy it is Said fell back at the same time. Gen Lee was compelled to fall back for two reasons first he had at least sixty thousand Stragglers Second the men were in a Starving condition, The enemy has not crossed the Potomac since in force, is conclusive evidence they were cut to pieces very much, They did attempt to follow old Stone Wall- 10 thousand of them, old Jack ambushed them and killed and wounded at least one half of them, those remaining leaped over a Bluff 60 feet high, But the most Brillant Victory of the war was the last Battle of Manassas, our men could see their whole army while our Artillery played upon them from every part of the Battle field, they could see the yankees as they would throw down their arms and break to the rear like White cattle as Boom Shell after Shell would burst in their midsts. Wilcox is now Maj Gen, Col Roysten of the 10th ala is our Brigadier gen.[33] We are now in Andersons Division Longstreats corps, well I must stop until after general Review. Since writing the above we have had General review. Gens Lee, Longstreat were presant. It was a grand sight to see a column of men 2 miles long march by company While the soul stirring notes from 20 splendid bands revived the trooping spirits of the Battle worn veterans of Andersons division. Just to the left of Gen Lee on a beautiful Bay sat the Rebel Spy Bell Bay [Boyd] looking as innocent as a Lamb.[34] When we fell back from Martinsburg Miss Bell fell in with Gen Wilcox- they rode together to Winchester where She put up at a Hotel, She it seems fell in Love with the Gen. She pays him 2 or 3 visits a week, Miss Bell is a large portly Lady features rather coarse- always having a smile for a friend or foe, it is said She is as chaste and pure as any Lady in Virginia. She dresses as fine as a fiddle and knows as much about Military matters as any, Gen Lee not excepted. We also had 3 English nobleman on review who were highly pleased with our army. They said we were in a greatdeal better fighting condition than our enemys and they had seen both armys since the fight at Sharpsburg. one of them who rode with Gen Lee down our lines said to him you have the finest Army ever Marshalled on the continent by far. We are now six miles North of Winchester on a hill called Bunker Hill. every thing is perfectly quiet so far as the yankees are conserned. this country is a perfect desert Armys having been here ever since the war commenced, no meats no corn no nothing, I think we will fall back towards Staunton to Winter quarters it being impossible to haul supplyes for our army so far, no R. Road any nearer than Culpeper courthouse. The Enemy have done all the damage they can do this country, they may again possess it then have ample room to flank them again will be the long and short of it. It turns out that Bragg did not gain a victory in Ky at last, but is leaving the State having accomplished nothing at all in Kentucky.

your affectionate son
W. C. McClellan—Winchester

William Cowan McClellan to his sister

Culpeper, Court House
Nov 10th 1862
Dear Sister,

Since writeing we have fallen back 62 miles. we are now at ,CC, House under marching orders destined for gordonsville I suppose to Winchester. We were not pursued in our retreat. Al Martin arrived last night bringing my Pants & gloves they were just in time as I had put the last patch on my old ones they would have. Tell Mother I am very thankful to her for them. I am barefooted but hope I will get some shoes before long.[35] Fielding has not come yet Hal Malone left him in Rich probably he is at Gordonsville with his kinfolks, Fletcher has my cloths in Richmond. W. Jones has not arrived yet. The letter by Martin is the first & and [*sic*] only one I have received from home since last May. I am glad you have received my Letters. Sergeant Batts[36] will start to Montgomery to morrow for conscripts, I will send this Letter by him, probably he will get to go home if so he will give this to you, My respects to all, Your effectionate Brother

W. C. McClellan, C.C. House, Va

Direct your Letters to Gordonsville Virginia, Wilcox Brigade, I think we will go in a day or two to that place. Al Martin tells me some strange yarns about Alabama, have you got the letter I sent by Tom McDonald yet, have you got my picture sent by Ben Williams,

Your Brother,
W. C. McClellan
Culpeper Court House State of Virginia

William Cowan McClellan to Thomas Joyce McClellan

Culpeper court House
Nov 14th /62
Dear Father-
I have received 4 letters and all of the clothes sent me except those sent by Fielding, he has not arrived yet. My uniform is admired and prized by every body. I cannot express my thanks to my good old Mother for them. They fit me splendidly. I have ben offered 10 dollars for my co. Davis gloves. I need nothing now save boots or shoes. I am compleately barefooted. we have been expecting to draw shoes for some time but failed so far. I have just read my letters from home. They contained much of interest to me. I was very much gratified to hear from your own hands that the enemy had been less destructive in our neighborhood than almost any where in North ala. God grant they may never return to our country. If they do I think you all had better take your negroes and move South of Tennessee River, and give them to some man for what they eat. when they come again they will run off all the negroes in the county big and little old and young. In Matildas letters She frequently alludes to Billy Richardson as having acted a Scoundrel with John. She does not say what he has done but I have no doubt it was something very mean as I always thought he was capable of doing-almost all of that stock are treacherous and unreliable. the best trait of their character before the war commenced was courage and this revolution has proven them cowards and traitors. It will be a pleasure when this war is ended to meet such gentlemen and tell them they are cowards. This is the treatment John received at the hands of one whose family you have befriended in a thousand ways. There is but few men in the world upon it which do to defend. We are camped

in one mile of CC House, there is some Skirmishing going on in our front probably we will have a fight here in a few days. As you see proper relative to my transfer, if I can be spared I would like to join Bobs company, but as far as Bobs being elected Lt. and giving up his position to me, I could not think of executing it on the other hand I would be perfectly satisfied to remain a private. I wrote about a month ago to C. C. Clay[37] to use his influence for a transfer. I have no idea that anything of the sort will do any good. My health is now very good gaining flesh everyday.

Your affectionate son,
W.C. McClellan
Culpeper Court House Va

William Cowan McClellan to Thomas Joyce McClellan

Culpeper Court House
Nov 15th/62
Dear Father,
Haveing failed to get my letter off in time I will write a few more lines, Old Stonewall Jackson is still at Bunkers Hill north of Winchester six miles, he has offered the enemy Battle several times but they have failed to fight. I now hear very cannonading in the direction of Manassas I expect he has attacked them, every body here is very glad the Northern government has deposed McClellan, he is by a long shot the best general the North has, Burnside is a hotheaded impetuous man and will run head long into the first trap old gen Lee sets for him. Seargeant Batts of our company has gone to montgomery to get conscripts, I told him to hunt you up. Fred is a clever Boy, and a good Soldier if you see him write back about him, he can tell you Something of the late campaigning in Va.

your affectionate Son
W.C. McClellan C.C. House, Va.

Let me heare from you as soon as possible. The weather is warm and dry at preasant, roads very good fine weather for fighting heavey cannonading towards Manassas.

W C McClellan
Culpeper Court House

William Cowan McClellan to Matilda McClellan

Culpeper, Court, House
Nov 18th/62
Dear Sister,
All of my things except those Mr Fielding has have come to hand, I read your Letters over and over again each time with interest, I cannot express my thanks to you all for the things you sent me, my cloths fit me first rate it is decidedly the finest suit in the Regt all I need now is Shoes and the Shirts Fielding has for me, I think I will draw Shoes in a day or two, I went down to the 4th ala a day or too ago for my cloths they are carried 7 miles below us, I saw 2 or three gentlemen from Huntsville but I do not remember their names, They said they knew Father very well one of them told me he saw him leave Huntsville in a hack for Montgomery. Pat Moore Ben Love and other Boys you know are all in good health & spirits, Rufus Moore was either killed or taken prisoner at Sharpsburg, Md.[38] But have never heard a word from him. I have just received a letter from John Fletcher informing me of the clothes he sent me by Scruggs[39] which I have received, he extends to me a pressing invitation to come to the 3rd ala hospital if I get wounded or Sick which I will gladly except if I am so unfortunate as to get in either situation. We have just received orders to cook up 3 days provisions and be ready to march at a moments notice, probably before this reaches you we will have fought another Bloody and desperate Battle the result of which whether in our favor or against us brings the war no nearer to a close. This war will never be desided by fighting in my opinion we have too much territory for either army to subdue the other, We have defeated them in almost every single fight in Va and still they occupy a considerable part of the State. We are encamped one mile north of Culpeper court house, Some of our troops are 10 miles South of here. Gen Anderson has recovered from his wounds,[40] and taken charge of his division. Gen Wilcox has come back to his Brigade. We have had the 14th ala Regt annexed to our Brigade, we now have the 8th, 9th___10th___11th__ 14th Alabama Regiments in our Brigade, Wilcox was recommended by Lee & Longstreat for Maj Gen but the war department appointed Forney at Mobile over him. Forney was the Col. of the 10th ala.[41] Matilda I was glad to hear that the yankees done no more mischief to you all than they did, I hope to the Lord they will

never visit our county again. If they do I think you had better take the negroes a little farther South as they will be much wary the next time they come. I wish you could get Bob Mills to stay with you all the time when Father is gone, You say the war has made a change in you,[42] It has made a very great change in me, I am not the gleeful Boy I was two years ago the Bloody deeds and tragedies of war has taught me a Solem lesson. We Boys have all changed but I have undergone a greater change than most of them. you Say in your letter that Billy Richardson acted like a scoundrel with John just as I expected. well if we all live and get home John, Bob, and I he and others will have to account for injuries done us, I have to Settle accounts as I go along but in some cases it is impossible. Jack Thompson[43] & Al Martin left here a day or two ago to try for another furlough as they where not able for duty yet, Tell Henry I have his durable pipe. tell Mother to save that Suit of cloths for me, I gave Bud Cartwright those pants Fletcher had, I will give you the names of my mess now as it has ben sadly changed. Bud C[artwright], Tom C[artwright], W. B. Vaughn and Black Bill Eagin.[44] Tell Nick Davis if he desires to do me a favor he can do so by seeing C. C. [Clement Claiborne] Clay and get him to use his influence for a transfer as he goes to Richmond in January next.

your affectionate Brother
W C McClellan
C.C. House Va
Wilcox Brigade co F, 9 ala, Vol

WRITE SOON

1. William Cowan McClellan

2. Robert Anderson McClellan

3. Thomas Joyce McClellan

4. Martha Beattie McClellan

5. Thomas Nicholas McClellan

6. Matilda Joyce McClellan

7. Charlie McClellan White

8. Willie McClellan

8
The Fredericksburg Campaign
December 3, 1862–February 9, 1863

I am now compleatly bare footed.

—William Cowan McClellan

On November 9, 1862, Maj. Gen. Ambrose E. Burnside assumed command of the Army of the Potomac, and on November 15 he began moving Union forces southward toward Richmond. Burnside was under immense pressure from Washington to assume the offensive again and to force Lee to defend Richmond. The most direct approach to Richmond was to move due south and through Fredericksburg, Virginia, so that city became his first objective. As Burnside moved troops out of Warrenton toward the city, Robert E. Lee responded by putting his army into motion from Culpeper to Fredericksburg.

Once there, Lee positioned the Army of Northern Virginia along Marye's Heights above the town. Burnside and the Army of the Potomac took up positions at Falmouth across the Rappahannock River. The river created a formidable barrier for Burnside in his attempt to take the city. Although he planned to use pontoon bridges to cross the river, the needed pontoon delivery was delayed for weeks, and he was thus late in beginning his attack. As William Cowan McClellan observed, the Union bombardment of Fredericksburg started at midmorning on December 11, 1862, with the hope of knocking out the Confederate sharpshooters attached to Brig. Gen. William Barksdale's command in the town. Barksdale's Mississippians, acting as skirmishers, had delayed the construction of the pontoon bridges across the river by nearly eight hours. The construction under fire continued as the Confederates were slowly pushed from the vicinity of the river.

Burnside launched wave after wave of almost suicidal attacks against the Confederate position. The main Confederate line along Marye's Heights held, and Burnside broke off the attack with heavy casualties. The Northern press was highly critical of the Union defeat at the Battle of Fredericksburg. While Lee knew that Northern morale was low after the victory, he also realized that he had failed once again to destroy a significant portion of a

Federal army and that Burnside was still in motion attempting to cross the Rappahannock River further upstream.

The 9th Alabama Regiment was assigned to Richard H. Anderson's division, which was holding the far left of the Confederate line across the river from Beck's Island. Cadmus M. Wilcox's brigade now consisted of all Alabama regiments: 8th, 9th, 10th, 11th, and 14th. The 9th saw little or no action during the Battle of Fredericksburg, and later Wilcox's brigade went into winter quarters near Scott's Dam in log buildings with tent roofs.[1] As the Battle of Fredericksburg opened, William McClellan was assigned to the position of provost guard at Richard Anderson's headquarters.

While William reflected on the past year, he was informed that his older brother, John, had been wounded in the Battle of Murfreesboro, Tennessee, and had lost an arm. Throughout the month of January, intermittent skirmishing occurred between Confederate cavalry and Union troops occupying northern Alabama. The Southern newspapers chronicled the Union troop movements into northern Alabama and the depredation that was occurring there. Citizens from northern Alabama petitioned the Confederate government for more protection against the Union troops that were harshly oppressing them, and they noted in their petitions that the area was populated now only by the aged and the infirmed.

William Cowan McClellan to Matilda McClellan

Fredericksburg, Va,
Dec 3rd/1862
Dear Sister,
I have just received your very kind letter of the 22nd, I cannot express my thankfulness to you for so many interesting letters it is indeed gratifying to read Them, I have written two or three letters since I have ben at this place informing you of the state of affairs in and around Fredericksburg, we are listening every hour for the signal gun to fire when the Southern Army is to meet the invading hords of the north and repell them as usual with great slaughter of the best men of the South. The Yankees are still on the North bank of the Rappahannock threatening to cross everyday. I suppose our Gens. are going to let some of them cross before the fight commences, let them come we will meet them as we always have done

determined however great their numbers to whip them or die in the attempt, with this determination we can never be whipped. The inhabitants of Fredericksburg are scattered all over the county. night before last 4 little children froze to death out in the woods. they could not get a house to stay in. the Ladys of Fr[edericksburg] are very patriotic they say they are willing or had rather see Fredericksburg burned to the ground than for the Vandals to occupy it, they are extreamly Southern in their views and actions sentiments. As I have stated in a former letter we can see the whole yankee army, I tell you there is a many a one of them. mornings the country for five miles around sounds with music from a thousand Bands, and ten thousand drums. The two armys are on better terms at presant than they have ben since the war began. they frequently meet and exchange Sugar & coffee for Tobacco. one of them gave a man in our Reg a fine over coat. But this familiarity will all disappear when the first gun fires and they will fall back into the Savage feelings of war, a feeling better than ever existed among men before. Since writing the above I have ben on Patrol. I was up at the church last night[.] the 16th Miss Band consisting of 24 peaces[,] the finest band in the confederacy[,] seranaded the ladys in camped at the church, we had a grand old time of it, if we are in the war. I have received Fathers letter from Montgomery conveying the news that it is impossible to get a transfer by any other means than the consent of all my officers from 4th corporal to Lee. It is as much impossible to get consent of any of these gentlemen from Lee to 4th corporal, as it is for me to fly without wings. And so far as a furlough is concerned, that has played out. no my destiny is east in old Virginia, and by the way to make the state of my adoption as pleasant and agreeable as possible[.] I am going to Marry before long. Capt Fetherston's siting by petitions to wait upon me provided he can get Boots if not he says he will go it barefooted, I am fully sadisfied Father has done all in his power for me, for which I am truly greatful. probably it wont be long before I will be better satisfied to stay in Virginia. it is true my desire for home has ben stronger than any earthly desire, but when the ruleing Powers of the army of Va. say I must not go home I must knuck under. The Small Pox are in our company we have had one case in our Brigade 8th ala. Matilda says She wishes the army of the West had a Jackson or a Longstreet to inspire them with an enthusiasm, I understand old J E Johnston has taken command of that army my opinion is that he is the best Gen in the confederate States; he has kept this army from being captured twice every body admits, at Harpers Ferry in July .61. on the Peninsula in May .62. he planned the great Battle of Richmond and was prevented from going through the Battles by wounds, although the papers have ben down on him for being so slow, The army of Virginia has as much confidence in him as they have in Lee, I have heard the expression ten thousand times among the Soldiers give me old Joe Johnston. I feel confident if he takes command of Braggs army Alabama will never be invaded. I was very sorry to hear of Capt Thams death. I am disposed to think he was a good old man not with standing his vanity and thirst for drink. Since I left home many of those with and around whoom I was raised have past silently away, how many more will be laid into the cold grave god only knows. Tell Tom I kept his marble until a day or two ago I gave it to a little Virginia girl, about the size of Mae Davis one of the Prettyest little thing he ever saw, a little Sister of my dearly beloved Virginia, three cheers for old Va better State than you heard it was. Poor aunt Mary I am Sorry for her children. give my respects to Cleopatra[2] The lord be with her for I cant, Featherston says here Mc take annother drink of Wine, all right Capt[.] me and C. F. [Captain Featherston] have a good time on Provost guard. Plenty to eat, drink. The [9th Alabama] Reg is about 3 miles from here[3] boys all well. I suppose this is one of the shortest Pen Staffs you ever saw, did you get my pictures sent by Ben Williams. Give my love to Sallie and Little Sue. all inquiring Friends Mr. Vaughan & Moore & direct your letters to Fredericksburg Va.

Yours truly
W C McClellan

William Cowan McClellan to Thomas Joyce McClellan

Fredericksburg, Va December 10th 62
Head quarters Wilcox Brigade Andersons division Longstreets Core left wing
Dear Father
I am now doing Provost guard duty in the city taking up stragglers in town with out papers from Lee or Longstreet. we get many a

one, I have received your letter from Montgomery. I was not at all disappointed relative to a transfer. It is impossible to get a furlough. They would see a man dead forty times first. Capt Holcomb left here this morning on furlough home to fix up his home. Bill Cartwright went with him. I would have written by them but I did not know they were going until I met them as I was going over to the Reg after my rations on their way to the Depot. I told Holcomb to tell you to send me a pair of Boots. I am now compleatly bare footed. The snow two inches deep raw hides have been issued to the troops to make masking which last about a weak or ten days. Please have a pair of boots maid and send them too as soon as possible. my feat have been wet for two or three weaks and surprising to say my health was never better. Gen. Lee has issued an order that no man will be excused from duty having no shoes. Go in Lemons and get squeezed.

Dec 11th, 1862.
The sun is about one hour high. At five o'clock this morning our Signal guns fired. all those who heard them knew before one now the great Armys of the South and North would be ingaged indeed by conflict. Nor were they mistaken. As I have said I was in the city on Provost guard duty. We were in a house the first Shell the enemy threw fell within 20 yards of our Shanty. We came back to Andersons head quarters where I am now writing.[4] It was dreadful to hear the Screams and pitiful cries of the Women and children as those terrable Shots came crashing through Brick walls and Shingle roofs. At this moment there is 70 peaces of artillery flying upon either side. Also great deal of infantry. The enemy attempted to throw Pontoon Bridges a cross. Just opposite the town our pickets let them get half way cross before they fired upon them. Father you can not imagine the dreadful clamoring that is going on at this moment. They may cross but the tug of War has just begun with them then. I suppose the guard will be kept in the rear to drive up stragglers. We may be sent to our Reg- if, so I intend to give them the best I have in my shape. The Bloody Drama has begun at last. Your son W.C. McClellan. One hour later, our men are cheering vocifferously giving it to them. I see the Smoke rising from the city. poor Fredericksburg will soon be in Ashes. If the Dead could rise from the grave what would Old Mother Washington think to see her grand children exchanging Shots over her grave.

December 15th
Since writing the above the enemy have crossed the river in two places at the city and some distance below. at boath places they where repelled and driven back with heavy loss. Longstreet corps fought at town on the left while old Stonewall Slayed them at the rite wing. But little of our division has been engaged our Brigade has not fought any yet. Gen. Lee says we have lost one thousand men. The enemy five thousand. They charged our Batterys at city Three times each time being repelled.

William Cowan McClellan to Thomas Joyce McClellan

Fredericksburg Va
Dec. 15th 62
Dear Father
Another year has almost past and no peace yet. We have wild reports of the resignation of Seward & Son and other resignations in Lincolns cabinet.[5] I have just read the full Northern account of the late Battle at Fredericksburg. For the first time since the war began they admitted a dreadful defeat. With great Slaughter. The New York Papers say let us look to god for assistance. There seems to be no power in man. This was sertainly the cheapest Victory of the war. The enemy admit a loss of 15,500. While ours is but 2000 in killed wounded and prisoners.[6] Our men fought behind Rifle Pits and a stone fence. They charged our positions seven different times and each time with fresh troops every time being driven back with terrible loss. in a small lot that stood in the edge of the city, not as large as our yard, I counted one thousand dead Bodys. some of them fell in 10 paces of the Stone fence. At this point we had but 12 men killed. Was this not glorious after being repulsed several times. Our men heard the Col of the 49th N York Reg[7] Say men will you charge again. all silent. Says he I will carry the Flag from one end of the line to the other. Our Boys looked at each other and smiled, now we will give it to them Boys. aim low; down goes the Brave Col. and his colors, men begin to fall thick and fast now. Stop and lie down. Our Boys still pepering it to them. up they went and off to the rear. After this they all grounded arms and swore they would charge no more nor could they be induced to do so by all the Patriotic appeals of their officers. They fought well but could not win.

Three miles below the city old Stone Wall fought them on equal ground opposed by three times his number he drove them the two miles they had advanced back into the River and across Slaughtering them terribly. I have it from good authority that we did not have nothing like half of our men engaged. while the fight was going on our Brigade Stationed a mile above the city was Swapping Tobacco for coffee. The North admits that Lee set a trap for Burnside and he walked into it. They said that Lee fired but Seven Shots at them when crossing the River when he could have brought to bair upon them one hundred gun. The Enemy Bombs did, F[redericksburg]. with one hundred and seventy peaces of Artillery, While he had 100 guns playing upon their Batteries. This was one of the grandest sights the world ever Saw indeed. It was grand glory and peculiar in the true sense of the word. I was on a high hill where I could see the flames as they ascended from the house tops and distinctly heard the crash of timbers as those 20 pounders would strike them.

W.C. McClellan

William Cowan McClellan to Thomas Joyce McClellan

Camp Near Fredericksburg Virginia
Dec 28 /62
Dear Father
I have written a letter or two that I have failed to get off by mail which I will send by Mr. Broyls[8] who intends starting home in a day or too. This is Christmas and about the dullest one I ever saw. Nothing to drink nothing to eat save beef and cow. Though Yesterday me and the mess dispatched an old Turkey Gobbler that cost us six dollars. We intend repeating the experiment to morrow. I have just been reading extracts from Northern papers. They set up a pitiful account of their defeat at Fredericksburg. They Say God help us. There seams to be no help in man. Fifteen thousand of the Grand Army of the Potomac Swept off in a day. Oh what shall we do says the New York Herald and winds up by saying Abraham and all his cabinet there being devils calling them fools and idiots. We have certainly gained one of the greatest victories of the war.[9] The last letter received from home was dated the 9th of this month. I have received a good many letters recently most of them however a month

or two old. I am glad you are thinking of moveing to Wills valley in the event the yankees are likely to occupy our county again. I think by the middle of January the Northern cabinet will be composed intirely of radical Abolitionists. Wo be unto the slave holders of the invaded county. My health is very good at present. I am in fine order and in tolerable spirits. I was at a big dance last night composed of refugees from F[redericksburg] and Soldiers. You must remember I am with Provost guard and have been ever since we visited at this place. We go where we pleas pretty much. Featherston was Capt of the Provost Guard until a weak ago he got sick and left for Linchburg and Floyd Fathers. Capt H [ouston] is a very poor soldier and especially in times of Noise. We stay at Gen Andersons head quarters, the Brigade is stationed about three miles from here. Roysten is not our Brigadier as you suppose. He acted in Wilcoxs stead while Wilcox acted in Andersons place. No we have old Wilcox yet. Please send me some boots or shoes. I am barefooted and have been ever since we left Culpeper. I have given up all hope of getting a transfer or furlough in Virginia. I am bound to stay until the war ends. I have just read Jim Moores Obituary, it is very good. Some talk of our Division going to South Carolina.

Your Affectionate Son
W. C. McClellan F. Va.

William Cowan McClellan to his sister

Fredericksburg-VA-
January 1st 1863
Dear Sister
The sun has set for the last time in the Bloodiest year the world ever saw. 1862 will only be remembered and associated with sighs and regret by the American people. Many a fond parent will turn aside from the perusal of the History of this horrid year of war and Bloodshead with the said remembrances of the loss of a beloved son, Husband, or Friend. Oh that we could blot out for ever the Bloody deeds of the last 20 months. This morning the sun arose in all the beauties of nature herralding fourth the first day of 1863. God grant that it may be a year of peace-making and the first year of our independence as a nation. But if the enemy continues to in-

vade our soil and pilage our homes, I hope the Soil of old Virginia may be made fertil with their Blood & Bones but they say dog manure is not good to enrich land. You have before this time heard of the dreadful defeat of the Yankees at Fredericksburg. This was the most glorious victories of the war. Our loss was very slight while that of the enemy was tremendous. I saw one thousand of the blue bellys lying in a smaller place than our yard. I still stick to what I said at Manassas, that the army of Virginia cannot be whipped. Our gens. May retreat to gain better positions and keep between the enemy and Richmond, but whenever the two Armys meet in force the Confederate States Army is always victorious. Have we not whipped them 19 times in 20 months while they have gained but one victory, that was at Roan Oak [Roanoke] Island where we had but a few companies engaged. Christmas has just gone and a very dull one it was too, though we guards went to dinner or too out in the country. One of our guards shot and killed a man. He halted him and he did not stop. He fired and killed the man dead, in which he was perfectly justifiable but it looks very hard to kill a brave Mississippian who has faced death in 40 battle fields for the independence of the South. About a weak ago Maj. Gen. Stewart [Stuart] of cavalry went around towards Manassas in the enemys rear with 4000 men to capture Burnsides Christmas presents. I saw some of Stewarts men yesterday who have returned. They captured 500 prisoners a good many horses & waggons and government stores and returned without any loss of men.[10]

William Cowan McClellan to his sisters

Fredericksburg Va
Jan 3d 1863
Dear Sisters,
This the third day of January is a mild clear day. The tall Pines under which I am camped gently waives as a gentle wind sweeps through them, Just now I saw Gen Longstreet passing along the road Solitary and alone with that old head of his a little inclined downward. no doubt thinking how long it would be before he would have an opportunity to Slaughter the Grand army of the North again. They say old Lee pats him on the shoulder and calls

him his old war Horse, well he may. longstreet has done more hard fighting than any other gen in the confederate States. Longstreat has command of 4 divisions making in all over one hundred Regiments, Anderson, McClaws, Hood, Pickett command the divisions in Longstreats corps. Send on the boots as soon as possible. Old Stonewall has the two Hills [A. P. and D. H.], Walker, Ewell are under his command.[11] these are the too mighty wings that old Lee flayed the Boasted Army of the Potomac with. Under these three Gen is the best army ever martialed on this continent, They have never ben whipped or ever will be, We may fall back to keep the enemy from out flanking us- can never be whipped. no such letter in the Books as defeat. It dont make any difference if the enemy have got 3 to one, no more about war, How does the gals get along. how long since you heard from my beloved Maggie of Indian creek,[12] Cleopatra or any other girls. Matilda tell old Mrs Robinson[13] when I come home I intend to give her a map for her other daughter.

I am very uneasy about John and Bob. though I do not believe Bob was in the fight as he was just got into the service. I would like to see Bob before he goes into a fight I could give him some good ideas how to dodge bomb shells also a minie Ball occasionally, The first fight Soldiers go into they always suffer most. It will not do to Stand up in battle unless you are charging. The infernal yankees have destroyed several Bridges in east Tennessee so my letters and yours will be a long time reaching their destination. I hear some talk about furloughs but I have no idea we will ever get a furlough. Bud & Tom Cartwright are both well, Bud makes a splendid Soldier, Buds health is very fine. Tom is a good Soldier too but he is a little devilish occasionally. Day before yesterday the officers of our Reg met and resolved that Col Henry Should not take command. Yesterday the Privates met and got up a petition for him to take command, nearly every Private in the Reg Signed the Petition, I dont know how it will turn out, but hope they will take command. They have been trying to supersead Williams and Henry both with Capt King.[14] Well Matilda I have scribbled long enough, give my love to every body or those at least that have not forgotten me. Tell Sally I will answer her kind letter of the 13 Dec. soon, yours of the 12 has come safely to hand.

Affectionately, Your Brother
Wm C McClellan Fredericksburg

William Cowan McClellan to his sister

Fredericksburg, Va.
Jan 3d 1863
Dear Sister,
I will attempt to write you a letter on this dirty paper. My health is very good at presant. Christmas has passed and gone, I was at two or three parties and enjoyed myself as well as could be expected. There is quite a contrast between the ladys of Alabama and Virginia as a general thing the women of our county are a greatdeal more dignified and reserved than those of Virginia. I have yet to find a lady about Fredericksburg that will not let a man kiss and hug them, a Soldier of the 19th Miss Reg married a young lady New years night. it was quite a novel sight to see this veteran Soldier arm in arm with one of the fair sex. I think She has driven her ducks to a bad market. He will have to leave her behind when we leave here. Yesterday we got the Richmond Dispatch containing a dispatch from Gen [Braxton] Bragg at Murfresboro stating he had assailed the enemy at 7 oclock on the 31st after 10 hours hard fighting have driven him from every position except his extreme left where he has been successfully revisited. We captured 4 thousand prisoners including two Brigadier Generals, Thirty Pieces of Artillery and some hundred Waggons and teams,[15] This is all very good except the extreme left, I hope this dispatch will not be modified like all the dispatches we have received from the West of Battles, from Perryville Ky we received a dispatch from Braggs army that he had taken 15 thousand prisoners and captured the entire wagon train of the enemy and the remaining yankee army was fleeing in disarray. gen Bragg must drive back the enemy on his left before he claims a victory or a decided one at least, Lee would not have dispatched until this was done.

William Cowan McClellan to Thomas Joyce McClellan

Head Quarters Provost Guard
Jan 7th, 1863
Dear Father
Sergeant [James D.] Tucker leaves for home tomorrow. I will send this letter by him. His Father was killed in a fight at home and he

got a furlough to go and see about it. We first received flaming dispatches from Bragg Stating he had gained a glorious victory, in a day or too after we hear that Bragg has fallen back 30 miles. Will we never gain a victory in the west at a time when our prospects where brightening and brightening all over the confederacy. Braggs retreat cast a dark Shadow over our gayns.[16] last night I could not sleep for thinking of the desperate condition of my home and all I hold dear in consequence of this retreat. it may all be for the best but it looks to me to be a very bad sine. We understand the loss of the enemy was very heavy. But old Bragg tells so many lies we do not know whether or not to believe him.[17] I am very uneasy about John & Bob you must let me know of them as soon as possible. Oh if we could have whipped them at Murfreesboro we would have had peace. The enemy were staggering awfully under the dreadful defeat. They sustained at this place every Northern paper was filled with lamentations of the loss of life in the slaughter pen of Fredericksburg. You may look out for a fight before long. Braggs defeat in the west will encourage the enemy. So they will be tempted to try old Bob Lee again if they do they will get a thrashing as usual although their army is so large. Again no sun. All is perfectly quiet along the Rapidan some say that the enemy have retired though it gives me the creeps. [Maj. Gen. J. E. B.] Stewart was in the rear of the grand army a few days ago capturing 400 prisoners destroying a great many government Stores going within 6 miles of Alexandria. My health is very good at presant though it is surpising to me I have ben bare footed for two months all the while performing hard duty. furloughs transfers and very things of the sort has played out. There is only one way to get on furlough and that is to go home to get married a pretext I have an idea of taking advantage of as I can produce pretty strong proof of the fact. Let me know in your next letter whether or not you intend to move in the event the enemy are likely to occupy our vicinity which I look upon as almost sertain. If you don't move your self, send all your negroes that can get about to some place of safety down South. This I think will be the best plan though you know better than I do. there is one thing surtain the enemy are going to attempt to free all the Negroes they find in the country they occupy. You must excuse this hastily written letter. I am afraid Tucker will get off before I can see him now as it is three miles to the Reg

Affectionately. Your son
William C. McClellan

William Cowan McClellan to Thomas Joyce McClellan

Fredericksburg Va Headquarters
Provost Guard Anderson Division
January 12th 1863
Dear Father

I wrote a letter a day or to ago to send by Sear[geant] Tucker but failed to see him before he left consequently I will have to mail it. Gen. Lee has ordered two men to be furloughed from a company subject to the choice of company commanders in most of the Reg. they draw for it but in our Reg. officers of the co. say whoo Should have furloughs. Floyd has applied for two Married men in our company Steward & Holland,[18] There is three more men in the .co. they will go in 15 days and then I will have a chance with the 65 single men which is a very slim chance. I have no idea I will get home until the end of the war, which will be about 1870. By the time the second squad starts home Lee will countermand the order. [F. J. "Ted"] Batts has arrived with my clothing and Boots. the Boots I am afraid are too small, I can get them on but they are too tight in the in step. I exchanged with Lt. Gilbert for a while but his are too small also, I expect I will have to sell them if I do I will send the money home and get a pair a little larger probably I can get Shoes for the presant, tell Mother I have got as many clothes as I want, if we had to march I would have to throw away some of them, I am very sorry I cant ware those nice new Shirts She sent me if I was to put one on in less than two days I would have a pint of Body Lice on me, I am wareing the linsey drawers sent me, I am wareing the vest Batts Brought me, with this suit on I will not suffer much. There is not a man in the army officer or Private that does not have from a Batallion to a Brigade of Body Lice on him, I could soon get most of them but there is always some filthy man in the camps that perpetuates the race. When they first got on me they pestered me almost to death but now I cannot sleep sound unless I have a few on me well enough of Body lice, We are haveing very pleasant wether now, we have had scarsely any rain this winter but little snow. All is quiet about Fredericksburg the enemy have retired some distance back from the River towards Stafford Court House. the Yankee Pickets say they are tired of the war & opposed to crossing the Rappahannoc. It seems France has a very strong idea of recognizing our Government if She has to go it alone, judgeing from the latest news from Europe, Napoleon tells England She must join him in mediating or he will acknowledge our independence alone. With the Navy of France We can whip, yes subjugate the North in a short time. I have just ben reading Northern extracks. they claim a victory at Murforsboro [Murfreesboro] but admit it was dearly bought. they Say Bragg retired with the air of a conqueror than a Gen that had ben whipped. Batts tells me he heard that John was wounded in the arm in the late fight. arm was not broken, I also heard Bob's Horse was Shot under him, I hope to god it is no worse with them. I am afraid Bob will be too daring in a fight, it will not do to be too bold[.] such men always get killed. Fight as other men fight is the idea, keep in line neither going before or lagging behind do nothing to attract the enemys attention only let them know there is a Solid line of men that can be gaped but cant be broken, is the best policy a man can pursue. Tell some of the gals to write me a love letter and I will Show it to old Bob and get a furlough to go home to get Married. What is Clint Davis doing has he got his company reformed yet or not. What is the letter of Bobs company, whoo is his Col.-Brigadier Gen &—

Write Soon
Your Affectionate Son, W C McClellan

Fredericksburg, Va. January 13
Some talk of another fight at this place, The enemy have ordered all the people out of the city preparing to a big Shelling of the place. Mr Steward & Holland will start home tomorrow on furlough. Fetherston in ala. give my respects to Billy Vaughan and company. tell Old Mrs Robinson I will give her another map for remaining Daughter as soon as I can get home as I understand She is in the Market.

Your Son,
W C McClellan

William Cowan McClellan to his sister

Fredericksburg
Febuary 6th 1863
Dear Sister,
As Sergeant King[19] starts home on furlough to morrow I will write you a few lines by him. I have not received a letter from you since

the third of January, having written repeatedly. We have had dreadful weather in the last few days, had two large snows. last night we had torrents of rain. We had orders last night to listen for signal guns, it appears old [Gen. Joseph] Hooker[20] meditates a night attack as they always get whipped in the day time. the fight will be postponed for a week or two on account of the dreadful condition of the roads. Hooker is bound to fight before long or be recalled and superseaded. I am still on Provost guard at Andersons Head quarters. We sometimes have a gay time pressing Whiskey Brandy, wrestling men Stragling in the country. I am very anxious to hear from John, Bud Cartwright got a letter from his sister stating that John was at Mr Beaties- and was expected to be at home in a day or two. I infer from this that he is at Uncle Davids doing very well. Let me hear from him as soon as possible- furloughs continue to come in slowly in the Reg now. Though Floyd says he will send me next- but in our company as well as all others there are a great many "boot licks"- and an independent white man stands but little chance[.] this paper has no lines concequently it is written a little slanted. Our government has offered 500 dollars bounty to a certain number of men in this army to join the navy, and go over to England and bring over a lot of Iron clad gun boats. the whole army is applying for the transfer to that department.[21] If there was not so many applicants- I would apply my self. Several have applyed in our Regiment. The Richmond papers are lauding our Western Cavalry to the Skyes, probably I can get a transfer after a while if they continue to do well- I am for anything to get out of my present predickament. I have ben away from home so long I have forgotten the names of our nearest neighbors. What is that old fellows name a cross the road oh, up on reflection Brunswick be him. I have ben in Brunswick [County][22] since I landed in Virginia. Where is that little black [illegible] Bill Vaughan. how does he look in lines of a bloody revolution, Poor Smith is among these things that were; So is poor old uncle Harry Davis. John Milton Ancient Poet [John Milton Moore], Still lives. my respects to all of them, and to all the girls in the county- tell them God be with them for I cant- my respects to old Heartwell and the balance of the negroes.

Affectionately your Brother
W. C. McClellan,
Fredericksburg Virginia

William Cowan McClellan to Thomas Joyce McClellan

Fredericksburg Virginia
February 9th 63
Dear Father,
I was very much surprised yesterday to step out of my tent and find Dr. [Richard M.] Dick Fletcher and Sid. The Dr. told me you where all well and getting on very well generally. He said John is at Uncle David Beaties doing very well. This was very gratifying to me. Dick only stopped for ten minutes. to day is Sunday. I am going to try and get a pass tomorrow and go down to the 4th ala. and see him. If I succeed in getting my pass I will send this letter by him. I have written several letters recently sent them all by hand. From all the indications we are going to have a fight here before a great while. Hooker seams determined to do something if he gets a whipping while he is doing it. We have full confidence in our ability to meet successfully any advance the enemy can make. He has the largest Army ever assembled on earth but numbers frequently become the element of weakness rather than strength. We have as many men as can be handled to advantage upon a field. Maj. Gen Stewards [Stuart's] Cavalry Started on some unknown expedition this morning before long we will hear him thundering in the rear of the grand army of the Potomac. They have two or three aids with them. Lee, Longstreet & Jackson are frequently walking around the lines. Jackson and Lee have two or three aids with them. Longstreet is always alone with old head a little inclining, he rides a horse very much like Clint Davis horse Nay. Now is the time to strike for a transfer to Malones Cavalry co. as the western cavalry has made some reputation. I have known several men to be transferred to the west to fill the appointment of Sergeant. I can stand the Winter very well in Infantry but cant stand long marches in the summer. My back is too weak to toat nap Sacks and gun waying 50 pounds. Just use your own pleasure about applying through Col [Thomas Hill] Watts[23] to the Sec of War. If I could I would go to Richmond to see Col Watts on this matter but it is impossible and I dislike the idea of you going if it will cost you money and time boath of which are very precious to you. Well I will dismiss the subject it is very unpleasant. I am glad to hear John is well and fast recovering from his dreadful and unfortunate wound. John will now go study-

ing law for which he has a talent. How would it be with me if I was to loos an arm, poor ignorant man who has misapplied all of my youthful days. I would starve or have to rely on the efforts of somebody else a thing I will never do again if I can possibly help it. My respects to all.

Affectionately your Son
W.C. McClellan

This is Sunday, tomorrow Monday. I will try and go down to the 4th ala and send this letter home by Dr Fletcher. He starts Wednesday for home.

9
Chancellorsville, Virginia, to Gettysburg, Pennsylvania
February 20–July 9, 1863

> It must be very humiliating to the yankees to be whipped so often by our army . . .
>
> —William Cowan McClellan

Athens and Limestone County, Alabama, were occupied again by Union forces in 1863, and in this year the Confederacy reached its zenith before the defeats at Gettysburg and Vicksburg in July. Very few of the original recruits from 1861 hadn't "seen the elephant" by now. In January 1863, the Army of Northern Virginia (including the Valley District of the Shenandoah Valley) numbered 144,614 men and still faced the Army of the Potomac now commanded by Gen. Joseph Hooker.[1] After the successful campaign at Fredericksburg, the Army of Northern Virginia was probably at its peak in terms of manpower, leadership, and effectiveness.

Lee still kept an eye on Hooker, who was threatening to turn Lee's left flank near Chancellorsville, while he also maintained some pressure in the direction of Fredericksburg. The Army of Northern Virginia was spread out in a line between Fredericksburg and Chancellorsville, and the Union commander opened the battle by trying to execute a turning movement on the Confederate left. The 134,000-man Union army held a two to one ratio over Lee's army as Hooker crossed the Rappahannock River on April 29 and positioned his forces between the Wilderness and Chancellor crossroads. On May 1 he advanced his army with the goal of driving Lee southward toward the South Anna River. Lee was able to stop Hooker's turning movement with one of his own, and on May 2 Thomas Jonathan (Stonewall) Jackson's flanking movement drove in Hooker's right flank. Hooker retreated across the river, but Lee was unable to further punish the Union forces.

Also on May 2, Union general John Sedgwick drove Jubal Early's Confederate defenders out of Fredericksburg and toward Chancellorsville, threatening Lee's right flank. The next day Lee ordered a portion of his line to turn and face Sedgwick. Wilcox's brigade, which was a mile upriver, was sent back in time to face the Union attack. The brigade moved eastward down the turnpike to Salem Church, where they went into line across the road by the old church. The 9th Alabama was in the middle of the fight that lasted until dark when the Union forces were halted. Union losses at the Battle of Chancellorsville numbered 17,304 (between April 27 and May 11), and Confederate losses totaled 13,460. Wilcox's brigade suffered 535 casualties, with 113 in the 9th Alabama.[2]

With the victory at Chancellorsville, Robert E. Lee decided to press his advantage into Pennsylvania, and the Confederate troops immediately began to move in that direction. The 9th Alabama was assigned to Richard H. Anderson's division of A. P. Hill's Third Corps. They left Fredericksburg, Virginia, on June 14 to begin the long march to Pennsylvania, sometimes covering as much as thirty miles a day.[3] Crossing the Potomac River, they proceeded to Hagerstown, Maryland, and then on to Greencastle and Chambersburg, Pennsylvania, on June 27. That same day, just before sunset, the 9th reached Fayetteville, Pennsylvania, just at the eastern foot of the Blue Ridge, where they remained until the early hours of July 1.[4] Upon hearing that the Union army had crossed the Potomac, Robert E. Lee instructed A. P. Hill and James Longstreet to proceed east to Gettysburg. The Confederates passed through Cashtown, Pennsylvania, on June 30 and were approaching Gettysburg on July 1. A premature engagement by Henry Heth's Confederate division led to an escalating battle that ended with the Confederates driving the Union forces through the town and onto the ridge beyond it. Anderson's division of 7,100 men (which included the 9th Alabama) was ordered there early to support the growing offensive by Heth's division, but Anderson's division was then ordered by Lee to go into camp as reserves that afternoon.[5]

On the second day of the battle, the 9th Alabama and Wilcox's brigade took up their position near Pitzer's Woods, with the rest of the line running to the south end of Spangler's Woods.[6] Anderson's division was assigned to attack toward the Union right on Cemetery Ridge, after Longstreet's attack began on the Union left flank.[7] Wilcox's brigade was to attack the Union flank after crossing Emmitsburg Road just past the Staub and Spangler farmhouses.[8] The brigade struck Andrew A. Humphrey's Union division, driving them back up the ridge and momentarily opening holes in the line. As successful as they were, the attack started to break down as Wilcox's, Brig. Gen. Carnot Posey's, and Barksdale's brigades became disoriented.[9] Wilcox's brigade was finally halted in its attack by the 1st Minnesota.[10] Wilcox later blamed the failure of the attack on Anderson's inability to provide a supporting line and said that Anderson's brigades attacked "in one thin line."[11]

On the third day of the Battle of Gettysburg, during Pickett's charge, Wilcox's and Brig. Gen. Edward Aylesworth Perry's brigades were supposed to support the advance of General Pickett's forces, and they occupied a position just to the right and in front of the first advancing brigades. According to Edward Porter Alexander, Lee expected Wilcox's and Perry's brigades to provide support for Pickett during his attack on Cemetery Ridge.[12] However, as Pickett's charge unfolded, Wilcox's brigade set out to its right later than it was supposed to (with the 9th Alabama on the extreme right) and came under heavy artillery fire which they were unable to neutralize. In his report, Cadmus M. Wilcox noted, "The advance [by Pickett] had not been made more than twenty or thirty minutes before three staff officers in quick succession (one from the major general commanding division) gave me the orders to advance to the support of Pickett's Division . . . not a man of the division that I was ordered to support could I see."[13] When two lines of Union infantry threatened to flank and destroy them, Wilcox ordered his men back to their starting point at Seminary Ridge. That night the Confederate forces remained in their positions on Seminary Ridge and withdrew the next day to retrace their steps through Cashtown and Chambersburg for Virginia.

The battle of Gettysburg was over, and so was the invasion. However, the Confederates did not see it as a devastating defeat. Many believed that Lee had ordered the withdrawal due to a lack of provisions and ammunition. Anderson's division suffered 2,157 casualties out of 7,136 engaged. Wilcox's brigade had suffered 777 casualties out of 1,726 engaged. The 9th Alabama had 306 men engaged with 3 killed and 55 wounded.[14]

In the same way that he had viewed the Battle of Sharpsburg, William looked at the Gettysburg retreat as a planned withdrawal due to a shortage of ammunition. He gave no indication that he believed it was anything more than just another battle. Some of the other members of his company, however, thought that the North might be successfully turning the tide of battle. As the letters reveal, William still had the spirit to poke fun at his appearance and even the audacity to ask his family to spare one of the slaves on the farm to help him out for a while.

William Cowan McClellan to his sister

Head. Quarters Andersons Division
Fredericksburg Va.
Feb 20 1863
Dear Sister,

Two days ago the enemy crossed the Rappahannock 18 miles above here. that is a cavalry force. They were met promptly by one Brigade of Gen Stewards [Stuart's] Cavalry. A desperate fight insued in which we were Victorious after three hours hard fighting.[15] the enemy were driven a cross the River with great Slaughter. it is Said that the enemy had 4 Brigades of Cavalry engaged. They captured several pieces of Artillery from us but were recaptured.[16] All the indications are at present that the Scene of operations will be changed in the neighborhood of orange courthouse. The Rapidan River will then be the line. At this moment I heard the roar of cannon directly opposite Fredericksburg. Some believe they are fighting among themselves. I believe the Yankees have got Gen. Lee a little puzzled for one time. Two Divisions of our army have been in Petersburg for some time, But I understand this morning that they were ordered back to this place. All the indications are that we will have a desperate fight here in a few days. The Yankees keep two balloons up all day. Send up rockets and beat drums all night. They are a noisy people. Our guard as I said in a former letter has charge of seven convicts who were to be shot on the 14th but all of them have ben respited by the President for an indefinite time or until further orders. One of them an 8th Alabamian's mother arrived here from Mobile a day or two ago. It was an unpleasant sight to see this old lady embrace her condemned son. Some of them will be bound to be shot. I think so. Young Edgeworth a Brother in law of Senator [John W.] Lewis of Georgia one of the best families in Geo. will be shot. His brother Dr Edgeworth ate dinner with me yesterday. It must be awful for parents to know that their children are to be tied to a Stake and Shot like a dog. Capt W. L. Wayland has arrived here, having failed to give bond for his office. Floyd has been appointed in his Stead having given the requisite bond.[17] Poor Wayland. I might rejoice at his down fall if I was as mean as some people but I do not. he never liked me while in the company for opposing him so strenuously when he ran against Gilbert for Lieutenant. My health is very good at present. I weigh 200 pounds and a perfect model of a soldier as far as physical powers are conserned. I am very popular among the Misses of F[redericksburg] and vicinity.

Affect. your Brother
W. C. McClellan

yours of the 31st January came to hand a day or two ago. Write soon tell me something about Uncle William [McClellan]. Ask Mrs Moore what size man Gen Longstreet is the color of his eyes hair. There is a reward out for him.

William Cowan McClellan to Thomas Joyce McClellan

Fredericksburg, Virginia
Head quarters Andersons Division
Provost guard
March 1st 1863
Dear Father,
We have ben preparing to move for several days, somewhere south of town betwean Petersburg and Suffocks [Suffolk]. Hoods and Pickets divisions of Longstreets corps have arrived somewhere not far from Petersburg.[18] Andersons & McLaws[19] will move as soon as the roads will admit of it. Some say we will go to South Carolina. but I dont believe we will go further than Petersburg. The enemy have all left the North bank of the Rappahannoc, supposed to have gone to fortress Monroe and the coast of North and South Ca, Georgia and Alabama. The enemy I think are going to make a desperate effort to gain the southern rout, R. Road at or near Welden N. Ca, by so doing they think they can take Charlestown and Savannah before our forces can reach those points having no railway communication but this like all there plans will be knocked in the head by old Bob Lee and Longstreet both of whoom are down there somewhere. The on to Richmond Song of two years will cease for awhile, it is on to Charlestown and Savannah. The yankee congress has made Lincoln King of their nation haveing power to draft every man in the North Black or White, big old little or young, bartering him five hundred millions of dollars, you will see all this before you receive this letter. the New England yankees are perfectly desperate knowing as they do that they are a doomed people Nationally, commercially and Politically and they are determined to wreck

the remainder of the continent if it is in their cowardly power. I believe as Valingdingham[20] says the North West will eventually withdraw from the eastern States, but I think it will be some time first after too more years of bloodshead and distructions of life and property then the West will join the confederacy they have ben fighting so long if our government will let them. Capt [John P.] Featherstone returned from Linchburg last night after an absence of 70 days having courted all the rich pretty ladys of that city. Miss Anderson, daughter of Maj Anderson was there, She sent me a great many messages of one sort and another. I dont think I ever saw her, Featherstone no doubt tells a great many yarns on me. I think F is after Miss Floyd, a Sister of N.J. Floyd. Capt F. [Featherston] has taken command of the Provost guard, Shelton has gone home on furlough. We have had a greatdeal of Snow in the last month, the last snow we had a week ago Sixteen inches on a dead level. It has not gone yet, night before last we had a big rain makeing the roads impassable. All of our Artillery has gone on the cars to Richmond, Infantry will march to Richmond .60. miles distance. We have had some very exciting times Snow Balling recently. Brigades with generals and cols came out and fight- as thou they were fighting yankees. Hood brought out his division and fought McLaws the fight lasted 6 hours when Hood drove McLaws from his camp achieving a splendid Victory. it is one of the grandest Sights you ever saw to see several thousand men filling the elements with snow. My health is very good at presant. a few days ago I was down with my back, have gotten well. I received a letter from Matilda & Bob. Kittie one dated 23d January the other 9th Febuary, all well John doing very well and at home, the letter stated Rip Daviss children had the measles. poor little Mae likely to die. I have received all my cloaths. I Swapped Boots with Gilbert and got a pair to suit me. I have plenty of cloaths to last me sometime needing nothing. Billy Holcomb has quit the commesary department will be Adjutant of the regiment. Col Henrys time of suspension expired the first of January. the officers of the Reg objected to his taking command. Wilcox Saw the Sec of War and had him indefinitely suspended again. the poor old fellow has Sold his Horse and gone home,- reputation of a lifetime destroyed a[nd] disgraced man,- my opinion is this man has ben rascally treated.- he may not be competent to command a Reg, but he is no coward. he took a musket at Sharpsburg and fought like a turk. some of our men saw a cannon ball cover him up with rails, he scrambled out and kept fireing at the enemy- We will stay here probably several days longer roads being so bad we cant march, direct your letters to this place until we move or you heare from me.

your Affectionate Son
W C McClellan co F 9th ala Vol

William Cowan McClellan to Thomas Joyce McClellan

Fredericksburg. Virginia.
March 3d.63
Dear Father,
I have written time and again to you all scarsly getting a reply. I know it is not negligence on your part that I fail to get letters but the irregularity of the mails. I have given out all idea of a furlough. I have a new plan to propose in order to get home and a transfer also. I understand Clint Davises company is at Huntsville on conscript duty. If he would be so kind as to have me elected or appoint me Seargeant in his co. and draw up a document stating the facts in the case and send it to Col. Watts in Richmond to present to the Sec of War. I have no idea but what it would meet with success. If I could maik such an arrangement I could after getting to the company throw up the office which I would not care a cent about. If circumstances are such that I cannot get a transfer to Clint's company probably I could make the same arrangement in Capt Malones company as I wrote you some time since. No general in the army can prevent me from going to any company in the confederacy to which I have been promoted even to a Seargency. I would write to Capt Davis upon the Subject: but he would do more for you than he would for me asking a favor directly. Our congressman Foster does more for The Soldiers from our State than all the other men from the state put together. I have never known or heard of a letter from an Alabamian going unanswered by Foster always doing something for the Boys as he called them. If you have any Business with Congress call on him and it will be attended to. The enemy have again appeared in strong force on the North bank of the Rappahannock don't think we will leave here for some time. A yankee Pickett told our men yesterday that Vixburg had fallen. Rebel replyed

that is a lie. Hood & Picketts Virginians are down at Petersburg. Nothing more at present.

Affectionately yours
W.C. McClellan
9th Reg ala Vol F. Va

William Cowan McClellan to Thomas Joyce McClellan

Fredericksburg, Virginia
March 8, 1863
Dear Father, Having nothing to do at preasant I will address you a few lines, nothing of any importance to communicate at this time. We have five men in our guardhouse sentenced to be shot on the 14th of this month to death with musketry. The courtmartial of our division sentenced 8 men in the division to be shot, but two of them have been repreaved by Gen. Lee, & President, two are to be shot in the 8th ala. All for cowardice on the Battlefield. They are tightening down on this army on all sides[.] one of the men to be shot is young [Clarence A.] Edgeworth of the 3rd Georgia Reg. he is of a good family[.] Senator [John W.] Lewis of Georgia is his Brother-in-law. I am very sorry for this Boy as I have got well acquainted with him since he has been under guard, a man in our Reg. knocked a man down day or two ago and cut his throat from ear to ear. So you see if they can't get to fight on the Battlefield they will kill one another. It is said now that the Provost Guard will have to shoot these condemned prisoners. I would not do it for five hundred dollars if I could help it. We are listening every day to hear of a battle commencing at Vixburg, and I fear the fall of that place as the enemy has succeeded in the digging of their canals and flooding of the city. The enemy have again reappeared in strong force on the north bank of the Rappahannoc. Consequently we will not leave this place for some time yet, at least not until they do. We have had an immense quantity of rain the last month and several large snows, one 16 inches deep, the largest I ever saw but quite a moderate snow for the country, so say old men. Featherston has arrived from Linchburg where he says he has had a good time with the girls. He is on the guard now but has been ordered back to his company by Wilcox and approved by Lee, so I expect he will have to go. Lt. [Robert R.] Scott of the 8 ala. Will then be in command of

the guard. he is a Scotchman and a very clever gentleman, thorough Soldier having served in the English army 8 years before he joined the confederate army. he is said to be the best Swordsman in our army, great favorite with gen. Wilcox, Anderson, and a strong friend of mine. [Maj. Gen. Earl] Van Dorn has been giving the Yankees thunder in Tennessee, if reports are true. I have written you several letters recently but have not received any in reply. The last one I wrote to you I stated that Clint Davis will appoint me Sergeant in his company, and have me transferred to his company. I have known several men to get transfers on the same grounds. I don't care a [illegible] a bout an office if I will get down in the west with him. Some of these days I will taik a Frenchman's furlough for home. Send me a pair of pants by the first good opportunity. My respects to Bill Vaughan & family, all friends. Tell Kittie I will write to her in a day or too.

Affectionately, Your son,
W. C. McClellan
CO F 9th Reg ala Vol Fredericksburg, Virginia

William Cowan McClellan to his sister

Fredericksburg
March 16th 1863
Dear Sister,
Your kind and lengthy letter that Father kept in his Pocket too weaks has ben received. Bobs account of the Battle of Fort Donelson and M[urfreesboro]. It appears to me we could have taken that place with half the forces we had engaged. I suppose Van Dorn has maid another dash upon them near Franklin, Tennessee capturing we heare it 23 hundred prisoners.[21] I went to a concert in the city last night,- it was a very grand thing. The actors were all from Barksdale Miss[issippi] Brigade. One play was a burlesque on the Yankee generals. Burnside took his seat at his table, called a courier, sent for Gen Sumner [Maj. Gen. Edwin Vose Sumner], consulted Sumner muttering all the time about the Rebel Stewart being in his rear, called again for the courier, whoos spurs rattled powerfully, tell gen Hooker to come here immediately. Hooker came up: Gen Burnside I want to cross the Rappahannoc 20 miles above Fredericks and gain possession of the so Hills on the South Side and the

whole Rebel army cant whip me. Well general I cant spare you from the front, those Rebels might attack me and I have not got more than 200 thousand men and you know it takes 3 to one to whip those Rebels. Hooker says gen I want the place in front. Very well general my place is in the rear, Here comes a courier out of breath with a dispatch. Sumner remarks, guess they are advancing[.] whoo advancing: Jackson, Stewart, Longstreat. Burnside: good God Sumner do you heare the Picketts fireing- useing a big Ball churn for a cannon, firecrackers for musketry. Sumner, Hooker, Burnside are running from one side of the stage to the other, in comes the Rebels, they Shoot down Burnside, Sumner & H. make their escape, instantly they Shift Burnside of his Shoes, coat, Pants and in fact all he has on then drag him behind the Curtain. All break up With applause, of course a very good many ladys in attendance, that is they Wore dresses not much of the Lady. Nothing more at presant, but remain your dearest Brother,

William Cowan McClellan

William Cowan McClellan to Thomas Joyce McClellan

Head quarters 9th Ala Reg.
March 23, 1863
Dear Father
Mr. Neal[22] of our company starts home tomorrow on a furlough having been disabled by a wound received in front of Richmond. Mr. Neal will be a candidate for Judge in Limestone. I will try to speak a good word for him provided John [McClellan] does not run for the office. Neal has a petition from both of the Limestone camps asking the people of said county to vote for him for the office. If I were in Johns place I would run for the office regardless of any body. If he does conclude to be a candidate let me know and I will do all I can for him here. Mr. Neal was shot through the mussle of his right arm at Franklin Farm. I have just received Matildas letter of March 18th speaking of John's health. All of the indications are now that we are to have a bloody time of it this summer. I expect the first move will be made against North Alabama. I think the weakest point in our whole line of defence. I have had a talk with a man from Savannah Georgia from the yarns he tells it will be impossible for the enemy to take that place, he says it is the best fortified city in the world. A gentleman on the Provost Guard who

lives in Petersburg received a letter from there yesterday stating that Longstreet had ordered preparation to be made to receive ten thousand wounded. Hoods Division was at Petersburg but ordered back to this place where within 12 miles of here was ordered back to that city. So you may look for a big fight down on Blackwater south east of Petersburg 20 miles. Our army is in a better condition to fight than it ever was and will make a much better fight than it has ever done. Gen. Lee is in command of this part of the army. Our Division is under command of Longstreet but for some cause or other we were left behind when Longstreet went to Petersburg. My health is now very good better than it has been in my life almost. My affairs with the Ladys are bright and prosperous. I circulate with fish of the first waters. They say I am the best looking Alabamian they ever saw and firmly believe I am one of the biggest cotton farmers in the Gulf states. One lady asked the other day how many negroes I had lost by the Yankees. I told her I did not know exactly but on one of my Plantations I had two and three hundred to leave. A soldier has his pleasures as well as sorrows.

Your Devoted Son
W.C. McClellan

Be careful when you unfold this letter Gilbert put too much sugar in his ink, I suppose he was writing to his sweet heart and put in too much sweeting.

William Cowan McClellan to Matilda McClellan

Fredericksburg, Virginia
March 24th 1863
Dear Sister,
I wrote to Father yesterday all the news. I received your letter of March 9th & 11th. was very glad to hear from home. Sorry to heare of the rapid manner in which our neighbors and friends are departing this life. Have you ever read the Rev. N. T. Davis Book called the campaign from Texas to the Potomac. I am now reading it[.] the parson does not knock the black out every time, as he Says the 4th Texas was the first to break the enemys line at Gains Mills, this was not so. the first hole ever made through the enemys lines was made by the 8th & 9th Alabama Reg. I dont care how many histories they write, this is so because I was there and helped to do it and

saw it with my own eyes. Tell Father to let me know as Soon as possible what he can do for a transfer for me. if he can do nothing let me hear from him and I will never pester any one again on this vexing subject, not that I think he has not done all in his power to aid me in obtaining a transfer. You must write Uncle Will [McClellan] and tell him to write to me. he seems to have forgotten me or I have forgotten him, far from it I think he is one of the best men I ever saw. Tell Uncle David Beatie to write to me also and let me know. you I mean what has become of old Uncle Bery [Beattie] and his charming wife. How does that Bill Wright come on, you must excuse this disconnected and badly written letter.

Your Affectionate Brother
W. C. McClellan

P.S. I have waited two or three hours for Mr. Neal to come by for this letter. I suppose he will go by Fredericksburg concequently I will have to mail it. I was over at the Reg yesterday and wrote a letter by Neal to Father, I have carried your miniature in my pocket so long it has worn out I will have to get a new case for it. I received a letter some time ago from . . . informing me of Johns misfortunes[23] and Bobs exploits, losing the two horses, catching a cannon Ball and throwing it back at the insolent foe, who dared to shoot at him, killing a large number of them. well I am writeing just writeing to be writeing as the boys say have played out,- what has become of old Rush. oh have you heard anything recently of the adorable Fannie Bibb.[24] if you ever see her give her my regards, no doubt you have come to the conclusion that I have gone deranged.

Yours till death,
W. C. McClellan

William Cowan McClellan to Matilda McClellan

Head Gen. Andersons Division
First Army corps.
March 28th 1863
Matilda
Your kind letter of the 15th of March was gladly received yesterday haveing made the trip in ten days. Also one from Bob of a very

recent date giveing me the troubles and bad management of the Malone Battalion from all accounts he is a very presummtious man. Bob says they are all ways overpowered or whipped in every fight that is the Batt[alion] Wiley Webb[25] has got back to the company somewhat crest fallen relative to the Lieutenancy he was to get in the Malone .Bat. they must be hard run in the west if they want such men as Webb for officers, Wiley is about the weakest member in Comp F. Webb says Bob is a buster, very popular with the company & if an election was submitted to the company, would get an office. You say in your letter that John has concluded to run for Judge. I dont think Neal will be much in his way. He is a very ordinary man. You say Mrs Bibb is hard at work making money, dressed out in homespun. I am very glad to hear it. I have come to the conclusion She was the best Friend I ever had at least I have long since forgiven her of an imaginary wrong. tell old Mrs. Graves howdy for me, tell her that William is in fine health, good spirits. In your letter you speak of cloaths, all I need at presant is a pair of Pants, two cotton Shirts, two pair cotton drawers. Pants I need worse than any thing else. I bought an over coat from Featherston for 45 dollars, it is a very warm coat. I never had a coat in Richmond as Fielding told you. Capt. Clint Davis is having a good time collecting conscript. I would give a gooddeal to belong to that squad for a month or so. I would then be close to my dearly beloved. She wrote me all about the death of her Brother, you must not say any thing about this to any one. I am betraying her confidence now but you must not tell this to any one for fear she gets hold of it. I also wrote to Miss Cleopatra a few days ago, by her own request Mr Thompson of our company having seen her while on furlough communicated the fact on his return. I wrote her a very good, friendly letter of about 4 pages of fools cap. no doubt you will hear from this letter but keep silent that you may hear, Miss Maria sends you her kindest regards, Tell Miss Mollie Pettus I frequently think of her and strange to say dreamt the other night that she was desperately in Love with me. Please ask her if this be so. Nothing more at presant.

Your Affectionate Brother
William C McClellan esq,

William Cowan McClellan to Matilda McClellan

Camp Near Fredericksburg, Va
April 13th-1863
Dear Sister,
Your letter of the 31st inst was received a day or two ago concerning the welcome news of the welfare of those at home. I have nothing to write that would interest you, times have never ben so dull to me in the army, no indications of a fight, though the roads have almost dryed up sufficiently to admit of military movements, Why Hooker does not advance is curious to all, probably the Pontoons failed to arrive again. We have ben expecting to hear of the commencement of the fight at Vicksburg, Also an attack on Bragg in Tennessee. I think you are a little too hard on Capt. Clint Davis, he is doing the duty assigned to him, every Soldier will take advantage of Soft places in the army no matter what the people say of them. Maj. Dick Fletcher has just left here, I was asking him something about north Ala. he said every d—n-ed one of the Fletcher Boys had managed to get out of the reach of Bullets. To morrow I will take a squad of men and go about 30 miles up the country hunting Stragglers, deserters, conscripts & whiskey. I will be gone about a week, I have ben acting Sergeant of the Provost Guard for 3 months, a position I do not like as well as Private. This squad is composed of the most moral and intelligent men in the division. Floyd is now quartermaster, there will be an election for Third Lt in our company, there is several candidates for the office among them: Bud Cartwright. I will not run, I will tell you why, before long Cartwright will Stand a very good chance to be elected, My health is very good at this time my respects to all friends.

Your Brother,
W. C. McClellan
Fredericksburg Virginia

Tell mother all I need very bad at this time is a pair of Pants. I have had these I have on patched 3 times, old Mrs Mills says they wont bare it any more, yours W C McClellan Write often

William Cowan McClellan to Matilda McClellan

Head Quarters Andersons Division
April, th22, 63
Dear Sister,
Your kind favor of the 8 of this month came to hand yesterday, apprising me of the good health of you all & Bob being at home on furlough, his scout around Nashville & Murf[reesboro], Safe return to our lines again. Dink Thach. glowing description of the Same. poor Dink is a great hypocrit, better writer than Soldier. he will pray one day to God for forgiveness of his sins, the next day he will get drunk, waller in a mud hole, curse the world and the balance of mankind. Dink is one of the biggest cowards you ever saw. All very quiet along the Rappahannoc at presant. we have had several days fine weather of late, roads in good order. but still old Jo. Hooker fails to advance. We have a report in camp that Longstreet with 4 divisions has completely surrounded the enemy at Suffolk, escape being impossible[26] Also that D. H. Hill has the yankees cut off at Washington N. C. & but neither report can be relyed on. Vicksburg being abandoned. Bragg giving way inch by inch to the enemy in Tennessee, Signal repulse of the Yankee fleet at Charlestown, S. C.[27] By a letter one of the Cartwrights received from home I learn that Neal of our co. has declined running for the office of Judge. the Boys, most of them will write to their friends to vote for John. In the last number of Illustrated News you will find a likeness and Sketch of the life of Brigadier Gen. C. M. Wilcox in the battles of Mexico and the present Revolution. Speaking in high terms of the Gallantry of his old Regt the 9th Alabama. Why Wilcox does not get promoted is a mistery to every body, to day he ought to be in command of Braggs army in the west. I think the people of North Ala ought to petition to the President to transfer him and his Brigade down there, he would show those gens. how to flank a Hill, and charge a Battery. My health very good, cloaths good save pants. They have ben patched three times now show a little too much of my person. Body Lice are very plentiful now, I pulled off a Shirt last night and threw it down, this morning I saw it moveing first one way, then another. I thought at first that it was a rat under it, but upon inspection found it was the lice moveing about hunting a poor Soldier.

Your Affectionate brother
W. C. McClellan
Fredericksburg, Virginia

William Cowan McClellan to his sister

Fredericksburg, Virginia
April 30th 1863
Dear Sister,
Your letter of the 16th inst came to hand a few days ago, giveing me the news of the country. All is in a bustle here now, the enemy have crossed the River in two places, 4 miles below the city and at Elys Ford 15 miles above, So they have turned our left flank without any resistance. our line of Battle is 4 miles up the plank road.[28] We are looking for Longstreet to land at Orange courthouse. if he can make the connexion, the Yankees will be the worst whipped people in the world, all agree that a dreadful struggle is at hand, the army of Northern Virginia is called upon to meet superior numbers. they will prove equal to the task. Stonewall is confronting a large number of the enemy below town, they are formed clost to the banks of the River. Jacksons line in full view a mile and a half off awaiting the proper time to strike. In five days from now annother great Battle will be recorded in the history of this Bloody revolution- hope a victory to the Southern confederacy. This is the lull before the Storm old Stonewalls guns will signal the attack. I wish old Jim L[ongstreet] would hurry up, he is the man that always takes the Bull by the horns, I will wait a few minutes and see what turns up. 2 oclock P.M. fireing has commenced on Jacksons lines boom boom goes the cannon, bang bang the musketry, come on Longstreet. the pride of Alabama, the fighting cock of the confederacy, come on and take the Bull by the Horns. While Stonewall and the ballance of the little dogs nibble at his tail legs and flanks, Wilcox Brigade is Still at Bankses' ford six miles above the city. All quiet at that point. You will receive on the wires the result of this mighty Struggle be fore this reaches you.

W. C. McClellan

William Cowan McClellan to his sister

Fredericksburg. Virginia
May 8th 1863
Dear Sister,
Again the army of Northern Virginia is engaged in conflict with the foe. Some days ago Longstreet & Ewells corps crossed the Rap-

pahannoc at Kellys ford, makeing for the rear of Hookers army. They have had an engagement with the enemy resulting in our favor;[29] it is said A. P. Hills corps remained here day before yesterday. The enemy crossed a mile and a half below Fredericksburg. We offered but little resistance to their crossing. They have not advanced from the River all day yesterday. they lay under the banks afraid to show themselves on the open plains in front of our rifle pits and Batteries. last night they threw up a line of Rifle pits, along the River for a mile. I dont think they will advance on our fortifications, if they do certain distruction awaits them. They are not ready for aggressive movements- They have crossed the River to delay our movement & to keep us from joining Longstreet & Ewell, between Culpeper and Manassas our army is on the forward movement all of our force from the Black water & Suffolk have come up, the yankees have with drawn their forces from those two points. They are evidently uneasy about Washington. We have all lost sight of Vicksburg,[30] let her Slide. My health is very good, in closed you will find a communication in the Richmond Sentinel relative to Wilcox Brigade, no reply to a piece written some time ago by our chaplain relative to our Regiment and the Brigade in the Battle of Salem Church. There is a greatdeal of feeling between theas two Regt, our Boys devil the 10th Ala Boys all the time. you will see by this document that our Regt is looked upon as the most gallant Regt in the Services by the admission of one of the other Regts, the 10th ala is a very good Regt but she always runs. Send me some cloaths by Lt Gilbert when he comes, Pants, Jacket, two shirts, two drawers.

Yours in great haste
W. C. McClellan

William Cowan McClellan to Thomas Joyce McClellan

Fredericksburg, Va.
May 10, 1863
Dear Father,
By the blessings of god the army of Northern Virginia has gained another glorious Victory. by far the most Signal victory of the war [at the Battle of Chancellorsville]. The enemy utterly demoralized driven across the River at all points, for seven long days did our noble army beat back the foe from hills, from rifle pits, swamps and all natural barriers that obstruct our passing. On the 29 of April Hooker

crossed his army over the Rappahannock 4 miles below the city. Same place they crossed in December fronting Jackson having but little difficulty in getting his force across. He remained quiet all day on the bank of the River not daring to advance on a Stonewall, that night Hooker crossed the River 12 miles above F . . . [Falmouth] driveing our men who were building a bridge across the River at Elys Ford before them finally capturing the whole party. On they came down the plank road driveing [William] Mahone, Poseys Brigade[31] of our division rapidly before them towards Fredericksburg. Thease Brigades were stationed at U.S. Ford two miles down the River from Elys Ford. On the 13th the enemy withdrew his forces 4 miles below the city. Seaming to concentrate his Whole army at Chancellorsville on the plank road 10 miles from F. [Falmouth]. Jacksons army came on up Also A. P. Hills corps. We formed our line five miles east of Chancellorsville, ran half way around between Chancellorsville and Falmouth. On the first day of the month they appeared in site of our Works Which were hastily thrown up. We waited all day and night old Stonewall came up looked at the map a few minutes, asked a few questions about the direction of the plank road and He studied about five minutes and said forward your division Gen. Anderson. over the works and in went Andersons Division Save Wilcox Brigade which was left two miles above town to guard Banks Ford. Anderson drove them 4 miles. They having fell back to a very strong position in a mile and a half of Chancellorsville. On Saturday evening Gen. Anderson took Poseys Miss. Brigade charged a powerful Battery of the enemy. A Regt supporting the Battery threw down their arms and surrendered. The Miss. so eager to pursue others that ran on started after them they had got about 30 paces when an officer of the Yankee Reg that had surrendered told his men to fire into them. They did so killing a great many of the Mississippians. Old Posey ordered them to about face, they then turned upon the Scoundrels and killed one thousand of them. Sunday our forces drove the enemy back to Chancellorsville where they threw up fortifications and placed in a good position 50 pieces of Artillery. We brought up an equal number in position not quite so good as theirs. The Ball opened and never I reckon since the invention of gunpowder has so much ben burned in an hour and a half. The enemy gunners many of them ran and left their Batteries While every few minutes our shells would Blow up their casions. amid this terrible conflict of arms both large and small. Stonewall Jackson the greatest man probably on the continent threw a shell directly from their flank in their Rifle Pits directly another came from their rear. Jackson went forth from every Yankee tongue as they broke pellmell for the woods. Three Yankee Regt surrendered to Jackson. Stonewalls guns fired rapidly and so did ours. I saw many an oak tree as large as my body shot in two three times while the ground was plowed up in all directions. I counted 36 very fine Battery Horses lying in a field. One of them I noticed received a Bomb in his Bowells his guts hung in strings in the tops of trees while their contents was probably scattered over hundreds of acres. Here we captured one of the finest Batteries the enemy had, all Napolean guns.[32] Hooker now found himself driven back to the River with no alternative save a hollow square. With one Side resting on the River. Wagons and ordinance trains in the distance. In this dreadful condition Hooker like a good gen[eral] ordered his 10th army corps commanded by Sedgewick & Meade[33] across the River at the city at night, to storm Marees [Marye's] Heights and come up in Bob Lees rear. We had one division to defend this point of the line commanded by Maj. Gen. Early. he managed the affair very badly and let them flank him on the rite. consequently he had to give up the Stone fence and heights.[34] Wilcox Brigade which was a mile up the River was almost surrounded. When they received orders to fall back to the brick church 2 1/2 miles from town. Earlys men fought very badly running like scared cattle. Wilcox formed his men at Salem Church the enemy in full view coming at a double quick. up they came. the 10th Ala whose right wing rest on the left wing of the 9th Ala gives way. They can't stand and face 4 columns of Yankees. They run at Drainsville and in front of Richmond. The only ala Reg I ever saw to run. Wilcox voice rang out look at that damned 10th. The 9th ala the enemy had now got within 30 paces of our Regt- one solid sheet of flame arose from this noble Reg. the enemy waver and return the fire with great effect. Our Boys send another volley into their thick ranks they seem to be paunch thick. Our Boys brings a loud yell, the 8th, 11th, 15th and part of the tenth reply and they charge through three quarters of a mile only stopped by Wilcox. When the 9th was delivering her volley into the enemy ranks Maj. Gen. McClaws asked Gen. Wilcox what Regt that was. General Wilcox told him he says that is the best Regt I ever saw old W[ilcox] yes Gen that is the best Reg on the American continent.[35] Next day

Gen Lee came down to F[redericksburg] With Andersons and the balance of McLaws divisions. The enemy were flanked and driven pell mell into the River cleaning out the whole concern upon our return to Chancellorsville found that A.P. Hill had driven fighting Jo Hooker in and across the River. Since writing the above I have been to Guinea Station 12 miles distance from here to bring back some stragglers. I still belong to the Provost Guard consequently I did not have to go into the fight. Though we were under the shelling all of the time. Spurning up the stragglers and receiving yankee prisoners. I am Seargeant of the Guard. On Sunday after the fight I took down the names, co. and Regt of 11 hundred and fifty yankees, guarded them with 20 men. Our Regt had 24 men killed dead on the field 83 wounded. the heaviest loss of any Regt in the division. Our company had one man killed 18 wounded. Orderly Sgt Batts was killed, he was one of the best friends I ever had, as brave and generous as a man can be. He told me all of his plans. I told him mine. Poor Ted is no more. Oh what feelings crawled upon my memory yesterday as I stood beside his shallow grave and thought of the words he spoke to me a few days ago. While talking a week together he says Mc the next fight I get into I am going to distinguish myself or fall. Poor Ted has paid dearly for going beyond most men. The Cartwrights- both came out safe. Lt. Gilbert slightly wounded in the breast. Poor Bob Menefee was killed.[36] Jimmy Cane[37] slightly wounded in arm. Capt [W. C.] Murphey of Mobile killed. The worst is to be told yet. Gen. Jackson lost an arm left arm shot through rite hand. he was expected to die yesterday. he and Gen. Hill rode up within 30 paces of the enemy. Two of Jacksons aides were killed. A. P. Hill slightly wounded in hand.

Your son,
W.C. McClellan
Fredericksburg Virginia

William Cowan McClellan to Thomas Joyce McClellan

Fredericksburg Virginia
the 15th May___63
Dear Father,
We have won a glorious victory yet heaviness is on the heart of our people. The laurel is twined with cypress and the keen sense of joy

which the news of the Rappahannoc is now carrying to every home in the land will be dulled and damped by the feeling that this triumph has cost us the life of Jackson.[38] Upon every Soldiers countenance in the army rests a Shade of sadness not withstanding we have just gained one of the greatest victories of the war. A Seargeant that came over the River yesterday to attend to his wounded, said Burnside met with a reverse in December, but says he Hooker has got the worst whipping a man ever toated. When you consider the fact that Hooker had 160 thousand men while Lee had but 60 thousand, does it not look surprising that we should whip them. The enemy up to last accounts Say Longstreet was here, when they find their mistake that Gen Longstreet and three Divisions of his corps were at Suffolk it seems to me it will be very humiliating, but he and all of his troops are here now for I saw the old war horse ride by an hour ago looking as fat as a hog and Stern as a mud fence. God grant that he may live till the end of our troubles. All quiet along the River, the enemys Balloons up looking to see if Old Bob is crossing. The wounded have all been sent off, the dead burried and the Army of Northern Virginia ready to whip the Army of the Potomac again if General Lee Says So. Tell old Gen Bragg for Gods Sake not to let the Yanks whip him as he generally does when his army gains a victory. no doubt he has better fighting men to contend with than we have, but the cause of this is we have whipped the yankees so much they cant fight, prisoners Say that if our men start at a Battery they had just as well leave, that our Boys were never known to Stop. Northern papers speaking of the fight Says Rodes and his gallant Alabamians drove their eleventh corps over a mile, by the by Rodes has ben made a Maj. Gen. Since the Battle.[39] Wilcox Brigade lost more men than any Brigade. the division and our Division did more fighting than any other Div in the army. the loss of our Reg was 108 killed & wounded. I am very anxious to hear how John came out, I received Matildas letter of the first of this month, I got a good pair of Pants during the fight, our Brigade killed many a yank in Miss Mumas yard. She escaped While Shells were screaming through the yard. I went over yesterday and found her up Stairs, While the lower floors were covered with wounded bodys of the Jersey Boys.

William Cowan McClellan to his sister

May 15th 1863
Dear Sister,
Your kind letter of the first may came to hand yesterday, from reports during the fight here I feared the enemy had again occupied our country, how glad I was when I learned Forrest[40] had driven them back, So far you may consider yourself fortunate, compared with the ladys of this section, during this fight Some of them were between the artillery of the too armys running to and fro like horses not knowing which way to go. My health is very good, got tolerable good clothes & My respects to all

Your Affectionate Brother
W. C. McClellan
Fredericksburg Virginia

—till the cows come home.

William Cowan McClellan to Sarah Anne McClellan Davis

Fredericksburg, Virginia.
May 19th 1863
Dear Sister, Sallie Davis
I received your kind letter of the 26th ult. and would have replyed to it ere this but have not had time to turn around, having gone through one of the biggest Battles of this war. Also as usual gained a glorious victory for almost the 20th time. We fought this time over three hundred men to our one, all of the same if there had been five to one this army cant be whipped. The Yankees say Jackson outflanked a flank movement of theirs. I tell you Sally it was grand when Jackson came up in their rear or flank and faced to the east while A. P. Hill faced to the west. At the dawn of the day Stonewall Jacksons men raised a shout that went from one end of his line to the other, it was answered by Hills and too Divisions of Longstreets corps on this side. Some yanks knew they were gone up, they now admit that our soldiers are better fighting men than theirs in the open fields. They say Brigadier Gen Rodes and his gallant Alabamians ran their eleventh corps too miles. This was a mistake. Rodes was acting Maj. Gen. during the fight. Col. Oneal was in command of his Brigade that did this glorious fighting, you must re-

member that Oneal was Major of our Regt ages ago.[41] Alabama has nobily sustained her reputation in the war this last fight. So has the gallant Boys from our Sister state Mississippi. They love each other more probably than any other state. Confide in each other. When in line of battle you will hear the Boys begin to inquire who is on our rite. Poseys Missippians all rite go ahead. Give my respects to Mr. Davis Mac, Jesse P. and little Sue. Write soon and often

Your affectionate Brother,
W.C.McClellan,
Provost Guard. Andersons Division

P.S. We have heard that we had won a glorious victory at or near Jackson Mississippi. dont believe it is so. Such news from the west another mistake in the printer.[42]

William Cowan McClellan to his sister

Fredericksburg Virginia
May 19th 1863
Dear Sister,
Your kind letter of May first came duly to hand giving me a great deal of news of importance[.] Stamppeed of the citizens of Athens & we have just received the account of Forrests brilliant exploits through Ala and the capture of the thirteen hundred prisoners with only five hundred men near Rossie Georgia.[43] We have news here that the enemy has advanced within a few miles of Jackson Miss. driveing our forces before them. if they advance 10 miles further they will take the R. Road over which our army at Vicksburg gets their Supplies. I understand by a letter Bud Cartwright received dated the 6th of May that John was beaten by Tyus[44] for Judge 19 votes, this Shows how the enlightened people of Limestone appreciate the Services of a man who has lost his right arm fighting for their liberties, this world is a huge mass of ignorance and our ungreatfulness. Bud Cartwright has been elected third Lieutenant in our company, you will be a little surprised at this as he was a recruit having left home a year after the company did, too of the old members of the co[mpany] ran against him for the office: Sart. Tucker, Labreere [William Lebarreare]. I knew nothing of the election until too days after it was over. We have got three of the easi-

est, slowest Lts. now out, Gilbert, Baugh, Ca.[Cartwright] good fellows though neither of them has been mad Since the war commenced. All quiet along the lines, no demonstrations of the Part of Poor fighting Jo Hooker, old Bob has settled his hash for him, If the army of the West were worth a goober, we would soon have Peace on our own terms. Send my clothes by the first man passing. I need them now when I go to see Miss Maria. Bless her sweet little soul, the yankees came a very near getting her. I believe my transfer to Cavalry has died a natural death, well it does not matter a great deal. I dont want to go home half as bad now as I did a few months ago, probably by the end of this year I would not go home if I had an opportunity. I received Bobs letter to the Advocate, very good letter. yours truly

W. C. McClellan

William Cowan McClellan to his sister

Fredericksburg
May 28 1863
Dear Sister,
Your kind favor of the 22d came to hand yesterday, having maid the trip in five days. I have no news of importance to write relative to the army or anything else. All quiet although we had orders yesterday to be ready to move out at a moments notice. This is election day with the Virginians for congressmen and Governor. Col. extra Billy Smith is a candidate for Governor of this state.[45] We poor Alabamians stood by with our fingers in our mouths not a word to say we have been in the State two years and I think ought to be allowed to vote in the old dominion. I was very much surprised to hear of Johns defeat for Judge, glad to hear that Bob has got an office. Yesterdays dispatch paper stated that Pemberton had repulsed the enemy six times at Vicksburg with great slaughter, while Joseph Johnston was clost in their rear.[46] All of our army have great confidence in gen. Johnston. I feel however down. more depressed in Spirits than I have for many a day, why I do not know. I hope it is no forboding of evil. The future looks Black, the past Brown, presant Brown.

your Brother
W.C. McClellan

William Cowan McClellan to his sister

Fredericksburg. Virginia.
June 11th. 63
Dear Sister,
All quiet here, occasionally a Shell comes screaming across the valley from the enemys Batteries on this side of the River. What the enemy intends to do is a mistery to all, I suppose, save Lee. Three or four days ago, the yankees crossed the River and commenced throwing up breast works along the River bank. this is a mile and a half below Fredericksburg, here the River bottom is a mile wide, our line of fortifications extend along the heights. They certainly dont expect to dig us out of our Rifle pits, and so far as storming our works are concerned, that is preposterous in the extreme. we can whip them in the open field. The day before the yankees crossed here Longstreet and Ewells forces crossed the Rapidan at Raccoon ford. this is a flank movement on the part of our men consequently we are looking every day to see these lads cross the River and Skedaddle towards Washington; We have about 28 thousand men here and one third of our army commanded by A. P. Hill. Gen Lee is up in Culpeper with Longstreet & Ewell. Wilcox Brigade is at its old position, Banks ford two miles above the town. Balloons were up all day yesterday in front of the ford. Wilcox last night ordered two long range guns to a commanding point to give them a Shot, but the wind has ben blowing so much they cant go up in the Balloons. It must be very humiliating to the yankees to be whipped so often by our army, only one third their number. See them now as I lookout of this window cowering in their ditches afraid to move hand or foot. See then how they Scamper when our Shell flys over their heads, pulling down their tents, the only protection they have from the hot rays of the sun, poor devils you have got no sand in your craw. look at our Boys as they mount the embankment waiveing their hats, come on you d—n cowardly scoundrels, face the music you blue bellys. dispatches from Vicksburg of the 9th state that Pemberton was Still holding out boldly,[47] Banks, Stonewall Jacksons commessary had ben defeated at Port Hudson.[48] Kirby Smith taken Millikins Bend[49] cutting (I write this in very great haste, you might suppose) off Grants Supplies & Great Peace meetings in New York. 30 thousand people in attendance, Fernando Wood made a Peace

speech.[50] Times look a little bright now Richmond papers talking of an armistice being proposed by our enemys. They Say we ought to expect it as a respite could do us no harm, I am like Col. Parham of the .41.st Va[51] who was in the last fight, his men fired two or three Volleys into the yankees and they fell back, they Started to advance, he said hold on boys, by god let them brown awhile and come again, by god we can whip hell a mile and forty. They were in an open field. My health is very good. I am still on Provost Guard.

Your Affectionate Brother
William Cowan McClellan

William Cowan McClellan to Thomas Joyce McClellan

Culpeper Court House
June 17th [1863]
Dear Father,
We left Fredericksburg three days ago, arrive at this place last night. Will move on towards Winchester in a few minutes. A courier just from Winchester says Ewell thrashed Milroy out of his Boots a day or two ago, capturing 3 thousand prisoners, 11 hundred head of horses, all of the Artillery belonging to Milroys command.[52] I think Ewell will prove a second Jackson, the enemy have fallen back near old Manassas, probably another great Battle will be fought on the old stomping ground. I dont think the enemy will stop this side of the Potomac, if they do they will get a glorious thrashing. old Bob Lee frequently rides by with his hat off for a mile while the Rebels send up cheer after cheer. Well I must close and put on my napsack for Winchester I suppose, &

Your Affectionate Son,
W.C. McClellan

P.S. I just saw Bud Mc. he is well, Maj Buchanan & Miller, Blake.[53] Weather very hot. off we go good bye

William Cowan McClellan to Thomas Joyce McClellan

Gettysburg Pa.
July 4, 1863
Dear Father,
We left Fredericksburg on the 14th of last month traveling from 10 to 12 miles a day, by Culpeper C. H. across the Blue Ridge up the Shenandoah valley to Winchester where Gen Ewell captured nearly all of Milroys army. [Gen. Robert Huston] Milroy made his escape by assuming the garb of a Citizen. We crossed the Potomac on the 24th, stayed on the Battlefield of Sharpsburg that night, next day we Struck out up the Pike for Hagerstown. Md. from Hagerstown to Chambersburg Penn., from C, to Fayetteville at the foot of the Blue Ridge on the Baltimore Pike, next day we crossed the Ridge and found the enemy in a powerful Position 5 miles from the foot of the mountain. Gen Lee attacked them on the first of July, drove them through Gettysburg. on the 2nd our army charged the powerful position of the enemy, took nearly all of their guns, by some means or other we had no Support, the consequence was a Brigade to the right of Wilcox gave way, this compelled Wilcox to fall back to keep the enemy from flanking him and comeing up in his rear. Barksdales Miss Brigade was the one that gave way, so you may judge that it was a hot place. On the third days fight we charged them again in the breast works, our men took the works but could not hold them. Wilcox Brigade planted their flag on the fortifications again but had to fall back. our loss was very heavy. Bud Cartwright was missing, Some say he had his leg Shot off in falling back, he fell into the hands of the enemy. Capt [Gaynes C.] Smith was wounded and taken prisoner. Capt King commanding the 9th was wounded. Featherston was wounded, in fact all of the officers in the Regt Save 7 were wounded or killed. Night of the 4th we fell back towards Hagerstown Maryland.

Hagerstown Maryland, July 8
We have arrived here safe & the Potomac is six miles off and very much swollen, cant cross for several days yet. One of the reasons of our fall back was we had no cannon shot, whether or not we have got any yet I cant say, it is still raining. Two of our guards were

wounded by shells. Thank God I am still alive and ready to go into the foremost ranks if need be.[54]

Nothing more at Presant, Your Devoted Son
W C McClellan Hagerstown, Maryland

William Cowan McClellan to his sister

Hagerstown, Maryland.
July 9th 1863
Dear Sister,
I wrote to Father yesterday as there is a mail going out tomorrow. I will write again. we have ben lieng still for a day or two awaiting the approach of the foe, but he does not come, some man saw a Northern paper which admits a loss of 40 thousand men. So I dont blame them for not following up. I have it from a good source that Gen Lee fell back because his Artillery ammunition gave out. We were only repulsed chargeing their entrenchments, not defeated either, but after takeing them we were not able to hold them.[55] Our line of march through Pennsylvania was attended with many amuseing incidence. The people seemed to think that the Rebel army would eat them up without salt or bread, many of them actually begging for their lives. We played the wild with all of the Featherd tribe: Onions, all garden vegetables, pressed all the Horses & Cattle. The people in this part of Penn have the finest Barnes, largest Horses, fattest Cattle, finest grass and more whiskey than any people in the world, it is the same case in West Maryland. I am now sitting in a barn 60 by 40 feet, basement story used for Stable, third story filled with hay clover, while the second story has a beautiful poplar floor ready to receive the presant crop of wheat, which is fast being destroyed by the dirty Rebels, now in the proper state for harvesting. The people think it is awful to have to submit to this destruction of property, but we point them to the desolate plains of old Virginia and various places in the confederate states of America. they then curse old Abe Lincoln and his government and say they ought to be hung. The mass of the people in Southern Penn are the most ignorant beings in the world. They dont care how long the war lasts so they are not troubled, but do as we take their cows, and horses, chickens. if you want to see their dutch temper show to advantage have an old fellow say, god darn. Hell took all mine tinks, me dont

fight, me say no fight, me Secess[ionist]. When we first got to Chambersburg Penn the women would not look at a Rebel, they would turn up their nose and toss their heads to one side as contempuously as if we were high way Robers, we stayed three days at C. when we left many of them would ask the Boys to come back and see them the first opportunity. many of the Boys where engaged to be married to them and doubtless would have Married them in three more days. We are now encamped in a mile of Hagerstown Maryland, one of the most fertile and beautiful countries in the world. The people in this part of the State are about divided, some for the North some for the South. Gen Lee makes no difference in his treatment towards them, union and disunion, all receive the same treatment, property all respected and protected. Some Soldiers will depredate occasionally in spite of orders. Alabamians very bad at this, so Mississippians. The Boys Say old Abe has ben trying to bring us back into the union a long time, has at last succeeded. You would laugh now if you could see me, elbows out, seat of my pants out, a great big greasy Spot on my hip where my haversack hung, an old yankee cap, one shoe worn out, beard about an inch long, have the Same, thin in order, all of that flesh I had on me at Fredericksburg has ben marched off. If you all could spare Henry a while, he could be of great benefit to me to bring me some cloaths out here and help me along a while, until next winter when I intend to go home, if it coast me a barrell Shirt. Head shaved and so on. Bud Cartwright was among the missing in the late Battle. One man said he saw him with his leg shot off but it is uncertain. Capt [Gaynes C.] Smith was wounded and a prisoner. [William] Hub Malone & Marion Harvey,[56] Bart Eagin were killed, great many wounded. Tom .C. [Cartwright] was not hurt. A. Martin unhurt. Write soon and often, our letters are carried 125 miles by Horse back, Staunton, Va.

Your Brother
W C McClellan

10

Orange, Virginia, to Petersburg, Virginia

August 22, 1863–October 1864

> A temporary gloom now spreads itself over the country . . .
>
> —William Cowan McClellan

With the losses at Gettysburg and Vicksburg in July 1863, the Confederacy faced its darkest hour. By September, Confederate general Braxton Bragg was forced to evacuate Chattanooga as Union major general William S. Rosecrans flanked his defenses. Pres. Jefferson Davis and Gen. Robert E. Lee sent Gen. James Longstreet to Tennessee to help Bragg shore up his forces. On September 18, the Confederates under Bragg attempted to cut off Rosecrans from his Chattanooga base at Chickamauga Creek in north Georgia. It was a tactical victory for the South and a lift for the Southern public. The South, however, had taken 18,454 casualties (and the North 16,170)—numbers they could not afford to lose. Rosecrans still had Chattanooga, and Bragg would fail to follow up on his victory at Chickamauga.[1]

With Longstreet in Tennessee and Lee still suffering from the losses at Gettysburg, Lincoln and Maj. Gen. Henry Wager Halleck pressured Maj. Gen. George Meade to take direct action against Lee. Halleck, tired of hearing from Meade that Richmond and the Shenandoah valley were the army's objectives, warned that "Lee's army is the objective point."[2] Meade preferred to push Lee away from Washington and the Shenandoah Valley and back to the defenses of Richmond. After the Union loss at the Battle of Chickamauga, however, Halleck sent reinforcements west to Rosecrans, which removed the pressure for Meade to move forward. In the meantime, hoping to catch Meade out in the open and crush his army, Lee began his own flanking movement on October 9 against Meade. Lee also hoped the movement would discourage further reinforcements of Union troops being sent west.[3]

Meade fell back and avoided Lee; and, at the same time, he was able to inflict heavy casualties on A. P. Hill's lead division that blundered into a trap at Bristoe Station on October 14.[4] Around Thanksgiving Day, Meade attempted to turn Lee's position to the east but ran into a firmly entrenched Confederate position at Mine Run and was forced to withdraw across the

Rapidan River.[5] Throughout the late summer and into the first week of December, both Lee and Meade attempted to turn the other's flank and to drive each other back toward their respective capitals. What resulted was a continuation of the stalemate that had plagued Union operations in Virginia since the start of the war. Lincoln could not find a general who understood that Lee's army was the target and not Richmond.

Throughout late 1863 and 1864, William remained with the provost guard in Anderson's division, and the 9th Alabama was still in Wilcox's brigade of Richard H. Anderson's division of A. P. Hill's 3rd Corps. With Wilcox's promotion to major general, replacing Dorsey Pender who was fatally wounded at Gettysburg, Col. John Caldwell Calhoun (or J. C. C.) Sanders was put in temporary command of the brigade. But on September 10, 1863, Abner M. Perrin was promoted to brigadier and assumed command of Wilcox's brigade.[6] Along with Wilcox's promotion, the promotion of J. Horace King to colonel of the regiment led to a great dissatisfaction among the men, which contributed to low morale and a string of desertions continuing for the next year. The men had great respect for Wilcox, more than they would have for any other officer, and Wilcox's promotion was difficult for the men to accept. King was one of several commanders of the 9th that the men did not respect. In the battles during the fall of 1863, the 9th was not directly involved in the actions at Bristoe (October 9–22); at Rappahannock Station on November 7; or at Mine Run (November 26–28). At the end of November the brigade went into their winter cabins about two miles from Orange Court House.

William got a real morale booster when he received a furlough to go home in December 1863. His furlough was for thirty days, but it took him one week each way to travel to and from Virginia. In addition to visiting his parents, he stayed with relatives and friends while traveling through Alabama. Although he wanted to remain longer at home, William was concerned about overstaying his leave and arriving late back at the front.

In March 1864, everything would change when Maj. Gen. Ulysses S. Grant assumed command of the Union army and came to Virginia to personally lead the assault on Lee's army. In Grant, as opposed to Meade, Lincoln found the general that understood how to beat Robert E. Lee and the Army of Northern Virginia: constant fighting and the destruction of Confederate communications and railroads.[7] By late 1864, Grant would have forced Lee into a defensive perimeter around Richmond, extending from Williamsburg Road on the east side of Richmond to Hatcher's Run to the southwest of Petersburg.

In May 1864, the 8th, 9th, 10th, 11th, and 14th Alabama regiments served in Perrin's brigade of Richard H. Anderson's division.[8] On May 5–6, the armies of Ulysses S. Grant and Robert E. Lee collided along the Orange Plank Road in the Battle of the Wilderness, beginning what would be thirty days of hard fighting and a longer confrontation between the two armies that would last until Appomattox Court House. During the Overland Campaign, which saw fighting between May 4 and June 12, one battle led to another at the Wilderness, Spotsylvania Court House, the North Anna River, Cold Harbor, and Trevilian Station. Whether he lost or won, Grant kept constant pressure on Lee, and he spent the summer of 1864 maneuvering to turn Lee's right flank in an attempt either to destroy Lee's army or to force it to go into the ground in defense of Richmond.

During the Battle of the Wilderness, the 9th was on the extreme left of the Confederate line and saw little action. At Spotsylvania C Court House on May 12, the 9th followed the rest of the brigade into the Bloody Angle, where Brig. Gen. Abner M. Perrin was killed (J. C. C. Sanders would replace Perrin as brigade commander). The 9th was not directly involved with the fighting at North Anna and Cold Harbor between May 20 and June 3. Wilcox's late brigade (Sanders's brigade) left Cold Harbor on June 15 and camped at Chaffin's Bluff. They were later marched to the defenses at Petersburg on June 18, and upon arrival, they were placed in the division of Gen. William Mahone.[9]

For the rest of the war, the 9th Alabama would remain along the Richmond and Petersburg line, being moved periodically from one end to the other in response to Union attacks. The regiment (as part of Sanders's brigade) participated in stopping the Union drive on the Weldon and Petersburg Railroad on June 22.[10] Grant had attempted to extend the siege lines to the southwest of Petersburg, only to be turned back by A. P. Hill's 3rd Corps.

On July 30 at 5:45 a.m., the powerful explosion of a Union mine occurred beneath Elliott's Salient on the east side of Petersburg. The explosion left a crater 170 feet by 80 feet and 30 feet deep, and it killed about 300 soldiers. The Union attack that followed was repulsed by a counterattack led by General Mahone, which included the 9th Alabama.[11] The 9th was also involved with the actions at Poplar Springs Church (Battle of Weldon Railroad) on August 21,[12] when Union general G. K. Warren occupied more than a mile of the Weldon Railroad south of Petersburg. Warren's forces were attacked by A. P. Hill's corps that included Sanders's brigade. The Confederate attack was not successful, and Union forces kept possession of the Weldon Railroad. On October 27, Maj. Gen. Winfield Scott Hancock's and Warren's corps attempted to move on the South Side Railroad about twelve miles southwest of Petersburg. Confederate infantry under Henry Heth and William Mahone (including the 9th Alabama) stopped the Union drive at Burgess's Mill (also known as Boydton Plank Road or Hatcher's Run).[13]

Gradually, after earlier invasions into Pennsylvania, Kentucky, and Tennessee, the Confederate armies were now pushed back into their own inner defenses. The war would now be fought in and around the cities of Nashville, Atlanta, Richmond, and Petersburg. By 1864, the hopes early in the war for a quick victory and a Union collapse were gone.

Northern Alabama stayed under constant occupation and at the mercy of Union forces throughout most of 1864. Confederate forces were powerless to repel the occupation, although cavalry raids and skirmishing by Gen. Nathan Bedford Forrest and Gen. Philip D. Roddey created havoc for the Union forces in and around Athens and northern Alabama. Morale wavered at home—a result of the constant occupation by Union troops and the prolonged shortages, but also from the reversals of fortune the Confederate soldiers were facing on the battlefield.

This wavering frustrated the soldiers at the front and made some question their allegiance to the Confederacy.[14] Groups such as the Peace Society were more prominent in their efforts to end the fighting and to reconcile with the North.[15] Adherents not only attempted to reach the local populations in Alabama, but they also carried their influence through the soldiers returning to the front from furloughs. Complicating the matter was the fact that the population of northern Alabama was very fractured; divisions that had persisted before the war were now more pronounced. Several kinds of white Southerners competed for power in Limestone County: Unionists who quietly hoped for a Union victory, Tories who openly rebelled against Confederate authority, mossbacks who hid from Confederate conscription officers and supported neither side, and loyal Confederates who continued to support the Confederate cause. Thus families such as the McClellans could suffer at the hands of any of these groups. William was as concerned for the welfare of the folks back home as he was for himself at the front. The pull to go home and take care of his family remained very strong.

Declining morale at home and on the battlefield led to an increase in desertions during 1864. For instance, on September 30, 1864, the Army of Northern Virginia counted 155,820 aggregate present and absent for duty, but only 51,045 were actually present for duty.[16] The 9th Alabama had only 90 men present for duty. One historian believed that the Confederate defeats of 1863 plunged the Confederate morale to a low that didn't reverse until mid-1864.[17]

As the events of 1864 unfolded, William Cowan McClellan took pride in the fact that the Army of Northern Virginia was able to fend off the larger Union army of Ulysses S. Grant for so long. At times he felt as if the war would never end, but he put his faith in the idea that the Northern people and the soldiers were tired of the war as well, and that if George B. McClellan was elected president in the 1864 election, peace might be close at hand. However, as more time went by, William did not see a favorable ending for the Confederacy. Among the soldiers, the lack of furloughs led to more desertions from the ranks of the 9th Alabama as well as from the provost guard. This dampened William's enthusiasm for his own regiment, and his loyalty and respect went to the men and officers who remained to fight in the trenches around Petersburg and Richmond.

William Cowan McClellan to Martha Catherine McClellan

Orange CH
August 22d 1863
Dear Sister
Your kind letter of the third of this month came to hand several days ago you complained of my not writing to you. I assure you it is not because I dont think of you. I frequently write a letter and think for some time which one of my sisters to direct it to. Matilda gets the most of them because she usually manages to write. We are still quietly encamped at Orange CH No Yankees closer than 28 miles. You must excuse me for this letter while I cant write much. at last fight I had my five fingers mashed very badly by an old prisoner. Gen Lee has given one man from each fifty to be [furloughed] subsequently one for every hundred if not found detrimental to the service no doubt will prove detrimental to the Service.

WCM

The Yankees maid the bricks fly from Fort Sumpter yesterday in about three weeks you may listen for the fall of Charleston. I believe it would be best to give up both Mobile & Savannah. Capt. King of our Regt. Has been made colonel over Maj. [Jeremiah] Williams, Capt. [Gaynes C.] Smith. There is a great dissatisfaction in the Regt. Night before last 20 heroes of the Gettys[burg] fight all raffled up them selves with 80 rounds of cartridges strapped on nap sacks and in all one hundred had their names drawn to go but 20 got off, the men have always said they would not serve if King was put over Williams, it has been his only fight save Gettysburg, Wilcox was the cause of it. by the by Wilcox was maid Maj. General a few days ago and assigned to Gen. [Dorsey] Penders Div. who was killed at Gettysburg. We have lost him at last- he has been our commander ever since we left Richmond. Wilcox has traits of character that no man can like, but he is a better General in our army than he was at his Brigade when he left it- I can't find appropriate words he told them- they had won for themselves a great name. He regretted to leave them but duty to his country called him away and he never expected to command any more of his men. He would try to get them transferred to his Division. Col. Royster- if he recovered from his wound- will become Brigadier. I drew a very good suit of clothes [next three lines are illegible] You don't state in your letter whether or not Bruce & Elias came back. I was very glad to hear that John beat those skallawags for the Legislature. I am still on Provost Guard, Second Sergeant, very good position to save my bacon in times of Perile. Well Kittie I would like to see you all very much but it will a long time before I see Alabama again. yesterday was a day of fasting and prayer- it was also by our army. I heard general Pendleton [Brig. Gen. William Nelson Pendleton] Chief of Artillery of the Army Preache. He is as good at preaching as he is at throwing bomb shells. Generals Lee, Longstreet, Ewell, gallant [Maj. Gen. Robert Emmett] Rodes of Ala. And many others present. Rodes is the finest looking man I ever saw, The Ladys would give him bouquetts, he would smile and say Brig Gen. [J. E. B.] Steward was the man for flowers. my finger pains and so I will quit, Good bye Kittie.

Your brother,
W.C. McClellan.

Write to me as soon as you get this.

William Cowan McClellan to Matilda McClellan

Rapidan River
Sept 20th, 1863
Dear Sister
You can hardly imagine the pleasant position I now occupy sitting on the top shelf in a Green House, while the bright rays of a Sab-

bath sun Streams in at the long glass walls, While without doubt it is one of the finest gardens I ever saw, we are placed here for the purpose of guarding the guards who guard this place and Mr. Jones, property genuinely of Which he has an abundance. The Yankees drove our Cavalry from Culpeper courthouse about a week ago with but little resistance as our Cavalry knew our infantry was just South of the Rapidan R. they fell back promptly with the old cry over powered by Infantry, Artillery and Cavalry. Andersons Division advanced and by a few well directed shots from their Infields stopped their on ward progress. Established our line half mile on the north side of the River where it now remains undisturbed. We now occupy one of the strongest positions in Virginia, the position Gen Johnston chose when we fell back from Manassas in sixty one, and would have held had the enemy not attempted to flank us by way of the Peninsula. Our army feels Master of the position withstanding the best corps on the best third of the army of Northern Va has ben sent to the west to reinforce that old set fast & retreated Braxton Bragg, General Longstreet has had almost time to get in position in front of Rosencrantz [Gen. William S. Rosecrans],[18] if so he will move him back on Nashville so fast it will make his head swim. You can have Gen Longstreet until we lose old uncle Bob, then you will have to give him up to command this army. They would put up with no body else, old Bob looks like he would live as long as any body but he might get killed some day, and especially if he exposes himself like he did at Gettysburg where Minie Balls and shell grape rained in torrents. Matilda I sometimes think this Bloody war will soon come to a close, and then I conclude it never will. I know it never will by the consent of that infernal old scoundrel Abe Lincoln and cabinet. But the people of the North are getting awfully tired of the War and more especially the Soldiers. Night before last one hundred and thirty deserters came over the River and said 800 more would come the first opportunity. This will end the war quicker than decisive victorys, We have had a great many deserters in our own army but they have ben by ones and twos, men who could not resist the temptation to go home and spend a few days with their Friends and relatives they have not seen since the war commenced. great many will return, some have already returned.[19] This desertion was caused by the leniency of Gen Lee and the Pardon of the President.[20] In Johnsons Division a few days ago ten men were Shot for desertion, 6 or 8 will be shot in ours; and other Div. the same which will break up Desertion. I wrote to you some time ago Stating we were allowed furloughs on the guard by order of General Anderson, we sent two mens furloughs up. They were returned by Gen Lee with the question: did they come under order 82, which orders furloughs one man out of every fifty for duty as we had but 47 men in the guard, General Anderson said it did not come under order 82 which knocked it all in the head.[21] Gen A.[nderson] has ordered us to be furloughed from our companys, or to draw for furloughs. it will be a very hard matter to get a furlough from companys as officers and men all envy the position of Provost Guard.[22] Officers all want to command the guard while the men all want to belong to it. Capt Featherstone has returned from Lynchburg, looks tolerable well, recovered from his wound & I wrote to you some time ago asking if those two negroes came back, if so to send me one if you all could spare him. I could get along a greatdeal better with a Negro. He could help me along in a great many ways, if I had him he could do my cooking, Washing, bat a blanket occasionally. I have tried time and again to Wash but cannot. I blister my hands before I get a Shirt Washed. I have most of my Washing done 50 cents a garment, cant get many garments Washed at 11 dollars a Month, buy my tobacco & little Soda to go in my bread .&. frequently cant get Washing done at any Price. A Soldiers life is a very hard one any way you fix it. I have bourn the hardships, trials and trouble as well as most men, but of late I have been low spirited, dejected, worn out. But I am trying to rally and will do so if Possible, I sometimes think that Poore Jim Bailey was a fortunate man in being killed in the beginning of this war, in Which we all must go down eventually, by one means and another, after undergoing all the hardships human nature can stand for years. I understand there is a letter over at the Regt for me. I will not seale this until I go and read it. You must send me some cloths by the first good opportunity, dont send them unless you are certain they will come through, cloths are too scarce to be lost now. Write soon,

youre Affectionate Brother
W. C. McClellan

Monday Sept 21, 1863
I went over to the Regt last night and received a letter from John dated Sept. 7th, Carterville Georgia. he was well, and had paid a visit

to Braggs army, found it in fine condition, haveing been reinforced by most of Johns[t]ons army. John says Elias & Bruce have never come back, Yankees in Limestone again. He says a letter will reach him at Summerville, So I will answer his letter to day,- tell him to send this one on to you.

your Brother,
W C McClellan

William Cowan McClellan to John Beattie McClellan

Orange Court House, Virginia
Sept. 21, 1863
Dear Brother,
Your kind letter of Sept 7 came to hand today, apprising me of your welfare, whereabouts, etc . . . I am glad to hear that Braggs army is in good fighting condition. You say Bragg has been reinforced by most of Johnstons army. You will be surprised to learn that he has received large reinforcements from the Army of Northern Virginia. Longstreet has gone to the west with his corps consisting of three Divisions, Hoods McLaws and Picketts Divisions, the latter is a Virginia Division principally, and very small, consequently it was left at Richmond and Petersburg and Jinkins [Gen. Micah Jenkins] and old Henry A. Wises Brigades sent instead. These two Brigades number over seven thousand men, making Longstreets forces 30,000. So we may look for better times in the West. Longstreet will fight or run old Rosy [Rosecrans] out of the Confederacy. Longstreet is a man who will beat the long roll in the morning from line of battle in an hour in two hours more force them from their positions. He has done this numbers of times since the war began. He is decidedly the fastest fighting man of his day. The enemy are directly in our front at present, threatening to advance at any moment. We have a good position, the south side of the Rapidan River, Our first line is a half mile south of the river. You say Elias and Bruce have gone with the yankees. I am sorry to hear of it. I have just written home if they could spare a negro to send me one. I fear they cannot do it. I understand that Bull Nelsons Brigade is at Athens now. If so he will make raids on the south side of the Tennessee River and I fear get all the people of our section run off. You had better be careful how you dodge about or you will get an invitation to visit Camp

Chase.[23] John I am not near as big a scamp as I used to be in days gone by. I have quit most of my rudeness and as you used to say, my monkey antics, but I will turn Jack from the bottoms on the boys sometimes. I was tricky if not lucky. I had my fun while in Pennsylvania, out of those old Dutchmen. I would go up to a fellows house and ask him if he would take Confederate money. He would say no so quick it would make your hand shake. I would then tell him that if he didnt have dinner ready in fifteen minutes I would confiscate all his property and in a few minutes he would have one of the finest dinners in the world. They are a God-for-saken wicked set in Penn. Woman all curse like men All the ladies in Penn. wear their shoes without stockings. They look very nice sitting astride of an ox with a pole in their hand about 30 feet long. You must write soon and let me know when you start to Montgomery. My respects to all.

Your Brother,
Wm. C. McClellan

P.S. 2 Oclock Monday. I hear pickett firing very briskly over the river. Occasionally a shell explodes with that same old sound.

Yours- W. C. Mc

William Cowan McClellan to his sister

Orange C.H. Va
November 17th, 63
Dear Sister,
Your kind letter of the 16th Oct was received yesterday. I was very glad to learn you all were well. I know you all see a great deal of trouble among the yankees hope by this time they have left you. You say in your letter that by this time I have received my clothes by Mr Ryan. I have not nor do I ever expect to see them or Ryan either. I did see a day or two ago in the Richmond paper where one Robert Ryan was up before the Mayor of Richmond. we are now camped near Orange C.H. putting up winter quarters that is bunks with Flys stretched over them. The enemy are just across the River some Picketts fighting. I sent you some time ago Gen. Lee's report of the late campaign to the Northern Border, his plans were very fine but his Lieutenants did not execute them well. Old Wilcox

ambushed a Brigade or two of Yankees a few days ago took seven hundred prisoners, killing a great many. Wilcox is one of the best Maj. Gen. in our army a great favorite with Gen Lee. I wish I could be in Ala a few days to help the yanks press horses & negroes. give my respects to all the girls, Miss Davis, Peter Cartwrights family, Miss Robinson all you see in fact. tell them they had as well marry not to wait for me any longer. I will settle in Virginia. Tell Mollie Pettus to quit that way she has of flirting with young men and be serious for once and marry. Tell her to marry that Moore fixer & confederate Balloon Mr. King or send him to the Army. Another squad of old Braggs deserters came in to our Brigade last night. Some also for the first Tennessee- bad soldiers I expect. you must write to me as often as you can. I will have to close as this pen is used up. We had snow several days ago very cold at present. Tell Father to taik matters as cool as possible no use to fret about war matters.

Your affectionate Brother
W.C. McClellan

William Cowan McClellan to Matilda McClellan

Orange. C. H. Va
Nov 25th, 63
Dear Sister,
It is with extreme felicity that I seat myself this beautiful sabbath morning to write you a Short letter, not that I have anything of importance to communicate, but merely to let you know I am in the land of the living. After carefully peruseing the past, the presant and future I cannot see how or when this cruel war will be ended. we have fought too much to give up now, too many gallant Spirits have been Slain; too many voices would cry out from their graves for revenge to give up the Boon for which they died. No we must fight on, fight ever until the end of time. In the language of Roger A. Pryor, Speaking to the Florida Brigade a few days ago: can eight millions of people be subjugated, if so all history is a fable. Gen Pryor once commanded this Brigade. He is now a Private in the 4th Va. Cavalry, the only instance of a Gen going into the ranks we have had in this war.[24] I am just recovering from a long spell of the back ache or kidney affection consequently I have to lie down to write. I have had several attacks of this painful disease recently,

bouts last very long. All very quiet here at presant, no demonstrations on either side of a move, Meade knows he will get a sound thrashing when he crosses the Rapidann. Chancellorsville is the only place he can get any thing like a fair fight, and around that clusters some bitter recollections, probably old Jo. Hooker could tell him something about the old Tavern, how he felt when the cannon Ball knocked down the Pillers.[25] Mr. Ryan has not made his appearance yet with my clothing nor never will in my opinion. He is about as no count as any man that ever came from that god forsaken country Maryland, oh yes my Maryland, my Maryland, as grand an abolitionist state as ever existed on earth. as our army passed through Sharpsburg this last time, there was not a single countenance but what wore a sneer, yes one alone a beautiful young lady about 16 wafted her kerchief to the gallant army of the South. Gens. lifted their hats to her while all Privates cheered, hollered why dint you move South among the noble, the Generous and the free. tears were the only reply to the salute of every Banner in the army. Same case at Boonesborrow, Hagerstown & Frederick city. All over Maryland we met the cold shoulder. But I did not intend to Say any thing about Maryland in this letter, I am no Maryland man. We have all built Winter quarters consisting of logs four or five feet high, little yankee tents stretched over them with little chimneys at one end, very comfortable dwellings indeed. There is scarcely a Soldier in this army that has not captured his House top from the yankees, Canteens, Haversacks. Tell Sallie I think her Bubby has a beautiful name, Williametta. I believe you say, if She had ben born in Virginia they would have named it Loretta. all the children in Va. Are named Lee, he or she. Give my Respects to Tom Nick and tell him to count his years as slow as possible or they will have him in the army. Well Tony Says I must get about Supper. So no more for the presant.

Yours truly
W.C. McClellan O. C. H. Va

William Cowan McClellan to Matilda McClellan

[Orange Court House]
November 26th 63
Since writing the above I have received a letter from you dated Nov 1st eight pages in length, giving an account of Fathers and

Johns pursuit of the horse thiefs and the recovery of them. Things are coming to a nice pass in North ala from all accounts. exposed as the people are to thieves, both friend and foe. The people will have to form in small squads and hang every scoundrel they can get hold of. Each ought to be hung to the first tree they could get him to. I wish I could be in Limestone a few days. I think I could kill a few just such scoundrels as those you mention in your letter. Mr Ryan has not yet arrived with my clothes yet you must let me know by letter what you sent by him. We are expecting a move of some kind in a day or two, ordered to listen for Signal guns, cook up 3 days rations. Gen Ewell has been suffering with out his short leg for some time. Rumor says this morning that he is dead-[26] if so another such blow has befallen the confederacy, and one of its best generals gone. Jackson, Ewell the natural guardians of the Valley of Virginia lie cold in the graves. Wiley Webb received a letter a day or two ago from home stating that Bud Cartwright was at home which is very strange news if so.

Affectionately Your Brother
W.C. McClellan

William Cowan McClellan to Matilda McClellan

Camp Near Orange C. H. Va.
December 8, 1863
Dear Sister
We have just returned from line of Battle to our winter Quarters from which we had to leave a few days ago to meet the cruel yankees. The enemy crossed over the Rapidan River in two places on the 31st of last month. We met them on the Plank Road 6 miles from the old Battle field of Chancellorsville, fronted them in line of Battle, contrary to our rule threw up Breast works and waited for them to attack us. They shelled our works for two or three days and retreated a cross the River under cover of the night, not haveing the courage to give Battle. We have the news of Braggs defeat in front of Chattanooga, driven back beyond the Chickamauga, badly whipped generally, with the loss of several thousand prisoners and 52 Pieces of Artillery.[27] army demoralized Bragg given up his command, quit the Service. What he ought to have done long ago if he had considered the good of his country. We dont know who could

command the army of the west better than Bragg, but most assuredly somebody can. Longstreet I think is the man to command that army. If Gen Lee was killed this army would unanimously request Longstreet as its commander. I am not at all surprised at Braggs defeat, when he sends such men as D. H. Hill to Richmond under arrest.[28] Hill was the best Maj Gen we had in this army, [Leonidas] Polk also has the reputation of being a good General, and most assuredly [Nathan Bedford] Forrest was a good commander. The latest news we have from Longstreet is that he had Burnside compleately surrounded at Knoxville and a fair chance to capture his entire command. He will do it if it can be done by man with the force he has. Longstreet in my opinion has but few equals and no superiors in this war. I suppose by this time you are completely surrounded by the yankees, no liberty, no Peace for some time to come if ever, probably they will send our corps and old Bob down to your assistance, if so you will be redeemed, Tennessee delivered, Kentucky menaced, until then it is farewell Home, Friends, and country. I have not seen my long looked for clothing yet, or a furlough this winter. but I believe furloughs have played out, so many have not returned that got furlough some time ago. They ought to be shot, every one of them, if they would return promptly we would all get home this winter. Private R. E. Deal of our company is now at home a month over time, he is a man that cared but very little for his Reputation.[29] Tom Cartwright Al Martin & John Boyd[30] all of your acquaintances are well. We have had a snow, Several hard rains of late. I will direct this to Summerville. Gen. Ewell is not dead as I wrote, but on the contrary is now on duty, he is too ugly to die. poor old fellow.

Your Affectionate Brother,
W. C. McClellan

William Cowan McClellan to Matilda McClellan

Orange C.H. VA.
Feb. 17th 1864
Dear Sister,

I arrived in camp on the 25th precisely the day my furlough [ended].[31] The commander of the guard did not look for me under 40 days. I am sorry now I did not stay at home longer regardless of the consequences but probably I did best by returning in time.

I stayed with Uncle Andrew [Beattie] two days found him well, Mr. Allison[32] was there and accompanied me to Atlanta. I lay over in Talladega three days the train having run off the tracks smashing up several Boxes very badly, killing one or two soldiers which was the cause of my delay at that huge hole. I was delayed one day in Montgomery from that place I made it to Richmond in three days making all the connections. John [McClellan] went with me to Summit Ala at which place he sold two horses for 1,250 dollars. went with me ten miles beyond summit and concluded to turn back. As I rode over that bleak barren region called Sand Mountain I resolved a half dozen times to turn back to Sommerville and stay a month, but duty called- reason triumphant over desire. I found all quiet in this department. One corps of yankees appeared over the Rapidan on the 6th of this month. Johnson & Rodes Divisions drove them back after a small fight with but little loss on either side.[33] The yankee papers say the object of this move was to attract Lees attention while [Maj. Gen. Benjamin Franklin] Butler with most of the troops from Charleston was to take Richmond and liberate their prisoners which he signally failed to do of course. the yankee papers say this is the worst failure they have ever maid to capture Richmond. This accounts for his departure of the forces in front of Charleston indicated in the papers a few days ago. John says he can get Col Gilbert[34] to give me a position in his Regt of Cavalry. I would be very glad of such a swap or transfer as it would give me a chance to do something in the World for my self. My love to all. Sallie and all the children.

Affectionately your Brother,
W.C. McClellan Orange C.H. Va.

William Cowan McClellan to Thomas Joyce McClellan

Orange, C. H.
February 27th. 1864
Dear Father,
Willie Holcomb will start to Ala to morrow. I will send this letter by him & others to the Family. All quiet in Virginia, army reinlisting very rapidly. Our Brigade has reinlisted for the War.[35] Cavalry, Artillery and Infantry all going it for the War. We are getting plenty to eat: Bacon, corn meal, lard, sugar & coffee plenty.[36] Mo-

rale is splendid, not with out thinking some are deserting, every day several have left our Regiment in the last month and John told me he would try and get Col Gilbert to give me an appointment in his Regt which will be a very great favor on the part of Col Gilbert. You must all write as often as you can to me. This trip home has made a perfect child of me.

your Affectionate Son,
W C McClellan

William Cowan McClellan to Robert Anderson McClellan

Camp Near Orange C. H. Va
April 27th, 1864
Dear Brother,
Your very kind favor of the 4 of this month has just ben handed to me. It met with a warm reception, being the first I have received from you or any one else in two months. You speak of my saying but little about my brief visit home, you have not received the letter I first wrote to you after returning to camp. I presume in that letter I gave you the full particulars of my stay in that down trodden land. I will not reiterate again as you have before this learned later news than I could give you-I suppose you have before this ben down to see Uncle Andy at Kelsos farm 12 miles North west from Talladega, he is living a gay old time of it, as the Boys say he is beating the war badly. you have doubtless also seen John before this as he is stirring around pretty considerably over the country. I have no news of importance to Write, we have had some very good news of late which you have heard. Capture of Fort Pillow by Forrest,[37] Plymouth N.C. by Brigadier, now Maj general Hoke,[38] victory in La. by Kirby Smith over Poore Banks.[39] I believe every body whips Banks that wants to. Gen Forrest is gaining a glorious name for his dareing exploits. The Soldiers of this army say he is the best Cavalry gen in the confederacy. The Northern papers and congressmen are making a terrible fuss over the slaughter of the garrisons at fort Pillow. Old Abe in a speech in Baltimore said he would have the mater thoroughly investigated, if proven that Forrest had killed out the garrison he would retalliate. We have the great hero of the west [Ulysses S. Grant] confronting us at this point, it remains to be seen wether or not old Bob will cull his plumage and turn him upon

the commons to recruit his fallen fortunes, different from all the ballance of his generals, they cant send him to the west as he is just from that country. You of the Cavalry will soon have a hard Horse to contend with from the yankee army of the Potomac. the great Cavalry Gen Kilpatrick who has given Stewart [Stuart] the devil on several occasions, made a raid in three miles of Richmond a few weeks ago.[40] I wrote you a letter a few days ago and directed it to Blue Mountain, not knowing there was an Office at Oxford. We are getting terribly good rations at this time, that is we make them hold out by gathering wild onions, little turnip salle & as soon as we commence a march we will have our rations increased,- you must write to me as soon as you receive this, let me hear from home, the news generally. Nothing more at Presant.

Your Brother,
W. C. McClellan 9th Regt ala Vol
Wilcox old Brigade O. C. H. Va a, N Va

William Cowan McClellan to Robert Anderson McClellan

Head Quarters Provost guard
Andersons Division
Orange C.H. Va May 1st, 1864
Dear Brother,
Twelve months ago today the old Army of Northern Virginia was contending in deadly strife with an enemy three times their number which resulted in the most glorious victory ever achieved on the continent against greater odds. The boasted Army of the Potomac numbering 150 thousand men was driven in consternation and dismay from their chosen position by our army numbering 48 thousand veteran soldiers. But the fortunes of war are various. amid sunshine there is sorrow. we returned to camp not with our accustomed shout of victory, but gathered in groups and in awe sat staring stone faced the above the result of the wound the immortal Jackson had received. No soldier in this army but inquired hourly of the welfare of one of our great commanders. On the 10th day of this month his spirit took its flight to the blessed land of eternity leaving behind a sorrow stricken family & condoling army & one of the most brilliant careers ever allotted man since the days of Napoleon. We

are now quietly awaiting the movements of the hero of the west [Grant] The man that has subjugated the people of Tenn and Miss carrying by storm every impediment in his way. his plan is to take Richmond by the eastern shores of Virginia by the South West and North not giving us the least hole to crawl out at. in a word Grant proposes to do just what McClellan did- capture Richmond and Lees army and break up the Rebellion. We are drawing our corn meal and bacon. We have a very disagreeable time of it when the wind gets in leeward of the sinks[41] the elements are filled with brand mixed with onions makes an odor few can with stand. I see by the papers you have had a big Show and Cavalry Review near Oxford and we have too much of the scalling here to deal in the show. I still have a great desire to be a cavalryman you must not let any chance of my swap transfer exchange promotion pass untried. I am heartily tired of Soldiering in this frigid zone of a Va. I do not care much about the 9th ala in the honors they gained on the Battle field they have lost this Winter by desertion but dont talk this out or I would have to fight the gallant Boys of Co F. our company has always numbered as much any other two almost despite the deserters. This is the reason [for] picketts now they have to send co F in front of the balance of the Regiment to keep them from going to the yanks. has been great dissatiafaction in the Regt ever since Capt. King was maid Col. over Maj. Williams.[42] Also in Col. Henrys old company. I have not heard a word from home since I left here. The Yankees have been tightening down on them worse than ever. Yesterdays paper states Forrest had a fight not far from Winchester day or too before a letter from some big man South stated a yankee division 7 thousand strong passed from Athens to Huntsville en rout to reinforce [George Henry] Thomas at Chattanooga[43] last accounts say Loring Division was at Montavello destination North ala. where the great disposer of events will determine whether or not Bob Lee can do anything to avert this sad calamity to our capital and country, his strong arm and clear-head has never failed us in time of need- Grant will never martial as large an army for the capture of Richmond as old Jo. Hooker had at Chancellorsville without giving up the hard earned advantages gained in the West for the last too years. One of Grants plans has been to land troops at Plymmouth N.C. advance up the Rone Oak River to Weldon take the R. Road cut off our supplys & reinforcements from the South, advance upon us Ric[hmond] south side of the James River. This plan has been defeated by the capture of Plymmouth by Gen. Hoke, two thousand prisoners a Brigadier gen. and a very large lot of provisions and camp equipage. We now have several Rebbel Rams stationed at that point guarding the garrison. Indeed the Spring campaign has so far been greatly in our favor. Plymouth, Fort Pillow and the victory in La. are good omens of the future. In a few days the big guns in Virginia will thunder forth to awake the courage, energy and zeal of the nation to a last desperate struggle for independence and freedom. when the smoke shall have cleared away and the Pane of the Battle has been hushed in silence, We will then turn our eyes to the dome of the capitol to see if our beloved colors still flote to the breeze. turn and look to see if the beloved Washington still sits upon his charger, if so Peace must follow beside Washington. we will place our commander in chief R. E. Lee. Such feelings sometimes cross my immagination when I get my belly well filled with wild onions. You said in your letter if I saw Miss Maggie [Lipscomb]. I did not see or hear of her suppose the Yankees have suppressed freedom of speech, liberty of actions almost The privilidge of breathing. The only ladys I saw north of the River. was the Nick Davises, Miss Annie Cartwright & Mrs Vaughan. The ladys were as glad to see me as if I had been a Brother. I look upon her as a true and good friend- polite and sedate as in days past. I suspect coloring for the cheeks is not so plentiful in these days of Revolution. These ladys all seem glad to see me the day after getting home. The greatest change to me about the place was the absence of those too trees one at the gate and the old tree providing foilage that stood between the [illegible] under whose protecting limbs I and you have played when we were young with the old grey mule, the only remaining member of that family of Horses. I saw George, Jim, Rosie and others had gone back into the Union. give my kindest regards to Floyd, John Moore. Buck Lane, Davis & all the Boys of my acquaintance. you must write to me as often as you can conveniently. I suppose this will be about the last letter I will have an opportunity to write from camp. Think we will be on a march in a day or too. When peace again unfurls her benign wing over the war-torn fields of our dear Confederacy I hope clever young miss to return to your side to prove the fidelity of my purpose to wed you to [last line illegible] . . .

W.C.McClellan
Org C.H. Va. a.n. Va.

William Cowan McClellan to Matilda McClellan

In front of Richmond in Line of Battle,
June 2nd 1864
Dear Sister,
Your very kind letter of April 25th was received a day or two ago, bringing me the first tideings I have received from that place since Febuary 10th. On the same day I received a letter from John, one from Bob, and one from John Fletcher. I have no news to write you at this time, we have ben fighting 30 days with unbroken success to Southern arms.[44] We now occupy a position in three miles advance of our old position at the commencement of the seven days fight around Richmond.[45] I was of course very much grieved to hear of the death of Uncle John [McClellan], he will be sadly missed by his family. John Fletcher informs me that Jennie Davis has married the yankee Col Phillips.[46] Is it possible that a daughter of old Nick Davis can be so vile a traitor to her native South as to marry one of the Hell bound persecutors of the Soil that gave her birth. This is another Stigmas upon the Davis family, you say Matilda, Nick Davis says he intends to conduct himself in such a manner that he will not be ashamed to Fish on Limestone with we boys when we get back, you say he has adopted a manly course. I beg to differ with you, I think his present position very humiliating, cowardly and disgraceful. A big strong, young man with no family save a wife, to stay at home and have his nose pulled by every yankee that comes along. poor fellow, also Nicholas your days are over. Jennie has payed the oppresser of her Evil the greatest complyment in her power; married him. In Va there has ben a few ladys that have married Federal Officers, but they were all of this kind, they were poor, hand to mouth, barefooted and undereducated. I have never heard of a woman of any respectability Marrying a Blue Son of a yankee yet in this country. I have said to much on this subject, it does not concern me but it is very provoking to see neighbors doing this way. My health is not very good at presant, bowells out of order. You must tell Bob Davis to be sure and save those fine Runts for me. I understand he and Dick Allen have gone into the trade pretty extensively, tell Bob he must save me a good hat, pants and vest so I can have a little start when the war is over. My regards to all.

Your Brother
W C McClellan

9 miles from Richmond, you must excuse mistakes. I wrote this letter in a great hurry. Battle expected every day. Write soon and often.

William Cowan McClellan to Thomas Joyce McClellan

Camp Near Petersburg, Va
July 16th, 64
Dear Father,
Mr. Eppy Fielding starts home tomorrow on furlough, he promises to convey this letter to you. I have no great news to write you, all around looks gloomy in the extreme. Our armys of the most have all ben defeated as you are forcefully aware. we have but one army able to present any thing like a front to the progress of the enemy. No telling how soon that we will be overwhelmed and defeated by brute force. Hoods defeat at Nashville[47] has cast the darkest shadow over our prospects the country ever fancied ever dampening the spirits of the a [Alabamians], & 'va' [Virginians] causeing many to depart which have fought like Heroes on fifty Battle fields. Asa Moore has blocked any passes. I am needing clothing very bad. If you can send me something now it would come in the nick of time, but do not send clothes unless in care of a reliable person. Boots, Pants, Jackett worn. Need all artickles. getting dark have no candle.

Your Affectionate Son.
W. C. McClellan

William Cowan McClellan to Robert Anderson McClellan

Right Wing A.N.Va. Petersburg
August 10th, 1864.
Dear Brother
Your very kind favor of July 17th was received a day or too ago and I read with great pleasure Old Virginia has been shook from centre to circumfrence by the shock of arms for the last 90 days.[48] No county in the state but has heard the screaming of shells and rattle of small arms. but Richmond still stands in defiance of the largest army ever martialled on the continent of America, lead on by the hero of the West. This powerful army has been beaten, failed, decimated and demoralised. We crossed the James River at Chaffins

Bluff on the 16th of June[49] marched in quick time to the assistance of Beauregard who was contending with the combined forces of Grant & Butler in front of Petersburg.[50] early in the morning of the 17th our old chieftan and his veteran army commenced fileing through the city amid the tears and smiles of the frightened populace. many would point to Gen. Lee and say our homes are safe. We went to the front formed our lines, precisely where they are now. On the 22nd of June the enemy commenced extending his lines in the direction of the Weldon R.Road,[51] his cavalry crossed this road, made directly for the Danville R. Road 30 miles farther west. Infantry came up within a half mile of the Weldon Road, threw up breastworks of a very formidable nature. Three Brigades of our Division under command of Brigadier Gen. Mahone. Mahone threw out a heavey line of skirmishers in front of the Yankees while he charged the yanks on the flank and rear. The result of this fight was the stampeade of Hancocks corps and a Division of Wrights corps, numbering in all 20 thousand men. We captured 17 hundred prisoners 4 pieces of Artillery 10 stands of colors. held their works all night fell back to our line next morning too thousand stands of small arms. A week later our Brigade and too others of the Div were ordered down to Va. R.Road 10 miles from Petersburg to intercept the raiders retiring from the Southern country of Va. loaded down with stolen plunder, scarsly thrown out skirmishers. When they maid their appearance pursued by Wade Hamptons Cavalry,[52] [the] 10th and 14th ala Regt were thrown out too far in advance of support. The yankees charged their line of Skirmishers front and flank throughout several times capturing 36 men. Billy Mahone now arrived and charged the aspect of officers and immediately ordered forward the balance of the Brigade also Finegans Florida Brigade. Yankees supposing them to be dismounted cavalry presented a front. but they were soon undeceived when our old Brigade poured in one of those low deadly volleys that has sent so many yankees to their final accountability before a frowning god. a charge was ordered by Infantry and Artillery. a scene now ensued that beggars all description- caissons blowing up, Yankee artilleryman going at a two 40 lick through the woods, strike a tree and cut loose horses mount and off he goes. Negroes of all color age sex size flying in disarray in every direction, some of the waggons were on fire, countless numbers of carriages, buggeys caryalls chickens, turkeys, every conceivable species of property centered in confusion.

The fruits of the victory to our division was twelve pieces of Artillery Plundered and 70 prisoners & hundred stolen negroes, carriage waggons and ambulance train horses and carriages enough to bring the wounded back to the lines, recaptured our 36 men. On the 31st of last month Grant sprang one of his mines at a Salient in our lines. In this mine he had six tons of powder, which is twelve thousand pounds. The explosion took place about daylight shaking the earth for miles around. This cavity swallowed up a Battery of ours and most of the 18th S. C. Regt & created a good deal of confusion in our lines, but the flanks held out stubbornly against an infilading fire from the yankees who made a rush at the point the explosion occured under a destructive fire from our Batterys on the flank. This part of the line belonged to Bush Rod Johnsons Division Beauregards army. about twelve o'clock in the day Mahone and Wrights Brigades were ordered to charge and retake the works. Mahones Virginians succeeded in gaining the Rifle Pits on the left of the Salient. fought hand to hand until they drove them back to this huge hole in the earth caused by the explosion. The Georgians did not have the Gallant Wright to lead them consequently they made a failure, but I am too fast. Just as our men started to charge a Brigade of Negroes leaped from our last line tossing their hats in the air cried out no quarter, our Boys gave them a volley sent them skedaddling back into the ditches upon top of their White friends. Well Mahones Brigade held the line to the left of the explosion some of Wrights Brigade charged up behind them. others did not go, an hour passed off in the broiling sun. A. P. Hill told Mahone to bring up the old Wilcox Brigade. They were soon in position. Mahone walked to the crest of the Hill and showed General Saunders the position he wanted to take. Sanders came back to the Brigade said Boys I wont deceive you. you have a powerful position to take. We will meet Negroes and Yankees by the thousands. The eyes of the commander in chief are upon you. They walked slowly to the top of the Hill. Sanders clear voice rung out trail arms cross on the centre double quick. The earth trembled with the sound of artillery not a sound uttered by the Brigade while within ten paces of the enemy. They gave a yell and fired a deadly volley into the Negroes and yankees now commenced a hand to hand fight soon killed all the negroes and drove the Whites into the cavity of the explosion. our men then ran up to this big hole throwing clods of dirt, yankee guns. with bayonetts and cannon balls over in the hole.

The poor fool negroes would stick their heads over the works to look for our Boys, next moment his hat would fly about 6 feet in the air while his brains would fly on like [illegible]. They all surrendered to Gen. Sanders. Mahone requested our men to stop killing the negroes. Our Division was all that was in the fight.[53] We have taken twelve hundred prisoners 75 commissioned officers among them Brigadier Gen. Bartlett 51 Regt was represented among the prisoners.[54] 21 stands of colors this makes for our Division since escaping the James 41 hundred prisoners, 256 Negro soldiers 31 stands of colors 16 Pieces of Artillery. Several of their flags had ben scorched upon view. This last victory has made Brig. Gen Mahone a Maj. Gen[eral]. Capt. V. J. Genarely[55] a.ct.g. to Mahone a Brigadier gen. assigned to Wright's Georgia Brigade. Col. Sanders of the 11th ala has been commanding our Brigade since the death of Gen. Perrin at Spotsylvania, C.H. was made Brigadier on the field Dec. 31st. Sanders is 22 years of age a rigid disciplinarian. Northern papers say their loss in the last fight was five thousand seven hundred. We had lost men in the fight, seven hundred yankees died left on the field. Excuse this very hasty and unconnected letter. if you can read it remail it to Matilda—buy some paper.

William Cowan McClellan to Robert Anderson McClellan

[William repeated the story of the Battle of the Crater for his brother during the first part of this letter, which will not be repeated here. This letter does provide additional information about the battle, beginning with the pushing back of the black troops into the Crater.]

Petersburg Va
August 15th, 1864
. . . Our Boys soon drove them [the black troops] back into the tremendous cavity made by the explosion formed in a circle around it, commenced Pitching clods of dirt cannon Balls, muskets with Bayonetts on while they hoisted a white flag and surrendered. Our men burried eight hundred and fifty in and around our works, while between the two lines of Battle they lay in files. These were killed by our Artillery as they would run out. We captured 11 hundred prisoners, one Brigadier, three Cols. Yankees report a loss of 6 thousand men. next day we struck a flag of truce to bury the dead.

They were the worst looking set you ever saw, yankees layed the defeat to the Negroes, Negroes were disposed to lay it on the yankees. We captured 250 Negroes, all of whom were wounded in some way: Bayoneted, knocked on the head by the butts of muskets. all would have ben killed had it not ben for Gen Mahone, who would beg our men to spare them. one fellow in our Brigade killed several. The Gen told him for gods sake stop. Well, Gen. let me kill one more, he deliberately took out his pocket knife and cut ones throat. Great many of the yankees officers, even Negroes, were killed on the spot. Our loss including the Brigade and Artillerymen that were blown up, was one thousand men. None done any fighting save our Brigade and Mahones. We also captured 20 stacks of colors. Our division since crossing the James has captured 41 hundred prisoners, 30 stacks of colors, 16 Pieces of Artillery. At the time of this fight we had but three divisions on this side of the River to meet a part of the enemy. Longstreets corps never returned. They have gone to reinforce Early in the Valley. Most of Grants army has gone to the Potomac, Grant among them. Think all of his force will soon follow. This will end the mammoth plans for the capture of Richmond, not withstanding the great gallantry of our Regt. Great dissatisfaction has prevailed every since the appointment of King Col., two nights ago 25 men & and [*sic*] officer Fuller of the Regt deserted.[56] They took their guns and accoutrements now on them, raced to Ala. via Knoxville or Cleveland. 10 of our company are in these crowds. Never had a deserter brought before . . . [57]

[The rest of the letter is missing.]

William Cowan McClellan to Thomas Joyce McClellan

Petersburg, Va.
August 23rd, 1864
Dear Father,

We have had one continuous Battle ever since we crossed James River the 16th of June. Our Division has occupied the rite wing of the army covering our rear and protecting the Weldon R. Road. On the 22nd of June the enemy made a demonstration to our rite.[58] Gen. Mahone com[manding the] Div took three Brigades, Wilcox ala, Wrights georgia, Mahones Va. Brigade of our Div attack Hancocks corps in flank and rear capturing 17 hundred and fifty prisoners 4 pieces of Artillery 10 stands of colors capturing the yankee works. Two thousand five hundred stands of small arms. Cavalry having preceded this expedition. They crossed the Weldon Road struck out for the Farmville R. Road 25 miles to the west our only remaining line of communication. Our Cavalry being North of Richmond they pushed forward and tossed this road doing it some damage. first of July Mahone moved down to the Weldon Road to intercept the raiders returning to Grants army loaded down with negroes and plunder of all description. this time had our old Brigade [Brig. Gen. Joseph] Finegans Florida Brigade. Our lines were securely formed before the enemy made his appearance. They charged our Brigade from each flank front & center but they maintained their position against all opportunities until Finnegan came to support. Mahone saw, ordered a charge. Now was seen a sight that seldom ever met even the eye of a soldier. Yankees flying in dismay through the woods with Artillery, Negroes of all ages size and sex running to an froe in the Wildest confusion. Artillery would run until they would strike a tree and cut loose and, my kingdom for a horse, clucking turkeys Pigs and Negroe Babys strewed the country. This continues until our Infantry broak down when Wade Hamptons Cavalry took up the war cry and continued the chore. Our Division captured six hundred raiders 12 Pieces of Artillery 8 hundred negroes 4 stands of colors [. . .]

[At this point in the letter, William again relates the story of the Battle of the Crater, which will not be repeated here.]

. . . All of this fighting was done by our Brigade and Mahones Va. Brigade. This fight was on the 30th of last month. Five days ago the yankees crossed James River.[59] Three Brigades of our Division went over to help old Wilcox to stop their progress towards Chaffins Bluff. They were formed on the extreme left. The Yankees broak through Wrights Georgia Brigade and came down on the rear of our Brigade. They stepped over the works on the rim of the Brigade while the left swung around now poured volley after volley into them but still they came on but our Boys would not run. They turned the buts of their guns on them and held the ground until one of Wilcoxs Brigade came to their assistance and drove them from the works. Seven hundred prisoners were the fruits of this victory. We lost a few prisoners among them. There was the gallant John Rawlings, Lt Baugh and Cas Minney of our company. So our little Division has captured since crossing James River 48 hundred prisoners 34 stands of colors 16 pieces of Artillery. Wilderness and Spotsylvania one thousand five stands of colors. This is just the number of our Division when we left Orange C.H. Our Regt has won immortal honor for gallantry but she has lost it all by desertion. Lt [Richard B.] Fuller of Houstons old company Deserted a few days ago taking with him 25 men of the Regt ten of whom went from our company.[60] none had ever gone before. They took their guns and accoutrements will no doubt go to the North ala via Knoxville Tennessee. Fullers idea is to go to Limestone and be a regular freebooter & Jayhawker[61] worse than any yankee. say nothing of this. Fuller and myself have been good Friends through the war. would do you a favor if by accident he was to be thrown in the way. Our Regt now numbers 50 men for duty about five hundred on the roles.[62] Great many of them now at Home. This last move of the old Fuller squad was the boldest thing I ever knew men to undertake. My regards to all Especially to galls of no scruples.

Affectionately Your Son
W.C. McClellan

Since writing the above we have had another fight. The gallant young Sanders was killed dead on the field.[63] great loss. Gen Sanders was the youngest gen. in the army being only 22 years old, formerly of the 11th ala Regt. He died leading the Brigade over the breast works of the enemy.

William Cowan McClellan to his sister

Petersburg, Va.
September 25, 1864
Dear Sister,
Having plenty of Yankee paper on hand I will write you a short letter in this my first leisure hour for some time. A temporary gloom now spreads itself over the country in consequence of the fall of Atlanta. we have suffered a great reverse in Georgia comeing as it does on the Heels of the nomination of McClellan by the democratic party for Presidency of the United States. This is a sad blow to the only party the confederacy can back for sympathy or friendship. If McClellan is elected I think this dreadful war will be brought to a speedy close.[64] Peace will dawn upon our bloody coun-

try both honorably and satisfactory to the confederacy. With their usual crudeness the democrats have nominated the strongest man of the party with a platform upon which you can put two constructions as they always do. One clause union on the old basis of the Union, another Peace on any terms and an acknowledgement of states rights. Democracy. It has been a charmed recourse in days gone by. Why may it not be successful again. God grant it may be. bitterly as I have hated that recourse. any thing to beat that monster Abe Lincoln and [illegible] of New England. Had Hood stood firm at Atlanta McClellans election would have been inevitable. Atlanta was but little importance to us after the R. Road connections were destroyed being nothing more than a small town. But this is not the question. The enemy looked upon it as the most vital point in the Confederacy save Richmond hence its capture will cheer the sagging spirits of Lincoln and his war dogs. Lincolns draft of a half million was to take place on the 5th of this month. Armed resistance was looked for in the north west. In Indiana great many arms and munitions of war was discovered. By the fall of Atlanta I fear this resistance will disappear like mist before the wind. The army of Northern Va. has met and beat back the most numerous and powerful army ever martialled upon a field for some months. They have fought day and night being victorious in every engagement. At last-being masters of the field they hoped to wrest from their labors turning hopefully to Atlanta praying earnestly that the army of Tennessee would stand firm to their poast one time. Alas for all human calculation Atlanta is gone. Grant until now a dead cock in the pit, gathers fresh hope and tells Lincoln to give him one hundred thousand more men and he will destroy the last Rebel army in the field. Let him come no hundred thousand men can whip the noble army of Va lead by the immortal Lee The Greatest among generals living or dead. The Soldiers of this army don't doubt the courage or gallantry of the army of Tennessee but deplore the misfortunes that has followed them from Fort Donaldson to this day. probberbly this has ben in the incompetency of their generals. It appears Hood was looking over the fortifications at Atlanta for Sherman while Sherman with nearly all of his army was fighting Hardee[65] 25 miles in his rear. This is an awful slur on the gallant Hood. Some one else will now be put in command of the army west, currently reported Beauregard will be put in command. Some may say Gen. Lee has already gone to see what he can do for Sherman if so I believe he will drive him to his gun Boats wherever they may be in the Tennessee or Ohio. No more war at preasant. I received a letter from Bob dated August 9th written at Social circle, ga after the capture and expulsion of the two yankee raiders in georgia. They captured old Stoneman[66] an old Puppy that used to give us thunder in the rear. Bob was in fine spirits and expecting to start on a raid on Sherman's communications in Tennessee. was gratified in a day or too after writing. I suppose as Wheeler soone made his appearance not far from Chattanooga. too much praise cannot be awarded the Cavalry of the West. I also received a letter from John written at Coosa Valley St. [Clair] County. Men well but had heard nothing definite from home in too months. Since hearing by letter from Bud Martin to Al [Martin] that he was up at Atlanta to see Bob. Our Regt now has 75 muskets for duty.[67] 22 of which belong to our county company. Houstons old company has one man[,] no officers. This mans name is Dock Lane. he has had an election and elected himself Capt. of the company. A month ago Lt Fuller of Co H deserted as I have before stated takeing with him 25 of the best men in the Regt, 10 of our company, but two of the crowd have been brought back. Adkins and Wolley came in yesterday. Worst looking Boys I ever saw. The way they were caught Adkins was snake bit Wooley remained with him and both arrested. Fuller was making for H[untsville] to plunder and bushwhack. They left him in Western Virginia. very little desertions in the Brigade save in our Regt. All details are ordered to report to their commands with muskets. I expect the Provost guard will be broken up. No one straining every nerve to meet Grants new Levees. Col. King is now in command of the Brigade. Baugh captured, Featherston in Lynchburg, Gilbert in command of the Regt. Wiley Webb, McWilliams, Tandy Lewis, Pinkney Neal[68] been killed during the campaign. [John M.] Rawlings captured. News came last night that Gen. Early had ben defeated in the Valley of Va. and forced to pull back 12 miles.[69] Gen. Rodes of Ala was killed, also [Maj.] Gen. [John Brown] Gordon of Alabama the Maj. Generals of great romance. Grant ordered one hundred guns to be fired in honor of the victory, guns to be sighted. Gen. Lee issued an order two hours before the firing took place for his men to get in the ditches. how he knew Grant was going to open his artillery is a great mystery to all. I believe he knows what Grant has for dinner every day. Mrs. Grant and all the little Grants are down on a visit to the city. every body can gain victory but Grant, poor general is too smart to continue against Robert E. Lee. Just ben over to the 4 ala saw Trible, Bob Hughes, Allen Walls, John Hawkins, Dock White, Cockrun of Huntsville, Wilson[70] all well, wish me so to state in my letter home. Currently reported in the 4th ala that Nick Davis had killed Col. Phillips, his brother in law, now in Huntsville jail awaiting trial.[71]

William Cowan McClellan to Matilda McClellan

Camp near Petersburg, Va.
October 1864 [no day noted]
Dear Sister,
Your very kind and interesting letter of September 27th was received to day. giveing me more news as usual than all the letters from Limestone put together. I agree with you that Wheeler accomplished but little in his great raid that was to cut off [illegible] and capture the monster of the world W. T. Sherman.[72] glorious man. almost equal to U.S. Grant who according to yankee pickets on the Rapidan last spring has been let down a button hole or two- Lee oh that we had a few more like him. We heard three days ago of the capture of Athens that Huntsville Decatur and several other small garrisons had surrendered to Forrest but turns out only Athens was captured.[73] Bully for Forrest. I believe he is the greatest Cavalry commander on the continent- now commander in chief of all the Cavalry of the West. This is commensurate with his genius and ability as a great and successful commander a bright future opens before Forrest and his men in the West- an open field of six hundred miles over which the enemy receives his supplies if they can successfully blockade hold destroy his line of communication. Sherman will have to leave georgia. If not the enemy will stay in georgia until the end of the war. I was very sorry to hear the infernal yankees is still plundering the people of their scarce means of subsistance. Tell Father to play yankee on them when ever he can save a dollar by it. take the oaths to save his family from poverty and ruin, many have, Good Southerners have done this all over the Confederacy. Speaking of Mr. Phillips. good. Lane Martin supposed Peace was made and these nice yankees purpose was to visit Limestone. We Boys of the 9th and 4th happened upon them would we not have a gay old time hanging the infernal Scoundrells. Why

Matilda a yankees smile is worse than a minks hole why a Southern Lady would marry one of them I cant see to save my life- I will write to Mrs Brock and tell her where to direct her letters to her Brother. Suppose she lives in Richmond. Give my kindest regards to Pat Ragland and tell him I am now soldering around the city of which I have so often on days gone by heard him describe and talk of by the house. little dreaming I would be so soone called upon to do Battle in their defence against a savage foe. Such the fate of nations, such the lot of man. drifted in a few short years from the Peaceful Valley and happy fireside of home, to the rude theatre of war where nothing is heard but the thunder of Artillery. The rattle of small arms, the groans of dieing and the glassy eyes of the dead. This is a sad picture upon which it will not do to reflect. I will get two or three days leave before long and go to Richmond and get my over coat which I left at Mrs Ann Hooker, [William Eppa] Fielding's kinswoman. Will also call upon Mrs. Brock and Pat's [Pat Ragland's] stiff brothers up on Broad Street. I have received several messages from The Miss Anderson in Lynchburg to call upon when the first opportunity. suppose they feel a sympathy for all the Boys from Limestone. Capt Featherton is now in Lynchburg sick. has been there for some time. N.J. Floyd has been transferred to Houston Texas on provost duty at that place. Our lines now extend from the Darby Town road North of the James River to the Weldon R. Road South of Petersburg a distance of 30 miles, all along this line boath sides have powerful Siege gunns and frequently make the earth tremble with their unearthly sounds. false alarms are of frequent occurance when both parties open all the Artillery while small arms sing the tenor note to perfection. They commence a great sight- mortar shells by the thousand ascend several hundred yards high describing a half circle blowing light following in their wake a foot long and as broad as your hand. Some explode high in the heavens some fall to the ground with a crash louder than thunder. These huge monsters unexploded are worth at the Ordinance Department 8 dollars. you will see a half dozen confederate soldiers running at a fearful rate to claim the prize. Some ingenious soldiers take the trap fuse of the shell and make finger rings for which they have realized the sum of one hundred dollars. one poor jew in Petersburg was broken up before he found all that shined was not gold. Gen. Early has again ben whipped in the Valley of Va. with a loss of 23 pieces of Artillery.[74] I received a letter from John written at Montgomery dated of October 3rd stating he was just starting home as Forrest had captured the country west of Huntsville.[75] Very likely heard he would hold until a negotiated peace resolution had been introduced and resolved in the House of Representatives, but did not take very well, that is being opposed by a majority, See through the Selma papers that Mingo [Marengo] county was the leader in the matter. I have also received too letters from Bob one written at Summerville before the assembling of his fight 24th of September, the other Jackson ala en rout for Hoods army at or near Dalton georgia. I think I will get a furlough this winter if nothing happens. tell Father to have me a good horse Bridle and Saddle and spurs I am going to ride the remainder of this war- turn about is fair play said the equestrian to the Pedestrian. you say Pat Ragland thinks Nancie Cartwright is the nicest gal in the county. Tell Patrick I disagree with him- Cleopatrice Indiana Ohio [Cleopatra Indiana Cartwright] is the gal for me. I can even now hear the gentle cooing of that dove like voice falling in soft melodies upon my eager ears, while my head throbs with the wild emotions of pleasure and happiness. oh sad sad eyes. war cease thy burning and let me go home where the spring time comes gentle Annie- and you say Bettie R. has been over to see you. is She as pretty as Miss Flora. Mrs Bibb use to be. you must excuse this unguarded expression of feelings as I have on about two drinks of the mud dip fresh from No. Ala., pine tops and all, it is well calculated to me we have not only the secrets of a mans sole but the contents of his heart also. My regards to Sallie, L. R. D., and children around in general. your affectionate brother, W.C. McClellan. Mr. Yankee if you get your fangs on this just take it to the address and the old lady will give you a turkey & Watermellon or a spade or nigger.

yours with considerable
WCMc.

11

Prison and Home Again

January 2–June 5, 1865

I can see but little hope for these confederate states in these times.
—William Cowan McClellan

By 1865, there were few men on either side who didn't believe the war was almost over. With a Confederate victory seemingly no longer possible, the only question was when the Confederate states would be brought back into the Union. The Army of the Potomac had finally forced the Army of Northern Virginia to go into the ground around Richmond, and Ulysses S. Grant's main concern was to prevent Robert E. Lee from escaping Petersburg and joining up with Gen. Joseph E. Johnston in North Carolina.

In January 1865, the Army of Northern Virginia numbered 150,554 aggregate present and absent, but with only 61,748 present for duty.[1] Lee's army had been greatly reduced by casualties in battle, desertions, and the loss of key officers. It had been pinned down for nearly a year in the trenches around Petersburg and Richmond and could not openly mount an effective offensive against Grant's forces. As one historian has observed, Lee found out how much his army had changed during the Petersburg campaign.[2] Their weakness also showed on March 25, when Confederate major general John B. Gordon launched his offensive at Fort Stedman; Gordon's forces overwhelmed the Union defenders in the morning but were unable to maintain the momentum after the initial assault. The Confederates were quickly pushed back to their own lines with more than two thousand casualties.[3]

On March 29, Union general Philip Sheridan and two divisions of cavalry, supported by two infantry corps under G. K. Warren and A. A. Humphreys, moved on Lee's right flank, extending the Confederate lines to the breaking point. Rain slowed the Union advance, but skirmishing occurred at Hatcher's Run on March 30, and heavy fighting continued the next day on White Oak Road. Despite a spirited Confederate resistance, on April 1 Union forces overwhelmed George Pickett's division at Five Forks and succeeded in almost encircling Petersburg.[4] Lee had no choice but to abandon Richmond on April 2, as Grant ordered an assault all along the Petersburg line that day. The Army of Northern Virginia, along with William Cowan

McClellan and the 9th Alabama, began the long journey toward Appomattox Court House.

All during this time, Union occupation forces and the many cavalry raids through Alabama tightened the Union's grip on the northern part of the state. Many Limestone County citizens were suffering. They still supported the troops in the field, but they were in deep despair. Mary Fielding of Athens, Alabama, mentions in her diary on January 7, 1865, that a Union cavalry force had paid a visit to her area: "They have neither the rations nor the forage for their horses & are taking literally everything from the people. They have been to our house and taken all of the corn, some meat, clothes . . . I don't see where the people are to get provisions, especially corn . . . I have never thought that I'd starve, but I don't know where the bread is going to come from now."[5] It was clear that morale was low at home, due in part to conditions there but also to the continual losses by Confederate armies in Virginia and Tennessee. No home was safe, and few—including that of the McClellans—were untouched by visits from both Union and Confederate soldiers. Generally meeting weak resistance from ill-equipped and demoralized troops, James Harrison Wilson's raid through Alabama in March and April of 1865 laid waste to factories and mills from Lauderdale County to Selma.[6]

In March, William McClellan's brother Robert was en route from Charlotte, North Carolina, to Gen. Joseph Wheeler's command near Raleigh. Wheeler was attempting to hook up with General Johnston, or possibly to head for Virginia to support Lee. Robert McClellan hoped he might have an opportunity to get to Petersburg and see William. In a letter to his father on March 18, 1865, Robert comments on the large numbers of former Confederate prisoners making their way home, and he notes, "the hour is dark but I think a better time is coming. The big battle of the war will come off soon which will certainly decide the question of liberty and subjugation . . . "[7] The Army of Northern Virginia, as well as Wheeler's forces, surrendered before Robert could get to Petersburg.

William and the other members of his company who remained in the lines outside of Petersburg and Richmond no longer fought for the Confederacy or even for the folks back home—they fought for Robert E. Lee, and they fought for each other. Desertions and combat had reduced troop totals to the point that regiments did not mean very much by 1865. The 9th Alabama could muster fewer than one hundred men—with one hundred men being one-tenth of a regiment's ideal size—and some regiments had almost disappeared altogether. Rations were scarce, and clothing was greatly needed by the troops, although most men had shoes. The mail and passenger service between Virginia and Alabama was deteriorating, with rail service continually rerouted through the Carolinas in response to Union advances.[8] The uncertainty of mail service and the increase in desertions (which decreased the chance for furloughs) reduced the opportunity for soldiers to receive mail and send return mail home. Coupled with the fact that soldiers were writing fewer letters home, this explains why so few letters survive from William McClellan during late 1864 and 1865.

Sarah Anne McClellan Davis to William Cowan McClellan

Home, [Athens]
January 2, 1865
My dear brother,
The year has come around with excitement and trouble for the poor downtrodden people of Alabama. Sunday night four yankees came by and tried to press a pistol [on Pa] to go to their camp down at the mill. Pa evicted them and got off- but yesterday we had three thiefs to day has been worse. They took Bonaparte[,] a yankee horse we have had for sometime, and killed our last three turkeys- making twenty two in all they have taken from us- and fruit- tin vessels and shot nearly all the chickens besides taking several pieces of meat and all the sausage. They robed two bee farms and as they had filled all their buckets they undertook to get another to put their honey in. Tommy hid one water bucket, and Pa ran in mother's corn with the other, and left it with me. Directly a yankee came and took a general search for it swearing every breath. I quietly kept my seat which was the water bucket and of course the gent. Had to leave without it. Yesterday I went to the dairy to get a bucket with a little milk in it- a yankee came cursing half-bent asking "what you got." I turned it bottoms upwards and kept on- he was very angry, swore he would do ten times worse. Pa was very uneasy- thought he might bring on a crowd; but they had all gone on and those today were a different set. Of all the senseless squabbles, these today were the worst- full of their impudent, insulting remarks- fired off their guns in [our] yard many times. They took thirty pieces of meat from Mr. Fletcher, a hundred pounds of sugar, spading utensils-combs-provender-flour-clothes and robed all the negroes. Broke him up in the way of horses. Mr. Vaughan came off even worse. Lost all

of his horses-four- forty pounds of coffee- all they had. Mrs. Smith lost some provisions, but no stock. Mr. Davis was here when they came yesterday morning, and they asked him if he had two fine grey mules. He told them he had, that he would show them where he had hauled them off- both having [been] sick with glanders. Pa thinks the horse they got here has it. All the horses in the county are aging with it.[9] They hadn't been to Mr. D nor Mr. Moore's. Mr. M. has not lost anything yet, neither has Mr. Sam P. We think the Ishoms are sending them on this creek. The yankees say they have been told that people down here lost nothing. Pa is worried nearly to death. J. B. M. [John Beattie McClellan] sent his bond in last night by R. A. M. [Robert Anderson McClellan] who wanted to come anyway to get some men who dodged him when he had to leave before, but with the yankees so thick he can't do anything now. The bond I speak of is the one he gave a Probate Judge having evidenced the appointment- Tyus being dead.[10] he left to find the circuit judge to have it approved by the Circuit Court Clerk who is not here. The time allowed by the law for making it is almost out. [The rest of the letter appears to be missing as there is no closing.]

William Cowan McClellan to Robert Anderson McClellan

Camp Near Petersburg, Va
March 24, 1865
Dear Bob,
I was very agreeably surprised yesterday at the reception of your letter of the 18th inst. This is the first news I have had from you in five months since your letter written at Gadsden. I received a letter a day or too ago from Matilda dated Dec 2 giving me the news in North Al up to that time. She generally gives me as much news as a couple of news papers tells me you had a gay time at a party at Esq Robertsons, your efforts to raise a company haveing a position for me & last but not least of the reported marriage of Miss M.[aggie] Lipscomb to Hiram Faulks. My hopes have departed like the glory of the noon day sun. My heart has again been wrecked for the 20th time upon the matrimonial sea. About two weeks ago we moved from the extreme right of our lines South of Petersburg to this position between the Appomattox and James River. Relieving Picketts Division which have had a good time and no fighting for the last

10 months. The left of our Brigade rests on the James. The right of the Lines are all aflame from attacks. Our Division has been commanded for a long time by Maj. Gen. Wm. Mahone formerly of the Va. Brigade of the Div. He was just today presented with a sword by the ladys of Petersburg. I will send you his remarks on the occasion. Also his report of the campaign. Some how or other I have been thinking a great deal presently about home, particularly about Father and Mother. They are getting old and feeble as Matilda says and I have a longing to be with them to comfort support and protect them. Suppose you and I will fall [in] this duty for this reason you must not expose yourself to numerous dangers. As for me I am in no danger at preasant as I now hold and have now for a long time a Bomb proof position but one I would gladly exchange for your Branch of service. We all expect here to see before long the army of Tennessee & georgia to the right the army of Va. We will commence the last great struggle for Richmond. Grant is perfectly quiet seems to be waiting for Sherman to win all the glory. You will excuse me for saying that Grant has had to contend with the greatest gen. the world ever produced. Napoleon acknowledged. The latter was sometime defeated with equal numbers, [Lee] fought even with overwhelming odds against him. No matter if our country goes down tomorrow Lees name will stand to repose at the pinnacle of fame, as the greatest of commanders living or dead. If your army was not on the move I would apply for a few days leave of absence to pay you a visit but under existing circumstances would be doubtful finding you. Bob I am low down. I can see but little hope for these confederate states in these times. My kindest regards to all the Boys. Write each opportunity possible.[11]

Your brother
W.C.McClellan

From Richmond to Sayler's Creek: April 2–6, 1865

On April 2, 1865, Gen. Ulysses S. Grant began his assault all along the Confederate lines outside of Richmond and Petersburg, which forced Lee to the western outskirts of the city. That night, Confederate office clerks burned what couldn't be carried away, and soldiers attached explosive charges to ironclad ships in the James River and to buildings near the capitol grounds. Lee's army moved westward toward Amelia Court House, as they hoped to reach much-needed supplies there before attempting a rendezvous with Gen. Joseph E. Johnston's forces somewhere in North Carolina. The army turned southwest as first Lee attempted to reach the Raleigh-Durham area; but, cut off by advancing Union cavalry, he turned toward Farmville, Virginia, with a view of reaching the mountains around Lynchburg. On April 6, Grant caught up with the rear of Lee's army at Sayler's Creek, to the east of Farmville.

With the death of Gen. A. P. Hill at Petersburg, the 3rd Corps, including Maj. Gen. William Mahone's division and the 9th Alabama, were transferred to Lt. Gen. James Longstreet's 1st Corps. On the morning of April 6, Longstreet's corps was already to the west of Sayler's Creek and approaching Rice's Station. Around 11 a.m. the rear of Longstreet's column, under Mahone, became separated from the head of Lt. Gen. Richard H. Anderson's forces, as Anderson responded to an attack by Union cavalry on his line of march near Holt's Corner. Federal cavalry under Gen. George Armstrong Custer and Maj. Gen. Wesley Merrett concentrated to block Anderson, while Gen. Horatio G. Wright's 6th Corps came up behind Gen. Richard Ewell's corps. This was a hopeless situation for the Confederates, and after several hours of fighting, more than 7,600 Confederates were forced to surrender.[12]

Lee and Longstreet were unaware of the disaster at Sayler's Creek. Lee, wondering why the other corps had not arrived at Rice's Station, selected Mahone's division to ride back with him to investigate. After viewing the disaster from a knoll overlooking the creek, Longstreet and Lee returned to Farmville that night. Mahone was instructed to remain at Sayler's Creek to delay the Union advance and then to burn the railroad bridge, High Bridge, over the Appomattox River after his forces crossed over. Mahone put some of his men into the line within sight of the approaching enemy.[13]

As Mahone's division prepared to cross the High Bridge at midnight, orders were given for two companies of the 9th Alabama to guard the bridge and set fire to it after the division had crossed. The 8th Alabama skirmishers were also in support. At dawn, the bridge was yet to be burned, and Mahone had to send back a detail to fire the bridge. Just as the Confederates were starting to set fire to it, Union forces arrived at the bridge and captured the guards and the skirmish line of the 8th Alabama.[14] Because only one or two spans of the bridge were damaged, the Union forces could cross it and continue the pursuit. The remaining Confederate forces made their way to Appomattox.

Point Lookout Prison: April 14–June 7, 1865

Documents from both the National Archives in Washington, D.C., and the St. Mary's County (Maryland) Historical Society indicate that William

Cowan McClellan was a prisoner of war at Point Lookout Prison in St. Mary's County, Maryland. According to the records, he was captured on April 6, 1865, at Burkeville, Virginia, and was transported to City Point, Virginia, on April 14.[15] While at Point Lookout, he was mustered into the camp hospital (for unknown reasons), and the hospital record indicates that he had been captured at High Bridge on April 6.[16] High Bridge was on the railroad to Appomattox Court House near Burkeville, and it was the bridge that the 9th Alabama was supposed to help burn; thus it was probably the site of his capture.

On Sunday, April 9, 1865, Gen. Robert E. Lee surrendered the Army of Northern Virginia at Appomattox Court House. During nearly four years of war, almost 1,600 men had served in the 9th Alabama Regiment, and they had marched more than 2,400 miles through six states, had fought in twenty battles, and had seen their ranks dwindle to just 75 men by the surrender. Along with William Cowan McClellan, several other members of the 9th Alabama were captured before Appomattox, and they were marched to Burkeville, Virginia, on April 7.[17] The Union troops who had confronted these men for four years showed them much respect and many kindnesses; they gave them food, clothes, and blankets as the prisoners were marched out. Eight thousand prisoners were marched to City Point (Hopewell), Virginia, by the 48th Pennsylvania, the 9th New Hampshire, and 39th New Jersey regiments.[18] There, they boarded ships for Point Lookout, Maryland, and Washington, D.C.

Point Lookout Prison sits at the very tip of St Mary's County, Maryland, on forty-five acres of land between the Potomac River and the Chesapeake Bay. It is completely surrounded by water, except for a small isthmus of land about a mile across. The Confederate "prison pens" were encircled by a fifteen-foot-high board fence along the edge of the bay. Atop the board fence was a catwalk along which the guards patrolled. Ten feet inside the wall was the "deadline," a line no prisoner was allowed to go beyond. The climate was hot and damp, and the land swampy. The base hospital was situated in the very point of the peninsula and consisted of twenty buildings "forming a circle . . . arranged like the spokes of a wheel."[19] The hospital was frequently found to be lacking in sufficient clothing and sanitary conditions. One prisoner reported in his journal that most prisoners who entered the prison hospital died there.[20] William was fortunate to have been an exception to that rule. The prison operated from August 1863 through 1865 with 52,264 prisoners imprisoned there. During those years, nearly four thousand of them died.[21]

On June 5, 1865, William reported with other prisoners to take the oath of allegiance and to receive his parole papers. By the time William received his parole, he had been a prisoner of war for nearly two months—two months after Lee had surrendered the Army of Northern Virginia. He may have boarded a ship to Mobile Bay for the return home (ships were provided to take some of the former prisoners back home by sailing around Florida to Mobile Bay), or he may have gone across country by train or on foot as other Confederate soldiers did. No records indicate how William traveled home. A family legend told that one summer day some of the townspeople of Athens, Alabama, looked up the road leading to town and saw William Cowan McClellan walking toward home.

Epilogue

William Cowan McClellan returned to a desolated Limestone County countryside whose homes and businesses were mostly pillaged, burned, or destroyed. There was a shortage of livestock and crops, and the scarcity of food threatened parts of the population with starvation. As one soldier described the scene, "most of the fields . . . were covered by briars and weeds, the fences were burned or broken down. The chimneys in every direction stood like quiet sentinels and marked the site of once prosperous and happy homes. Long since reduced to heaps of ashes. No cattle, hogs, horses, mules, or domestic fowl were in sight."[1] The McClellan family was fortunate—their home was still standing. Like most Alabamians, the McClellans faced a new world during the Reconstruction years as they tried to rebuild their lives.

Despite the difficulties, some normalcy returned to their lives. On October 15, 1866, William married Susan Strong of Madison County, Alabama, at her father's house. They bought a small farm adjacent to the McClellan farm, and within the next three years they had two daughters, Charlie Alice McClellan and Willie McClellan. Willie never married and became a successful businesswoman in Huntsville, Alabama. Charlie married Tony Arthur White of Pulaski, Tennessee, and had three children, including my grandmother Nancy Susan White (Carter).

William McClellan, however, did not have long to live. Perhaps it was the strain of four years of hard marching, battle, sickness, and constant deprivations; or perhaps it was the unsanitary prison conditions and poor food. But by late 1869, his body finally gave out. The family said he died of consumption, but the official record listed the cause of death as "congestion of the kidneys." The backaches that leveled William for weeks at a time during the war were probably the beginning of his fatal ailment. His final days were spent in his father's house, where he died on December 9, 1869. His young wife, Susan, raised her two children alone over the next ten years but later married David K. West of Pulaski, Tennessee. She remained in Pulaski, close to her children and grandchildren, until she died.

Thomas Joyce McClellan continued as a successful farmer and businessman, although he never again sought political office. John Beattie McClellan became a probate judge and a state legislator in Alabama. Robert Anderson McClellan became a state legislator, an attorney, and later the mayor of Athens. Thomas Nicholas McClellan became the attorney general of Alabama and later the chief justice of the Alabama Supreme Court. Matilda McClellan never married but cared for the family and oversaw two of her brothers' law offices. The other two daughters, Sarah Anne and Martha Catherine (Kate), both married and raised families. After the elder Martha's death in 1883, Thomas Joyce McClellan retired from the farm and moved a short distance into the town of Athens before he died in 1887. Robert McClellan died in 1898, and Thomas in 1906. Matilda died at her sister Kate's home in Fayetteville, Tennessee, in 1917.

A paved country road runs along the outer edge of the old McClellan estate outside of Athens in the section of the county called "Capshaw." This is still mainly farm country, although a large state corrections facility now occupies some of the land. From the road you can look out across about two hundred yards of bean fields to a line of trees along Limestone Creek where the McClellan children once played. The old home, as well as the large gates William remembered, is gone, destroyed by fire in 1901. Within the tree line is a small clearing surrounded by a modern chain fence, within which William McClellan is buried with his father and mother. The rest of the family are buried elsewhere: his brothers, John, Robert, and Thomas, and sisters Matilda and Sarah Anne are buried in Athens; his sister Martha Catherine is buried in Fayetteville, Tennessee; and his daughters are buried in Pulaski, Tennessee, and Huntsville, Alabama.

In Limestone County and the state of Alabama, the McClellans are remembered for the way they lived their lives and their contributions to their community, rather than the relics they left behind. They supported Alabama's stand in 1861; and when that failed, they turned their efforts toward rebuilding their lives and community. They served in the courts and the legislatures of Alabama and in the courts and government offices of Athens into the first two decades of the twentieth century. The McClellan family saw their state and country through the periods of Reconstruction, the First World War, and the rise of America as a national power.

William's letters, and especially the letters to him from home, form a narrative of a Southern family's life in a time of great trial. Mixed with the routine family events of birth, death, school, and marriage were the exceptional events of war, separation, sustained loyalty, and fear of destruction and loss. The letters offer a look at Southern culture through the eyes of a family living within that culture as it faced radical challenges to its very existence. Even more, the letters represent a documentary about a young man coming of age as both a man and a soldier, and about the family relationships that were strained by distance and events beyond their control.

William went away to war in June 1861 as a young, carefree boy who had never been more than thirty miles from home. While in the army, he grew as a person and assumed responsibility for his own life and for the men who served around him. He saw the horrors of war and endured its deprivations: the frequent sickness, the death of friends, and wounds received in battle. His boyish exuberance and thoughts of heroic victory at the start of the war changed to an understanding of how to live with the constant presence of death and the realization that, despite his best efforts, there was no hope for the Confederacy. William's morale and sense of patriotism changed from his initial excitement about fighting for the Confederacy to a belief in the cause inspired by regional pride and sacrifice. Finally, through combat and the emotional bonds of shared suffering, his loyalty and morale became more associated with the men who were still left in his company, the regiment, and the provost guard.

William was a late casualty of the war, one not recorded in the official statistics since his death neither occurred on the battlefield nor was directly attributable to a wound. Yet the war did kill him—if nothing else, it wore him down after four harsh years and his short stay at Point Lookout Prison. His letters reveal how an average soldier saw the war and how he dealt with the events that confronted him. They also show that William constantly reevaluated his position in the army throughout the war, and that his morale and values changed as he became caught up in the uncontrollable forces and events of the war. Regardless of his accomplishments on the battlefield or of his growth as a person and a soldier, the most significant thing is that he served his homeland from the beginning of the war to the very end.

Appendix A

List of the Letters

Date	Letter from	Letter to	Source of letter
Jan. 14, 1861	Thomas Joyce McClellan	Martha Beattie McClellan	LIMA
June 15, 1861	Matilda McClellan	William Cowan McClellan	UNC-SHC
June 20, 1861	William Cowan McClellan	Thomas Joyce McClellan	FAM
June 21, 1861	William Cowan McClellan	Robert Anderson McClellan	UNC-SHC
June 23, 1861	William Cowan McClellan	Matilda McClellan	UNC-SHC
June 30, 1861	William Cowan McClellan	Nicholas Davis Jr.	UNC-SCH
July 4, 1861	William Cowan McClellan	Thomas Joyce McClellan	FAM
July 4, 1861	Thomas Joyce McClellan	William Cowan McClellan	FAM
July 6, 1861	William Cowan McClellan	Thomas Joyce McClellan	UNC—SHC
July 8, 1861	William Cowan McClellan	Robert Anderson McClellan	FAM
July 21, 1861	Matilda McClellan	William Cowan McClellan	UNC-SHC
July 21, 1861	William Cowan McClellan	Thomas Joyce McClellan	FAM
July 22, 1861	William Cowan McClellan	Thomas Joyce McClellan	FAM

Date	Letter from	Letter to	Source of letter
July 29, 1861	William Cowan McClellan	Thomas Joyce McClellan	UNC-SHC
July 30, 1861	William Cowan McClellan	Robert Anderson McClellan	FAM
Aug. 7, 1861	William Cowan McClellan	Robert Anderson McClellan	FAM
Aug. 7, 1861	Lawrence Ripley Davis	William Cowan McClellan	FAM
Aug. 8, 1861	Thomas Joyce McClellan	William Cowan McClellan	UNC-SHC
Aug. 12, 1861	William Cowan McClellan	Sallie Anne McClellan Davis	UNC-SHC
Aug. 13, 1861	William Cowan McClellan	Robert Anderson McClellan	UNC-SHC
Aug. 18, 1861	William Cowan McClellan	Matilda McClellan	UNC-SHC
Mid-Aug.	William Cowan McClellan	Thomas Joyce McClellan	FAM
Aug. 22, 1861	Matilda McClellan	William Cowan McClellan	FAM
Aug. 24, 1861	William Cowan McClellan	Robert Anderson McClellan	FAM
Aug. 30, 1861	William Cowan McClellan	Robert Anderson McClellan	FAM
Aug. 31, 1861	William Cowan McClellan	Matilda McClellan	FAM
Aug. 31, 1861	Matilda McClellan	William Cowan McClellan	UNC-SHC
Sept. 6, 1861	William Cowan McClellan	Robert Anderson McClellan	FAM
Sept. 6, 1861	William Cowan McClellan	Thomas Joyce McClellan	FAM
Sept. 9, 1861	Sallie Anne McClellan Davis	William Cowan McClellan	UNC-SHC

Date	Letter from	Letter to	Source of letter
Sept. 10, 1861	John and Matilda McClellan	William Cowan McClellan	UNC-SHC
Sept. 13, 1861	William Cowan McClellan	Robert Anderson McClellan	UNC-SHC
Mid-Sept., 1861	William Cowan McClellan	Thomas Joyce McClellan	FAM
Sept. 16, 1861	Robert Anderson McClellan	William Cowan McClellan	DUKE
Sept. 19, 1861	William Cowan McClellan	Robert Anderson McClellan	FAM
Sept. 21, 1861	William Cowan McClellan	Thomas Joyce McClellan	FAM
Sept. 27, 1861	William Cowan McClellan	Matilda McClellan	UNC-SHC
Sept. 28. 1861	Robert Anderson McClellan	William Cowan McClellan	DUKE
Sept. 30, 1861	William Cowan McClellan	Robert Anderson McClellan	UNC-SHC
Oct. 3, 1861	William Cowan McClellan	Thomas Joyce McClellan	FAM
Oct. 5, 1861	Robert Anderson McClellan	William Cowan McClellan	FAM
Oct. 6, 1861	William Cowan McClellan	Robert Anderson McClellan	FAM
Oct. 10, 1861	Thomas Joyce McClellan	William Cowan McClellan	FAM
Oct. 11, 1861	Matilda McClellan	William Cowan McClellan	FAM
Oct. 17, 1861	Robert and Thomas Joyce McClellan	William McClellan	UNC-SHC
Oct. 18, 1861	Robert Anderson McClellan	William Cowan McClellan	FAM
Oct. 22, 1861	William Cowan McClellan	Thomas Joyce McClellan	FAM

Date	Letter from	Letter to	Source of letter
Oct. 26, 1861	William Cowan McClellan	John Beattie McClellan	FAM
Oct. 31, 1861	William Cowan McClellan	Robert Anderson McClellan	FAM
Nov. 3, 1861	William Cowan McClellan	Martha Beattie McClellan	FAM
Nov. 9, 1861	William Cowan McClellan	Martha Beattie McClellan	UNC-SHC
Nov. 9, 1861	William Cowan McClellan	Robert Anderson McClellan	FAM
Nov. 14, 1861	William Cowan McClellan	Robert Anderson McClellan	FAM
Nov. 16, 1861	William Cowan McClellan	Thomas Joyce McClellan	UNC-SHC
Nov. 21, 1861	William Cowan McClellan	Thomas Joyce McClellan	FAM
Nov. 22, 1861	William Cowan McClellan	Matilda McClellan	FAM
Nov. 23, 1861	William Cowan McClellan	Matilda McClellan	FAM
Nov. 25, 1861	William Cowan McClellan	Robert Anderson McClellan	UNC-SHC
Dec. 6, 1861	William Cowan McClellan	Robert Anderson McClellan	UNC-SHC
Dec. 10, 1861	William Cowan McClellan	Matilda McClellan	UNC-SHC
Dec. 18, 1861	William Cowan McClellan	Thomas Joyce McClellan	UNC-SHC
Dec. 20, 1861	William Cowan McClellan	Thomas Joyce McClellan	FAM
Dec. 25, 1861	William Cowan McClellan	Matilda McClellan	FAM
Dec. 31, 1861	William Cowan McClellan	Thomas Joyce McClellan	FAM

Date	Letter from	Letter to	Source of letter
Jan. 8, 1862	William Cowan McClellan	Thomas Joyce McClellan	UNC-SHC
Jan. 10, 1862	William Cowan McClellan	Matilda McClellan	FAM
Jan. 14, 1862	William Cowan McClellan	John Beattie McClellan	UNC-SHC
Jan. 15, 1862	William Cowan McClellan	Thomas Joyce McClellan	FAM
Jan. 17, 1862	William Cowan McClellan	Matilda McClellan	FAM
Jan. 17, 1862	William Cowan McClellan	Robert Anderson McClellan	FAM
Jan. 19, 1862	William Cowan McClellan	Thomas Joyce McClellan	FAM
Jan. 22, 1862	William Cowan McClellan	Robert Anderson McClellan	FAM
Jan. 25, 1862	William Cowan McClellan	Robert Anderson McClellan	FAM
Jan. 31, 1862	William Cowan McClellan	Matilda McClellan	FAM
Feb. 4, 1862	William Cowan McClellan	Robert Anderson McClellan	FAM
Feb. 7, 1862	William Cowan McClellan	Robert Anderson McClellan	FAM
Feb. 9, 1862	William Cowan McClellan	Thomas Joyce McClellan	FAM
Feb. 10, 1862	William Cowan McClellan	Matilda McClellan	UNC-SHC
Feb. 15, 1862	Robert Anderson McClellan	William Cowan McClellan	DUKE
Feb. 15, 1862	William Cowan McClellan	Thomas Joyce McClellan	FAM
Feb. 20, 1862	William Cowan McClellan	Matilda McClellan	FAM

Date	Letter from	Letter to	Source of letter
Feb. 27, 1862	William Cowan McClellan	Thomas Joyce McClellan	FAM
Mar. 4, 1862	William Cowan McClellan	Robert Anderson McClellan	FAM
Mar. 20, 1862	William Cowan McClellan	Thomas Joyce McClellan	FAM
Mar. 21, 1862	William Cowan McClellan	Robert Anderson McClellan	FAM
Mar. 24, 1862	William Cowan McClellan	Robert Anderson McClellan	FAM
Mar. 25, 1862	William Cowan McClellan	Matilda McClellan	FAM
Apr. 13, 1862	William Cowan McClellan	Robert Anderson McClellan	FAM
Apr. 15, 1862	William Cowan McClellan	Thomas Joyce McClellan	FAM
Apr. 16, 1862	William Cowan McClellan	Matilda McClellan	FAM
May 26, 1862	William Cowan McClellan	Thomas Joyce McClellan	FAM
June 16, 1862	William Cowan McClellan	Thomas Joyce McClellan	FAM
July 6, 1862	William Cowan McClellan	Thomas Joyce McClellan	FAM
July 8, 1862	William Cowan McClellan	Robert Anderson McClellan	UNC-SHC
July 27, 1862	William Cowan McClellan	Thomas Joyce McClellan	UNC-SHC
July 27, 1862	William Cowan McClellan	Robert Anderson McClellan	FAM
Aug. 9, 1862	William Cowan McClellan	Martha Beattie McClellan	UNC-SHC
Aug. 20, 1862	William Cowan McClellan	Robert Anderson McClellan	FAM

Date	Letter from	Letter to	Source of letter
Sept. 24, 1862	William Cowan McClellan	Robert Anderson McClellan	FAM
Oct. 2, 1862	William Cowan McClellan	Robert Anderson McClellan	FAM
Oct. 3, 1862	William Cowan McClellan	Matilda McClellan	FAM
Oct. 21, 1862	William Cowan McClellan	Thomas Joyce McClellan	FAM
Nov. 10, 1862	William Cowan McClellan	Sister	FAM
Nov. 14, 1862	William Cowan McClellan	Thomas Joyce McClellan	UNC-SHC
Nov. 15, 1862	William Cowan McClellan	Thomas Joyce McClellan	FAM
Nov. 18, 1862	William Cowan McClellan	Matilda McClellan	FAM
Dec. 3, 1862	William Cowan McClellan	Matilda McClellan	FAM
Dec. 10, 1862	William Cowan McClellan	Thomas Joyce McClellan	UNC-SHC
Dec. 15, 1862	William Cowan McClellan	Thomas Joyce McClellan	UNC-SHC
Dec. 28, 1862	William Cowan McClellan	Thomas Joyce McClellan	UNC-SHC
Jan. 1, 1863	William Cowan McClellan	Sister	UNC-SHC
Jan. 3, 1863	William Cowan McClellan	Sisters	FAM
Jan. 3, 1863	William Cowan McClellan	Sister	FAM
Jan. 7, 1863	William Cowan McClellan	Thomas Joyce McClellan	UNC-SHC
Jan. 12, 1863	William Cowan McClellan	Thomas Joyce McClellan	FAM

Date	Letter from	Letter to	Source of letter
Feb. 6, 1863	William Cowan McClellan	Matilda McClellan	FAM
Feb. 9, 1863	William Cowan McClellan	Thomas Joyce McClellan	UNC-SHC
Feb. 20, 1863	William Cowan McClellan	Sister	UNC-SHC
Mar. 1, 1863	William Cowan McClellan	Thomas Joyce McClellan	FAM
Mar. 3, 1863	William Cowan McClellan	Thomas Joyce McClellan	UNC-SHC
Mar. 8, 1863	William Cowan McClellan	Thomas Joyce McClellan	FAM
Mar. 16, 1863	William Cowan McClellan	Sister	FAM
Mar. 23, 1863	William Cowan McClellan	Thomas Joyce McClellan	UNC-SHC
Mar. 24, 1863	William Cowan McClellan	Matilda McClellan	
Mar. 28, 1863	William Cowan McClellan	Matilda McClellan	FAM
Apr. 13, 1863	William Cowan McClellan	Matilda McClellan	FAM
Apr. 22, 1863	William Cowan McClellan	Matilda McClellan	FAM
Apr. 30, 1863	William Cowan McClellan	Sister	FAM
May 8, 1863	William Cowan McClellan	Sister	FAM
May 10, 1863	William Cowan McClellan	Thomas Joyce McClellan	UNC-SHC
May 15, 1863	William Cowan McClellan	Thomas Joyce McClellan	FAM
May 15, 1863	William Cowan McClellan	Sister	FAM

Date	Letter from	Letter to	Source of letter
May 19, 1863	William Cowan McClellan	Sallie Anne McClellan Davis	UNC-SHC
May 19, 1863	William Cowan McClellan	Sister	FAM
May 28, 1863	William Cowan McClellan	Sister	UNC-SHC
June 11, 1863	William Cowan McClellan	Sister	FAM
June 17, 1863	William Cowan McClellan	Thomas Joyce McClellan	FAM
July 4, 1863	William Cowan McClellan	Thomas Joyce McClellan	FAM
July 9, 1863	William Cowan McClellan	Sister	FAM
Aug. 22, 1863	William Cowan McClellan	Martha Catherine McClellan	UNC-SHC
Sept. 20, 1863	William Cowan McClellan	Matilda McClellan	FAM
Sept. 21, 1863	William Cowan McClellan	John Beattie McClellan	DUKE
Nov. 17, 1863	William Cowan McClellan	Sister	UNC-SHC
Nov. 25, 1863	William Cowan McClellan	Sister	UNC-SHC
Nov. 26, 1863	William Cowan McClellan	Matilda McClellan	FAM
Dec. 8, 1863	William Cowan McClellan	Matilda McClellan	FAM
Feb. 17, 1864	William Cowan McClellan	Matilda McClellan	UNC-SHC
Feb. 27, 1864	William Cowan McClellan	Thomas Joyce McClellan	FAM
Apr. 27, 1864	William Cowan McClellan	Robert Anderson McClellan	FAM

Date	Letter from	Letter to	Source of letter
May 1, 1864	William Cowan McClellan	Robert Anderson McClellan	UNC-SHC
June 2, 1864	William Cowan McClellan	Matilda McClellan	FAM
July 16, 1864	William Cowan McClellan	Thomas Joyce McClellan	FAM
Aug. 10, 1864	William Cowan McClellan	Robert Anderson McClellan	UNC-SHC
Aug. 15, 1864	William Cowan McClellan	Robert Anderson McClellan	FAM
Aug. 23, 1864	William Cowan McClellan	Thomas Joyce McClellan	UNC-SHC
Sept. 25, 1864	William Cowan McClellan	Sister	UNC-SHC
Oct. 1864	William Cowan McClellan	Matilda McClellan	UNC-SHC
Jan. 2, 1865	Sarah Anne McClellan Davis	William Cowan McClellan	UNC-SHC
Mar. 24, 1865	William Cowan McClellan	Robert Anderson McClellan	DUKE

Sources: FAM—McClellan, Family Letters, Carter family, Tullahoma, Tennessee; LIMA—McClellan, Family Papers, Limestone County Archives, Athens, Alabama; UNC-SHC—Buchanan-McClellan Papers, 1816–1917, Accession #1850, Manuscript Department, Southern Historical Collection, Library of the University of North Carolina at Chapel Hill; DUKE—Robert Anderson McClellan, Papers, Special Collections, Duke University Library, Durham, North Carolina

Appendix B

9th Alabama Regiment Casualities/Enlistment Totals

Battle/Location	Date of Battle or Arrival at Camp	Size of Regiment	Size of Company F	Number in Regiment Killed-Wounded-Captured	Number Died by End of Year from Illness, Wounds, Other
Departure from Alabama	June 6, 1861	1,005	110	Not engaged	
Richmond, VA camp	June 13, 1861	1,000	100	Not engaged	
En route to Strasburg, VA	July 15, 1861	980	108	Not engaged	
First Battle of Manassas, VA	July 21, 1861	980	108	Not engaged	
Bristoe Station camp, VA	Aug. 12– Sept. 21, 1861	963	82	Not engaged	
Centreville, VA, camp	Sept. 22–Dec. 30, 1861	934	79	Not engaged	62
Broad Run, VA, winter camp	Dec. 31, 1861–Mar. 8, 1862	575	75	Not engaged	
Siege of Yorktown/ Warwick, VA	Apr. 1–16, 1862	550	82	1-3-0	
Battle of Williamsburg, VA	May 5, 1862	550	124	10-48-15	
Battle of Seven Pines, VA	May 31, 1862	595	100	0-6-1	
Battle of Gaines's Mill, VA	June 27, 1862	425	90	44-92-9	
Battle of Frayser's Farm, VA	June 30, 1862	295	80	30-91-4	
Second Battle of Manassas, VA	Aug. 29–30, 1862	220	70	1-6-0	
Battle of Sharpsburg, MD	Sept. 17, 1862	220	60	10-18-9	

Battle of Fredericksburg, VA	Dec. 13, 1862	165	60	1-1-0	219
Battle of Salem Church, VA	May 3, 1863	165	60	23-89-2	
Battle of Gettysburg, PA	July 1, 1863	325	46	6-58-105	
Battle of Bristoe Station, VA	Oct. 14, 1863	262	46	0-0-3	
Orange Court House winter quarters	Nov. 17, 1863	262	46	Not engaged	
Battle of Mine Run, VA	Nov. 26–27, 1863	262	46	0-2-0	43
Battle of Spotsylvania, VA	May 8–21, 1864	250	46	1-5-1	
Battle of North Anna River, VA	May 23–26, 1864	200	45	0-1-1	
Battle of Cold Harbor, VA	June 1–3, 1864	125	45	2-2-0	
Battle of Petersburg, VA	June 15–18, 1864	125	30	5-2-9	
Petersburg siege	June 19–July 28, 1864	100	30	3-9-16	
Battle of the Crater, VA	July 30, 1864	95	25	2-9-0	
Battle of Burgess's Mill, VA	Oct. 27, 1864	90	25	1-5-2	48
Battle of Sayler's Creek, VA	Apr. 6, 1865	85	20	0-0-10	
Appomattox	Apr. 9, 1865	75	13	Not engaged	9

TOTALS

22 engagements

Enrolled during war in 9th Alabama	1,657	Discharged	176
Died in Battle	142	Deserted/AWOL	153
Died of illness, wounds, or other causes	229	Transferred	39
Wounded	455		
Missing/captured	242		
Total casualties	1,068		

Appendix C

9th Alabama Regiment Officers and Infantry Assignments

Principal Officers of the 9th Alabama after the First Battle of Manassas in 1861

Col. Cadmus M. Wilcox	Lt. Col. Samuel Henry	John N. Hayes, asst. surgeon
Maj. Edward Asbury O'Neal	Maj. Jeremiah Henry Johnston Williams	Adj. J. R. B. Burwell
Col. J. Horace King	Lt. Col. Gaynes Chislom Smith	Adj. D. F. Boyd
Maj. James McCullough	Adj. John C. Featherston Crow	Nicholas J. Floyd, asst. quartermaster
L. H. Anderson, surgeon	Henry A. Minor, surgeon	E. R. Till, ensign
M. L. Witten, chaplain	Solomon Stephens, commissary	Adj. William R. Holcomb
Steptoe Picket Jr., asst. quartermaster	J. F. Martin, asst. quartermaster	E. N. Thomson, asst. surgeon
William L. Wayland, asst. quartermaster	W. J. Gannon, asst. quartermaster	Aaron A. Burleson, quartermaster

9th Alabama Infantry Assignments

Date	Colonel of 9th AL	Brigade	Division	District/Corps
July 1, 1861	Cadmus M. Wilcox	Edmund Kirby Smith		Shenandoah/ Johnston
Oct. 22, 1861	Cadmus M. Wilcox	Edmund Kirby Smith	James Longstreet	Potomac/P. G. T. Beauregard
Nov. 1, 1861	Samuel Henry	Cadmus M. Wilcox	Gustavus Woodson Smith	Potomac/P. G. T. Beauregard

Jan. 14, 1862	Samuel Henry	Cadmus M. Wilcox	James Longstreet	Potomac/P. G. T. Beauregard
June 1, 1862	Jeremiah Henry Johnston Williams	Cadmus M. Wilcox	James Longstreet	No. Virginia/ James Longstreet
Aug. 1, 1862	J. Horace King	Cadmus M. Wilcox	Cadmus M. Wilcox	James Longstreet
Sept. 1, 1862	J. Horace King	Cadmus M. Wilcox	Richard H. Anderson	James Longstreet
May 1, 1863	J. Horace King	Cadmus M. Wilcox	Richard H. Anderson	James Longstreet
Aug. 31, 1863	J. C. C. Sanders	Abner M. Perrin	Richard H. Anderson	James Longstreet
Jan. 1, 1864	J. C. C. Sanders	Abner M. Perrin	Richard H. Anderson	James Longstreet
Apr. 1, 1864	J. C. C. Sanders	Abner M. Perrin	Richard H. Anderson	James Longstreet
May 12, 1864	J. Horace King	J. C. C. Sanders	Richard H. Anderson	James Longstreet
May 31, 1864	J. Horace King	J. C. C. Sanders	William Mahone	Ambrose Powell Hill
July 29, 1864	J. Horace King	J. C. C. Sanders	William Mahone	Ambrose Powell Hill
Dec. 1, 1864	J. Horace King	William H. Forney	William Mahone	Ambrose Powell Hill
Apr. 1, 1865	James McCullough Crow	William H. Forney	William Mahone	Ambrose Powell Hill

Source: *Compiled Records Showing Service of Military Units in Confederate Organizations,* Alabama 1st Infantry–11th Infantry (National Archives Microfilm Publication M861, roll 2)

Appendix D

Pvt. William Cowan McClellan's Military Record

Company H left Athens, Alabama, on June 6, 1861, for Lynchburg, Virginia, with the rest of the 9th Alabama Regiment. They were mustered into Capt. David Houston's company, the Limestone Greys, on June 18. William transferred to Capt. Thomas Hubbard Hobbs's company, Company F, the Limestone Troopers, on July 31, 1861.

Battle/assignment	Date
Missed the First Battle of Manassas (sick)	July 21, 1861
Regiment posted to Manassas Junction and Centreville, VA	July–Dec. 1861
Peninsula Campaign: Lebanon Church, VA	Apr. 1, 1862
Lee's Mill, VA	Apr. 16, 1862
Wynn's Mill, VA	Apr. 16, 1862
Burnt Ordinary, VA	May 6, 1862
Companies D & F on picket duty on Charles City Rd. (slightly wounded)	June 17, 1862
Battle of Seven Pines, VA (slightly wounded)	(May 31, 1862)
Gaines's Mill, VA	June 27, 1862
Battle of Frayser's Farm, VA	June 30, 1862
Regiment posted to Orange Court House and Centreville, VA	summer–fall 1862
Missed Second Battle of Manassas, VA, and Sharpsburg, MD (sick)	Aug.–Sept. 1862
Detailed provost guard at Fredericksburg, VA	winter 1862–63
Salem Church, VA	May 3, 1863
Companies A & F put into rifle pits at Chancellorsville, VA	June 14, 1863

Detailed provost guard at Gettysburg, PA	July 1863
Detailed provost guard at Anderson's headquarters	July 1863–Feb. 1864
Orange Court House, VA	Mar.–Apr. 1864
Detailed provost guard at Anderson's headquarters	Sept.–Oct. 1864
Detailed provost guard at Mahone's division	Oct.–Nov. 1864
Petersburg, VA	July 1864–Apr. 2, 1865
March to Sayler's Creek, VA	Apr. 2–6, 1865
Sayler's Creek/High Bridge, VA	Apr. 6–7, 1865
Arrived at City Point (Hopewell), VA	Apr. 14, 1865
Imprisoned at Point Lookout, MD	Apr. 15–June 5, 1865
Took oath and released	June 5, 1865

Source: *Compiled Service Records of Confederate Soldiers Who Served in Organizations from the State of Alabama,* 9th Alabama Infantry (National Archives Microfilm Publication M311, roll 187)

Appendix E

9th Alabama Regimental Roster for Companies F and H

Name	Co	Rank	Age	Occupation	Date enrolled	Notes	Died	Times wounded	Left co	Captured
Adkins, Thomas W.	F	Pvt	22	farmer	6/4/1861	wounded at Salem Church; deserted 8/12/64		1	1	
Allen, James H.	F	Pvt	27	farmer	6/4/1861	wounded at Gaines's Mill; captured at Gettysburg		1		1
Andrews, Benjamin F.	F	Pvt	25	farmer	6/4/1861	wounded at Gaines's Mill, Salem Church; deserted 7/2/63		2	1	
Andrews, Thomas B.	F	Pvt	23	farmer	6/4/1861	wounded at Salem Church, Gettysburg; deserted 7/2/63		2	1	
Andrews, William S.	F	Pvt	27	farmer	6/4/1861	wounded at Sharpsburg, Salem Church; deserted 8/12/64		2	1	
Atkins, Thomas W.	F	Pvt	22	farmer	6/4/1861	captured at Fussell's Mill				1
Bailes, James E.	F	Pvt	21	farmer	6/4/1861	wounded at Frayser's Farm, died of wounds	1	1		
Baker, John Council	F	Pvt	23	farmer	6/4/1861	deserted 3/10/62			1	
Bass Jr., Thomas	F	Pvt	35	"loafer"	6/4/1861	discharged: surgeon's cert. 9/15/61			1	
Batts, Frederick J.	F	1st Sgt	25	student	6/4/1861	killed at Salem Church	1			

Batts, Benjamin H.	F	Pvt	21	farmer	6/18/1861	killed at Gaines's Mill	1			
Baugh, John M.	F	Pvt	19	student	6/4/1861	died of typhoid 10/3/61 at Broad Run	1			
Baugh, Thomas B.	F	Lt	27	teacher	6/4/1861	captured at Fussell's Mill; sent to Fort Delaware prison				1
Bentley, David C.	F	Pvt	41	shoemaker	6/4/1861					
Bentley, Thomas H.	F	Pvt	22	farmer	6/4/1861					
Bibb, Henry C. (Hal)	F	3rd Lt	35	doctor	5/24/1861	wounded at Frayser's Farm; resigned 12/29/61		1	1	
Blansett, Elias A.	F	Pvt	25	farmer	6/4/1861	deserted 8/25/62; died 12/13/62	1			
Brackeen, Joseph	F	Pvt	23	farmer	3/1/1862	wounded at Gaines's Mill; died of wounds	1	1		
Braswell, David B.	F	Pvt	24	farmer	6/4/1861	wounded at Gettysburg 7/2/63; deserted 10/63		1	1	
Bridgeforth, David	F	Pvt	20	farmer	6/4/1861	wounded at Gaines's Mill; killed at Frayser's Farm	1	1		
Bridgeforth, John M.	F	2nd Cpl	23	merchant	6/4/1861	discharged 9/18/61 for disability			1	
Brooks, Albert M.	F	Pvt	23	farmer	6/4/1861	wounded at Frayser's Farm; captured at Gettysburg; discharged for disability		1	1	1
Brown, Joseph L.	F	Pvt			6/3/1861	Appomattox parole				

Name	Co	Rank	Age	Occupation	Date enrolled	Notes	Died	Times wounded	Left co	Captured
Broyles, Benjamin F.	F	Pvt	20	farmer	1/1/1863	wounded at Salem Church; Appomattox parole		1		
Broyles, George W.	F	Pvt	22	farmer	6/4/1861	appointed color guard corporal				
Broyles, Joseph M.	F	Pvt	25	farmer	10/6/1862	died 4/3/62 in hospital of typhoid fever	1			
Brundige, James W.	F	Pvt	22	farmer	6/4/1861	wounded at Frayser's Farm, Gettysburg; courier at brigade HQ; Appomattox parole		2		
Burleson, Dr. Aaron A.	F	Qtrmst			6/1/1861	Quartermaster of the 9th Alabama				
Carter, Alpheus B.	F	Pvt	29	farmer	3/24/1862	captured at Fussell's Mill 8/16/64				1
Carter, Thomas J.	F	Pvt	25	farmer	6/4/1861	wounded at Sharpsburg, Wilderness; deserted 8/14/64		2	1	
Cartwright, Hezekiah J.	F	2nd Lt	22	farmer	3/24/1862	captured: Gaines's Mill, Gettysburg; sent to Johnson's Island				2

Cartwright, Matthew Thomas	F	Pvt	22	farmer	6/4/1861	Appomattox parole				
Chapman, Calvin T.	F	Pvt	24	farmer	3/27/1862	killed at Gaines's Mill	1			
Clay, Samuel M.	F	Pvt	19	farmer	3/24/1862	wounded at Gettysburg 7/3/63, lost arm; captured at Gettysburg		1		1
Coleman, Daniel	F	Pvt	23	farmer	6/4/1861	aide to Gen. St. George Cocke; discharged at his death 1/16/62; transferred to GA artillery			1	
Cook, Francis Marion	F	Pvt	23	student	6/4/1861	Appomattox parole				
Cook, Napoleon Bonaparte	F	Pvt	23	student	6/4/1861	Appomattox parole				
Crenshaw, Freeman N.	F	Sgt	27	farmer	6/4/1861	captured at Charles City, VA, 7/10/62; deserted at Fussell's Mill 8/10/64			1	1
Crouch, Solomon	F	Pvt	47	laborer	6/4/1861	wounded at Richmond 1862		1		
Cruse, Sam (Henry)	F	Pvt	21	farmer	6/4/1861	wounded at Williamsburg, Gaines's Mill; died of wounds	1	2		
Culps, Robert L.	F	Pvt	22	farmer	3/24/1862	wounded at Gaines's Mill, Spotsylvania		2		
Dasson, Thomas D.	F	Pvt	27	stonecutter	3/10/1862					

Name	Co	Rank	Age	Occupation	Date enrolled	Notes	Died	Times wounded	Left co	Captured
David, Amos L.	F	Pvt	23	farmer	6/4/1861	wounded at Salem Church; deserted after 10/63		1	1	
Davis, Henry H.	F	Pvt	21	student	6/4/1861	transferred to Co. B, 9th Alabama			1	
Davis, Wilbur F.	F	Pvt	24	farmer	6/4/1861	discharged 10/2/62			1	
Davison, Thomas L.	F	Pvt			3/10/1862	wounded at Sharpsburg; captured at Burkeville, VA; sent to Point Lookout Prison		1		1
Deal, Robert C.	F	Pvt	29	farmer	6/4/1861	absent since 9/27/63				1
Dement, James D.	F	Pvt	27	teacher	3/10/1862	discharged by surgeon 7/14/62			1	
Dollar, William (Moses)	F	Pvt	41	black-smith	6/4/1861	discharged by surgeon 12/1/61			1	
Eagin, Bertrand	F	Pvt	25	doctor	3/24/1862	wounded at Salem Church, captured at Gettysburg; died at Point Lookout Prison	1	1		1
Eaves, Jack	F	Pvt								
Evans, Joseph	F	Pvt	24	farmer	6/4/1861	deserted at the Crater			1	

Ezell, Edward Press	F	Pvt	23	jockey	6/4/1861	wounded at Gaines's Mill; captured at Spotsylvania		1		1
Ezell, John T.	F	Pvt	21	student	6/4/1861	captured at Spotsylvania 5/13/64				1
Featherston, John C.	F	Capt	25	farmer	6/4/1861	wounded at Gettysburg		1		
Fielding, William Eppa	F	Pvt	24	teacher	6/4/1861	wounded at Gaines's Mill		1		
Fields, Billy	F	Pvt								
Fields, Thomas	F	Pvt								
Floyd, Nicholas J.	F	Capt	31	editor	6/4/1861	Captain in QM department 11/1/63			1	
Fogg, William Rufus	F	Pvt	22	farmer	6/4/1861	captured at Gettysburg; Appomattox parole				1
Garner, Andrew J. (Duck)	F	Pvt	23	farmer	6/4/1861	discharged 7/17/63 for disability			1	
Gilbert, George A.	F	1st Lt		farmer	6/4/1861	wounded at Gettysburg		1		
Gilbert, Thomas H.	F	Pvt	21	farmer	3/12/1862	wounded at Frayser's Farm; killed at the Crater	1	1		
Goodman, John	F	Pvt				Appomattox parole				
Graham, G. G.	F	Pvt			2/25/1862	wounded at Gaines's Mill		1		
Graves, Joel L.	F	Pvt	24	farmer	3/24/1862	wounded at Gettysburg 7/3/63; AWOL since Gettysburg		1	1	

Name	Co	Rank	Age	Occupation	Date enrolled	Notes	Died	Times wounded	Left co	Captured
Gray, Emmanuel (Tobe)	F	Pvt	21	farmer	1/22/1862	died in hospital 5/1/62	1			
Gray, Thaddeus	F	Pvt	22	farmer	3/10/1862	died of measles in hospital 5/1/62	1			
Green, Adam W.	F	Pvt	21		4/6/1861					
Greeson, Nathaniel A.	F	Pvt	30		6/4/1861	wounded at Gaines's Mill		1		
Greeson, Sam	F	Pvt				killed at Gaines's Mill	1			
Greeson, Thomas L.	F	Pvt	25			wounded at Frayser's Farm; deserted at Fussell's Mill 8/12/64		1	1	
Griffis, James Franklin	F	Pvt	22		6/4/1861	wounded at Gettysburg 7/3/63; captured at Gettysburg; discharged for disability		1	1	1
Grissom, Frank L.W.	F	Pvt								

Hamilton, Elam C.	F	Pvt	20	farmer	6/4/1861	wounded at Gaines's Mill, Salem Church, Wilderness; Appomattox parole		3		
Hammond, Joseph G.	F	Pvt	31	farmer	3/10/1862	wounded at Salem Church; captured at Gettysburg; died at Point Lookout Prison	1	1		1
Haney, Francis Marion	F	Pvt	25	farmer	6/4/1861	wounded at Gaines's Mill; killed at Gettysburg	1	1		
Haney, Isaac Boyd	F	Pvt	25	farmer	6/4/1861	wounded at Williamsburg; deserted 8/1/63; captured 10/9/63 at Sugar Creek, TN		1	1	1
Haney, J. Gid	F	Pvt	30	farmer	3/2/1862	wounded at Spotsylvania		1		
Hanserd, William R.	F	4th Sgt	32	teacher	6/4/1861	discharged for disability 10/61			1	
Hapner, John B.	F	Pvt			6/1861	wounded at Gaines's Mill		1		
Harmon, J. C.	F	Pvt				captured at Gettysburg				1
Harmon, Thomas W.	F	Pvt				Appomattox parole				1
Harmond, J. G.	F	Pvt				died at Point Lookout Prison	1			1
Harn, James M.	F	Pvt	21	farmer	6/4/1861	deserted at Fussell's Mill 8/16/64			1	
Harper, John	F	Pvt	28	farmer	3/24/1862	wounded at Gaines's Mill		1		
Harris, William	F	Pvt								

Name	Co	Rank	Age	Occupation	Date enrolled	Notes	Died	Times wounded	Left co	Captured
Harwell, Levi S.	F	Pvt	30	farmer	3/24/1862	wounded at Frayser's Farm, Salem Church, Wilcox Farm		3		
Harwell, William C.	F	Pvt	37	farmer	2/12/1863					
Hepner, John	F	Pvt				wounded at Gaines's Mill		1		
Hepner, William	F	Pvt								
Herg, Isaac	F	Pvt								
Hern, Joseph	F	Pvt				Appomattox parole				
Herring, James	F	Pvt								
Hide, Len	F	Pvt								
Hill, James H.	F	Pvt	27	farmer	6/4/1861	left ill at Fayetteville, PA, en route to Gettysburg and feared dead				1
Hill, John W.	F	Pvt	27	farmer	3/19/1862				1	
Hobbs, Thomas Hubbard	F	Capt	34	farmer	6/1861	wounded at Gaines's Mill; died of wounds	1	1		
Hogg, W. M.	F	Pvt								

Holcomb, William R.	F	Corp	22	merchant	6/4/1861	captured at Weldon Railroad; sent to Fort Delaware prison				1
Holland, Tilman H.	F	Pvt	35	school-teacher	6/4/1861	AWOL since 12/29/62; in Roddy's cavalry 2/63			1	
Holt, J. H.	F	Pvt				wounded at Salem Church		1		
Holt, John E.	F	Pvt	25		2/24/1863	AWOL since 8/63			1	
Holt, John Marion	F	Pvt		farmer	3/10/1862	died in hospital 12/1/62	1			
Howell, L. S.	F	Pvt								
Harn, James M.	F	Pvt	21	farmer	6/4/1861	deserted at Fussell's Mill 8/16/64			1	
Hughey, James N.	F	Pvt	21	farmer	3/3/1862	died of measles in hospital 6/4/62	1			
Hughey, R. Benjamin	F	Pvt		farmer	3/3/1862	deserted 8/10/64			1	
Hurn, James M.	F	Pvt			6/4/1861	wounded at Frayser's Farm, Gettysburg; deserted 8/12/64		2	1	
Ivon, T. P.	F	Pvt				Appomattox parole				
Johnson, George W.	F	Pvt			6/4/1861	medical discharge 11/11/61			1	
Johnson, J. E.	F	Pvt			6/4/1861	captured at Gaines's Mill; deserted 9/21/64			1	1

Name	Co	Rank	Age	Occupation	Date enrolled	Notes	Died	Times wounded	Left co	Captured
Johnson, Joseph G.	F	Pvt			6/4/1861	wounded at Sharpsburg; captured at Frayser's Farm; sent to Fort Delaware; deserted 9/21/64		1	1	1
Johnson, R.	F	Pvt				deserted 8/12/64			1	
Kelly, P. O.	F	Pvt								
Kelly, Thomas B.	F	Pvt	22	printer	6/4/1861	discharged by surgeon 7/12/62 for tuberculosis			1	
King, Tilman A.	F	Sgt			6/4/1861	wounded at Salem Church; deserted 1/64		1	1	
Lebarreare, William	F	4th Sgt			6/4/1861	captured at Petersburg				1
Larten, A. B.	F	Pvt								
Larvin, Owen	F	Pvt			5/19/1863					
Ledbetter, William H.	F	Pvt			7/26/1862	wounded at Salem Church		1		
Lewis, F. W.	F	Pvt								
Lewis, Tandy W.	F	Pvt			6/4/1861	killed at Petersburg 7/64	1			

Lleland, George	F	Pvt								
Lovelace, J. A.	F	Pvt								
Loveless, Thomas A.	F	Pvt				discharged 12/62			1	
Lynch, Noble	F	Pvt			9/17/1863	Paroled Greensboro, NC 5/2/65				1
Malone, Henry W.	F	Pvt			6/4/1861	wounded at Frayser's Farm		1		
Malone, Joab C.	F	Pvt			6/4/1861	wounded at Frayser's Farm; Appomattox parole		1		
Malone, Spaulding Cecrops	F	Pvt			6/4/1861	wounded at Richmond, Sharpsburg, Salem Church; escaped from Elmira prison		3		1
Malone, William Hub	F	Pvt			12/13/1862	killed at Gettysburg 7/3/63	1			
Martin, A. M.	F	Pvt			10/2/1861	hospitalized at 3rd AL hospital Rich. 10/31/62		1		
Martin, Alfred H.	F	Pvt			10/21/1861	wounded at Gaines's Mill		1		
McClellan, William Cowan	F	Pvt	22	farmer	6/10/1861	wounded at Gaines's Mill, Williamsburg, Seven Pines; captured Sayler's Creek; sent to Point Lookout Prison		3		1
McCormack, F. M.	F	Pvt			3/12/1862	wounded at Williamsburg; captured 11/14/63		1		1
McDonald, John R.	F	2Lt			6/10/1861					

Name	Co	Rank	Age	Occupation	Date enrolled	Notes	Died	Times wounded	Left co	Captured
McDonald, John W.	F	Pvt			6/4/1861	wounded at Gaines's Mill, killed at Frayser's Farm	1	1		
McDonald, William A.	F	Pvt			6/4/1861	wounded at Gaines's Mill; captured at Petersburg 8/25/64		1		1
McIlhany, George	F	Pvt								
McWilliams, Andrew	F	Pvt/ Sgt			6/4/1861	wounded at Salem Church, killed at the Crater	1	1		
Miller, Robert	F	Pvt			6/4/1861	discharged 11/27/61			1	
Minney, Cas	F	Pvt								
Minor, H. A.	F					surgeon; captured at Gettysburg				1
Minor, Peter	F	Pvt			3/21/1862	wounded at Gettysburg 7/3/63; Appomattox parole		1		
Moore, Asa W.	F	Sgt			6/4/1861	wounded at Gaines's Mill; captured at High Bridge 4/6/65		1		1
Mooreland, James H.	F	Pvt				died at Bristoe Station 8/5/61	1			

Moreland, Johnson H.	F	Pvt			6/4/1861	died at Manassas 8/6/61	1			
Morris, John F.	F	Pvt			6/4/1861	killed at Frayser's Farm	1			
Murrah, L. K.	F	Pvt			3/12/1862	killed at Richmond 8/64	1			
Murrah, William B.	F	Sgt				Appomattox parole				
Nabors, G. M.	F	Pvt				killed at Gaines's Mill	1			
Neal, Thomas A.	F	Pvt	33		6/4/1861	died in Richmond 7/30/61	1			
Neal, William Pink	F	Pvt			6/24/1861	wounded at Gaines's Mill; wounded in Petersburg and died 6/24/64	1	1		
New, A. M. Rudd	F	Pvt				killed at Gaines's Mill	1			
Nichols, W. A.	F	Pvt				killed 10/18/64	1			
Odom, Alex P.	F	Sgt	18		6/4/1861	wounded at Petersburg; discharged 8/4/64		1	1	
Panson, E.F.	F	Pvt								
Pearson, Birgin G.	F	Pvt	22	farmer	6/4/1861	wounded at Gaines's Mill, Salem Church, Gettysburg; captured at Gettysburg		3		1
Pearson, James S.	F	Pvt			6/4/1861	discharged 5/24/62			1	
Pettus, William D.	F	Pvt	16	farmer	6/4/1861	discharged for epilepsy 10/17/61			1	
Phelan, William	F	Pvt			6/1/1861					

Name	Co	Rank	Age	Occupation	Date enrolled	Notes	Died	Times wounded	Left co	Captured
Phillips, David L.	F	Sgt		farmer	6/4/1861	wounded at Gettysburg, disabled, and transferred to conscript duty 9/64		1		
Powell, William L.	F	Pvt								
Ragland, G. W.	F	Pvt			6/4/1861	discharged for insanity 4/20/63			1	
Ragle, George W.	F	Pvt				discharged 4/30/62			1	
Rambo, J. Mike	F	Pvt			6/4/1861	died in hospital	1			
Rambo, William M.	F	Pvt								
Rawlings, John M.	F	Pvt			6/4/1861	wounded at Salem Church; captured at Deep Bottom, VA; sent to Point Lookout Prison		1		1
Ray, William W.	F	Pvt				captured at Petersburg; Appomattox parole				1
Rayle, G. W.	F	Pvt			3/24/1862	discharged for dementia			1	
Redus, Thomas H.	F	Pvt			6/4/1861	died 11/7/61 of typhoid fever	1			
Riddle, Robert S.	F	Pvt			3/12/1862	died of typhoid fever at hospital 7/2/62	1			

Roberts, N. J.	F	Pvt							
Robertson, Nathaniel Terry	F	Pvt			6/4/1861	discharged 10/9/61			1
Roden, Leanderson C.	F	Pvt			6/4/1861	killed at Gaines's Mill	1		
Roden, L. C.	F	Pvt			6/4/1861				
Roden, William	F	Pvt							
Rogers, Arthur Mac	F	Pvt	22	railroad agent	6/4/1861	discharged for tuberculosis 10/17/61			1
Rollins, J. M.	F	Pvt							
Rudd, A. M.	F	Pvt				wounded at Gaines's Mill		1	
Runnels, Riley	F	Pvt			6/4/1861	died in gunshot accident 10/21/61	1		
Sandifer, Thomas B.	F	Pvt			6/4/1861	discharged 10/6/61			1
Scott, T. T.	F	Pvt			9/17/1863				
Scott, W. D.	F	Pvt							
Sheldon, Parson	F	Pvt							
Shelton, Mark	F	Pvt			6/4/1861	killed at Frayser's Farm	1		
Shelton, William A.	F	Sgt			6/4/1861	wounded at Frayser's Farm		1	
Sloan, James S.	F	Pvt			6/4/1861	transferred to the Navy 7/1/64			1

Name	Co	Rank	Age	Occupation	Date enrolled	Notes	Died	Times wounded	Left co	Captured
Sloan, Milton J. (Paddy)	F	Pvt			6/4/1861	wounded at Gaines's Mill; died of wounds in right lung	1	1		
Smelley, W. J.	F	Pvt			6/4/1861					
Smith, E. M.	F	Pvt				captured in Tennessee; sent to Camp Chase prison				1
Smith, John	F	Pvt			6/4/1861	died in hospital 6/10/62	1			
Smith, John Pinkney	F	Pvt			6/4/1861	wounded at Gaines's Mill		1		
Smith, Thomas M.	F	Pvt			6/11/1861	killed at Sharpsburg; decapitated by shot	1			
Snodgrass, Thomas D.	F	Pvt	18	farmer	6/4/1861	discharged 7/10/61			1	
Stephenson, Simpson	F	Pvt			6/4/1861	died in hospital	1			
Steward, J. N	F	Pvt			6/4/1861	died of typhoid fever in Richmond 5/26/64	1			
Stewart, G. H.	F	Pvt			6/4/1861	wounded at Salem Church		1		
Stewart, James N.	F	Pvt			6/4/1861	died of typhoid fever 5/26/64	1			

Streat, George Harris	F	Corp				wounded at Salem Church, the Crater		2		
Terry, John	F	Capt				captured at Orange Court House				1
Terry, John T.	F	Pvt			6/4/1861	captured 3/20/64 in GA				1
Thompson, Dandridge B.	F	Pvt			6/4/1861	wounded at Frayser's Farm; died of wounds 7/9/62	1	1		
Thompson, Henry	F	Pvt	47	farmer						
Thompson, John W.	F	Pvt			6/4/1861	wounded at Warwick River 4/62; deserted 3/17/65		1	1	
Trimble, Bob	F	Pvt	19	farmer		wounded at Gettysburg, the Wilderness; Appomattox parole		2		
Trimble, Charles S.	F	Pvt			6/4/1861	deserted 3/62			1	
Tucker, James D.	F	Sgt			6/4/1861	wounded at Frayser's Farm, Gettysburg; captured at Gettysburg		2		1
Turner, J. J.	F	Pvt								
Tweedy, Thomas W.	F	Pvt	38		6/4/1861	discharged 1/22/62			1	
Vaughan, W. B.	F	Corp			6/4/1861	wounded at Gaines's Mill, Salem Church; Appomattox parole		2		

Name	Co	Rank	Age	Occupation	Date enrolled	Notes	Died	Times wounded	Left co	Captured
Venable, Andrew J.	F	Pvt			6/4/1861	wounded at Gaines's Mill; discharged 7/14/62		1	1	
Venable, Joseph	F	Pvt			6/4/1861	Appomattox parole				
Vincent, Allen J.	F	Pvt			6/4/1861	ambulance driver; wounded at Frayser's Farm; died of typhoid fever 9/8/64	1	1		
Vinson, Leonard	F	Pvt	21	farmer	6/4/1861	wounded at Gettysburg 7/3/63		1		
Waley, Burns	F	Pvt			6/4/1861					
Wayland, William L.	F	Lt			6/4/1861	wounded at Gaines's Mill; transferred to cavalry		1	1	
Weatherford, Thomas L.	F	Pvt			6/4/1861	discharged 1/2/62			1	
Webb, Wiley R.	F	Pvt			6/4/1861	wounded at Gaines's Mill; killed at the Wilderness	1	1		
Wilkerson, Y.Y.	F	Pvt			6/10/1861					
Wilson, James G.	F	Pvt			6/4/1861	discharged 7/3/63			1	

Wooley, Augustus T.	F	Pvt			6/4/1861	wounded at 2nd Manassas; deserted 8/12/64		1	1	
Young, Francis M.	F	Pvt			5/27/1861	wounded at Gaines's Mill; Appomattox parole		1		
Bailes, S. R.	H	Pvt			6/10/1861	wounded at Gaines's Mill		1		
Bates, Lewis R.	H	Pvt	24	farmer	6/10/1861	wounded at Frayser's Farm; disabled		1	1	
Bates, S. B.	H	Pvt								
Bates, William	H	Pvt	21	farmer	6/10/1861	wounded at Frayser's Farm; deserted 8/19/63		1	1	
Beckham, Cassill G.	H	Pvt	22		6/10/1861	discharged 9/12/61 for hernia			1	
Berry, Clifton	H	Pvt				captured at Orange Court House				1
Black, James L.	H	Pvt	25	farmer	3/22/1862	wounded at Gaines's Mill		1		
Booth, Sam	H	Sgt	27	planter	6/10/1861	wounded at Gettysburg; captured at Gettysburg; died at Point Lookout Prison 1865 from wounds in right leg	1	1		1
Bradshaw, James J.	H	Pvt	24	farmer	6/10/1861	deserted 12/1/63 at Mine Run			1	
Bullington, William	H	Pvt				died at Richmond	1			
Butts, Benjamin H.	H	Pvt				killed at Frayser's Farm	1			

Name	Co	Rank	Age	Occupation	Date enrolled	Notes	Died	Times wounded	Left co	Captured
Cain, James H.	H	Pvt	25	student	6/10/1861	wounded at Frayser's Farm, Sharpsburg		2		
Chambers, William	H	Pvt	24		6/10/1861	deserted 5/24/64			1	
Chandler, George	H	Pvt								
Clem, Hiram	H	Pvt	27	farmer	6/10/1861	wounded at Salem Church; deserted at Gettysburg		1	1	
Clifton, G. Benjamin	H	Pvt	23		6/10/1861	captured at Gettysburg				1
Cline, John I.	H	Pvt	32	carpenter	6/10/1861	wounded at Gaines's Mill; lost arm		1	1	
Cochran, James	H	Pvt		lawyer		Appomattox parole				
Colbert, Frank	H	Lt			6/4/1861					
Cox, James M.	H	Pvt			6/10/1861	deserted after 5/12/64			1	
Cox, W. R.	H	Sgt	26	farmer	6/10/1861	wounded at Salem Church; deserted 8/19/63		1	1	
Cox, William	H	Pvt	26	farmer	6/10/1861	wounded at 2nd Manassas; discharged 2/63		1	1	

Cox, William J. (Jr.)	H	Pvt	18	farmer	6/10/1861	wounded at Gettysburg; captured at the Wilderness		1		1
Cox, William J. (Sr.)	H	Sgt		farmer	6/1/1861					
Crabb, Sam	H	Pvt	30		6/10/1861	killed at Gaines's Mill	1			
Crayton, James J.	H	Pvt								
Davis, John	H	Pvt	25	farmer	3/22/1862	killed at Salem Church	1			
Dean, Jerry D.	H	Pvt	23	farmer	10/15/1861	wounded at Sharpsburg and permanently disabled		1	1	
Euton, Abner B.	H	Pvt	28	mechanic		brigade blacksmith; deserted at the Crater			1	
Evans, Daniel	H	Pvt		farmer	6/10/1861					
Evans, Oren	H	Pvt	23	farmer	6/10/1861					
Everett, William P.	H	Pvt	28		6/10/1861	wounded at Williamsburg; captured at Williamsburg; died in prison of wounds 5/17/62	1	1		1
Ewton, Albert B.	H	Pvt			6/1861	wounded at Gaines's Mill		1		
Fain, William B.	H	Pvt	23	farmer	6/10/1861	Appomattox parole				
Freeman, Julius R.	H	Corp	24	farmer	6/10/1861	killed at Frayser's Farm	1			
Freeman, William S.	H	Pvt								
Fuller, Richard B.	H	Lt			6/10/1861	wounded at Gaines's Mill; capt. of Co. H; deserted 8/12/64		1	1	
Gallet, Madison	H	Pvt								

Name	Co	Rank	Age	Occupation	Date enrolled	Notes	Died	Times wounded	Left co	Captured
Glover, John N.	H	Sgt	21	clerk	6/10/1861	died at home	1			
Goldsmith, Levi	H	Sgt	24	merchant	6/10/1861	wounded at Salem Church; deserted 1/4/64		1	1	
Graham, George T.	H	Pvt			6/10/1861	wounded at Sharpsburg, Salem Church		2		
Gray, James	H	Pvt			6/10/1861	transferred to 50th AL			1	
Grayham, J. A.	H	Pvt			6/10/1861					
Green, D.	H	Pvt			6/6/1861					
Gresham, Joseph	H	Pvt	45	farmer	3/22/1862	deserted 8/62			1	
Grier, David	H	Pvt			6/10/1861					
Griffin, H. M.	H	Pvt								
Grisham, George	H	Pvt			6/10/1861	wounded at Gaines's Mill		1		
Gullett, Madison	H	Pvt			6/10/1861	discharged 4/65			1	
Hardy, John H.	H	Sgt	24	carpenter	6/10/1861	wounded at Gaines's Mill, Gettysburg; captured at Gettysburg		2		1
Harris, Watkins	H	Pvt								

Harvy, John	H	Pvt			5/24/1861	wounded at Gaines's Mill		1		
Hawkins, William	H	Pvt			6/10/1861	captured at Gettysburg				1
Henderson, Perry	H	Corp	25	schoolteac her	6/10/1861	wounded at Gaines's Mill; captured at Gettysburg		1		1
Hendrix, George W.	H	Pvt	22	clerk	6/10/1861	died of acute diarrhea in Manassas 1861	1			
Hill, Ezekial H.	H	Pvt			6/10/1861					
Hill, Marion	H	Corp	21	farmer	6/10/1861	wounded at Gaines's Mill; died of wounds	1	1		
Hill, Thomas H.	H	Corp	26	farmer	6/10/1861	deserted 8/12/64			1	
Hill, W.	H	Pvt			6/1861	wounded at Gaines's Mill		1		
Hobbs, Dallas	H	Pvt	17	farmer	3/22/1862					
Hobbs, William S.	H	Sgt	24	carpenter	6/10/1861	wounded at Frayser's Farm; captured at Gettysburg		1		1
Holman, J. H.	H	Pvt								
Houston, David	H	Capt	24	farmer		resigned 9/31/61			1	
Hurley, G. E.	H	Pvt								
Isbell, James R.	H	Pvt	29	farmer	6/10/1861	teamster				
Isbell, William M.	H	Pvt	24	farmer	6/10/1861	wounded at Williamsburg, Gaines's Mill; captured at Rapidan Station; deserted at Sharpsburg		2		1

Name	Co	Rank	Age	Occupation	Date enrolled	Notes	Died	Times wounded	Left co	Captured
Isbell, Zachariah	H	Pvt			6/10/1861	captured at Sugar Creek, TN, 10/9/63				1
Jackson, Calvin	H	Pvt	34		6/18/1861	killed at Petersburg 7/30/64	1			
Jackson, Henry	H	Pvt								
Jackson, Van Buren	H	Pvt	34	farmer	6/18/1861					
Jackson, William H.	H	Pvt	18			killed at Salem Church	1			
Johnson, James	H	Pvt			6/18/1861	captured in Tennessee 4/14/65				1
Johnson, Jason	H	Pvt			6/4/1861					
Jones, Rufus Cary	H	Pvt/Lt	21		6/4/1861	captured at Gettysburg; sent to Johnson's Island and escaped 1/6/64				1
Kline, John	H	Pvt	34	mechanic	6/6/1861	wounded at Gaines's Mill; discharged 10/24/62		1	1	
Lindsey, Jeff	H	Pvt								
Love, Orin P.	H	Pvt	22		3/22/1862					
Lovell, C. P.	H	Pvt			5/3/1862	wounded at Gaines's Mill		1		

McCabe, William	H	Pvt			6/4/1861	wounded at Williamsburg; deserted 1/15/64		1	1	
McCaghren, F. A.	H	Pvt				paroled at Talladega, AL				1
McDonald, John R.	H	Pvt/ Maj	21		10/10/1861	discharged by surgeon 10/10/62			1	
McDonald, Thomas	H	Lt	23		6/4/1861	wounded at Williamsburg, Gaines's Mill		2		
Menefee, Isaac	H	Pvt	53		3/12/1862	detailed as nurse due to his age				
Menefee, Robert	H	Pvt			6/10/1863	killed at Salem Church	1			
Menefee, J. A.	H	Pvt								
Mingea, George D. (Dud)	H	Pvt	22	painter	6/10/1861	wounded at Williamsburg; discharged 9/16/62		1	1	
Modin, W. W.	H	Pvt								
Morgan, Dallas	H	Pvt			6/10/1861					
Morgan, David H.	H	Pvt			6/10/1861	died 9/24/64	1			
Morgan, George H.	H	Pvt			6/10/1861					
Morland, B. P.	H	Pvt								
Morris, Joseph	H	Pvt			3/10/1862	captured at Gettysburg; sent to Fort Delaware prison				1
Odair, William J.	H	Pvt			6/6/1861	wounded at Frayser's Farm		1		
Ogelsby, William	H	Pvt			6/10/1861	died of typhoid fever at Danville, VA 5/11/62	1			

Name	Co	Rank	Age	Occupation	Date enrolled	Notes	Died	Times wounded	Left co	Captured
Owens, David	H	Pvt			6/18/1961	captured at High Bridge 4/6/65; sent to Point Lookout Prison				1
Owens, E.W.T.	H	Pvt								
Pantell, William	H	Pvt			6/14/1861	discharged 5/24/62			1	
Patterson, James H.	H	Pvt			6/18/1861	wounded at Gaines's Mill; captured at Clarksville, WV		1		1
Patterson, John H.	H	Pvt			6/4/1861	wounded at Gaines's Mill; killed at Salem Church	1	1		
Patton, David	H	Pvt			6/10/1861	wounded at Frayser's Farm		1		
Patton, James D.	H	Pvt			6/10/1861					
Pierce, A.	H	Pvt				captured at South Mountain				1
Powell, John	H	Pvt			6/4/1861	died of phthisis at Chimborazo Hosp. 5/24/62	1			
Powell, William	H	Pvt			6/4/1861	died of typhoid fever at Chimborazo Hospital 7/7/62	1			
Rambo, G. M.	H	Pvt			6/4/1861	wounded at Gaines's Mill		1		

Rambo, Thomas	H	Pvt	26		6/18/1861	wounded at Frayser's Farm, Salem Church; captured at Gettysburg; died 1/9/64 at Point Lookout hospital	1	2		1
Roberts, James H.	H	Pvt			6/4/1861	wounded at Gettysburg		1		
Roberts, Wiley M.	H	Pvt			6/18/1861	wounded at Gaines's Mill; died at hospital #2 Lynchburg, VA 12/23/62 of meningitis	1	1		
Smith, A. B.	H	Pvt								
Smith, Gaynes Chislom	H	Lt Col	32		6/10/1861	wounded at Gaines's Mill; captured at Gettysburg		1		1
Smith, George R.	H	Pvt			6/10/1861	wounded at Salem Church; teamster		1		
Smith, James P.	H	Pvt			6/16/1861	wounded in service		1		
Smith, John	H	Pvt			6/10/1861	captured near Memphis; died in hospital 6/10/62	1			1
Smith, John Pinkney	H	Pvt			6/4/1861	wounded at Gaines's Mill; Appomattox parole; drummer		1		
Snodgrass, Thomas	H	Pvt	18	farmer	6/4/1861	discharged 7/10/61			1	
Steele, French H.	H	Pvt			6/10/1861					
Stephenson, Samuel D.	H	Pvt	21		6/10/1861	deserted 5/63			1	
Stevenson, Thomas	H	Pvt								

Name	Co	Rank	Age	Occupation	Date enrolled	Notes	Died	Times wounded	Left co	Captured
Stewart, Matthew	H	Pvt			6/10/1861	wounded at Gettysburg; captured at Gettysburg		1		1
Strange, Augustus	H	Corp	21		6/10/1861	discharged by surgeon 8/18/61			1	
Thach, Robert H. (Dink)	H	Pvt	27	lawyer	6/10/1861	discharged for tuberculosis 11/7/61			1	
Thomson, Hilliard	H	Pvt			6/4/1861					
Toone, William	H	Pvt			6/10/1861					
Twitty, John C.	H	Pvt	18		6/10/1861	wounded at Frayser's Farm; died of wounds	1	1		
Varrellman, Augustus D.	H	Pvt	30		6/10/1861	deserted 5/29/63			1	
Watkins, Harris	H	Pvt	18		6/10/1861	wounded at Gaines's Mill; captured at Gettysburg		1		1
Webb, Isaac	H	Pvt			6/10/1861	deserted 6/8/63			1	
Wilburn, Henry	H	Pvt			6/10/1861	died of typhoid fever 8/8/61 at Manassas	1			

						Died	Times wounded	Left co	Captured
Wilkerson, George	H	Pvt		6/10/1861	discharged for chronic bronchitis 2/9/62			1	
Williams, Benjamin R.	H	Pvt	29	6/10/1861	discharged for paralysis			1	
Yancey, Henry D.	H	Pvt		6/10/1861	wounded at Salem Church; captured at Petersburg; sent to Point Lookout Prison		1		1
Yarellman, G.A.	H	Pvt		6/10/1861					
Total men:	358					76	152	92	62

Notes

Introduction

1. James M. McPherson, *For Cause and Comrades: Why Men Fought in the Civil War* (New York: Oxford University Press, 1997), 16; and James M. McPherson, *What They Fought For, 1861–1865* (Baton Rouge: Louisiana State University Press, 1994), 11–18. McPherson believes that after the initial motivation to fight in a war, soldiers sustained their motivation by their belief in the cause and through primary group cohesion: "[F]or the Civil War soldier this group may have been as large as his company but was likely to be smaller: his messmates, the men from his town or township with whom he enlisted" (*For Cause and Comrades* 85). Bell Irvin Wiley saw the dominant urge to enlist as being the desire for adventure (*The Life of Johnny Reb, The Common Soldier of the Confederacy* [Indianapolis: Bobbs-Merrill Company, 1943], 17–18).

2. Randall C. Jimerson, *The Private Civil War: Popular Thought during the Sectional Conflict* (Baton Rouge: Louisiana State University Press, 1994), 16–17. Both sides claimed to be fighting for their own views of liberty. For a recent discussion of liberty and freedom in America, see David Hackett Fischer, *Liberty and Freedom: A Visual History of America's Founding Ideas* (New York: Oxford University Press, 2005), 308–28.

3. Joseph Allan Frank, *With Ballot and Bayonet: The Political Socialization of American Civil War Soldiers* (Athens, GA: University of Georgia Press, 1998), 8.

4. Gerald F. Linderman, *Embattled Courage: The Experience of Combat in the American Civil War* (New York: Free Press, 1987), 7–16.

5. Reid Mitchell, *Civil War Soldiers: Their Expectations and Experiences* (New York: Viking Penguin, 1988), 3–4.

6. Mitchell 58.

7. According to Mitchell, as the soldiers "became isolated from the old patterns of life, men had to make themselves new identities from the very military life that threatened to degrade them" (56–57).

8. Robert Anderson McClellan, "Early History of Limestone County" 15. Robert authored a series of articles in the *Athens Post* in 1881 and was attempting

to develop a more comprehensive history of Limestone County. The sudden death of his daughter put an end to the project.

9. Robert Henry Walker, *A History of Limestone County* (Athens, AL: Limestone County Commission, 1973), 48, 68.

10. Robert Dunnavant Jr., *Historic Limestone County Alabama* (Athens, AL: Pea Ridge Press, 1995), 39–46.

11. J. Mills Thornton III, *Politics and Power in a Slave Society: Alabama, 1800–1860* (Baton Rouge: Louisiana State University Press, 1978), 365.

12. Margaret M. Storey, *Loyalty and Loss: Alabama's Unionists in the Civil War and Reconstruction* (Baton Rouge: Louisiana State University Press, 2004), 1–17. Margaret Storey looks at the complex demographic features of the northern Alabama unionists and the multiple political and social factors that shaped Union loyalty on the Southern home front.

13. Compiled Service Records of Confederate Soldiers Who Served in Organizations from the State of Alabama, War Department Collection of Confederate Records, Record Group 109, M311, National Archives Building, Washington, D.C. (hereafter referred to as CSR, with the name of the specified individual following); Alabama Department of Archives and History, Alabama Civil War Service Cards File in the Alabama Civil War Service Database, Montgomery, AL (hereafter referred to as ADAH, with the name of the specified individual following). I did not add multiple woundings for each soldier to the casualty totals.

14. Steven M. Stowe, *Intimacy and Power in the Old South: Ritual in the Lives of the Planters* (Baltimore: Johns Hopkins University Press, 1987), 3–4.

15. Buchanan-McClellan Papers, 1816–1917, Accession #1850, Manuscript Department, Southern Historical Collection, Library of the University of North Carolina at Chapel Hill.

16. McClellan, Family Letters, Carter family, Tullahoma, TN (hereafter referred to as Carter family letters).

17. CSR, John B. McClellan.

18. Carter family letters.

19. CSR, Robert A. McClellan.

20. Buchanan-McClellan Papers.

21. Buchanan-McClellan Papers.

22. Thomas McAdory Owen, *History of Alabama and Dictionary of Alabama Biography* (Spartanburg, SC: Reprint Company Publishers, 1978), 4:1093.

23. Faye Acton Axford, *To Lochaber Na Mair: Southerners View the Civil War* (Athens, AL: Athens Publishing Company, 1986), 210 n.

Chapter 1

1. Thornton 420–21.

2. Clarence Phillips Denman, *The Secession Movement in Alabama* (Montgomery: Alabama State Department of Archives and History, 1933), 164.

3. Thornton 428–29.

4. Thomas Joyce McClellan to Martha Beattie McClellan, 14 January 1861 (McClellan, Family Papers, Limestone County Archives, Athens, AL; copy of the original document, which is at the Alabama Department of Archives and History).

5. Thomas Hubbard Hobbs (1826–62) raised Company F of the 9th Alabama Regiment and was its captain. He graduated with a law degree from the University of Virginia and was a respected leader of the Limestone County community. Hobbs was responsible for bringing the railroad to Limestone County before the war, and he served on the educational committee of the Alabama state legislature. He died from wounds received at the Battle of Gaines's Mill and was buried in Spring Hill Cemetery in Lynchburg, Virginia. Hobbs kept a diary before and during the war. See: Faye Acton Axford, ed., *The Journals of Thomas Hubbard Hobbs* (Tuscaloosa: University of Alabama Press, 1976), 236.

6. Walker, *History of Limestone County* 102.

7. Clement Eaton, *The Mind of the Old South* (Baton Rouge: Louisiana State University Press, 1991), 283.

8. Gen. George Smith Houston (1808–79) was a member of the Alabama House of Representatives in 1832, and twice a U.S. congressman beginning in 1841. He was elected governor of Alabama in 1874, and to the U.S. Senate in 1878 (Dunnavant, *Historic Limestone County Alabama* 109–11).

9. *The War of the Rebellion: A Compilation of the Official Records of the Union and Confederate Armies,* ed. Col. Robert N. Scott (Ann Arbor, MI: Edward Brothers, 1985), 2:798 (hereafter referred to as *OR;* citations are to series I unless otherwise noted). Smith (1824–93) was a West Point graduate who served in the Mexican War. He became lieutenant general in October 9, 1862, and was in command of the Trans-Mississippi Department through the end of the war (Ezra J. Warner, *Generals in Gray: Lives of the Confederate Commanders* [Baton Rouge: Louisiana State University Press, 1997], 279–80). Smith was also the brigade commander for the 9th Alabama during the First Battle of Manassas.

10. David Houston was appointed captain of Company H at the beginning of the war. He was later charged with drunkenness on duty and resigned his commission. Houston returned to Alabama and served with partisan rangers in north Alabama (Axford, *To Lochaber* 189 n. 8).

11. Gen. Leroy Pope Walker, from Huntsville, Alabama, became the first secretary of war for the Confederacy on February 21, 1861. He lacked the administrative experience required for the position and was the focus of much criticism, which forced him to resign on September 16, 1861. He was then appointed a brigadier general serving in garrison command at Mobile and Montgomery. Failing to secure field duty, he resigned on March 31, 1862. He finished the war as the presiding judge of a military court in north Alabama (Warner, *Generals in Gray* 320–21).

12. Gen. George S. Houston to L. P. Walker, 24 May 1861, 1173–1861, Letters Received by the Secretary of War, 1861–1865, War Department Collection of Confederate Records, Record Group 109, National Archives Building, Washington, D.C.

(National Archives Microfilm Publication M437, roll 3). Walker was following the policy of the Confederate government that recognized the supremacy of the states in controlling and providing their own arms, munitions, and forces. See Jefferson Davis, *The Rise and Fall of the Confederate Government* (New York: Da Capo Press, 1990), 1:264.

13. Axford, *Journals of Thomas Hubbard Hobbs* 235.

14. Axford, *Journals of Thomas Hubbard Hobbs* 236. The Reverend A. F. Lawrence was mentioned in the diary of Mary Fielding (a resident of Athens, Alabama, and the sister of William Eppa Fielding, a member of the 9th Alabama) as a preacher who preached in Limestone County but was stationed in Pulaski, Tennessee (Axford, *To Lochaber* 63–64, 97).

15. George Edgar Turner, *Victory Rode the Rails: The Strategic Place of the Railroads in the Civil War* (Lincoln: University of Nebraska Press, 1992), 69; Axford, *Journals of Thomas Hubbard Hobbs* 236–37.

16. Diary of William Eppa Fielding in Axford, *To Lochaber* 1. On June 15, 1861, Gen. Robert E. Lee reported to Virginia governor John Letcher that there were approximately 35,000 troops in Virginia (*OR* 2:928). On June 3, Brig. Gen. P. G. T. Beauregard had reported to Pres. Jefferson Davis that he had between 10,000 and 15,000 troops at Manassas, while Col. John Bankhead Magruder reported 3,400 at Yorktown (2:902).

17. Col. William Henry Fowler, superintendent for Alabama Military Records, estimated that 120,000 men from Alabama served in the Confederate armies, and that approximately 30,000 served in the Army of Northern Virginia (Walter L. Fleming, *Civil War and Reconstruction in Alabama* [Gloucester, MA: Peter Smith, 1949], 78–83). Fowler also stated that 9,000 Alabama troops serving in Northern Virginia had died while in service, and that half of the soldiers who had resigned or had been discharged were either dead or permanently disabled (251–52).

18. Dr. Nicholas (Nick) Richardson served in the 19th, 26th, and 26th-50th Alabama regiments as a surgeon and was married to Sarah Elizabeth Hine, possibly "Lady" mentioned in the letter (Axford, *To Lochaber* 205 n. 36; CSR, Nick D. Richardson).

Dr. Henry Booth (Hal) Malone (1825–68) practiced medicine in Cincinnati, Ohio, before the war. He attended to the wounds of Col. Egbert Jones of the 4th Alabama Regiment at the First Battle of Manassas (Axford, *To Lochaber* 207 n. 55).

Capt. William (Billy) Richardson was wounded at the Battle of Shiloh and would later serve with the 50th Alabama Regiment (Chris Edwards and Faye Acton Axford, *The Lure and Lore of Limestone County* (Tuscaloosa, AL: Portals Press, 1978), 214 n. 2; CSR, William Richardson).

"Mr Childs" may be a relation to Mrs. Jane Hamilton Childs, who came to Alabama from Maryland in 1842 to open a girls' school in Huntsville and then moved to Athens in 1856 to become the president of the Tennessee Conference Female Institute, now Athens State College. A known Union sympathizer, she wrote

President Lincoln to request that Union troops protect the college during the occupation of northern Alabama (Axford, *To Lochaber* 204 n. 23).

19. David Gilbert was a prominent citizen of Limestone County and the father of George A. Gilbert, a lieutenant in Company F of the 9th Alabama (Axford, *To Lochaber* 193 n. 50).

20. Alexander L. Blackburn was the son of Francis Blackburn and a farmer in Limestone County. His grandfather, Clement, was a Revolutionary War soldier (Axford, *To Lochaber* 191 n. 26).

21. Nathan Fletcher was born in Brunswick County, Virginia, in 1794. He moved to Limestone County and married Elizabeth D. Pruett. He was a family friend of the McClellans who lived nearby (Buchanan-McClellan Papers).

22. This was probably Andrew M. Beattie. Martha Fleming Beattie McClellan, William's mother, had several brothers who were mentioned in the letters: David M. Beattie, Josiah Beattie, William B. (Berry) Beattie, and Andrew M. Beattie. Their father, John Beattie (1763–1849), lived in the Nashville and Williamson County, Tennessee, area around 1800, but the family had moved to the Cane Creek section of Lincoln County, Tennessee, by 1840 (Carter family letters). David, Josiah, and William were listed as farmers in the 1850 Lincoln County census.

23. This was either James H. Moore, listed on the 1850 census for Limestone County, Alabama, as a farmer in District 3; or John Milton Moore, listed on the 1850 census for Limestone County, Alabama, as a farmer in District 3 with land valued at three thousand dollars. James H. Moore was married to Lizzie Fletcher, and he served for a brief time with Company E of the 26th-50th Alabama Regiment after unsuccessfully running for political office (CSR, James Henry Moore). John Milton Moore was the county court clerk for Limestone County in 1875 (Walker, *History of Limestone County* 197).

24. Robert Lane was the son of Judge George Washington Lane and Martha Nicholas Davis. He married Mrs. Mattie Goode and later died while serving as a member of Nathan Bedford Forrest's cavalry. Lane was appointed as a federal judge by President Lincoln in 1862 (Edwards and Axford 63).

25. Robert H. (Dink) Thach was a twenty-seven-year-old lawyer when he enlisted as a private in Company H on June 10, 1861. He was discharged on November 7, 1861, for pneumonia. Robert died in December 1866. One of his sons became the president of Alabama Polytechnic Institute, or Auburn University (CSR, Robert H. Thach; Axford, *To Lochaber* 220 n. 9).

26. Gen. Joseph E. Johnston had petitioned Richmond several times in late May and early June to evacuate the army from Harpers Ferry since he determined that it was too difficult to defend it against a strong enemy with the untrained troops under his command. While he saw it as an indefensible position, Robert E. Lee requested that Johnston hold out as long as he could, since the position was one that could hamper Union communications and troop movements. With permission from Richmond, Johnston evacuated Harpers Ferry on June 14 (James I. Robertson Jr.,

Stonewall Jackson: The Man, the Soldier, the Legend [New York: Macmillan Press, 1997], 241–43).

27. Company H was sworn in at Lynchburg on June 18, 1861, for the term of the war, and the 9th Alabama would be sworn in as a regiment on June 20, 1861, in Richmond (Stewart Sifakis, *Compendium of the Confederate Armies—Alabama* (New York: Facts on File, 1992, 68–69; *Supplement to the Official Records of the Union and Confederate Armies,* Part II, *Record of Events,* ed. Janet B. Hewett [Wilmington, NC: Broadfoot Publishing Company, 1994], 1:409 [hereafter referred to as *OR Supplement*]. The "splendid Spring" mentioned by William was Clark's Spring. The waterworks nearby the spring was later replaced in 1876 by a larger one farther upriver near Windsor Farms.

28. Both companies were in a pine grove at Camp Reservoir, one mile west of town near the city reservoir and waterworks, just west of Hollywood Cemetery (diary of William Eppa Fielding in Axford, *To Lochaber* 2–3). On June 21, Company F received seventy muskets for the 100-member unit (Axford, *To Lochaber* 4).

29. A mess was organized with about six to ten soldiers sharing a tent and responsibilities for providing for their own food and cooking. Cooking duties were usually shared. See Carlton McCarthy, *Detailed Minutiae of Soldier Life in the Army of Northern Virginia, 1861–1865* (Lincoln: University of Nebraska Press, 1993), 24–26. See also Wiley, *Life of Johnny Reb* 89–107. All of the men mentioned here were members of Company H: Rufus Carey Jones was captured at Gettysburg and sent first to Johnson's Island, Ohio, and then to Fort Delaware, where he escaped on June 6, 1864; James Cain was wounded at Frayser's Farm in 1862, and later at Salem Church in 1863; George Hendricks died of acute diarrhea on April 12, 1862, at the general hospital in Winchester, Virginia; George G. (Dud) Mingea was discharged on September 16, 1862; William Everett died on May 17, 1862 from wounds received at the Battle of Williamsburg; and Benjamin Williams was discharged in 1862 (CSR, Rufus Carey Jones, James Cain, George Hendricks, George G. Mingea, William Everett, Benjamin Williams).

Chapter 2

1. *OR Supplement* 1:783–93.

2. *OR Supplement* 1:401. On May 27, Thomas Jonathan (Stonewall) Jackson received orders to take command of all Virginia regiments at Harpers Ferry. However, all Confederate forces in the Shenandoah Valley would be under the command of Joseph E. Johnston (Robertson 230–50). General Smith had just been promoted and a fifth brigade formed under him that included the 8th, 9th, 10th, and 11th Alabama regiments, the 19th Mississippi Regiment, and Stannard's Battery (Joseph E. Johnston, *Narrative of Military Operations during the Civil* War [New York: Da Capo Press, 1990], 33).

3. Pres. Jefferson Davis visited the camps of the new recruits in Richmond

when he had time (William C. Davis, *Jefferson Davis: The Man and His Hour* [Baton Rouge: Louisiana State University Press, 1997], 346).

4. William's version conflicts with an Alabama historian who believes that Junius A. Bynum of Company C had been seriously wounded at Williamsburg in 1862 and was sent home to recuperate. While at home he joined another command and, during that time, killed one of his comrades. He was later arrested by the provost guard and was never seen again (Col. James Edmonds Saunders, *Early Settlers of Alabama* [Baltimore: Genealogical Publishing Company, 1969], 169).

5. This was either 2nd Lt. John R. McDonald or 2nd Lt. Thomas J. McDonald, both of Company F of the 9th Alabama Regiment (*OR Supplement* 1:398).

6. Tom T. Tweedy was a thirty-eight-year-old farmer from Limestone County. He was discharged on January 22, 1862 after procuring a substitute (CSR, Thomas T. Tweedy).

Samuel Booth was a twenty-six-year-old private who was reduced in rank from sergeant in 1863. He was later wounded in the leg and captured at Gettysburg, and he died from his wounds while in the prison hospital at Point Lookout on January 11, 1864 (CSR, Samuel Booth).

7. John C. Featherston (1837–1917) was a native of Limestone County. He was elected first lieutenant of Company F of the 9th Alabama Regiment and was promoted to its captain on July 13, 1862, with the death of Captain Hobbs (CSR, John C. Featherston). He married Letitia Preston Floyd of Lynchburg (Nick Floyd's sister) in 1864. Featherston resigned on October 24, 1864, due to bad health and the fact that only four officers and fifteen to twenty men were left in his company (CSR, John C. Featherston; Axford, *To Lochaber* 190n, 233 n. 12).

8. Second Lt. John R. McDonald of Company H was twenty-one years old when he enlisted; he resigned on October 10, 1862, with a certificate of disability (CSR, John R. McDonald).

9. Rufus Cary Jones was a private in Company H and was captured at Gettysburg but escaped from Johnson's Island, Ohio, on January 6, 1864 (CSR, Rufus C. Jones). Herbert has not been identified, and he is not listed on the roster of the 9th Alabama.

10. Lucy was probably one of the McClellans' slaves at home (Buchanan-McClellan Papers).

11. This may have been John A. Johnson, the publisher of the *Limestone News,* who went home on July 8, 1861 (Limestone County, Alabama, 1860 Census 123; Axford, *To Lochaber* 190 n. 18).

12. Edward Asbury O'Neal (1818–90) was a resident of Madison County and a leading advocate of secession. He enlisted in the 9th Alabama Regiment as its major and later became lieutenant colonel. In 1862 he was appointed colonel of the 26th Alabama Regiment and was later recommended for promotion to brigadier after leading Rodes's brigade at Chancellorsville. He was elected governor of Alabama in 1882 and 1884 (Warner, *Generals in Gray* 226).

13. Pat Ragland was a friend of Thomas Joyce McClellan, who frequently offered business advice to Ragland in his letters (Buchanan-McClellan Papers). The Raglands were originally from Virginia, and Pat's brothers ran a store in Richmond. Pat lived at various times in Limestone County.

14. The regiment of "Frenchmen" was probably one of the Louisiana commands—the 8th Louisiana Regiment, the 7th Louisiana Regiment, or Maj. C. Roberdeau Wheat's 2nd Louisiana Battalion (F. Ray Sibley Jr., *The Confederate Order of Battle: The Army of Northern Virginia,* vol. 1 [Shippensburg, PA: White Mane Publishing Company, 1996], 1).

15. The fight on the border probably refers to the clash between Union forces under Col. J. J. Abercrombie, 7th U.S. Infantry of Gen. Robert Patterson's command, and Confederate forces under Gen. Thomas Jonathan (Stonewall) Jackson at Falling Waters, near Martinsburg, Virginia, on July 2. Union losses were six to ten killed, eighteen wounded, and fifty captured (report of Maj. Gen. W. H. Keim, Pennsylvania Militia in *OR* 2:182; see also Robertson 247–50).

16. John N. Hayes was from Lauderdale County and was appointed assistant surgeon of the 9th Alabama in 1861. He transferred to the 26th Alabama Regiment along with Colonel O'Neal. Hayes was captured at Gettysburg after being left to care for the wounded, and he was sent to Fort McHenry prison in Baltimore, Maryland (CSR, John N. Hayes).

17. Gen. Winfield Scott married into the Mayo family of Richmond, who owned some of the land around the Richmond campsite. The land, named Powhatan estate, had been in the family for two hundred years (R. W. Wright, "Richmond since the War," *Scribner's Monthly Magazine* 14.3 [July 1877], 303–12). Some of the booming cannons are from the Thomas Artillery firing from Camp Chimborazo, according to the *Richmond Dispatch* of July 5, 1861.

18. The Confederate government had asked farmers to plow under some of their cotton to make room for more needed food crops. In 1862, a 10 percent tax was imposed on all cotton produced above the limit of 2,500 pounds of seed cotton per hand. Governor John Gill Shorter's March 1 proclamation implored Alabamians to produce only what cotton they needed for their own use (Malcolm C. McMillan, *The Alabama Confederate Reader* [Tuscaloosa: University of Alabama Press, 1992], 108–11).

19. Col. James Henry Malone (1812–76) was the captain of Company E, 26th-50th Alabama Regiment (CSR, James Henry Malone). He was from Athens, Alabama, and was the focus of William McClellan's attempts to transfer to a company back in Alabama. His son, Henry, was a member of Company F of the 9th Alabama and was wounded at the Battle of Frayser's Farm (CSR, Hal Malone).

L. R. Davis was Lawrence Ripley (Rip) Davis, the older brother of Nicholas Davis Jr. The Richardson boys were related to Dr. Nicholas Richardson (1832–95), the son of William and Ann Davis Richardson. He served as the surgeon of the 19th and 26th-50th Alabama regiments. Capt. William (Billy) Richardson (1839–1914) was the brother of Dr. Nicholas Richardson. Annie Richardson was their sister.

Several other members of the Richardson family served in the 26th-50th Alabama Regiment (Axford, *To Lochaber* 205–6 n. 36).

20. Capt. Edward Dorr Tracy (1833–63) was captain of Company I of the 4th Alabama Regiment, which was organized in Huntsville on April 1, 1861. Tracy was promoted to lieutenant colonel of the 19th Alabama Regiment and was made brigadier general in 1862. He was killed on May 1, 1863, at the Battle of Port Gibson (Jeffrey D. Stocker, ed., *From Huntsville to Appomattox: R. T. Coles's History of 4th Regiment, Alabama Volunteer Infantry, C.S.A., Army of Northern Virginia* [Knoxville: University of Tennessee Press, 1996], 228 n. 30).

21. On May 3, 1861, the surgeon general of Virginia ordered the immediate vaccination of all soldiers in Virginia for smallpox (H. H. Cunningham, *Doctors in Gray: The Confederate Medical Service* [Baton Rouge: Louisiana State University Press, 1993], 196–97).

22. Harpers Ferry, Virginia, was evacuated by Gen. Joseph E. Johnston on June 15–16. Despite President Davis's desire to maintain control of the strategic position at Harpers Ferry, Johnston had sent a memorandum to Robert E. Lee on May 31 stating, "This place [Harpers Ferry] cannot be held against an enemy who would venture to attack it" (*OR* 2:895–96).

23. Joseph Eggleston Johnston was born in Farmville, Virginia, on February 3, 1807, and was a classmate of Robert E. Lee at West Point. He served with distinction during the Seminole and Mexican wars. Johnston was commissioned a brigadier in the Regular Army of the Confederacy in May 1861 and was placed in command at Harpers Ferry (Warner, *Generals in Gray* 161).

24. "Lions" may be a mistake in both the spelling of Gen. Nathaniel Lyon's name and the fact that he was not in the Shenandoah Valley. This Union general was killed at the Battle of Wilson's Creek in Missouri (Hattaway and Jones 42). Gen. Robert Patterson had been instructed to recapture the arsenal at Harpers Ferry and ensure that the Confederate forces in the Shenandoah Valley did not come to the support of the Southern forces gathering around Manassas Junction (William C. Davis, *Battle at Bull Run: A History of the First Major Campaign of the Civil War* [New York: Doubleday and Company, 1977], 42–48). Johnston estimated the size of his forces at just under 9,000 and those of Patterson at 20,000 (Johnston 31). Winchester was a village of 4,500 people but held strategic importance as it was the gateway to northwest Virginia, where several main roads came in from Pennsylvania, Maryland, and Virginia (Robertson 221–22).

25. The number 190,000 was far more than the entire Confederate army could muster in July of 1861. According to Thomas L. Livermore, the Confederate army had 112,040 soldiers in July 1861 (Thomas L. Livermore, *Numbers and Losses in the Civil War in America, 1861–65* [Dayton, OH: Morningside, 1986], 42). There were 35,000 soldiers in all of Virginia on June 15, 1861 (*OR* 2:928).

26. Fannie Fern was the name of William's favorite horse at home (Carter family letters).

27. Matthew Thomas C. Cartwright enlisted on June 4, 1861, and served as a

private in Company F of the 9th Alabama. He would later be paroled at Appomattox (CSR, Matthew T. Cartwright). His brother Hezekiah John (Bud) Cartwright enlisted on March 24, 1862 and served as second lieutenant in Company F (CSR, Hezekiah J. Cartwright). He was captured at the Battle of Gaines's Mill and later at Gettysburg, being exchanged both times. Their parents were Hezekiah and Martha Cartwright (Limestone County, Alabama, 1860 Census 68).

28. This may have been Pvt. J. E. Johnson of Company F who was captured at the Battle of Gaines's Mill and sent to Fort Columbus, New York, and then to Fort Delaware on July 9, 1862. He would later desert and take the oath on September 22, 1864 (CSR, J. E. Johnson).

29. This may refer to George Burgwyn Anderson, who was the colonel of the 4th North Carolina Regiment (Warner, *Generals in Gray* 5–6). The 9th Alabama Regiment may have been under his temporary command. However, on July 29, Col. Cadmus Marcellus Wilcox was appointed colonel of the 9th Alabama (CSR, Cadmus M. Wilcox). Thomas Hubbard Hobbs mentioned incorrectly in his journal that Wilcox was appointed colonel of the 9th on July 12, 1861 (Axford, *Journals of Thomas Hubbard Hobbs* 237.)

30. This may have been Maj. James T. Hester, of Company D, 23rd Alabama Regiment (Janet B. Hewett, ed., *The Roster of Confederate Soldiers, 1861–1865* (Wilmington, NC: Broadfoot Publishing Company, 1996), 7:486.

31. William Berry Beattie was a brother of Martha Beattie McClellan (Buchanan-McClellan Papers).

32. Josiah Beattie was a brother of Martha Beattie McClellan (Buchanan-McClellan Papers).

33. Dr. Thomas Coleman Pettus (1816–90) moved from Virginia with his parents and settled in the area of Pettusville (Edwards and Axford 86).

34. DeWitt Clinton (Clint) Davis was a son of Capt. Nicholas Davis Sr., who was an early settler of Limestone County and the president of the Alabama senate from 1820 to 1829. Clint Davis was married to Susan Lowe (Edwards and Axford 62–63).

35. This may be Sgt. Levi Goldsmith of Company H who enlisted on June 4, 1861. Goldsmith was listed as hospitalized at Howard's Grove Hospital in Richmond in August 1863. He deserted on January 5, 1864, and took the oath of allegiance on March 14, 1864 (CSR, Levi Goldsmith).

36. The 1850 Limestone County census showed an Amos French as a sixty-three-year-old farmer married to Elizabeth with several children, including Amos, age 15.

37. This engagement was for the legislative seat from Limestone County, which Thomas McClellan won (Walker, *History of Limestone County* 191).

38. Warren Phillips was one of the earliest settlers of Elkmont, Alabama, in Limestone County. He was instrumental in bringing the railroad to Elkmont and was probably the father of David Phillips, who served in Company F of the 9th

Alabama Regiment (Axford, *To Lochaber* 192 n., 217 n. 27; Limestone County, Alabama, 1860 U.S. Census 38).

39. Col. Egbert Jones was the colonel of the 4th Alabama Regiment and would be mortally wounded in both hips at the First Battle of Manassas (Stocker 224 n. 2). Jones was born in Limestone County and lived in Madison County. He died at Orange Court House on September 2, 1861 (Robert K. Krick, *Lee's Colonels: A Biographical Register of the Field Officers of the Army of Northern Virginia* [Dayton, OH: Morningside, 1992], 213).

40. The Lincoln County troops were from Lincoln County, Tennessee. Just northeast of Limestone County, Alabama, Lincoln County was named for Gen. Benjamin Lincoln, a Revolutionary War hero. Company G was the Fayetteville Guards of the 1st Tennessee Provisional Regiment—not the same as the 1st Tennessee Regiment that returned to Tennessee in 1861 after the regiment was reorganized (Civil War Centennial Commission, *Tennesseans in the Civil War: A Military History of Confederate and Union Units with Available Rosters of Personnel,* vol. 1 [Nashville, TN: Civil War Centennial Commission, 1964], 170–71). The captain of Company F was Maj. Felix Grundy Buchanan. Major Buchanan would later lead the regiment and would marry Martha Catherine McClellan (William's sister) after the war (Capt. W. P. Tolley, "Mrs. F. G. Buchanan" *Confederate Veteran* [1894] 2:135).

41. Brock Clark may have been Capt. Davis W. Clark from Fayetteville, Tennessee (Civil War Centennial Commission 170).

42. Pierre Gustave Toutant Beauregard was born on May 28, 1818, in St. Bernard Parish, Louisiana. He graduated from West Point and served on Winfield Scott's staff during the Mexican War. Beauregard was appointed brigadier general, Provisional Army, C.S.A., on March 1, 1861, and was second in command at Manassas to Joseph E. Johnston (Warner, *Generals in Gray* 22).

Chapter 3

1. Turner 65.

2. There were several theories about the 9th Alabama's delay in getting to the battlefield. According to Edmund DeWitt Patterson of Company D, 9th Alabama Regiment, a number of railroad cars were run off the tracks by an engineer who was then put under guard at Piedmont Station (John G. Barrett, ed., *Yankee Rebel: The Civil War Journal of Edmund DeWitt Patterson* [Chapel Hill: University of North Carolina Press, 1966], 7). William C. Davis indicates that a train leaving Piedmont Station early on the morning of July 21 suffered a collision that prevented the train from proceeding (W. C. Davis, *Battle at Bull Run 140).* William Eppa Fielding of the 9th Alabama mentions in his diary that the 9th would have made it to Manassas sooner than July 22, "but some persons had torn up the tracks" (Axford, *To Lochaber* 10).

3. In his diary, William Eppa Fielding reports finding the knapsacks (Axford,

To Lochaber 11). The 4th Alabama Regiment had left its original position on Henry Hill to march to the support of the Confederate left in the early morning. They had marched to Young's Branch, where they briefly halted and then moved up Matthews Hill to a low fence surrounding a cornfield (Stocker 21).

4. Herman Hattaway and Archer Jones believe that the Confederate forces were too worn out and disorganized to mount a pursuit. President Davis, General Beauregard, and General Johnston met the evening after the battle and agreed that an organized pursuit of the retreating Union forces in the rain could not be made (Herman Hattaway and Archer Jones, *How the North Won: A Military History of the Civil War* [Urbana: University of Illinois Press, 1983], 48–49). Yet General Beauregard, while following the wishes of the two commanders, believed that Washington should have been attacked after the battle (Alfred Roman, *The Military Operations of General Beauregard in the War between the States,* [New York: Da Capo Press 1994), 1:114–19).

5. Wiley, *Life of Johnny Reb* 244.

6. James E. H. Bailey (1835–61) was a boyhood friend of William McClellan. He was the son of Martha A. Bailey and Elijah Bailey. When Elijah died, Martha married Hezekiah Bradley Cartwright and Hezekiah John C. Cartwright and Matthew Thomas C. Cartwright, who were members of Company F in the 9th Alabama. James Bailey lived in Madison County, Alabama, in 1860 and served with the 4th Alabama Regiment (Madison County, Alabama, 1860 Census 68). He was wounded in his right side and fingers at the First Battle of Manassas (CSR, James E. H. Bailey). He died from his wounds; was buried at the hospital in Culpeper, Virginia; and was later reburied in a mass grave in Fairview Cemetery in Culpeper.

3rd Lt. Robert N. Hughes was a twenty-two-year-old teacher from Huntsville, Alabama, and a member of the Huntsville Guards (Company F, 4th Alabama). William was mistaken about his death, as Hughes was later paroled at Appomattox (CSR, Robert N. Hughes).

Peter B. Fletcher was a private in Company I, 4th Alabama, the North Alabamians, from Madison County. He was sent to the hospital in Culpeper after the battle and was discharged by a surgeon on October 19, 1861 (CSR, Peter Fletcher).

7. The "first fight" at Manassas refers to the engagement at Blackburn's Ford on July 18. On the Union side, Gen. Daniel Tyler took two light companies and a squadron of cavalry forces to reconnoiter south of Centreville toward Manassas Junction, where they were drawn into a fight with Gen. James Longstreet's Confederate forces. Tyler was turned back, and there were relatively light losses on both sides: eighty-three Union and sixty-three Confederate (*OR* 2:83, 310, 461–62). Southern newspapers overplayed the engagement, with the *New Orleans Picayune* reporting Union casualties at four to five thousand (J. Cutler Andrews, *The South Reports the Civil War* [Pittsburgh: University of Pittsburg Press, 1985], 80). The main battle took place on July 21 as Gen. Irwin McDowell launched a flanking movement against the Confederate left. The Confederate forces were spread out from the fords of Bull Run near Manassas Junction to the Stone Bridge on the Warrenton Turnpike,

and the left flank at the bridge was lightly guarded by the small brigade of Col. Nathan George (Shanks) Evans.

8. Cadmus Marcellus Wilcox (1824–1900) was born in North Carolina but grew up in Columbia, Tennessee. He graduated from West Point, was a veteran of the Mexican War, and was also known for his work on infantry tactics (Warner, *Generals in Gray* 337–38).

9. Sherman's battery was actually Griffin's and Rickett's batteries that were moved from near the Stone House up the hill to the Henry House. The batteries were expecting infantry support to arrive but mistook the blue uniforms of Jackson's advancing troops as that support. Maj. William F. Barry, General McDowell's chief of artillery, twice instructed Capt. Charles Griffin and Capt. J. B. Ricketts to hold their fire on the advancing Confederates, exclaiming they were their support troops. The batteries were cut to pieces. The 69th New York of William Tecumseh Sherman's brigade was in support of Rickett's and Griffin's position (W. C. Davis, *Battle at Bull Run* 177, 203–12; Stocker 234 n. 21, 236 n. 32, 237 n. 35, 240 n. 1).

10. Gaynes Chislom Smith (1827–1910) would become the captain of Company H, 9th Alabama Regiment (replacing David Houston), and was later promoted to colonel of the 9th. Smith was captured at Gettysburg and later released. He was born in Giles County, Tennessee, and moved to Limestone County, where he was a farmer, a teacher, a justice of the peace, and a member of the state legislature (Krick, *Lee's Colonels* 351). The privates in David Houston's company had petitioned for Houston's removal but were unsuccessful. Houston, however, was arrested in early September 1861 for being drunk at recitation, and that incident would lead to his resignation a month later.

11. According to Bell Irvin Wiley, "Diarrhea and dysentery were the most prevalent forms of camp disease," accounting for one-quarter of all cases reported to the Army of Northern Virginia during the first nine months of the war (Wiley, *Life of Johnny Reb* 252). "During the summer of 1861, one out of every seven men serving in the Army of Northern Virginia had measles and total cases for three months exceeded 8,000" (251). According to Joseph Jones, one of the foremost authorities on Confederate medicine, "each southern soldier was ill or wounded six times during the war . . . for every soldier who died as a result of battle, there were three who perished from disease" (244).

12. Union casualties were 472 killed, 1,011 wounded, and 1,216 missing out of 35,732 men present (report of Brig. Gen. Irvin McDowell in *OR* 2:327, 309). Confederate casualties were 387 killed, 1,588 wounded, and 14 missing out of 30,167 men present (*OR* 2:570, 487).

13. Cadmus Wilcox did not command any of the Louisiana regiments. The regiments of his brigade throughout the war were generally from Alabama.

14. The 9th Alabama, like most regiments, was experiencing a loss in manpower due to illness. As many as one-half of the troops were not fit for service during the campaign. On August 17, 1861, Gen. Joseph E. Johnston reported to President Davis that "on my last morning report the total present is 18,718; the sick amount to

4,809" (*OR* 5:790). According to William C. Davis, President Davis was surprised when he learned that "the effective number of men present for duty at Manassas was under 40,000" (W. C. Davis, *Jefferson Davis* 364).

15. Dr. Elijah Hussey was the father of Elizabeth, who married William's brother John after the war (Limestone County, Alabama, 1850 U.S. Census 79B).

16. Dr. Syd Harris may be A. Sidney Harris of Limestone County (Dunnavant, *Historic Limestone County Alabama* 41). Dr. Richard M. Fletcher was a physician from Limestone County (Limestone County, Alabama, 1860 Census 101). Dr. Jonathan McDonald was one of the largest landowners in Limestone County and a longtime physician in the county (Axford, *To Lochaber* 191 n. 26).

17. This may refer to Capt. John D. Kirkpatrick of Company C, 9th Tennessee Cavalry (Civil War Centennial Commission 74).

18. Pvt. William Manning Lowe of Huntsville enlisted in Company I of the 4th Alabama Regiment on April 26, 1861. He was wounded at First Manassas; was discharged on December 7, 1861; and returned home (CSR, William Manning Lowe). He later became a lieutenant colonel and served in the U.S. Congress in 1882. His brother, Robert J. Lowe, a lawyer, served in the same company and was discharged on July 12, 1861 (CSR, Robert J. Lowe).

19. The town of Culpeper Court House, like Athens, Alabama, was a crossroads for both Confederate and Union troops marching to battle. It would change hands regularly during the war, and the effect of that change on the population can be seen in Daniel E. Sutherland's *Seasons of War: The Ordeal of a Confederate Community, 1861–1865* (New York: Free Press, 1995).

20. The "india rubber overcoat" was also called a poncho or a gum blanket. It could be used as a ground cloth, blanket, raincoat, or tent. See Gregory A. Coco, *The Civil War Infantryman: In Camp, on the March, and in Battle* (Gettysburg, PA: Thomas Publications, 1996), 51.

21. Mollie Pettus may be Mary Pettus, daughter of David and Elizabeth Pettus of Limestone County (Limestone County, Alabama, 1850 U.S. Census 23).

22. Jim Shelton was the Rev. James A. Shelton, whose sons, William A. and Mark, served in the 9th Alabama Regiment (Axford, *To Lochaber* 192 n. 34).

23. Donnell may be Maj. Robert S. Donnell, who served in Company E of the 22nd Alabama Regiment (Axford, *To Lochaber* 206 n. 44). He was the grandson of Rev. Robert Donnell of Limestone County.

24. Dr. Joshua Proutt Coman was listed as a forty-eight-year-old physician in the Limestone County, Alabama, 1860 Census (131). Bill Hundley may be William Henderson Hundley of Limestone County (Limestone County, Alabama, 1860 Census 105). Samuel J. Ragland was an early resident of Limestone County (Edwards and Axford 2).

25. John B. McClellan and Jim Malone would eventually raise a company that became Company E of the 26th–50th Alabama Regiment. The regiment was initially called the 26th Alabama Infantry; however, it was found that the designation had already been given to a regiment that had been sent to Virginia. Renamed the

50th Alabama, the regiment was often referred to as the 26th-50th Alabama Regiment. John McClellan was later appointed captain of Company H (CSR, John B. McClellan).

26. James Abercrombie was from Russell County and served in the state legislature. Lawrence Ripley Davis had made his acquaintance while also serving in the legislature. Davis married Abercrombie's daughter, Mary, who died in 1860 (Edwards and Axford 21).

27. Alex (Fletch) McKinney served as sheriff of Limestone County until 1865 (Axford, *To Lochaber* 203 n. 11). Thomas W. Hine came to Limestone County from New York around 1837 and served as tax collector during the war (Axford, *To Lochaber* 208 n. 63). Mace Gilbert served as county tax assessor again in 1868 (Walker, *History of Limestone County* 198).

28. Capt. Hiram H. Higgins was captain of Company A of the 40th Tennessee Regiment, which later was incorporated into the 37th Alabama Regiment. Higgins initially raised a company at Athens known as the "Confederate Bricks" (Philip Reyer, *The Heritage of Limestone County, Alabama,* [Clanton, AL: Heritage Publishing Consultants, 1998], 180).

29. This may have been Alexander McDonald, one of the leading citizens of Lynchburg, Virginia, and the editor of several newspapers. He was also a private in Company A, 9th Alabama Regiment (Axford, *Journals of Thomas Hubbard Hobbs* 206).

30. This may have been Robert Slone of Madison County, Alabama, who was listed as a farmer in the Madison County, Alabama, 1860 Census (13).

31. This was James Vaughan, the grandfather of James Bailey. Jim Bailey and his mother had lived with his grandfather before his mother remarried.

32. Pvt. Leslie W. Moore of Huntsville was nineteen years old and a member of Company I, 4th Alabama Regiment. Despite William's statement, Moore was wounded at the First Battle of Manassas. He died of disease on September 9, 1861 (CSR, Leslie W. Moore).

33. William reversed his earlier statement that Pvt. Peter Fletcher of Company I, 4th Alabama was wounded at First Manassas, although records show that he was wounded and later discharged (CSR, Peter Fletcher).

34. This is probably William R. Day, who was listed as a student in the Madison County, Alabama, 1860 Census 24.

35. Archibald Gracie Jr. was a West Point graduate who resigned his commission to enter into business with his father in Mobile, Alabama. He married Josephine Mayo of Richmond, Virginia. Gracie entered service with the 3rd Alabama Regiment but was promoted to major of the 11th Alabama Regiment and then to colonel of the 43rd Alabama Regiment, which he had recruited. He was promoted to brigadier general in 1862 and served under General Beauregard in Petersburg in 1864. He was killed by an exploding shell on December 2, 1864, in the Petersburg trenches (Warner, *Generals in Gray* 113–14).

36. Mark Shelton and William A. Shelton were members of Company F, 9th Alabama Regiment. Mark would be wounded at the Battle of Frayser's Farm and

would die of his wounds (CSR, Mark Shelton). William would also be wounded at Frayser's Farm and would be promoted to lieutenant in the 7th Alabama Cavalry (CSR, William A. Shelton).

37. On August 8, Prince Napoleon, who had just arrived in the United States from France, was escorted through the Union lines to meet with General Beauregard and General Johnston at Manassas. They spent the night at Lewis House, and the prince left the next day (William P. Snow, *Lee and His Generals* [New York: Fairfax Press, 1982], 235–36. Prince Napoleon was the cousin of French emperor Napoleon III (Donaldson Jordan and Edwin J. Pratt, *Europe and the American Civil War* [New York: Octagon Books, 1969], 230–32.

38. Corp. Augustus H. Strange of Company H was twenty-one years old when he enlisted and was discharged for a hernia on August 11, 1861, while in camp near Bristoe Station (CSR, Augustus H. Strange).

39. William's sister Sarah Anne, to whom he was writing this letter, was married to Lawrence Ripley Davis.

40. Pvt. John C. Carter of Company J enlisted on June 8, 1861, at the age of eighteen (CSR, John C. Carter).

41. On August 31, there were 33,713 troops under Gen. P. G. T. Beauregard at Manassas, and 8,678 under Gen. Theophilus Hunter Holmes at Fredericksburg (*OR* 5:824). General Johnston reported 82,553 troops in all of Northern Virginia in November 1861 (5:974).

42. George Roland Peck and his son, William L. Peck, were tailors in Athens, Alabama (Limestone County, Alabama, 1860 Census 121).

43. The Union general Nathaniel Lyon was a West Point graduate and a veteran of the Mexican War. Lyon was credited with being the man who saved Missouri for the Union in 1861. He was killed leading a charge on August 10, 1861, against Confederate forces under Ben McCulloch at Wilson's Creek, Missouri (Ezra J. Warner, *Generals in Blue: Lives of the Union Commanders* [Baton Rouge: Louisiana State University Press, 1992], 286–87).

44. This may have been the 1st Louisiana Battalion, whose members were outfitted in French Zouave uniforms and who carried knives similar to bowie knives (W. C. Davis, *Battle at Bull Run* 24–25).

45. Dr. William Tell Sanders (1824–65) graduated from medical school in Louisville, Kentucky, and served in the Mexican War. He raised the Molly Walton Guards on March 12, 1862; the unit originally joined the 35th Alabama Regiment (Edwards and Axford 193).

46. Pvt. Alfred M. Martin enlisted in Company F on October 2, 1861, in Athens. He was wounded at the Battle of Gaines's Mill and was frequently hospitalized during the war (CSR, Alfred M. Martin).

Nicholas J. Floyd (1828–1918), originally from Lynchburg, Virginia, was second lieutenant in Company F of the 9th Alabama Regiment, and first lieutenant after 1862. He served as adjutant of the 9th Alabama and later as captain of the provost guard. Floyd was a grand-nephew of Gov. John Floyd of Virginia. Before the war he was the editor of the *Athens Herald* (Axford, *To Lochaber* 190 n. 15).

47. Steptoe Picket Jr. (1816–84) had moved to Alabama with his family from Fauquier County, Virginia, and was a leading planter in Limestone County. He was appointed quartermaster for Company F in October 1861 and resigned on May 23, 1862 (Axford, *To Lochaber* 193 n. 52).

48. The drills William mentions can be found in Maj. William Gilham's "The School of the Battalion" in *Manual of Instruction for the Volunteers and Militia of the Confederate States* (Baltimore: Cushings and Bailey, 1861), 240–333. Gilham was instructor of tactics and commandant of cadets at the Virginia Military Institute.

49. This was probably John R. Fletcher, a physician from Limestone County (Limestone County, Alabama, 1860 Census 100).

50. Old Hartwell was one of the slaves on the McClellan farm (Buchanan-McClellan Papers).

51. The Edmondsons were from Lincoln County, Tennessee, and lived near the McClellans in the Cane Creek section of the county (Buchanan-McClellan Papers). "Mide" appears to be a nickname.

52. Besides making uniforms and flags for the Limestone troops, the girls at the Athens Training School were also hard at work in supplying homespun shirts, pants, underwear, and socks (Walker, *History of Limestone County* 103–4).

53. This was Company E of the 26th-50th Alabama (*OR Supplement* 1:786).

54. Heart, Lady, Willie, and Payne were slaves on the McClellan farm (Carter family letters).

55. This Matthew Buchanan may be the brother of Felix Grundy Buchanan, who lived in Lincoln County, Tennessee. Matthew joined Company E of the 44th Tennessee Regiment (CSR, Matthew Buchanan). It may also be Matthew Hay Buchanan of Washington County, Virginia, an uncle of Felix's who lived near Emory and Henry College at Glade Springs.

56. David Blackburn was a member of the 4th Alabama Regiment who was either wounded or sick and returned home, where he died (CSR, David Blackburn).

57. This may have been William Joseph Todd of Athens, who died during the war in 1861. His wife, Mary Jernigan Todd, sold all their belongings and joined a wagon train to move to Texas. A smallpox outbreak quarantined the train, and she returned to Athens to work as a nurse. She later moved to Texas (Reyer 429).

58. Little Sue Davis was the oldest child of Lawrence Ripley Davis and Sarah Anne McClellan Davis (Carter family letters).

59. Ira E. Hobbs was the father of Thomas Hubbard Hobbs, captain of Company F. He had come to the camp to visit Captain Hobbs and brought along the captain's wife, Annie (Axford, *Journals of Thomas Hubbard Hobbs* 240). Ira Hobbs also carried letters home for William Eppa Fielding (Axford, *To Lochaber* 15).

60. Immediately after the First Battle of Manassas, the Confederate troops suffered from a lack of provisions—especially meat and flour, which was not forthcoming from Richmond (W. C. Davis, *Jefferson Davis* 354).

61. Usually two companies from each regiment were selected to serve as skirmishers. Skirmishers moved ahead of the main body looking for signs of the enemy. The drill was taken from Gen. Winfield Scott's *Infantry Tactics: Or, Rules for the Ex-*

ercise and Manouevres of the United States Infantry (see Paddy Griffith, *Battle Tactics of the Civil War,* [New Haven: Yale University Press, 2001], 99–100).

62. This was William's uncle William A. McClellan, from Lincoln County, Tennessee (Buchanan-McClellan Papers).

63. Pvt. William D. Pettus, an eighteen-year-old farmer, enlisted in Company F on June 4, 1861. He suffered from fainting spells and was hospitalized at Centreville, Virginia, and later at the general hospital in Charlottesville. He was discharged with a certificate of disability for "epilepsia" on October 26, 1861 (CSR, William D. Pettus).

64. When soldiers were ordered to cook three days' provisions in case of a possible battle, the idea was to have enough food on hand for each day. Quite often, however, the Confederate soldiers ate three days of rations all at once rather than having to carry them into battle (McCarthy 27).

65. Pvt. Thomas Bass of Company F was discharged in September 1861 on a surgeon's certificate (CSR, Thomas Bass). Corp. John Rawlings (or Rawlins) of Company F was wounded at Salem Church and was later captured on August 8, 1864, at Deep Bottom, Virginia, and then sent to Point Lookout Prison (CSR, John Rawlings). Pvt. Thomas Sandifer of Company F was discharged on October 6, 1861 (CSR, Thomas Sandifer). Nathan M. Rogers of Company H was discharged on October 17, 1861, with tuberculosis (CSR, Nathan M. Rogers).

66. For most of the summer of 1861, the 9th Alabama went without tents—because the tents never caught up with the regiment. Historian Carlton McCarthy thinks the use of tents by the Confederates may have been overstated: "Tents were rarely seen . . . Two men slept together, each having a blanket and an oil cloth . . . the two laid on this . . . and slept very comfortably through rain, snow, or hail as it might be" (25). Armies frequently "bivouacked," or slept out in the open air on the ground.

67. Several Gills lived in Limestone County: Benjamin F., John Y., Peterson M., Robert M., and Thomas O. (Limestone County, Alabama, 1860 Census 8, 43, 64, 70, and 91).

68. The girl has not been identified, and the letter has not been found.

69. Southern women believed their role was to sacrifice their own feeling and doubt and to keep the men at the front in good spirits by writing cheery letters (Drew Gilpin Faust, "Confederate Women and Narratives of War," *Divided Houses, Gender and the Civil War,* ed. Catherine Clinton and Nina Silber [New York: Oxford University Press, 1992], 171–99).

70. Captain Francis has not been identified.

71. "Miss Sophy" may be Sophie Davis, daughter of Nicholas Davis Jr., and "Mr Firester" is probably Pvt. J. B. Forrester, a single farmer from Huntsville who enlisted in Company I of the 4th Alabama Regiment on April 26, 1861. He was severely wounded at First Battle of Manassas (ADAH, J. B. Forrester).

72. Burk Johnson has not been identified.

73. This may be the William Lowe listed as a twenty-year-old law student living with Nicholas Davis Jr. in the Madison County, Alabama, 1860 Census (152).

74. Dr. Hearns has not been identified.

75. "Elizabeth Douglas" was listed in the Madison County, Alabama, 1860 Census (21).

76. Alice Moore has not been identified.

77. This was the *Athens Banner* newspaper (Axford, *Journals of Thomas Hubbard Hobbs* 236).

78. Brunswood is one of the slaves from the McClellan farm (Buchanan-McClellan Papers).

79. The Confederates had advanced observation posts at Munson's Hill, Mason Hill, and Upton Hill overlooking Alexandria and Arlington on the ridge near Bailey's Crossroads (*OR* 5:182).

80. East Tennessee was heavily pro-Union in its sentiment. See Noel C. Fisher's *War at Every Door: Partisan Politics and Guerilla Violence in East Tennessee, 1860–1869* (Chapel Hill: University of North Carolina Press, 1997); and Daniel W. Crofts's *Reluctant Confederates: Upper South Unionists in the Secession Crisis* (Chapel Hill: University of North Carolina Press, 1989).

81. This was probably Mary E. Bronaugh of Madison County, Alabama (Madison County, Alabama, 1850 Census 24).

82. "Mrs Bibb" may be Mary Betts Bibb, wife of Capt. David Porter Bibb (Edwards and Axford 204).

83. This may have been Thomas F. Allen, the son of clergyman James Wilburn Allen (Limestone County, Alabama, 1850 U.S. Census 93B).

84. Andy Wright was the son of Julia Benson McClellan Wright (Thomas Joyce McClellan's sister) and James B. Wright of Fayetteville, Tennessee. William N. Wright was also their son (Buchanan-McClellan Papers). Puss Davis is probably the daughter of Henry Davis and Carolyn Charlotte McClellan Davis, another sister of Thomas Joyce McClellan.

85. Gen. Bartley Lowe was a prominent citizen of Limestone County. His daughter, Sophia, married Nicholas Davis Jr., a close friend of the McClellans (Edwards and Axford 63).

86. Many members of the 4th Alabama Regiment were at home recovering from wounds or illness related to First Manassas. Sickness had already reduced the 4th to 558 men before the battle (Stocker 24–25).

87. Charles C. Salle of Company I, 4th Alabama Regiment was appointed captain on August 1, resigned on August 6, and died of typhoid fever on September 9, 1861 (CSR, Charles C. Salle).

88. Gen. Felix Kirk Zollicoffer was born in 1812 in Maury County, Tennessee. While he served as a volunteer in the Seminole uprising, his background was journalism and politics, and he served as a state senator. He accepted a commission as a brigadier in 1861 and went to east Tennessee. He led a force that crossed the Cumberland River into Kentucky, where he engaged Gen. George H. Thomas. Zollicoffer was killed at Mill Springs on January 19, 1862 (Warner, *Generals in Gray* 349).

89. Pvt. James F. Griffis of Company F enlisted on June 4, 1861. He was wounded at Gettysburg and was left behind to be taken prisoner. From Letterman Hospital

in Gettysburg, he was sent to the USA hospital in Baltimore, Maryland. He was exchanged November 17, 1863 (CSR, James F. Griffis).

90. Pvt. Cassill G. Beckham of Company H enlisted on June 6, 1861, and was discharged at Bristoe for a hernia on September 12, 1861 (CSR, C. G. Beckham).

91. William H. Robertson of Athens came to Manassas to take care of his son, Nathaniel Terry Robertson, who was sick and was discharged October 9, 1861 (Axford, *To Lochaber* 192 n. 43).

92. James Edward Fletcher of Huntsville enlisted in Company F, 4th Alabama Regiment on April 26, 1861, and was discharged on April 20, 1862 (ADAH, James Edward Fletcher).

93. The sounds of cannon may have come from the engagement at Freestone Point on the Potomac River on September 25 (*OR* 5:215).

94. On September 7, Gen. George S. Houston arrived in the Manassas camp of the 9th Alabama. After meeting with Colonel Wilcox and his son, Houston planned to go to Richmond to see secretary of war Leroy Pope Walker about having David's resignation put aside (Gen. George S. Houston to L. P. Walker, August–September 1861, 4061 [National Archives Microfilm Publication M437, roll 9], Letters Received by the Secretary of War). Captain David Houston had been charged with drunkenness while on duty, and the charge had officially been communicated to both Walker's office and to Gen. Joseph E. Johnston. Captain Houston voluntarily submitted his resignation. Wilcox also had another company commander (Captain Ripley of Company A) under the same charge (C. M. Wilcox to L. P. Walker, August–September 1861, 4308 [National Archives Microfilm Publication M437, roll 9], Letters Received by the Secretary of War). Although Walker instructed Wilcox to reinstate Houston, Houston eventually resigned and his resignation was accepted. He left the 9th Alabama a short time later.

95. Lieutenant Floyd returned to Limestone County to recruit more troops for the 9th Alabama. The 9th Alabama had only 575 men fit for duty in September, as compared with the 1,000 that arrived in Virginia at the start of the war. The losses came from sickness, injury, and causes other than battle; in addition, some men who were unwell or unfit had been released from service, and some men were away on leave (Cadmus Wilcox to Mary Emily Wilcox, 11 October 1861, Cadmus Wilcox Papers, Manuscript Division, Library of Congress Washington, D.C.).

96. Hall's Hill is located in Arlington County, Virginia. The Confederates had entrenched along a line above Chain Bridge, and on August 31 Union forces reconnoitering the lines led to brief cavalry engagements as far as Hall's Hill (Eleanor Lee Templeman, *Arlington Heritage: Vignettes of a Virginia County* [Arlington: privately published, 1959], 118).

97. Daniel Burbage Coleman (1838–1906) was the son of Daniel Coleman (1801–57), who was a leading political figure in Limestone County, the editor of the *Athens Herald*, a circuit court judge, and a member of the Alabama Supreme Court. Daniel Coleman served as an aide-de-camp to Gen. Philip St. George Cocke (his cousin) but resigned after Cocke's death (Edwards and Axford 52).

98. Arlington Heights was the area now occupied by Fort Myer in Arlington, and the home of Robert E. Lee (Margaret Leech, *Reveille in Washington, 1860–1865* [Garden City, NY: Garden City Publishing Company, 1941], 57–58). The Army of the Potomac was using observation balloons launched along the Potomac River to survey Confederate forces in Northern Virginia (Leech 115).

99. While army regulations called for clothing issues twice a year—in the fall and in the spring—reality saw far less clothing issued even at the beginning of the war. The Confederate government could not supply uniforms for all of its men. Volunteer units were expected to provide their own uniforms, and at the start of the war women's organizations made most of the uniforms for their hometown boys (Wiley, *Life of Johnny Reb* 108–11).

100. The "battle at Leesburg" Robert McClellan refers to was neither the Battle of Ball's Bluff nor the First Battle of Manassas. There was no major battle in the region during this time with the kind of casualties he describes. The Cheat Mountain Campaign had begun in western Virginia on September 11, and the Confederates suffered light casualties in this early defeat (*OR* 5:184–86).

101. John H. Blackburn was a twenty-one-year-old physician from Huntsville who enlisted in Company F of the 4th Alabama Regiment. He was discharged September 6, 1861 (CSR, John H. Blackburn).

102. Jack may have been the brother of Pvt. David Bridgeforth of Company F, who was wounded at Gaines's Mill and was killed a few days later at Frayser's Farm (Axford, *To Lochaber* 192 n. 36). Jack Bridgeforth's name did not appear on the rolls of the 9th Alabama. Jack Bridgeforth may be John M. Bridgeforth of Company F who was discharged on September 18, 1861 (CSR, John M. Bridgeforth).

103. Newton Nash Clements was the captain of Company F of the 50th Alabama Regiment. He was wounded in the foot at Shiloh and was appointed lieutenant colonel on October 20, 1862 (CSR, Newton Nash Clements). After the war he became a member of the Alabama House of Representatives and served in the U.S. Congress in 1880–81.

104. It was possible to get a substitute to take one's place in a regiment, by getting someone at home to take your place or by offering as much as $500 for a replacement (Wiley, *Life of Johnny Reb* 125–26).

105. On September 22, the 9th Alabama Regiment with the rest of the brigade moved into Centreville, Virginia. According to Capt. Thomas Hubbard Hobbs, "We took a near road across the country [from Broad Run] and before we knew it, found ourselves upon the battlefield of July 21. A halt of a few moments allowed us to look around a little . . . Arrived at Centreville about 2 p.m. and pitched camp on a high hill east of town, and at the west end of wood" (Axford, *Journal of Thomas Hubbard Hobbs* 243). According to William Eppa Fielding, "the camp was near the pike [probably the Warrenton Turnpike, modern Route 29] with a commanding view to the west although the easterly view was blocked by the woods, which contained a great many chinquapin trees" (Axford, *To Lochaber* 19).

106. Gen. Leonidas Polk was a graduate of West Point who had resigned his com-

mission to attend the Virginia Episcopal Seminary in Alexandria. On September 3, 1861, Polk seized Columbus, Kentucky, on the Mississippi River and turned it into a Confederate stronghold. Kentucky had tried to remain neutral in the conflict, but the occupation by Polk and the occupation of Paducah, Kentucky, by Grant brought an end to the state's neutrality (James M. McPherson, *Ordeal by Fire: The Civil War and Reconstruction* [New York: Alfred A. Knopf, 1982], 154.

107. Gen. Leroy Pope Walker resigned his position as secretary of war on September 16, 1861, and later served as a brigadier general for several months in 1861 (Warner, *Generals in Gray* 320–21).

Chapter 4

1. Johnston 69–74.

2. Kim Bernard Holien, *Battle at Ball's Bluff: Leesburg, Virginia October 21, 1861* (Alexandria: Rapidan Press, 1989), 23–24.

3. The Lewis House, also called "Portici," was the home of Francis W. Lewis. It served as the headquarters of Gen. Joseph E. Johnston during the Battle of First Manassas (W. C. Davis, *Battle at Bull Run* 200).

4. Axford, *Journals of Thomas Hubbard Hobbs* 247.

5. Joseph Mills Hanson, *Bull Run Remembers . . . The History, Traditions, and Landmarks of the Manassas (Bull Run) Campaigns before Washington, 1861–1862* (Prince William, VA: Prince William County Historical Commission, 1991), 38–39.

6. Zebulon Pike Davis was a son of Nicholas Davis Jr. of Limestone County and was from Madison County, Alabama (Edwards and Axford 63).

7. Nicholas Davis Jr. unsuccessfully tried to raise a regiment of his own and served as lieutenant colonel with the 19th Alabama Regiment until he resigned for health reasons (*OR Supplement* 1:514). DeWitt Clinton Davis, brother of Nicholas Davis Jr., served as captain of the North Alabama Cavaliers cavalry company, which served in Col. Jessee Forrest's regiment in Kentucky.

8. "Venable" was either Joseph Venable, a private in Company F who was an Appomattox parole (CSR, Joseph Venable), or Andrew Venable, a thirty-five-year-old blacksmith who enrolled as a private in Company F. Andrew was wounded in the hand at Gaines's Mill and would be discharged at the general hospital in Danville, Virginia, for a physical disability—a dislocated shoulder (CSR, Andrew Venable).

9. This was probably the Thomas Artillery of Virginia. Stannard's Battery was assigned to Edmund Kirby Smith's brigade at Winchester in July 1861 (Sibley 2). General Johnston reported to acting Secretary of War Judah P. Benjamin on September 26 that there was an advance guard of eleven regiments of infantry and J. E. B. Stuart's cavalry stationed at Falls Church and at modern-day Bailey's Crossroads. This command was in front of another line that ran from near Vienna to Fairfax Station. Johnston further told Benjamin that his forces were not then in a strong defensive position to either fight a battle or hold the enemy in check, and that it was now time to decide whether they should advance or fall back to a more

defensible line (*OR* 5:881). Confederate forces pulled back to Fairfax Court House on September 28.

10. President Davis met with General Beauregard and General Johnston during the first week of October 1861 to discuss strategy. When Davis found out that there were fewer than 40,000 effective troops at Manassas, and that sick lists were growing longer due to the lack of good water and provisions, he was ill disposed to support Beauregard's suggestion for an assault on Washington or Maryland (W. C. Davis, *Jefferson Davis* 364). The generals believed they needed 50,000 to 60,000 seasoned troops to attack Washington (*OR* 5:884). The visit William describes was part of the president's tour of the outposts around Manassas and culminated in a general review of the brigades and the Washington Artillery before he left for Richmond on October 5 (Andrews 96).

11. Robinson and Graves have not been identified. They may have been friends from Lincoln County, Tennessee.

12. Both McDonalds in Company H did leave the 9th Alabama Regiment. Thomas McDonald transferred to the 14th Alabama Battalion, the Partisan Rangers (CSR, Thomas McDonald); Jonathan R. McDonald was medically discharged on October 10, 1862 (CSR, Jonathan R. McDonald).

13. No Confederate forces of this size ventured into Maryland in 1861. William may be describing a camp rumor based on General Johnston's plan to eventually invade Maryland.

14. The "big fight" in Missouri was the surrender of the 3,500 Union troops at Lexington, Missouri, on September 20, 1861, to Maj. Gen. Sterling Price's Missourians (McPherson, *Ordeal by Fire* 156–57). Funds from the state bank of Lexington, Missouri, had been buried in the fort at Lexington, and upon its surrender all but fifteen thousand dollars in bank notes was recovered (Robert Underwood Johnson and Clarence Clough Buel, eds., *Battles and Leaders of the Civil War* [Seacacus, NJ: Castle, n.d.], 1:313).

15. Humphreys has not been identified.

16. These men were probably Madison County residents: Thomas J. Foster, who was also a member of the First Confederate Congress (Thornton 441); George T. Jones (Daniel S. Dupre, *Transforming the Cotton Frontier: Madison County, Alabama, 1800–1840,* [Baton Rouge: Louisiana State University Press, 1997], 227); John Lindsay (Dupre 109); and Zebulon Pike Davis (Edwards and Axford 63).

17. James H. Clanton was born in Columbia County, Georgia, on January 8, 1827. He served in the Mexican War and served in the Alabama legislature. Clanton began service in the Confederacy as colonel of the 1st Alabama Cavalry and was promoted to brigadier general in November 1863 (Warner, *Generals in Gray* 50–51).

18. Bob Mills has not been identified. The 1860 Census for Limestone County, Alabama, does show an Ebeneezer A. Mills living near the McClellans.

19. The large battery waiting for the Union troops along the pike was located at the intersection of today's Routes 29 and 211 and Old Centreville Road in Centreville. It was located upon a high hill that was built up as the principal fort and

named "Artillery Hill" (B. Eugenia Smith, *Centreville Virginia: Its History and Architecture* [Fairfax, VA: Fairfax County Office of Planning, 1973], 55–56).

20. John Horace Forney (1829–1902) began the war as colonel of the 10th Alabama. He was born in North Carolina and educated at West Point. Forney was promoted to brigadier general to rank on March 10, 1862, and then to major general on October 27, 1862. Forney was wounded at the skirmish at Dranesville, Virginia, in 1861 and was captured at Vicksburg. His brother, William Henry Forney, commanded a brigade under William Mahone (Warner, *Generals in Gray* 90–91).

21. White Buchanan (1818–92) was the brother of Felix Grundy Buchanan of the 1st Tennessee Regiment. White Buchanan did not appear to be enrolled in any of the regiments and may have just been visiting when William saw him (Buchanan-McClellan Papers).

22. This was merely a camp rumor; there was no major activity in Northern Virginia during that time.

23. As noted earlier, William D. Pettus was discharged on October 26, 1861, for "epilepsia" (CSR, William D. Pettus).

24. Thomas B. Kelly enlisted in Company F on June 4, 1861, at age twenty-two. He was discharged on a surgeon's certificate on July 12, 1862, for tuberculosis (CSR, Thomas Kelly).

25. This is probably Emmanuel Isom, who lived south of Nick Davis Road and close to the McClellan home. He was the son of George Isom of Baltimore, Maryland (Edwards and Axford 59). Elisha Kimble French built his home along French's Mill Creek, just to the west of the Isom land (149).

26. William Fielding (1790–1855), William Eppa Fielding's father, built the Fielding house near Piney Creek to the west of the Frenches (Edwards and Axford 74–75). William Eppa Fielding was a member of Company F of the 9th Alabama.

27. This may have been James Newby (1788–1861), who was the father of Henry W. Newby (Edwards and Axford 69).

28. The scarcity of meat in Alabama was in contrast to the plentiful supply of beef for the Confederate troops in Northern Virginia in 1861 (see William Cowan McClellan's letter of October 31, 1861). This was a very hard year for agriculture in northern Alabama; an Alabama judge testifying before a Union court in 1862 called it "a bad year—for the grain crops were short in north Alabama" (*OR* 16.1:474).

29. "Kittie" was Martha Catherine McClellan, and "Tom" was Thomas Nicholas McClellan, the youngest McClellan child.

30. Davis's 2nd Alabama Battalion (*OR Supplement* 1.2: 783).

31. Thomas H. Gilbert raised a company that eventually became Company B of the 26th-50th Alabama Regiment.

32. Robert Johnson, John Goodman, and Lem Hide were members of Company E of the 26th-50th Alabama Regiment (ADAH). George W. McKinney served as captain and assistant quartermaster for the regiment (CSR, George W. McKinney). William L. Peck was the son of Athens tailor George Roland Peck (Limestone County, Alabama, 1860 Census 121).

33. William R. Holcomb enrolled as a private in Company F and was appointed adjutant on May 2, 1863. He was captured at the Battle of the Weldon Railroad on August 31, 1864, and was sent to Fort Delaware prison. He was released on June 12, 1865 (CSR, William R. Holcomb).

34. The five hundred Union prisoners were from the Confederate victory at Ball's Bluff near Leesburg on October 21. The battle had started out as a Union reconnaissance in force toward Leesburg but quickly escalated from a skirmish to a full-fledged battle, which ended before larger forces could be brought to bear. See Holien's *Battle at Ball's Bluff.*

35. Forty-five to fifty-five thousand Confederate troops were amassed in and around Centreville in December 1861 (*OR* 5:1015). The 9th Alabama was encamped along Braddock Road just northwest of town near Big Rocky Run, where they were guarding the road from Leesburg leading to the main camp at Centreville (diary of William Eppa Fielding in Axford, *To Lochaber* 25).

36. "Gen Bacon" was Col. Edward Baker, a United States senator from Oregon and a personal friend of Abraham Lincoln's. Colonel Baker was the ranking officer on the scene who directed the ill-fated action and was killed during the battle. Col. Nathan B. Evans commanded the Confederate forces. His quick thinking and proper assessment of the situation prevented the Union forces from establishing a foothold on the Virginia shore (Holien 37–38, 54–55). Union casualties were 49 killed, 158 wounded, and 714 missing; Confederate casualties were 36 killed, 117 wounded, and 2 missing (*OR* 5:308, 353).

37. Cadmus M. Wilcox was promoted to brigadier general of the 3rd Brigade on October 22, 1861 (*OR* 5:914, 922, 961).

38. "Acquitine" was actually Accotink Creek, a small creek that flowed through southern Fairfax County into the Potomac River just below Mount Vernon. The regiment moved to the Braddock Road ford of Accotink Creek near Annandale on October 15, where they relieved the 11th Alabama (Axford, *Journals of Thomas Hubbard Hobbs* 244). Company F was at the Roundhouse at the ford (Parker 25).

39. William was awaiting delivery of a package of clothing from two Athens tailors—George Roland Peck and his son, William—which would be delivered by Mr. Warren Phillips (Axford, *To Lochaber* 238 n., 192 n. 48).

40. Cub Run is a small stream three miles east of Bull Run and about three miles west of Centreville. It was the stream at which Union forces, retreating from the First Battle of Manassas, panicked when a Confederate artillery shell hit the suspended bridge and blockaded the roadway. As William writes this letter, the 9th Alabama Regiment was again on picket duty on Flatlick Run, a tributary of Cub Run, where it rained for twenty hours (Axford, *Journals of Thomas Hubbard Hobbs* 246).

41. Jonas Brittle was a forty-eight-year-old shoemaker who lived in Limestone County. He was originally from North Carolina (Limestone County, Alabama, 1850 Census 127).

42. Samuel Henry (1825–93) was born in Tennessee and was working as a mer-

chant in Gunter's Landing, Alabama, before the war. He was appointed lieutenant colonel on July 3, 1861, and colonel on June 1, 1862 (Krick, *Lee's Colonels* 190). Colonel Henry was arrested for misconduct and cowardice during the Battle of Williamsburg. While under arrest he continued to serve in the field, including fighting in the line at Sharpsburg. After a hearing and an appeal, he was relieved from office on March 19, 1863, and returned to Marshall County, Alabama (CSR, Samuel Henry).

43. Henry Chambers (Hal) Bibb (1837–78) was a physician and the grandson of Thomas Bibb, the second governor of Alabama. Hal Bibb resigned his commission on December 29, 1861 (Limestone County, Alabama, 1860 Census 107; CSR, Hal C. Bibb).

44. Jeremiah Henry Johnston Williams (1829–1912) was born in Jackson County, Alabama, and worked as a civil engineer. He was appointed captain of Company B of the 9th Alabama Regiment on May 23, 1861. Williams was appointed major on March 27, 1862, and commanded the regiment at Sharpsburg, where he was wounded (Krick, *Lee's Colonels* 399). Many privates of the 9th Alabama blamed Williams for the cashiering of Colonel Henry, and Williams in turn was found unqualified for promotion at a hearing; he resigned on September 21, 1863, and returned to Alabama (CSR, Jeremiah Henry Johnston Williams).

45. Dr. Aaron A. Burleson of Decatur, Alabama, was a member of one of the first families to settle in northern Alabama, and he worked with Thomas Hubbard Hobbs and Luke Pryor to bring the railroad to Athens, Alabama (Axford, *To Lochaber* 192 n. 41).

46. This was a reference to the use of foreign-born Federal soldiers. There was concern as early as 1860 that the North would use German (Hessian) troops, much in the same way the British had used the Hessian troops during the American Revolution (Eric W. Bright, "Nothing to Fear from the Influence of Foreigners: The Patriotism of Richmond's German-Americans during the Civil War," master's thesis, Virginia Polytechnic Institute and State University, 1994, 104).

47. The man William describes may have been Mathias C. Mitchell, a resident of Centreville, who served as a guide for the Union troops to Blackburn's Ford on July 18 (*OR* 2:329). However, William Eppa Fielding, a member of Company F of the 9th Alabama, mentioned in a letter on November 9, 1861, that "we turned to the left, about a mile from town [Centreville], and found a squad at work nearly a mile from the pike, near a man's house named Lane, who is said to be in jail in Richmond, for guiding the Yankees through the country at the battle of the 21st [Bull Run]" (Axford, *To Lochaber* 27).

48. Thomas Redus contracted pneumonia and died on November 7, 1861. Capt. Thomas Hubbard Hobbs, a friend of the Redus family, telegraphed Thomas Redus's father, Alfred, about the boy. The elder Redus arrived in Manassas on November 16 not knowing of his son's death. He was unable to obtain a burial case to return his son to Alabama and was forced to leave him buried in Manassas (Price Parker, *From Alabama to Appomattox: History of the Ninth Infantry* [Athens, AL: Athens News Courier, 1970], 28–30).

49. Pvt. Henry (Hal) Malone of Company F was the son of Capt. James Henry Malone of the 26th–50th Alabama Regiment. Hal was wounded in the right eye at the Battle of Frayser's Farm (CSR, Henry Malone; Axford, *To Lochaber* 222 n. 32).

50. Warren Phillips and Ira Hobbs, the father of Capt. Thomas Hubbard Hobbs, arrived from Athens, Alabama, carrying with them suits and clothing made in Pulaski, Tennessee, which included round jackets, pants, and overcoats. As Hobbs noted, "These came in good time, for some of the boys were getting very ragged" (Axford, *Journals of Thomas Hubbard Hobbs* 247).

51. William Phelan does not appear in the rosters of the 9th Alabama nor in the records of the National Archives.

52. Gen. Joseph E. Johnston's November 14, 1861, report to the adjutant general on his troops in Northern Virginia showed 44,121 effective total present, and 52,435 aggregate present and absent—which makes a total of 8,314 absent for duty (*OR* 5:932). An October 13 memo to Gen. Joseph Johnston from acting secretary of war Judah P. Benjamin noted, "your recent report to the Adjutant General developed the painful fact that nearly one third of your force is still prostrated by sickness" (896). Several months earlier on July 16, 1861, in regard to the troops at Winchester General Johnston noted, "measles, mumps, and other diseases, to which new troops are subjected, had been so prevalent that the average effective strength of the regiments did not much exceed five hundred" (Johnston 33).

53. William T. Allen ran the drugstore in Athens (Limestone County, Alabama, 1860 Census 128).

54. Port Royal, South Carolina, was captured on November 7, 1861, by Admiral Samuel Francis Du Pont and his Federal naval squadron. The squadron sailed into Port Royal Sound, and the outnumbered Confederates were forced to flee. Gen. Thomas W. Sherman's 12,000-man Union force then occupied the area (*OR* 6:168, 186, 311–12). While it "created but little excitement," according to William, this was an important Union victory in that it secured a foothold on the South Carolina coast.

55. William is probably recounting the capture of a Union foraging party at Doolan's Farm to the southeast of Falls Church. According to a report by Maj. William T. Martin of the 2nd Mississippi Cavalry, the Confederates captured 30 prisoners, 120 bushels of corn, and 5 wagons (*OR* 1:440).

56. Historians' conventional wisdom has portrayed South Carolina as dominated by powerful and anxious planters who "directed the state into a series of belligerent political stands which . . . helped earn the state a well-deserved reputation as a breeding ground for reactionary radicalism" (Lacy K. Ford Jr., *Origins of Southern Radicalism: The South Carolina Upcountry, 1800–1860,* [New York: Oxford University Press, 1991], 100). Ford, however, believes that the concept of radical planters forcing the state into secession is misleading. Ford sees a society that seceded because of its old country–republican ideal of personal independence for both the planter and the yeoman (Ford 372).

57. John Slidell and James M. Mason were Confederate diplomatic envoys—Slidell to France and Mason to England—who were en route to England on a dip-

lomatic mission seeking military aid. While on board the English steamer *Trent* on November 8, 1861, they were intercepted by a Union warship commanded by Capt. Charles Wilkes. Under his own authority, Wilkes captured the two envoys and returned with them to Boston. The event caused great tension between the United States and Great Britain, and for a while there was a threat of British intervention. An ultimatum from Great Britain forced President Lincoln and secretary of state William Henry Seward to release the two diplomats on January 8, 1862 (Jordan and Pratt 24).

58. The *Charleston Daily Courier* blamed the inactivity of the Confederate forces after the First Battle of Manassas on the "miserable political jugglery of President Davis" (W. C. Davis, *Jefferson Davis* 367). Jefferson Davis was also accused of preventing a march on Washington and the invasion of Maryland (367). The newspapers created problems for the president with his two generals Beauregard and Johnston, as well as with the Confederate congress. Despite William's confidence in his commanders, some of the early enthusiasm for them was waning. According to Douglas Freeman, "many still looked at Beauregard in the afterglow of Sumter and Manassas, but the South perplexed by his egotistical writings, no longer believed unanimously that in him it had found its Napoleon" (Douglas Southall Freeman, *Lee's Lieutenants: A Study in Command* [New York: Charles Scribner's Sons, 1944] 1:109–10).

59. Bethel Church, or Big Bethel, was one of the first battles of the war, fought on June 10, 1861, near Hampton, Virginia. Here, 3,500 Union troops engaged 1,200 Confederates (*OR* 2:91). There were seventy-six Union and eight Confederate casualties (2:82, 92).

60. During the first year of the war, both North and South returned prisoners of war and paroled them with an oath that they would not take up arms again. A cartel was worked out on July 22, 1862, that officially allowed for direct exchange and parole of all prisoners (Margaret E. Wagner, Gary W. Gallagher, and Paul Finkelman, eds., *The Library of Congress Civil War Desk Reference,* [New York: Simon and Schuster, 2002], 600–601).

61. According to the November 1861 returns for the Army of Northern Virginia, there were 8,824 men aggregate present and absent for duty in the Aquia District (*OR* 5:974). This included the 1st Tennessee and twenty-two other infantry regiments, cavalry, and several artillery batteries (5:1030). The Confederates hoped to effectively stop Union ships from using the Potomac River (Mary Alice Wills, *The Confederate Blockade of Washington, D.C., 1861–1862* [Shippensburg, PA: Burd Street Press, 1998], 63).

62. The troops began work on the Centreville Military Railroad to solve a nagging problem. The wagon roads between Manassas Junction and Centreville were so poor that the snow and mud left them impassable for military equipment and wagons. Gen. Joseph E. Johnston decided to run a spur line some six miles from the Orange and Alexandria Railroad at Manassas Junction to a point on the Centreville plateau about one mile south of town and within the fort, crossing Bull Run at

Mitchell's Ford (Hanson 40–41). Although the soldiers started to work on the railroad, slave labor was later brought in to finish the job, releasing the troops for other duties. Local historian Carol Freedman believes that the rail line was in use before the Confederate withdrawal to the Virginia Peninsula in March 1862 (Carol Freedman [Historic Centreville Society], interview by John C. Carter, 10 September 1999).

63. Henry was a slave on the McClellan farm (Carter family letters).

64. "Welkin" is probably a reference to Charles Wesley's carol "Hark! How All the Welkin Rings." "Welkin" is defined by *The American Heritage Dictionary* as "the vault of heaven; sky" (*The American Heritage Dictionary,* 2nd College Edition, s.v. "Welkin").

65. William is probably writing about the action at Doolan's Farm near Falls Church, Virginia, where 30 Union troops of the 30th New York Regiment were taken prisoner along with 120 bushels of "already shucked corn." Four Union soldiers were killed out of a force of fifty by the 2nd Mississippi Cavalry (*OR* 5:437, 439).

66. On December 2, Union pickets were driven in by 200 Confederate cavalry at Annandale on Little River Turnpike. Union losses were one killed and twelve missing; Confederate losses were two killed, seven to eight wounded, and two prisoners (*OR* 5:451–52).

67. Thomas B. Harris was a twenty-two-year-old, married private in Company I, Edward D. Tracy's company, 4th Alabama Regiment. Harris was sick and was sent to the hospital before being discharged on September 10, 1861 (CSR, Thomas B. Harris).

68. George A. Gilbert enlisted in Company F of the 9th Alabama Regiment on June 4, 1861, and was elected first lieutenant. He was slightly wounded at Salem Church and was transferred on May 14, 1863, to Huntsville, Alabama (CSR, George A. Gilbert). Charles S. Trimble was from Franklin County, Alabama, and enrolled in Company F on June 4, 1861. He was absent without leave since December 1861 and listed as a deserter in March 1862 (CSR, Charles S. Trimble).

69. David L. Phillips of Company F was severely wounded at Frayser's Farm on June 30, 1862, and was detailed to the ordnance department on September 1, 1863. He was later detailed to the conscript corps in north Alabama in September 1864, and to the invalid corps on December 12, 1864 (CSR, David L. Phillips).

70. The two soldiers executed were most likely Michael O'Brien and Dennis Corcoran of Company B, Wheat's 1st Special Louisiana Battalion. A marker stands in the cemetery of St. John's Episcopal Church in Centreville which reads, "Michael O'Brien Dennis Corcoran Wheat's 1st Special Battalion CO B Tiger Rifles Executed Dec. 10, 1861 at Centreville Exhumed and reburied Dec. 9, 1979" (author's visit to St. John's Episcopal Church, Centreville, Virginia, August 26, 1995).

71. Columbus, Kentucky, was one of the strong points on the western Confederate line. It protected the Confederate left flank, defended the left flanks of Forts Henry and Donelson, and controlled the Mississippi River. When Gen. Albert Sidney

Johnston abandoned Columbus, and Forts Henry and Donelson fell, the route was then open for the Union army to invade Nashville and then northern Alabama (Hattaway and Jones 67–74, 145–47).

72. The Montgomery council passed a code in 1861 that allowed the killing of dogs that didn't have registered collars and were not under the management of an owner at that time (ADAH).

73. For an ambrotype, the subject stood or sat with his head supported from the rear by a harness while the photographer removed a lens cap for several seconds to expose the plate to the natural light in the room or tent. A glass plate was used as a base for the image instead of the silver plate common in daguerreotypes. A paper or cloth backing was added, and a thin brass plate was folded around the plate. The ambrotype was then placed in a case or pad (Ross G. Kelbaugh, *Introduction to Civil War Photography* [Gettysburg, PA: Thomas Publishing Company, 1991], 15).

74. Capt. William L. Wayland was promoted to assistant quartermaster after being severely wounded at the Battle of Gaines's Mill. He was eventually dropped from the list of officers. After he recuperated, he sought to be reinstated. Although the secretary of war approved Wayland's request, Wayland was unable to come up with his bond in time, and Lt. Nicholas Floyd was put into the position (Capt. Jeremiah Henry Johnston Williams to the Confederate Secretary of War, 1 December 1862, W30WD (National Archives Microfilm Publication M437, roll 115), Letters Received by the Secretary of War). Sgt. Freeman Crenshaw of Company F enlisted on June 4, 1861. Crenshaw was detailed as a nurse at Camp Lee in Richmond in 1862. He was captured at Charles City, Virginia, on July 10, 1862. Crenshaw deserted in August 1864 and was sent to the Old Capitol Prison in Washington, D.C., on August 16, 1864 (CSR, Freeman Crenshaw).

75. This may have been the skirmish that took place on November 20 outside of Fairfax Court House. A Confederate foraging party was looking for corn near Fairfax Court House and was attacked by a Union cavalry squadron with light casualties (report of Capt. William H. Boyd, 1st New York Volunteer Cavalry, in *OR* 5:450). No skirmishes around December 18 were listed.

76. On December 20, a foraging party sent to Dranesville (between Leesburg and Centreville), and escorted by the 10th Alabama Regiment, the 6th South Carolina Regiment, the 1st Kentucky Regiment, the 11th Virginia Regiment, and a detachment of Brig. Gen. James Ewell Brown (or J. E. B.) Stuart's cavalry, were engaged by a large Union force and driven back with fifty-six men killed and sixty-eight wounded (*OR* 5:490–494). Stuart was surprised, according to Capt. John Forney, colonel of the 10th Alabama, "by finding an enemy where he did not expect him" (Axford, *Journals of Thomas Hubbard Hobbs* 250).

77. Pvt. John T. Ezell of Company F enlisted on June 4, 1861, at age eighteen and was discharged in December 1861 (CSR, John T. Ezell).

78. William's "shore nuff Sweetheart in Madison county ala." was probably Susan Strong, the woman he would marry after he returned from the war (Carter family letters).

79. "Jinney Miller" may be Miss Virginia J. Miller, who lived for a while in Leesburg, Virginia, and visited in the Centreville area. She left a diary recounting her stay at the Glenfiddich House in Leesburg and her travels between November 15 and April 17, 1862 (see Virginia J. Miller, "The Diary of Miss Virginia J. Miller, November 15, 1861–April 17, 1862," The Miles/LeHane Group, http://www.mileslehane.com/diary.html [accessed December 2001]).

80. Dr. Robert A. Tweedy lived near the McClellans in Limestone County (Axford, *To Lochaber* 194 n. 74).

81. William Eppa Fielding (1837–1917) was born near Athens, Alabama, and grew up near the McClellan household. He was promoted to sergeant major and later to assistant adjutant of the 9th Alabama Regiment. He was wounded in the eye at Gaines's Mill. Fielding would go home on furlough on January 16, 1865, and would be unable to return to the 9th as the war came to a close. Fielding kept a diary during the war (see Axford, *To Lochaber*). His sister, Mary Fielding, also kept a diary which is published, in part, in Axford's *To Lochaber* (vi, xi, 136).

82. The December 31 date is approximate. William moved into his cabin on January 13, 1862.

83. The Confederacy attempted to contract woodcutters to provide winter quarters for the troops at Centreville, but when that attempt fell through the troops were forced to build their own quarters. A November 2, 1861, memo from Gen. Joseph E. Johnston to adjutant general Samuel Cooper requested that James J. Hunter, who had entered into an agreement to provide wood to build the winter cabins, return to Manassas to complete the job (*OR* 5:896–97, 934). However, a member of Johnston's staff later met with Hunter and informed him that the regiments could take care of the cabins themselves and that his services would not be required (5:941–42).

84. This may refer to the Union raid on Fairfax Station and Dumfries on December 27–29, during which the Union forces were driven back (*OR* 21:708–9).

Chapter 5

1. McMillan 141–45.

2. According to Turner, "no military man seems to have anticipated the difficulties involved in speedily moving the incredible mass of accumulated property over a single-track railroad which had only very limited sidetrack facilities" (131). Col. Lucius Bellingrer Northrop, the commissary general of the Confederacy, noted that "two weeks before [Johnston's] move, he promised my officer, Major Noland, the transportation deemed sufficient and of which he had assumed direct control. Empty trains passed the meat that had been laid in piles ready for shipment. Empty trains lay idle at Manassas for days in spite of Noland's efforts to get them" (132).

3. Livermore 42.

4. Ash 20.

5. Pvt. Francis Marion Cook was a member of Company F of the 9th Alabama

Regiment (CSR, Francis Marion Cook). His brother, Napoleon Bonaparte Cook, also served in Company F (CSR, Napoleon Bonaparte Cook). Both men were schoolteachers from Limestone County; both enlisted on June 4, 1861; and both were paroled at Appomattox (Limestone County, Alabama, 1860 Census 122).

6. Thomas L. Weatherford served as a constable in Limestone County in 1860. He was an officer in Company F and was discharged in January 1862 (Axford, *To Lochaber* 193 n. 64; CSR, Thomas L. Weatherford).

7. Lt. William T. Couch was a thirty-year-old single farmer in Company C. He was wounded at Frayser's Farm and permanently disabled (CSR, William T. Couch). Capt. M. G. May was also from Company C and was discharged on May 18, 1864 (CSR, M. G. May).

8. Berry's Ferry was a crossing point on the Shenandoah River near Ashby Gap in the Blue Ridge. It was along the main road between Winchester and Piedmont Station (John W. Wayland, *Twenty-five Chapters on the Shenandoah Valley* [Harrisonburg, VA: C. J. Carrier, 1989], 53, and 126–27). "Long Green" may be a reference to Green Spring Farm near the intersection of Little River Turnpike and Braddock Road near Annandale (Nan Netherton, Donald Sweig, Janice Artemel, Patricia Hickin, and Patrick Reed, *Fairfax County, Virginia: A History* [Fairfax, VA: Fairfax County Board of Supervisors, 1992], 624–25).

9. As noted earlier, the Lewis House, also called "Portici," was the home of Francis W. Lewis and was located about one mile southeast of the Stone House near Lewis Ford on the Manassas battlefield. As William explains, it served as Gen. Joseph E. Johnston's headquarters during the First Battle of Manassas (W. C. Davis, *Battle at Bull Run* 200).

10. Union major general Ambrose E. Burnside sailed from Hampton Roads, Virginia, on January 11, 1862, heading toward Hatteras Inlet, North Carolina, where he and his men arrived on January 13 (McPherson, *Ordeal by Fire* 177).

11. Emmanuel Tobe Gray was a twenty-two-year-old farmer from Mooresville, Alabama, who was hospitalized at Chimborazo Hospital in Richmond with erysipelas, a streptococcal infection usually stemming from an infection of a wound (Alfred Jay Bollet, *Civil War Medicine: Challenges and Triumphs* [Tucson, AZ: Galen Press, 2002], 201). Gray transferred from the 9th Alabama on April 5, 1862 (CSR, Emmanuel Tobe Gray).

12. On January 19, Brig. Gen. George B. Crittenden of the Confederate army was defeated by Union forces led by Brig. Gen. George H. Thomas on the north bank of the Cumberland River at the Battle of Mill Springs, Kentucky (Hattaway and Jones 62–63). Brig. Gen. Felix Kirk Zollicoffer was a U.S. Congressman before the war. During this battle, Zollicoffer mistakenly rode into a Union regiment and was instantly killed by a volley of fire (Warner, *Generals in Gray* 350).

13. The reference to sixty thousand dollars is unknown.

14. The French family lived near the McClellans, and Trudy may have been one of the daughters of Elisha Kimble French, possibly Mary Prudence French (Limestone County, Alabama, 1850 U.S. Census 83).

15. In January 1862, Col. Roger A. Pryor, a member of the Military Committee

of the Confederate Congress, met with General Beauregard and informed him that he was being transferred in order to assume command of the defense of the Mississippi valley (but only with his consent). Beauregard's supporters contended that he was being transferred due to his conflicts with Gen. Joseph E. Johnston and with Pres. Jefferson Davis (Roman 210–11).

16. Leanderson C. Roden was a private who was later killed at Gaines's Mill.

17. Camp Wildcat was located on the Wilderness Road at the Rockcastle River. It was the site of the battle on October 21, 1861, at which Gen. Felix Kirk Zollicoffer's brigade attacked 7,000 Union troops at the camp on Rockcastle Hills. Zollicoffer was forced to withdraw with fifty-three casualties (*OR* 4:210).

18. This may be Pvt. Amos David who enlisted in Company F on June 4, 1861. He was wounded at Salem Church (CSR, Amos David).

19. With seven gunboats, Adm. Andrew Hull Foote, commander of the Union naval forces on the upper Mississippi River forced the surrender of Fort Henry on the Tennessee River on February 6, 1862 (McPherson, *Ordeal by Fire* 222).

20. Lt. W. C. Murphy of Company A was promoted to captain on April 12, 1862. He was wounded and captured at Williamsburg, and was exchanged on August 5. Murphy was killed at Salem Church on May 3, 1863 (CSR, W. C. Murphy).

21. Judge William Walker of Limestone County married Sally Ryan and had seven children, including Robert Henry Walker, who would marry Robert Anderson McClellan's daughter Memory Pryor McClellan (Edwards and Axford 12).

22. Gen. Gideon Pillow was the second in command at Fort Donelson to Gen. John B. Floyd, and Pillow helped repel the initial Federal assault by Admiral Foote's gunboats on February 14, 1862. The fort surrendered 13,000 men on February 16, but Floyd and Pillow along with 2,500 of their men escaped in boats down the river. The fall of Forts Henry and Donelson effectively opened up the Tennessee River Valley (McPherson, *Ordeal by Fire* 222–25).

23. Jimmie Harris may have been James A. Harris, the thirteen-year-old son of William and Caroline Harris (Limestone County, Alabama, 1860 Census 58).

24. Clement W. Johnson was listed as a fifty-eight-year-old wagon maker who was married with five children in the Limestone County, Alabama, 1860 Census (107).

25. After Forts Henry and Donelson fell, Nashville, Tennessee, was abandoned on February 23. Brig. Gen. Ormsby McKnight Mitchel's Union forces quickly moved into Florence and Huntsville, Alabama (Hattaway and Jones 206).

26. On February 8, Union forces under Maj. Gen. Ambrose E. Burnside (11,500 men) overran Roanoke Island, North Carolina, and forced the surrender of nearly 2,000 Confederate troops. This opened Pamlico Sound as a possible base for Union operations, threatening Richmond from the south (McPherson, *Ordeal by Fire* 177–78). Union casualties were 37 killed, 214 wounded, and 13 missing (*OR*, 9:85). Confederate casualties were 10 killed and 30 wounded (9:158).

27. Daniel Robinson Hundley of Limestone County was colonel of the 34th Alabama Regiment and was captured at Big Springs, Georgia, on July 15, 1864. Hundley kept a prison diary that he published as *Prison Echoes of the Great Rebellion*

(1874), and he authored a historical work titled *Social Relations in Our Southern States* (1860) (Axford, *To Lochaber* 226 n. 10).

28. This was not the 1st Provisional Tennessee Regiment under Col. Peter Turney. The 1st Tennessee Regiment ordered back to Tennessee was the one recognized in Sam Watkins's diary, "CO. Aytch" (Civil War Centennial Commission 1:170–71).

29. Simon Bolivar Buckner was appointed brigadier general on September 14, 1861, and was left by Generals Floyd and Pillow to consummate the surrender of Fort Donelson (Warner, *Generals in Gray* 38).

30. Union general Don Carlos Buell, occupied Nashville, Tennessee, without bloodshed on February 25. Union forces then began moving into northern Alabama near Athens and Decatur (Hattaway and Jones 76, 206; McPherson, *Ordeal by Fire* 225).

31. William Press Tanner was a merchant whose store was burned during John Basil Turchin's occupation of Athens (Limestone County, Alabama, 1860 Census 126; Axford, *To Lochaber* 235 n. 7).

32. It is not known what two men are represented by the initials.

33. Bullpen is a game in which players form a circle with one team on the outside of the ring and the other team inside the ring. Members of the outside ring throw a ball at the inside ring members, and anyone hit with the ball goes outside the ring.

34. John W. McDonald of Company F was wounded at Gaines's Mill and killed a few days later at Frayser's Farm (CSR, John W. McDonald).

35. The two railroads were the Orange and Alexandria Railroad and the Virginia Central Railroad (Turner 134).

36. "Pioneers" were enlisted men who were temporarily transferred into a pioneer corps, which worked on fortification, bridges, and roads. Slaves were often used as well (Katcher 147–48).

37. Gordonsville was an important point on the Virginia Central Railroad where it intersected with the Orange and Alexandria Railroad. This was a major railway to Richmond and a strategic point for covering the approach of Union forces from the north toward Richmond (Turner 37, 134).

38. Montpelier was built by James Madison's father in 1760 and improved over the years by James and Dolly Madison. After James Madison's death, the mansion passed out of the Madison family hands in 1844. During the war, the property was owned by Thomas J. Carson of Baltimore and his brother, Frank, who lived in the home. The cemetery is located on the edge of the property and includes President Madison's grave.

Chapter 6

1. Archibald Gracie, "Gracie's Battalion at Williamsburg in 1862," *Confederate Veteran* 19 (1911): 27. See also Axford, *To Lochaber* 32.

2. Gracie 27. While Company F was on special detail on the Warwick River,

the rest of the regiment was posted near the mouth of College Creek at King's Wharf (Barrett 16).

3. Stephen W. Sears, *To the Gates of Richmond: The Peninsula Campaign* (New York: Ticknor and Fields, 1992), 50.

4. The Confederates were strengthening their position at Dam number 1 behind the Warwick River when they were attacked by Union forces under Gen. William Farrar (Baldy) Smith. Early success by Smith's Vermont Brigade turned into a devastating rout from a Confederate counterattack led by a brigade of Georgians and Louisianans. There were 165 Federal casualties (Sears, *To the Gates of Richmond* 55–56).

5. Barrett 18–19; Earl C. Hastings Jr. and David S. Hastings, *A Pitiless Rain: The Battle of Williamsburg, 1862* (Shippensburg, PA: White Mane Publishing Company, 1997) 63–67.

6. Daniel Harvey Hill was born in York District, South Carolina, on July 12, 1821, and was a graduate of West Point. He served in the Mexican War and was breveted for gallantry. After resigning from the army, he became a college professor. He entered the Confederate service as colonel of the First North Carolina Infantry and was later appointed major general on March 26, 1862 (Warner, *Generals in Gray* 136–37). James Longstreet was born in Edgefield District, South Carolina, on January 8, 1821, and also graduated from West Point. He served in the Mexican War, during which he was twice breveted for gallantry. Longstreet was appointed brigadier general on June 17, 1861, and lieutenant general on October 9, 1862 (Warner, *Generals in Gray* 192).

7. Hastings and Hastings 125.

8. Hastings and Hastings 87.

9. Livermore 80.

10. *OR* 11.1:593.

11. However, Edmund DeWitt Patterson reported 67 casualties for the 9th Alabama in the battle (Barrett 22).

12. Diary of Thomas Hobbs in Axford, *To Lochaber* 35.

13. See Wilcox's report of the Williamsburg campaign in *OR* 11.1:589–93; and Col. Samuel Henry's report on the 9th Alabama in *OR* 11.1:594–95. See also Wilcox's report in *OR*, series 2, 2.1:337–38. According to Gen. Ambrose Powell Hill, "[my brigade] shared with the 9th Alabama the honor of taking eight pieces of artillery" (*OR* 11.1:577–78).

14. Richard Heron Anderson (1821–79),originally from South Carolina, was a West Point graduate and a veteran of the Mexican War. He was commissioned major of infantry at the start of the Civil War and was promoted to brigadier general, commanding Charleston, South Carolina. In early 1862, he was assigned a brigade in Longstreet's division and on July 14, 1862, was appointed major general. After Chancellorsville, he commanded the Third Division (Warner, *Generals in Gray* 8–9).

15. Sears, *To the Gates of Richmond* 93–94.

16. McPherson, *Ordeal by Fire* 239.

17. McPherson, *Ordeal by Fire* 242–43.

18. Livermore 81. According to Wilcox's report on Seven Pines, the brigade moved from Mechanicsville at 6:30 a.m. and onto the Charles City Road to support Maj. Gen. Benjamin Huger's division. They went into the line on the edge of the woods and relieved Anderson's brigade at 10 p.m. (*OR* 11.1:986–89). See also Wilcox's report of March 15, 1868, in *OR Supplement* 1.11:379–80. On June 17, Companies F and D were sent down the Charles City Road on picket duty (Barrett 27).

19. Ambrose Powell (or A.P.) Hill was born in 1825 in Culpeper, Virginia; graduated from West Point; and was a veteran of the Mexican War. He began his service in the Confederacy as colonel of the 30th Virginia Regiment and was appointed brigadier general on February 26, 1862. Hill was appointed major general on May 26, 1862, and served under Thomas Jonathan (Stonewall) Jackson until Jackson's death at Chancellorsville. Hill was appointed lieutenant general on May 24, 1863, and commanded the 3rd Corps at Gettysburg. He was killed when he mistakenly rode into the Union line on April 2, 1865 (Warner, *Generals in Gray* 134–35).

20. For a description of the Battle of Gaines's Mill, see Sears, *To the Gates of Richmond* 210–48. See Maj. Jeremiah Williams, captain of the 9th Alabama, and his article in *Confederate Veteran* 8 (1900): 443–44; and Barrett 28–36.

21. *OR* 11.2:771–75, 980.

22. Sears, *To the Gates of Richmond* 296.

23. *OR* 11.2:775–79. See Barrett 45–60 for an account of the battle by Edmund DeWitt Patterson.

24. *OR* 11.2:980.

25. McPherson, *Ordeal by Fire* 248.

26. President Davis had learned that Union major general Ambrose E. Burnside was off the coast of North Carolina threatening Roanoke Island. Davis agreed to dispatch two brigades from Gen. Theophilus Hunter Holmes's division See Jeffry D. Wert, *General James Longstreet, The Confederacy's Most Controversial Soldier: A Biography* (New York: Simon and Schuster, 1993), 99). Although the 9th Alabama was part of Maj. Gen. Gustavus Woodson Smith's division, it was apparently dispatched to North Carolina along with Holmes's division. By the time the troops reached Weldon, North Carolina, it became clear that General McClellan was advancing up the Virginia Peninsula from Yorktown, and they were quickly recalled.

27. John F. Morris of Company F enlisted on June 4, 1861. He was killed at Gaines's Mill on June 27, 1862 (CSR, John F. Morris). Dan B. Thompson was wounded in the head and leg at Frayser's Farm and died at Chimborazo Hospital of his wounds on July 9, 1862 (CSR, Dan B. Thompson).

28. Green's Landing was apparently located at the confluence of the Warwick and James rivers.

29. Lebanon Church was a crossroads located on the Virginia Peninsula between Skiff's Creek and Yorktown, just west of the Confederate line that was located along the Warwick River (Hastings and Hastings 34).

30. "Minny muskets" refers to rifled muskets that fired minié balls instead of the smoothbore rifles that were more common in the 9th Alabama during the beginning of the war. Many men had brought their own guns from home, and only about 10 percent were armed with modern weapons (Griffith 73–77).

31. Maj. Gen. John Bankhead Magruder reported to the adjutant general that he had 11,000 men, and also 5,000 on line holding back 100,000 of the enemy during the first week on April (*OR* 11.1:405–6).

32. The "news of a great victory" was the report of General Beauregard's success during the first day of the Battle of Shiloh. Gen. Albert Sidney Johnston was initially in command at Shiloh but was killed on the first day and replaced by Beauregard. After the defeat at Shiloh on April 7, General Beauregard withdrew his forces to Corinth, Mississippi (McPherson, *Ordeal by Fire* 226–28). Gen. Don Carlos Buell was not killed.

33. Lord Charles Cornwallis (1738–1805) was commander in chief of the British forces in North America during the American Revolution. The surrender of the British army at Yorktown, Virginia, to the American forces under George Washington effectively ended the war (Thomas H. Johnson, ed., *The Oxford Companion to American History,* [New York: Oxford University Press, 1966], 213–14). Cornwallis was not present at the surrender.

34. Sam Henry Cruse was a private in Company F who enlisted on June 4, 1861, and was killed at Gaines's Mill on June 27, 1862 (CSR, Henry Cruse).

35. On April 16, a skirmish occurred at Dam number 2 and at Dam number 1 (Lee's Mill or Burnt Chimneys). Gracie's battalion was composed of five companies of Wilcox's brigade—one for each regiment—and were posted on Warwick River near its confluence with the James. Lt. John C. Featherston was in charge of Company F, which was supplied by the 9th Alabama (Gracie 27). Union forces under Gen. Baldy Smith attempted a crossing of the Warwick River near Lee's Mill. Intense artillery barrages preceded attacks in the morning and afternoon by the 3rd and 4th Vermont regiments respectively. Both Union attacks were repulsed with close to two hundred Union casualties and seventy-five Confederate (Hastings and Hastings 20–21).

36. E. F. Ragland and Company was located at the corner of Marshall and Third streets in Richmond. The *Richmond City Business Directory of 1860* lists the company as a lumber dealer. Ragland and Brothers is also shown as operating a mercantile store and grocery at Main and Ninth streets. The gentlemen who ran the store were brothers of Pat Ragland of Limestone County, Alabama, who was a business associate and personal friend of Thomas Joyce McClellan.

37. As noted earlier, Emmanuel Tobe Gray was hospitalized at Chimborazo for erysipelas on March 17, 1862, and transferred on April 5, 1862 (CSR, Emmanuel Tobe Gray). Thaddeus L. Gray was a twenty-two-year-old overseer from Limestone County (Limestone County, Alabama, 1860 Census 113). He died in the hospital of measles (CSR, Thaddeus L. Gray).

38. D. W. Gillis replaced Edward A. O'Neal as captain of Company I. He was

mortally wounded at the Battle of Williamsburg and died on May 22, 1862 (CSR, D. W. Gillis).

39. Sterling McDonald was the sixteen-year-old son of Dr. Jonathan McDonald of Limestone County. He was not a member of the 9th Alabama Regiment (Limestone County, Alabama, 1860 Census 111).

40. Leanderson C. Roden enlisted in Company F on June 4, 1861, at Athens, Alabama, and was killed at Gaines's Mill (CSR, L. C. Roden). As noted earlier, John F. Morris of Company F enlisted on June 4, 1861; he was killed at Frayser's Farm on June 27, 1862 (CSR, John F. Morris). As noted earlier, John W. McDonald of Company F was wounded at Gaines's Mill, then killed a few days later at Frayser's Farm (CSR, John W. McDonald). David Bridgeforth was wounded at Gaines's Mill and was later killed at Frayser's Farm (CSR, David Bridgeforth). Sam Henry Cruse enlisted in Company F on June 4, 1861, and died from wounds received at Gaines's Mill (CSR, Henry Cruse). Milton J. Sloan was wounded in the shoulder at Gaines's Mill and died at Chimborazo Hospital on June 30, 1862 (CSR, Milton J. Sloan). Mark Shelton was a member of the 9th Alabama Regiment, Company F; Shelton was wounded at the Battle of Frayser's Farm and died of his wounds (CSR, Mark Shelton). As noted earlier, Sgt. David L. Phillips was wounded at Frayser's Farm on June 30, 1862, and was detailed to conscript duty in north Alabama in September 1864 and detailed to the invalid corps on December 12, 1864 (CSR, D. L. Phillips). Albert Brooks was severely wounded at Frayser's Farm and later was captured at Gettysburg, sent to Fort Delaware, and sent later to Point Lookout Prison (CSR, Albert Brooks).

41. The campsite was probably in the vicinity of Brook Hill, near Brook Church. Brook Church was south of Yellow Tavern and was on the Brook Turnpike, one of the first toll roads in Virginia and the road that Union colonel Judson Kilpatrick used to enter Richmond during his raid on March 1, 1864 (Emory M. Thomas, *The Confederate State of Richmond: A Biography of the Capital* [Baton Rouge: Louisiana State University Press, 1998], 158, 137). A plantation nearby was called "The Brook" or "Brook Hill" (George B. Davis, Leslie J. Perry, and Joseph W. Kirkley, *The Official Military Atlas of the Civil War* [New York: Gramercy Books, 1983] 42).

42. William T. Couch enlisted in Company C, the Pope Walker Guards of Lauderdale County on May 24, 1861. He was wounded and disabled at Frayser's Farm on June 30, 1862. Couch was promoted to captain and was assigned to duty with the invalid corps on February 27, 1865 (CSR, William T. Couch).

43. Maj. Felix Grundy Buchanan's (1838–1907) father, Andrew, was originally from Washington County, Virginia. He moved to Fayetteville, Tennessee, and married Bethia Line White. Although Felix Buchanan grew up in Fayetteville, he attended Emory and Henry College in Emory, Virginia, before the war. Buchanan enlisted in Company B of the 1st Tennessee Provisional Regiment and later commanded Company H; he commanded the regiment when it surrendered at Appomattox. He was wounded several times during the war, including at Gaines's Mill, Gettysburg, and Weldon Railroad. Buchanan married Martha Catherine McClellan

in 1874. His brother Matthew Buchanan (1822–62) served in Company E of the 44th Tennessee Regiment and died on March 12, 1862, in Lincoln County, Tennessee. Another brother, White Buchanan (1818–92), visited the regiment while it was in Northern Virginia (Buchanan-McClellan Papers).

44. Thomas R. Grimes was a sixteen-year-old farmer from St. Stephens, Alabama, who enlisted in Company E of the 11th Alabama Regiment. He was killed at Frayser's Farm (ADAH, Thomas R. Grimes).

45. Joseph Brackeen of Company F enlisted on March 1, 1862. He was wounded at Gaines's Mill and died of his wounds at the First Division Alabama hospital in Richmond on July 13, 1862 (CSR, J. Brackeen). Asa W. Moore enrolled as a private on April 4, 1861, and rose to sergeant. He was wounded at Frayser's Farm on June 30, 1862, and was captured at High Bridge on April 6, 1865. Moore was sent to Point Lookout Prison, where he was paroled on July 17, 1865 (CSR, Asa W. Moore).

46. James W. Brundige was a twenty-two-year-old farmer who was wounded at Frayser's Farm. He served as a courier at Gettysburg and was paroled at Appomattox.

47. On July 2, Robert E. Lee was convinced that George McClellan might attempt to cross the James River and attack Richmond from the southeast. Lee began to reinforce Drewry's Bluff with a division of Maj. Gen. Theophilus Holmes's troops (Sears, *To the Gates of Richmond* 339).

48. The Union army invaded northern Alabama and seized Huntsville in April of 1862. On May 1, the 1st and 2nd Louisiana Cavalry charged through Athens, routing the 18th Ohio Regiment and driving it from town. The Confederate cavalry was itself driven from town the next day by Col. John Basil Turchin's brigade. Turchin allegedly retaliated against the citizens of Athens and allowed his men to plunder the town for nearly two hours, resulting in nearly fifty-four thousand dollars in losses (Robert Dunnavant Jr., *The Railroad War: N. B. Forrest's 1864 Raid through Northern Alabama and Middle Tennessee* [Athens, AL: Pea Ridge Press, 1994], 40). Turchin was a Russian immigrant who settled in Chicago before the war and worked with the Illinois railroad. His brigades were always known for their disregard toward civilians and their property (Warner, *Generals in Blue* 511).

49. William Lebarreare enlisted in Company F on June 4, 1861, and was hospitalized with a disability at Chimborazo Hospital in Richmond in 1862. He was listed as missing since August 25, 1864 (CSR, William Lebarreare).

50. Braxton Bragg was a West point graduate who served in the Mexican War. He rose from brigadier general to major general, and in June 1862 he was named commander of the Army of Tennessee. He did not experience success in leading the Army of Tennessee and was transferred by President Davis to Richmond, where he was responsible for the conduct of Confederate military operations (Warner, *Generals in Gray* 30–31).

51. Complaints to Gen. Don Carlos Buell, commander of the Army of the Ohio, led to the arrest and court-martial of Col. John Basil Turchin for conduct unbecoming an officer. Although convicted by the court, he was promoted to brigadier general and was later returned to duty. As the commanding general, Brig. Gen. Ormsby

MacKnight Mitchel was blamed for allowing Turchin to sack Athens. He was also charged with engaging in the cotton trade for his own profits. General Mitchel resigned his command on July 2, 1862, and went to Washington, D.C., to answer the charges against him. He was later reassigned to a local command at Hilton Head, South Carolina, where he died a few months later from yellow fever (McMillan 147–48). Mitchel was born in Morganfield, Kentucky, in 1809 and graduated from West Point in 1829. While he was appointed a brigadier general in the Army of the Cumberland under General Buell, he saw no action in battle (Warner, *Generals in Blue* 327).

Chapter 7

1. Thomas Hubbard Hobbs's parents were Ira E. Hobbs and Rebecca Maclin Hobbs of Athens, Alabama.

2. These numbers were reported in the September 25, 1862, issue of the *Jacksonville [Alabama] Journal* (McMillan 179).

3. From the Mary Fielding diary, qtd. in Stephen V. Ash, *When the Yankees Came: Conflict and Chaos in the Occupied South, 1861–1865* (Chapel Hill: University of North Carolina Press, 1995), 39. For more on the nature of the Union occupation see Mark Grimsley, *The Hard Hand of War: Union Military Policy toward Southern Civilians, 1861–1865* (Cambridge: Cambridge University Press, 1996).

4. Qtd. in Ash 39. As noted earlier, Mary Fielding was the sister of William Eppa Fielding, who was a member of Company F of the 9th Alabama (Axford, *To Lochaber* vi–vii). She lived about six miles northeast of Athens, Alabama, and near the McClellans.

5. Hattaway and Jones 245–46.

6. Hattaway and Jones 220–23.

7. Hattaway and Jones 228–29.

8. Livermore 89.

9. See Joseph L. Harsh, *Confederate Tide Rising: Robert E. Lee and the Making of Southern Strategy, 1861–1862* (Kent, OH: Kent State University Press, 1998).

10. Harsh 67–71. See also Hattaway and Jones 231–32.

11. Hattaway and Jones 240–43.

12. John M. Priest, *Antietam: The Soldiers' Battle* (Shippensburg, PA: White Mane Publishing Company, 1989).

13. Thomas Joyce McClellan left Athens, Alabama, on July 26 to pay a visit to William. After saying goodbye to William near the beginning of August, Thomas spent more time in Richmond before returning home around August 22. He had received a pass from the Union provost in Athens for the trip (diary of Mary Fielding in Axford, *To Lochaber* 71, 82).

14. During the Second Battle of Manassas, the 9th Alabama Regiment was in Wilcox's brigade of Cadmus Wilcox's division of James Longstreet's corps. Thomas B. Baugh enlisted in Company F on June 4, 1861, and was promoted to corporal,

then to third lieutenant. He was captured on August 18, 1864, outside of Petersburg and sent to Fort Delaware prison (CSR, Thomas B. Baugh). Joseph Horace King, from Morgan County, Alabama, was captain of Company E of the 9th Alabama Regiment and was promoted to colonel on March 19, 1863. He was wounded at Frayser's Farm and later at Gettysburg (Krick, *Lee's Colonels* 223–24).

15. Lee was attempting to turn Pope's flank and cut off his forces at the Rappahannock River, potentially destroying the Union army. Pope discovered the trap and withdrew his forces behind the Rappahannock (John J. Hennessy, *Return to Bull Run: The Campaign and Battle of Second Manassas* [New York: Simon and Schuster, 1994], 48–49).

16. Maj. Gen. James Ewell Brown (or J. E. B.) Stuart was born in Patrick County, Virginia on February 6, 1833. He graduated from West Point and served on the Kansas frontier. Stuart was an aide to Robert E. Lee in the capture of John Brown at Harpers Ferry in 1859. Stuart was known for his exploits, such as his ride around McClellan's army during the Seven Days Battles in 1862 (Warner, *Generals in Gray* 296).

17. On August 22, J. E. B. Stuart raided the Orange and Alexandria Railroad at Catlett Station and Maj. Gen. John Pope's tent. Fitzhugh Lee's troops carried off the general's coat and hat, and Stuart later sent the hat to Gov. John Letcher in Richmond (Emory M. Thomas, *Bold Dragoon: The Life of J. E. B. Stuart* [New York: Harper and Row, Publishers, 1986], 146–47; Freeman, *Lee's Lieutenants* 2:71–72).

18. Bill Wallis and the Blackwells have not been identified.

19. Gordonsville was the site of a camp hospital commanded by Thomas H. Fisher. As Lee moved north, there was less need for the hospital, and the remaining patients may have been moved to private homes (Peter W. Houck, ed., *Confederate Surgeon: The Personal Recollections of E. A. Craighill,* 2nd ed. [Lynchburg, VA: H. E. Howard and Company, 1989], 33, 56).

20. When Gen. John Pope came to Virginia in July 1862, he issued general orders that authorized the arrest of local citizens and partisan rangers who supported the Southern cause and refused to take an oath of allegiance. The Confederate government reacted by declaring that Pope and all of his officers were not entitled to be treated as soldiers and therefore not entitled to be included in the cartel for the exchange of future prisoners of war (William Allan, *Stonewall Jackson, Robert E. Lee, and the Army of Northern Virginia, 1862* [New York: Da Capo Press, 1995], 2:155–59).

21. James E. Bailes was mortally wounded at Frayser's Farm on June 30, 1862, and died on July 8, 1862 (CSR, James E. Bailes). T. J. Foster, from Alabama, was a member of the First Confederate Congress (Thornton 441).

22. While William returned to his regiment after his illness, thousands of other Confederate soldiers who had fallen out of the ranks returned to Lee's army toward the end of the campaign. Lee had expected too much from his army, and it suffered from mass desertion and straggling (Michael A. Palmer, *Lee Moves North: Robert E. Lee on the Offensive* [New York: John Wiley and Sons, 1998], 33–34).

23. James W. Wilson was appointed acting adjutant of Company D on August

22, 1862. He was wounded at Sharpsburg and died of his wounds shortly afterward (CSR, James W. Wilson). James Rayburn from Company K of Marshall County, Alabama, was promoted to captain on September 17, 1862. He was killed at Antietam on September 17, 1862 (CSR, James Rayburn).

24. Thomas M. Smith of Company F was decapitated by a cannon shot at the Battle of Sharpsburg on September 17, 1862 (CSR, Thomas M. Smith).

25. Bunker Hill was twelve miles from Winchester, Virginia (McDonald 86).

26. The Sharpsburg campaign saw the beginnings of the Confederate troops' disaffection with the state of Maryland and its citizens, a disaffection that reached a final break with the Gettysburg campaign. For a discussion of the ebb and flow of Southern sentiment for Maryland, see William A. Blair, "Maryland, Our Maryland," *The Antietam Campaign,* ed. Gary W. Gallagher (Chapel Hill: University of North Carolina Press, 1999), 94–99. For individual Confederates' reactions to the campaign, see Gary W. Gallagher, "The Net Result of the Campaign Was in Our Favor: Confederate Reaction to the Maryland Campaign," in *The Antietam Campaign,* ed. Gary W. Gallagher, 27.

27. Spaulding Cecrops Malone of Company F was wounded at Frayser's Farm, Sharpsburg, and Salem Church. Malone was detailed as a brigade teamster on June 30, 1864, and he was captured at the Wilderness and sent to Elmira prison in New York on August 15, 1864. He escaped by tunneling out on October 7, 1864 (CSR, Spaulding Cecrops Malone). George H. Stuart was a twenty-six-year-old farmer who enlisted in Company F on June 4, 1861 (CSR, George H. Stuart). J. E. Johnson was captured at Savage's Station on June 26, 1862, and sent to Fort Delaware Prison. He was later captured on September 21, 1864, in Knoxville, Tennessee, after deserting (CSR, J. E. Johnson). James D. Tucker of Company F was wounded at Frayser's Farm, Sharpsburg, and Gettysburg. He was captured at Chambersburg, Pennsylvania, where he was left wounded at the hospital, and was sent to Harrisburg, Pennsylvania's West Walnut Street hospital, then to the USA hospital in Baltimore, Maryland (CSR, James D. Tucker). Thomas L. Davison enlisted in Company F on March 10, 1862. He would be captured at Burkeville, Virginia, on April 6, 1865, and sent to Point Lookout Prison (CSR, Thomas L. Davison).

28. The "Bluff at Botellers Mills" was Boteler's Ford, the site at which the Army of Northern Virginia crossed the Potomac River on the evening of September 18, 1862. Union brigadier general Fitz-John Porter sent three divisions across the river only to be met by A. P. Hill and the Light Division, who drove them back across (Gallagher, "The Net Result" 273).

29. The Emancipation Proclamation was issued by President Lincoln on January 1, 1863 (the preliminary announcement had been released on September 22, 1862). Many Confederates saw the proclamation as having a negative effect on the Union and its war effort (Gallagher, "The Net Result" 17).

30. This appears to be Augustus P. Wooley of Company F, who would later desert in 1864 at Petersburg. Before the war, Wooley was a farm laborer in Limestone County (Limestone County, Alabama, 1860 Census 39).

31. While Athens, Alabama, was occupied, many local citizens either showed their true Union colors or changed sides as convenient. Union major general Don Carlos Buell testified before a commission in Cincinnati, Ohio, in 1863 to the strong Union sentiment in occupied northern Alabama and believed "there was a large number of quiet Union men who were anxious to receive the protection of the United States" (*OR* 16.1:481).

32. As he will realize and acknowledge later in this letter, William was in error here in one respect. On October 8, Braxton Bragg faced Don Carlos Buell at Perryville, Kentucky, in a battle that both sides claimed as a tactical victory. Bragg, however, was forced to withdraw to Tennessee, lacking rearward lines of communication (Hattaway and Jones 257–60).

33. Cadmus M. Wilcox was promoted to brigadier general on October 21, 1861, and major general on August 3, 1863 (Warner, *Generals in Gray* 337). Young Lea Royston of Perry County, Alabama, was captain of Company A of the 8th Alabama and was later its colonel (Krick, *Lee's Colonels* 328). Wilcox missed the Sharpsburg campaign due to illness (Patterson 46), and Col. Alfred Cumming led the brigade (Stephen W. Sears, *Landscape Turned Red: The Battle of Antietam* [New Haven: Ticknor and Fields, 1983] 241). Cumming was wounded at Sharpsburg (Warner, *Generals in Gray* 66) and Royston may have been in temporary command of the brigade after the battle, which may have led William to assume he was their new brigade commander. Wilcox returned to duty after the campaign, but he temporarily replaced Richard H. Anderson as division commander while Anderson recovered from his wounds at Sharpsburg (Warner, *Generals in Gray* 49).

34. This was the rebel spy Belle Boyd, who was from Front Royal, Virginia, and brought information on Union troop movements to Stonewall Jackson during the Valley campaign (Boatner 76).

35. One Southern reporter following the Army of Northern Virginia at the end of August estimated that it would have taken forty thousand pairs of shoes to have shod the bare feet of Lee's army (Andrews 199).

36. Frederick J. Batts of Company H was promoted to first sergeant in July 1862 and was killed at Salem Church on May 3, 1863 (CSR, Frederick J. Batts).

37. Clement Claiborne Clay was from Huntsville and the son of former Alabama governor Clement Comer Clay. The younger Clay served as a U.S. senator from 1853 to 1861 and was elected to the first regular Confederate congress in 1861 (*Concise Dictionary of American Biography* 169).

38. Pat Moore may have been Corp. Hezekiah P. Moore of Company F of the 4th Alabama. He was captured while straggling at the Wilderness on May 9, 1864, and was sent to Fort Delaware prison. He was released on May 10, 1865 (CSR, Hezekiah P. Moore). Henry Benjamin Love enlisted in Company F of the 4th on April 26, 1861, and had a finger shot off at Fredericksburg, and was severely wounded in the foot at Spotsylvania. Love later transferred to the 4th Alabama Cavalry (CSR, Henry Benjamin Love). Rufus G. Moore was a nineteen-year-old farmer from Huntsville who enlisted in Company F of the 4th Alabama. He was missing after

the Battle of South Mountain, Maryland, and was listed as a deserter as of June 30, 1863.

39. John Fletcher may have been Dr. John R. Fletcher of Limestone County (Limestone County, Alabama, 1860 Census 100). Lt. Col. Lawrence Houston Scruggs from Jackson County, Alabama, was the captain of Company I, 4th Alabama Regiment. He was wounded in front of Richmond on July 1, 1862 (CSR, Lawrence Houston Scruggs).

40. Gen. Richard H. Anderson was severely wounded during the action in Piper's Orchard at Sharpsburg as he was attempting to position his men alongside those of D. H. Hill (Sears, *Landscape Turned Red* 241).

41. Brig. Gen. John Horace Forney was promoted over Cadmus M. Wilcox to major general on October 27, 1862. Wilcox was later promoted to major general on August 3, 1863, replacing Gen. Dorsey Pender, who was killed in battle (Warner, *Generals in Gray* 91; Douglas Southall Freeman, *Lee's Dispatches: Unpublished Letters of General Robert E. Lee, C.S.A., to Jefferson Davis and the War Department of the Confederate States of America, 1862–65* [Baton Rouge: Louisiana State University Press, 1994], 115–16). As noted earlier, Wilcox had missed the Battle of Sharpsburg due to illness and had been replaced by Col. Alfred Cumming of the 10th Georgia Regiment.

42. For the change in women's roles during the Civil War, see Drew Gilpin Faust's *Mothers of Invention: Women of the Slaveholding South in the American Civil War* and Catherine Clinton and Nina Silber's *Divided Houses: Gender and the Civil War.* (New York: Oxford University Press, 1992).

43. John W. Thompson enlisted in Company F on June 4, 1861, and was wounded in the thigh at Warwick River in 1862. He was sent to Farmville, Virginia's hospital on May 23, 1862, and was detailed to hospital duty. Thompson returned to the regiment in October 1863 but later deserted on March 17, 1865 (CSR, John W. Thompson).

44. W. B. Vaughan enlisted in Company F on February 24, 1862, and was paroled at Appomattox (CSR, W. B. Vaughan). Bertrand (Black Bill) Eagin was wounded at Salem Church and was later captured at Gettysburg and sent to Fort Delaware Prison. He was transferred to Point Lookout Prison and died there of chronic diarrhea on December 12, 1863 (CSR, Bertrand Eagin).

Chapter 8

1. Maurice S. Fortin, ed., "Colonel Hilary A. Herbert's 'History of the Eighth Alabama Volunteer Regiment, C.S.A.'" *Alabama Historical Quarterly* 39.5 (1977).

2. Cleopatra Indiana Cartwright was a sister to Hezekiah John and Matthew Thomas Cartwright, both friends and comrades of William Cowan McClellan.

3. According to Edmund DeWitt Patterson, the 9th was on picket duty between Scott's Dam and the dam at Dr. Taylor's near Bank's Ford on the Rappahannock River (Barrett 84).

4. William had been assigned to the provost guard at Brig. Gen. Richard H. Anderson's divisional headquarters. The duties of the provost included monitoring trains and transportation facilities for deserters and Union spies; checking passes at picket lines; guarding and transporting prisoners of war and Confederate deserters; arresting stragglers and deserters; and in battle, preventing the passing of soldiers to the rear without permission to do so (Kenneth Radley, *Rebel Watchdog: The Confederate States Army Provost Guard* [Baton Rouge: Louisiana State University Press, 1997], 6, 52).

5. On December 18, 1862, Secretary of State William A. Seward offered his resignation to President Lincoln. Secretary of the Treasury Salmon Chase also offered his resignation. Lincoln rejected both resignations (McPherson, *Ordeal by Fire* 306–7).

6. William understated the Confederate losses. Confederate losses were 4,656 killed and wounded, with 653 missing; Union losses were 10,884, with 1,769 missing (Livermore 96).

7. Daniel D. Bidwell was the colonel of the 49th New York Regiment. The regiment had four officers listed as injured and six as captured, but Bidwell was not listed among the casualties (*OR* 21:141).

8. Three Broyles served in Company F: Benjamin F., George W., and Joseph M. (CSR, Benjamin F. Broyles, George W. Broyles, Joseph M. Broyles).

9. While most Confederate soldiers and Southerners basked in the great victory at Fredericksburg, Robert E. Lee had his doubts about the effective outcome of the battle. For a full discussion of the reaction to the Union defeat at Fredericksburg, see Gary W. Gallagher, "The Yanks Have Had a Terrible Whipping, Confederates Evaluate the Battle," *The Fredericksburg Campaign, Decision on the Rappahannock,* ed. Gary W. Gallagher (Chapel Hill: University of North Carolina Press, 1995), 113–41.

10. On December 28, 1862, J. E. B. Stuart led 1,800 troopers on a raid for supplies at Dumfries and at Fairfax Court House. The Confederates suffered one wounded and one missing, and they captured about two hundred men (*OR* 21:731–35).

11. John George Walker was born in Cole County, Missouri, on July 22, 1822. He was commissioned in the United States Army in 1846 and served in the Mexican War. Walker was made brigadier general on January 9, 1862, and major general on November 8, 1862 (Warner, *Generals in Gray* 319–20). Richard Stoddert Ewell was born in Georgetown, D.C., on February 8, 1817, and graduated from West Point in 1840. He was breveted for gallantry in the Mexican War and was commissioned brigadier general in the Confederate provisional army on June 17, 1861. Ewell succeeded Thomas Jonathan (Stonewall) Jackson as lieutenant general on May 23, 1863 (Warner, *Generals in Gray* 84).

12. "Maggie" is probably Maggie Lipscomb, a friend from Limestone County.

13. "Mrs Robinson" may be a family friend from Lincoln County, Tennessee.

14. Col. Samuel Henry of Marshall County, Alabama, had been suspended on May 14, 1862, as charges were brought against him for his conduct during the Battle

of Williamsburg. The officers of the 9th Alabama Regiment had sent a letter to the secretary of war asking for Henry's removal; the privates had sent one asking for his reinstatement. The board of officers who heard the case found Colonel Henry in violation of the fifty-second Article of War—specifically of cowardice—and also of incompetence. For a complete account of the proceedings, see Special Order 11, 11 January 1863, R–111–1863, 111 (National Archives Microfilm Publication M437, roll 108) Letters Received by the Secretary of War. The incident at the Battle of Williamsburg leading to the charges seems to have taken place during the advance of the 9th Alabama, which was on the left of the 19th Mississippi Regiment. Henry was alleged to have hidden behind logs instead of leading his men who were engaged in battle. He had also ordered a retreat when no retreat was called for (Barrett 20–21). Maj. Jeremiah Henry Johnston Williams, commander of Company B, was in command of the regiment during Colonel Henry's absence. Williams himself would also be cashiered in July 1863 and would be replaced by Joseph Horace King of Morgan County, Alabama, the commanding officer of Company E. According to Robert K. Krick, Major Williams's resignation on September 4, 1863, was "accepted with relish" by his superiors (Krick, *Lee's Colonels* 190, 399).

15. In the Battle of Murfreesboro on January 1–2, 1863, also known as Stone's River, both sides attempted to turn the other's right flank, but the Confederates under Braxton Bragg struck first. The Confederate offensive, successful at first, gradually wore out as the Union defenses under Maj. Gen. William Starke Rosecrans stiffened. On January 2, Bragg launched a cautious attack that was inconclusive, and he chose to retreat as his casualties piled up (Hattaway and Jones 320–22).

16. Bragg's defeats in the west were exacerbated by his failure to get along with his subordinates and reports that he was unfit for his command. Men such as Joseph E. Johnston also recognized that Bragg needed more support for his too-weak army (Hattaway and Jones 354).

17. William's comment that "Bragg tells so many lies we do not know whether or not to believe him" should be tempered somewhat by the fact that the Southern press did not always report the facts before them. According to J. Cutler Andrews, "The press exaggerated the size of the enemy's forces, presented a wide range of estimates of the number of Confederate prisoners [taken], and minimized the scope of the disaster to preserve public morale" (131).

18. "Steward" was probably George Stewart of Company F (CSR, George Stewart), and "Holland" was probably Tilman H. Holland of Company F, transferred to Gen. Philip D. Roddy's cavalry in February 1863 (CSR, Tilman H. Holland).

19. Sgt. Tilman A. King of Company F would be seriously wounded in the right shoulder at Salem Church and was sent to the General Hospital at Charlottesville, Virginia, on March 28, 1862 (CSR, Tilman A. King).

20. Joseph Hooker was an 1837 graduate of West Point and had a distinguished career prior to and during the Mexican War. After resigning his commission in 1853, he was out of the army until the start of the Civil War, when he was commissioned a brigadier general of Union volunteers in 1862. He served as an effective combat

officer in charge of a division and later a corps from the Seven Days Battles through the Battle of Fredericksburg. Highly critical of Maj. Gen. Ambrose E. Burnside's efforts at Fredericksburg, his political connections helped to secure his command of the Army of the Potomac after Burnside was relieved (Warner, *Generals in Blue* 234).

21. Secretary of the Navy Stephen R. Mallory placed more hope in getting ironclads from England than in building them in the Confederacy, as they had done with the *Virginia,* which had been rebuilt in Virginia on the frame of an older sailing ship, the *Merrimac.* Pressure from the U.S. government on England and France prevented delivery of the ironclads (E. Merton Coulter, *The Confederate States of America,* vol. 7 of *A History of the South,* ed. Wendell Holmes Stephenson and E. Merton Coulter [Baton Rouge: Louisiana State University Press, 1950], 303).

22. Brunswick County, Virginia, lay along the Virginia–North Carolina border to the southwest of Richmond and Appomattox. William briefly passed through Brunswick County when the 9th was rushed by train to Weldon, North Carolina.

23. Thomas Hill Watts originally opposed secession, but after Lincoln's election he became a secessionist. He served as the Confederate attorney general until 1863, when he was elected governor of Alabama (*Historical Times Illustrated Encyclopedia of the Civil War,* ed. Patricia L. Faust [New York: Harper Perennial, 1991], 808).

Chapter 9

1. Livermore 45.

2. According to Stephen W. Sears, the returns for the Army of Northern Virginia as listed in *OR, The War of the Rebellion* 25.1:172–92 undercounted casualties by nearly 25 percent (Stephen W. Sears, *Chancellorsville* [Boston: Houghton-Mifflin Company, 1996], 475–501). For Wilcox's brigade's casualties, see Sears 493.

3. Edwin B. Coddington, *The Gettysburg Campaign: A Study in Command* (New York: Charles Scribner's Sons, 1984), 74–76.

4. Barrett 111–13.

5. Coddington 316–17. Henry Heth was born in Chesterfield County, Virginia, in 1865. He graduated from West Point in 1847 at the bottom of his class and served on the frontier until the start of the Civil War. He served as colonel of the 48th Virginia Regiment and was appointed brigadier general in 1862. He joined the Army of Northern Virginia in February 1863, when he was assigned a brigade in A. P. Hill's Division (Warner, *Generals in Gray* 133).

6. Harry W. Pfanz, *Gettysburg, the Second Day* (Chapel Hill: University of North Carolina Press, 1987), 351–52.

7. Pfanz 355.

8. Pfanz 363–66.

9. Pfanz 374.

10. Pfanz 410–12.

11. Qtd. in Coddington 425.

12. Gary W. Gallagher, ed., *Fighting for the Confederacy: The Personal Recollections of General Edward Porter Alexander* (Chapel Hill: University of North Carolina Press, 1989), 278–82. Edward Porter Alexander was a West Point graduate who served as chief of artillery for Longstreet's corps at Gettysburg. The support issue at Cemetery Ridge that Alexander described was corroborated by Col. Hilary Abner Herbert of the 8th Alabama Regiment, also a part of the Wilcox Brigade (Fortin 126–29).

13. Report by Cadmus M. Wilcox in *OR* 27.2:620.

14. John W. Busey and David G. Martin, *Regimental Strengths at Gettysburg* (Baltimore: Gateway Press, 1982), 186, 210.

15. No major engagements occurred on this date. The armies were generally inactive due to the snow. In early February, Federal cavalry attempting to burn the Orange and Alexandria Railroad bridge over the Rappahannock River were turned back by Wade Hampton's Confederate brigade. There were other cavalry engagements during February, and the "desperate fight" mentioned by William may be one of them (Edward J. Stackpole, *Chancellorsville: Lee's Greatest Battle* [Harrisburg, PA: Stackpole Company, 1958], 38–39).

16. When Joseph Hooker took over command of the Army of the Potomac in March, he reorganized the cavalry and operated it in a more aggressive manner (Michael C. C. Adams, *Our Masters the Rebels: A Speculation on Union Military Failure in the East, 1861–1865* [Cambridge, MA: Harvard University Press, 1978], 139–40).

17. As noted earlier, Capt. William L. Wayland was promoted to assistant quartermaster after being severely wounded at the Battle of Gaines's Mill. He was eventually dropped from the list of officers. After he recuperated, he sought to be reinstated. Although the secretary of war approved Wayland's request, Wayland was unable to come up with his bond in time, and Lt. Nicholas Floyd was put into the position (Capt. Jeremiah Henry Johnston Williams to the Confederate Secretary of War, 1 December 1862, W30WD [National Archives Microfilm Publication M437, roll 115], Letters Received by the Secretary of War).

18. As Union pressure on the Carolina coast built, two of General Longstreet's divisions, Pickett's and Maj. Gen John Bell Hood's, were dispatched toward Suffolk, Virginia, on February 15 (Wert 228–29).

19. Lafayette McLaws was a West Point graduate who was promoted to major general on May 23, 1862. He was a division commander in Longstreet's corps (Warner, *Generals in Gray* 204).

20. Clement Laird Vallandigham (1820–71) served as a Democratic congressman from Ohio. His strong opposition to all measures for national defense brought him the intense hatred of the Republican party. He was regarded as the leader of the Peace Democrats, or Copperheads. He was arrested and imprisoned for treason, but Lincoln banished him to the Confederacy instead. He escaped the South and went to Ontario, Canada. He returned to Ohio in 1864 and was active in politics, although he never again held office (*Concise Dictionary of American Biography,* ed. Joseph G. E. Hopkins [New York: Charles Scribner's Sons, 1964], 1098–99).

21. Gen. Earl Van Dorn surrounded Federal cavalry and infantry moving from Franklin, Tennessee, toward Spring Hill—the cavalry escaped, but the infantry was forced to surrender after heavy fighting on March 5 (*OR* 15.1:116–18).

22. This was probably Pvt. William Pink Neal of Company F, who was wounded at Gaines's Mill. He died of an unrelated illness on June 24, 1864, at Petersburg (CSR, William Pink Neal).

23. John Beattie McClellan, William's brother, was wounded and lost an arm at the Battle of Murfreesboro. The sender of the letter to which William refers was not identified.

24. The 1860 Limestone County, Alabama, Census shows a Fanny E. Smith living with Henry C. Bibb and Ada H. Smith (54). According to Edwards and Axford, Fannie Bibb was the daughter of Henry C. Bibb and a woman named Ella (204).

25. Wiley R. Webb enlisted in Company F on June 4, 1861. He was admitted to Chimborazo hospital and later to Farmville hospital on July 7, 1862. Webb was killed in the Battle of the Wilderness on May 5, 1864 (CSR, Wiley R. Webb).

26. Robert E. Lee sent General Longstreet to Suffolk, Virginia, on an expedition to gain supplies, as the Confederate forces were experiencing a shortage of food. On April 11, Hood's and Pickett's men crossed the Blackwater River into Suffolk and began what amounted to a siege. Longstreet's forces kept the Union forces occupied as they gathered supplies for the Confederate army. The length of the operation caused Longstreet's forces to miss the Battle of Chancellorsville (Wert 234–39).

27. On April 7 seven Federal ironclads and two other ships under Rear Adm. Samuel Francis Du Pont attacked Fort Sumter in Charleston. The Confederates surrounding the harbor returned fire and damaged all of the Union ships, forcing their withdrawal (Hattaway and Jones 361).

28. On April 27, Maj. Gen. Joseph Hooker moved the Army of the Potomac up the river from Falmouth, Virginia, and began the operation to turn the Confederate left flank and march on to Richmond. While Hooker crossed 70,000 men at Kelly's Ford, he left Maj. Gen. John Sedgwick at Falmouth with 40,000 men (McPherson, *Ordeal by Fire* 320).

29. This appears to be a camp rumor since Longstreet was just arriving in Petersburg, Virginia, on May 5 (Sears, *Chancellorsville* 400–401).

30. Vicksburg, Mississippi, was a strategic point on the Mississippi River in that it controlled the use of the river and kept the Confederacy from being split into two parts. Maj. Gen. Ulysses S. Grant's plan during the past winter was to find a way to turn Vicksburg and capture it for the Union, opening up the Mississippi River. Grant would later lay siege to the city, and it would fall on July 4, 1863 (Hattaway and Jones 342–45).

31. William Mahone (1826–95) was born in Southampton County, Virginia, and graduated from the Virginia Military Institute. He was an engineer of several Virginia railroads and was president and superintendent of the Norfolk and Petersburg Railroad. Starting the war as the colonel of the 6th Virginia Regiment, he was promoted to brigadier on November 16, 1861; and after the Battle of the Crater, he was

promoted to major general (Warner, *Generals in Gray* 208). Brig. Gen. Carnot Posey (1818–63) was named colonel of the 16th Mississippi Regiment in June 1861. He was promoted to brigadier general on November 1, 1862, and led his brigade in Gen. Richard H. Anderson's division of A. P. Hill's 3rd Corps. Posey died on November 13, 1863, of wounds received at the Battle of Chancellorsville (Warner, *Generals in Gray* 244–45).

32. A Napoleon gun was a smoothbore artillery piece that fired a twelve-pound projectile up to a range of 1,680 yards. It was one of the standard pieces used in the army (Philip Katcher, *The Army of Robert E. Lee* [London: Arms and Armour, 1994], 129–31).

33. George Gordon Meade was a graduate of West Point and an engineer. He served in the Mexican War. When the Civil War broke out, he quickly rose from brigadier to corps commander. He commanded the Federal army at Gettysburg but would later be overshadowed by Ulysses S. Grant (Warner, *Generals in Gray* 316–17).

34. On the morning of May 3, Major General Sedgwick and the 6th Corps attacked Gen. Jubal Early at Marye's Heights. Early did not believe the attack was a serious attempt to take the heights or to move on the Plank Road to Chancellorsville. After heavy fighting, the heights were taken and Early was forced out of Fredericksburg. Sedgwick was now in position to advance up the Plank Road and threaten Lee's right flank (Sears, *Chancellorsville* 348–57).

35. The 9th Alabama Regiment was in support of the 8th and 10th Alabama regiments south along the Plank Road. One company of the 9th was posted in the schoolhouse, with Company G in the Salem Church. They faced Brig. Gen. William T. H. (Bully) Brooks's 1st Division (Joseph Bartlett's brigade and Henry Brown's brigade) (Sears, *Chancellorsville* 376–83). The 9th Alabama had twenty-three killed, eighty-nine wounded, and one missing at Salem Church (493). Salem Church still stands alongside Route 3 just west of Fredericksburg. Near it is a marker erected to the 23rd New Jersey Regiment, but with an inscription honoring the Alabama brigade: "To the brave Alabama boys, our opponents on this field of battle, whose memory we honor, this tablet is dedicated" (A. P. Odom, "The Battle of Salem Church," *Confederate Veteran* 16 [1908]: 61). See also George Clark, "Chancellorsville and Salem Church," *Confederate Veteran* 18 (1910): 125–26; and N. B. Hogan, "The Virginia Campaign: A Touching Incident," *Confederate Veteran* 21 (1894): 51.

36. Robert Meneffee enlisted in Company H of the 9th Alabama Regiment on June 10, 1861, and was killed at Salem Church on May 3, 1863 (CSR, Robert Meneffee).

37. James H. Cain of Company H was wounded in the arm and shoulder at Frayser's Farm on June 30, 1862. He would be severely wounded at Salem Church the following May (CSR, James H. Cain).

38. While Jackson's flanking movement was a surprise, the Union army seemed to have adjusted. Lee was not as exuberant over the victory at Chancellorsville—he had suffered nearly 22 percent casualties and the loss of Jackson. He also said after the victory, "I was more depressed than after Fredericksburg; our loss was severe and

again we had gained not one inch of ground and the enemy could not be pursued" (Gary W. Gallagher, "Confederates Evaluate the Battle" 133). See also Gary W. Gallagher, Introduction, *Chancellorsville: The Battle and Its Aftermath,* ed. Gary W. Gallagher (Chapel Hill: University of North Carolina Press, 1996), xi.

39. Robert Emmett Rodes began the war as the colonel of the 5th Alabama Infantry and was later assigned to D. H. Hill's former division. Rodes was appointed major general for his services at Chancellorsville. He was mortally wounded at Winchester on September 19, 1864 (Warner, *Generals in Gray* 263).

40. Nathan Bedford Forrest was a self-made planter and a slave dealer. When the war began, he raised his own mounted battalion and would later be promoted to brigadier general. His cavalry raids and battles made him legendary (Warner, *Generals in Gray* 92–93).

41. Edward Asbury O'Neal began the war as the major of the 9th Alabama Regiment. He was promoted to colonel of the 26th Alabama Regiment in 1862 and was recommended by Lee for promotion to brigadier general on June 6, 1863. The document was never delivered to O'Neal, and Lee recalled his recommendation (Warner, *Generals in Gray* 226).

42. William is correct in suspecting that this was not a Confederate victory. As the Union corps of James B. McPherson and William Tecumseh Sherman advanced on Jackson, Mississippi, on May 14, Joseph E. Johnston ordered the evacuation of troops and supplies, leaving only a small guard behind that was easily overcome (Hattaway and Jones 392–93).

43. This account of Brig. Gen. Nathan Bedford Forrest's activities probably refers to the April 19 raid by Union colonel Abel D. Streight, who led a raiding party from Tuscumbia, Alabama, across the state to Rome, Georgia, in an attempt to cut the railroad. Forrest had moved his cavalry more than one hundred miles in thirty-six hours to reach Tuscumbia, Alabama, and join Gen. Philip D. Rodney in his fight against Streight on April 27–28. By bluff and maneuver, Forrest compelled Streight's 1,500-man force to surrender to his 600 men (McMillan 186–89).

44. Judge Thomas Tyus was the first probate judge for Limestone County, Alabama, serving from 1850 to 1862 (Axford, *To Lochaber* 226 n. 13). Judge Tyus died at home on November 15, 1862, after a two-month illness (97).

45. Maj. Gen. William (Extra Billy) Smith began a postal service in 1834 to Washington, D.C. He received his sobriquet "Extra Billy" from the rapid expansion of his mail service and the resulting extra mail payments. He served in the Virginia senate and a first term as governor. He was colonel of the 49th Virginia and was promoted to major general in 1863 (Warner, *Generals in Gray* 284–85).

46. On May 19, Maj. Gen. John Clifford Pemberton successfully repulsed Maj. Gen. Ulysses S. Grant's first assault on Vicksburg, inflicting one thousand Union casualties. A second assault by Union forces on May 22 also failed (Hattaway and Jones 395).

47. Major General Pemberton's Confederate forces were continuing to hold out against Grant's siege of Vicksburg, Mississippi.

48. During Jackson's Shenandoah Valley campaign, Union general Nathaniel Banks lost so many supplies to the Confederates that he was dubbed "Commissary Banks." See Robert K. Krick, *Stonewall Jackson at Cedar Mountain* (Chapel Hill: University of North Carolina Press, 1990), 48; McPherson, *Ordeal by Fire* 240; and Wayland 367). Port Hudson, Louisiana, under siege by Nathaniel Banks since May 21, would finally fall to the Union on July 9. The report William mentions in his letter of June 11 was in error reporting that Banks was defeated but correct in the success of Edmund Kirby Smith at Milliken's Bend. The Confederates had fortified Port Hudson, above Baton Rouge, because along with Vicksburg, it was a strategic point on the Mississippi River. The Union needed to take it before attempting Vicksburg (Hattaway and Jones 343).

49. Confederate forces were initially successful in attacking the Federal garrison at Milliken's Bend, Louisiana, but were eventually driven back (McPherson, *Ordeal by Fire* 354).

50. Fernando Wood was a leader of Tammany Hall in New York and served as a member of Congress. In January 1861, believing that the Union would be dissolved, he advocated that New York become a free city. He denounced the Civil War and advocated peace, joining forces with Clement L. Vallandigham in 1863 to organize the Peace Democrats (*Concise Dictionary of American Biography* 1243).

51. Col. William Allen Parham was born in Sussex County, Virginia, in 1830 and was a planter with more than one thousand acres. He served as colonel of the 41st Virginia Infantry and was wounded at Malvern Hill (Krick, *Lee's Colonels* 298).

52. Gen. Richard S. Ewell defeated Federal forces under Maj. Gen. Robert Huston Milroy at Winchester on June 15 (Coddington 81–88).

53. "Miller" was probably Pvt. Thomas K. Miller from Madison County, Alabama (CSR, Thomas K. Miller); and "Blake" was likely John R. Blake from Lincoln County, Tennessee. Both served in Company G of the 1st Tennessee Provisional Regiment. Blake was captured at Gettysburg and later deserted in December 1864 (CSR, John R. Blake).

54. The 9th Alabama Regiment followed a similar route to the one it had taken in June, going from Gettysburg back to Hagerstown, Maryland, where the regiment waited for the swollen Potomac River to go down and then crossed at Williamsport, Maryland, on July 13–14 (Coddington 52–53, 548–49, 570).

55. Despite their loss and retreat from Pennsylvania, the Confederate troops were far from demoralized and were capable of continuing the fight. The cavalry and artillery, as well as the infantry, had sufficient resources for one more day's battle or for punishing a pursuing Federal force (Coddington 536). According to A. Wilson Greene, "There can be no greater tribute to the discipline and morale of Lee's soldiers than their steadfastness following the army's most infamous tactical defeat" (A. Wilson Greene, "From Gettysburg to Falling Waters: Meade's Pursuit of Lee," *The Third Day at Gettysburg and Beyond,* ed. Gary W. Gallagher, [Chapel Hill: University of North Carolina Press, 1994], 183).

56. Francis Marion Harvey of Company F was killed near Devil's Den at Get-

tysburg on July 2, 1863 (CSR, Francis Marion Harvey). William Hub Malone was a private in Company F and was killed at Gettysburg on July 3 (CSR, William Hub Malone).

Chapter 10

1. McPherson, *Ordeal by Fire* 337–38.

2. Hattaway and Jones 467.

3. Hattaway and Jones 469–73.

4. Hattaway and Jones 472.

5. Beringer et al. 304.

6. Sanders was listed as brigade commander as late as December 1863 (*OR* 29.2:685). Abner Monroe Perrin was born in South Carolina in 1827 and served in the Mexican War. He served as colonel of the 14th South Carolina Regiment, and was commissioned a brigadier general to rank from September 10, 1863 (Warner, *Generals in Gray* 235). William Dorsey Pender was born in Edgecomb County, North Carolina, in 1834, and graduated from West Point in 1854. He commanded a brigade in A. P. Hill's Division during the Seven Days Battles and was appointed major general just before Gettysburg (Warner, *Generals in Gray* 233).

7. Beringer et al. 309–11.

8. *OR* 36.1:1025.

9. As of September 30, 1863, the 9th Alabama Regiment was in Wilcox's late brigade, commanded by Col. J. C. C. Sanders (8th, 9th, 10th, and 11th Alabama regiments) (*OR* 29.1:400). John Caldwell Calhoun Sanders was born in Tuscaloosa, Alabama, on April 4, 1840, and attended the University of Alabama until he enlisted in the 11th Alabama Regiment, of which he was elected captain. He was commissioned brigadier general on May 31, 1864 (Warner, *Generals in Gray* 268). Ninth Alabama veteran George Clark reported that the 9th Alabama and Perrin's brigade came to the support of Richard S. Ewell's troops in the Bloody Angle (George Clark, "From the Rapidan to Petersburg: Wilcox's Alabama Brigade in That Memorable Campaign," *Confederate Veteran* 17 [1909]: 381–382, 438). Col. James Edmonds Saunders, however, stated that the 9th had remained behind in the defensive works (Saunders 158).

10. For more on the Battle of the Weldon Railroad, see Noah Andre Trudeau, *The Last Citadel: Petersburg, Virginia, June 1864–April 1865* (Baton Rouge: Louisiana State University Press, 1993), 56–80.

11. Trudeau, 117–27, gives an account of the Battle of the Crater. Gen. Bushrod Johnson's report of August 20, 1864, showed that the 18th and 22nd South Carolina regiments suffered 354 casualties (*OR* 50:788–89).

12. Trudeau 158–74. See Robert E. Lee's report of August 22, 1864 (*OR* 42.2: 1194).

13. On October 27, the 9th Alabama Regiment was assigned to Sanders's Brigade in Gen. William Mahone's Division and was ordered to the junction of Cox

and Plank roads near Burgess's Mill to strike Maj. Gen. Winfield Scott Hancock's 2nd Corps. Gen. A. P. Hill then ordered Mahone to attack through the woods intersecting the Boydton Plank Road one-half mile west of Burgess's Mill (Trudeau 237, 243–44).

14. See especially chapter 1, "Popular Will," of Gary W. Gallagher's *The Confederate War: How Popular Will, Nationalism, and Military Strategy Could Not Stave Off Defeat,* (Cambridge, MA: Harvard University Press, 1997). Gallagher, however, believes that the Army of Northern Virginia's morale rallied by the spring of 1864 (Gary W. Gallagher, "Our Hearts Are Full of Hope: The Army of Northern Virginia in the Spring of 1864," *The Wilderness Campaign,* ed. Gary W. Gallagher [Chapel Hill: University of North Carolina Press, 1997], 36–65). Loss of will on the home front is supported by Coulter; and Richard E. Beringer, Herman Hattaway, Archer Jones, and William N. Still Jr., *Why the South Lost the Civil War* (Athens, GA: University of Georgia Press, 1986). See also Fleming 137–42.

15. Peace societies were well-organized, secret, treasonable societies that operated first to oppose secession and Confederate policies, and in the end to disrupt the Confederacy and bring the war to a close. There were organized peace bands throughout the Confederacy, and three well-developed peace societies: the Peace and Constitutional Society in Arkansas; the Order of the Heroes of America in North Carolina, east Tennessee, and southwest Virginia; and the Peace Society in Alabama, Georgia, Mississippi, and Florida (Georgia Lee Tatum, *Disloyalty in the Confederacy* [Lincoln: University of Nebraska Press, 2000], 3–6, 24).

16. *OR* 42.2:1243. The total present for duty would increase to 67,924 by October 31 (*OR* 42.3:1186) and would drop to 60,334 by December 31 (*OR* 42.3: 1362). The Confederacy was successful in replacing its casualties during the last year of the war, but more than half of the troops on the rosters were not present for duty. Even the provost guard had only 229 present for duty out of an aggregate total of 333 on October 31 (*OR* 42.3:1187).

17. Bell Irvin Wiley, *The Road to Appomattox* (Baton Rouge: Louisiana State University Press, 1994), 64. Wiley is typical of early historians who believed that Confederate morale fell after Gettysburg and remained low for almost a year. According to Gary Gallagher, however, optimism still pervaded the army; see Gallagher, "Our Hearts Are Full of Hope" 36–59. The letters of the troops also indicated a high level of optimism that Robert E. Lee would defeat Ulysses S. Grant in battle, and that independence was not far away. In late 1864, along with failing morale at home, soldiers' needs at the front led to increasing negative feelings. According to J. Tracy Power, many Confederate soldiers believed that the Confederate government was neglecting their needs as there were shortages of food, lack of good clothing and shoes, and few furloughs (J. Tracy Power, *Lee's Miserables: Life in the Army of Northern Virginia from the Wilderness to Appomattox* [Chapel Hill: University of North Carolina Press, 1998], 180–83). Confederate morale at the front continually changed as factors at home and on the battlefield affected their feelings and hope for the future.

18. The Battle of Chickamauga began on September 18. Longstreet's forces went into line opposing Maj. Gen. William Starke Rosecrans. It was eventually a Confederate victory, but the Union defense under Maj. Gen. George Henry Thomas prevented Braxton Bragg from following up on that victory (Hattaway and Jones 446–54).

19. Despite the increasing desertions, more men were returning to the ranks who had been absent since the Battle of Gettysburg. In addition, units were reenlisting for the duration of the war, and conscripts were filling the holes in the ranks (Power 3–4).

20. Lee and Davis were known for their leniency in dealing with deserters. Even as late as 1864, Lee suspended the death sentences of some of the deserting soldiers: those of extreme youth and those who showed previous gallantry in battle or good character (Freeman, *Lee's Dispatches* 149–58).

21. General Order 82 was an act of the Confederate congress of November 3, 1862, which dealt mainly with raising troops and conscripts and not with furloughs (*OR* series 4, 2:160–68). General Order 1 of January 1, 1862, authorized leave to be granted according to the distance of each volunteer from his home (*OR* series 4, 1:825–26).

22. According to Bell Irvin Wiley, "The matter of furloughs was a tremendous source of discontent. Any request . . . had to run a long gauntlet of approvals and frequently action came only after months of delay and . . . they were frequently refused" (*The Life of Johnny Reb* 139).

23. Camp Chase was a Union prison located west of Columbus, Ohio (Mark Mayo Boatner III, The Civil War Dictionary [New York: David McKay Company, 1961], 117). John McClellan rode with local partisan rangers after losing his arm in the Battle of Murfreesboro. William may be referring to the former brigade of Gen. William Nelson, who served in Don Carlos Buell's Army of the Ohio. Nelson, however, was killed by a fellow Union officer in September 1862 (Warner, *Generals in Gray* 343–44).

24. Roger Atkinson Pryor rose to command a brigade during the Sharpsburg campaign. His brigade was disbanded due to heavy losses in November 1862. Pryor resigned his commission after he could not obtain another command despite repeated promises from Lee. He took on independent scouting and intelligence duties under the command of Gen. Fitzhugh Lee (Warner, *Generals in Gray* 247–48).

25. During the Battle of Chancellorsville, Maj. Gen. Joseph Hooker was leaning on a pillar in the central doorway at the Chancellor House, his headquarters, when a shell struck nearby him and momentarily stunned him (Sears, *Chancellorsville* 336–37).

26. Richard Stoddert Ewell lost a leg at the Second Battle of Manassas and was later equipped with a wooden leg (Warner, *Generals in Gray* 85). Ewell's death was just a rumor.

27. On November 26, General Meade launched the Mine Run offensive as he crossed the Rapidan River and attempted to turn Lee's right flank. After heavy

skirmishing, Meade gave up his effort and recrossed the Rapidan. About the same time in the west, Gen. Braxton Bragg was badly defeated at Chattanooga, and Longstreet failed in his attempt to take Knoxville (Hattaway and Jones 460–62, 474, 478).

28. Daniel Harvey Hill was an outspoken critic of Maj. Gen. Braxton Bragg, the commander of the Army of Tennessee. On October 4, Hill, Gen. Simon Bolivar Buckner, and Longstreet met to prepare a petition to Jefferson Davis for Bragg's removal from command. The petition was telegraphed to Davis, who, after much investigation, supported Bragg. Hill was relieved of command, and Davis consented to it (Wert 326–29).

29. Pvt. Robert C. Deal of Company F, a married farmer, deserted September 27, 1863 (CSR, Robert C. Deal).

30. Pvt. John A. J. Boyd was in Company K of the 8th Alabama Regiment (CSR, John A. J. Boyd).

31. William's long-awaited furlough began around Christmas Day, and he returned to camp thirty days later. Most furloughs were for thirty days, a time limit that was a hardship for the Alabama soldiers. It took William nearly a week to return to Richmond from Alabama. To alleviate the rising problem of desertion, Robert E. Lee had initiated a system of furloughs on August 17, 1863—one per one hundred men present for duty (*OR* 29.2:650).

32. This was probably James Allison, who was a trustee of the Cumberland Presbyterian Church at Mooresville, Alabama (Edwards and Axford 226).

33. What William refers to is probably the 3rd Division under Gen. Rutherford B. Hayes crossing the Rapidan River on February 6 and being stopped by heavy Confederate artillery fire and Richard Ewell's infantry. Robert Rodes's and Edward Johnson's divisions were in Richard Ewell's 2nd Corps (*OR* 33: 114, 118, 141).

34. This was probably Maj. Thomas H. Gilbert of Limestone County who was formerly the captain of Company B of the 26th-50th Alabama Regiment. Gilbert was slightly wounded at the Battle of Shiloh on April 6, 1862, and he would later resign his commission on October 14, 1863 (CSR, Thomas H. Gilbert).

35. In a symbolic effort, the 9th Alabama Regiment reenlisted on February 10, 1864, at Orange Court House and was announced by the Congress of the Confederate States of America in a joint resolution on February 16, 1864 (*OR* 33:1182). The Confederate congress passed a joint resolution of thanks to the 9th Alabama.

36. The food supply for the 9th Alabama Regiment seemed to be good throughout 1864. On August 11, 1864, William Eppa Fielding would write from Fredericksburg that "vegetables and fruits are now getting to be plentiful, though at the most exorbitant rates" (Axford, *To Lochaber* 126).

37. On April 12, Maj. Gen. Nathan Bedford Forrest's cavalry captured Fort Pillow on the Mississippi River in Tennessee. Union casualties were 331 out of the 557 troops in the garrison. Nearly half of the troops were black. The Federal commander, William F. Bradford, claimed that Forrest's troops had continued to shoot Union troops after they surrendered, and it became known as the "Fort Pillow Mas-

sacre." Forrest claimed the soldiers who were shot were still resisting (Emory M. Thomas, *The Confederate Nation, 1861–1865,* [New York: Harper Torchbooks, 1979], 275).

38. Robert Frederick Hoke was born in Lincolnton, North Carolina, on May 27, 1837. He was promoted to brigadier general in January 1863 and sent to North Carolina, where he helped to capture the Federal garrison at Plymouth (Warner, *Generals in Gray* 140).

39. On April 8, Nathaniel Banks was defeated by Gen. Richard Taylor (part of Edmund Kirby Smith's command) at Sabine Crossroads, about forty miles south of Shreveport, Louisiana. This ended the Red River campaign that President Lincoln had ordered to invade Texas (McPherson, *Ordeal by Fire* 412–13).

40. On February 28, Brig. Gen. Hugh Judson Kilpatrick of the Union cavalry raided Richmond with 3,500 men hoping to free Union prisoners of war held there. On March 1, he was turned back by Confederate forces. Union colonel Ulrich Dahlgren, who had become separated from the main force, was killed in an ambush set by Fitzhugh Lee. Later it was claimed that papers found on his body had involved him in a plot to assassinate President Davis (Hattaway and Jones 505–6).

41. A "sink," or "sinkhole," is a natural depression in a land surface communicating with a subterranean passage (*The American Heritage Dictionary* s.v. "sinkhole").

42. Jeremiah Henry Johnston Williams briefly commanded the 9th Alabama after Col. Samuel Henry was suspended. After an examining board found him unfit to command the regiment, he resigned on September 4, 1863. The 9th Alabama Regiment then came under the command of Capt. J. Horace King and was placed in Brig. Gen. Abner M. Perrin's brigade (8th, 9th, 10th, 11th, and 14th Alabama regiments). Brigadier General Perrin would be killed in action on May 12 at Spotsylvania Court House (*OR,* 36 [1]:1030).

43. This probably refers to Brig. Gen. Glenville Mellen Dodge's 8,000-man force that left Corinth, Mississippi, in April to support Col. Abel D. Streight's raid into central Alabama (McMillan 186). William assumed incorrectly that Dodge's force was moving to reinforce Chattanooga.

44. During the Wilderness campaign of May 4–6 and the Spotsylvania campaign of May 8–21, the soldiers had little time to write, and those who did, according to J. Tracy Power, "were vague and imprecise . . . most simply provided an outline of what happened" (Power 41–42).

45. The 9th Alabama Regiment would soon leave Richmond and would arrive at Petersburg on June 18 and go into the breastworks.

46. Jennie Davis married Col. Jessee P. Phillips *after* the war (Axford, *To Lochaber* 227 n. 22).

47. Maj. Gen. John Bell Hood was defeated at Atlanta on July 22, not at Nashville. Hood's Army of Tennessee would be effectively destroyed at Nashville on December 16, 1864 (McPherson, *Ordeal by Fire* 434–35, 466).

48. This would include the Battles of the Wilderness and Spotsylvania, North Anna, Cold Harbor, Petersburg, and the Crater.

49. Grant crossed the James River near Drewry's Bluff on June 16. The Wilcox Brigade moved to Chaffin's Bluff and then to Petersburg on June 18. According to Power, "Most of the confidence in the Army of Northern Virginia came from the soldiers' belief that Lee had the situation in hand" (Power 87).

50. On June 15 and 16, Benjamin Butler led Union forces in an attack on Petersburg, Virginia, from the southeast at Bermuda Hundred. P. G. T. Beauregard's small force of 2,500 troops combined with civilians fought off 15,000 Federal troops until reinforcements arrived. Lee was forced to pull in troops from all around Richmond at Petersburg, including the 9th Alabama (Power 81).

51. Grant attempted to envelop Petersburg toward the Southside Railroad by driving against the Petersburg and Weldon Railroad on June 22. Mahone employed three brigades, including Sanders's brigade, to meet the Union 2nd Corps's advance. Wilcox's division also participated. The 2nd Corps folded under the Confederate attack with 2,392 casualties, as compared with 421 for Mahone's division and 151 for Wilcox's (Trudeau 56–80).

52. Gen. Wade Hampton was born in Charleston, South Carolina, in 1818 and was one of the largest landowners in the South. He served in the South Carolina legislature and organized the Hampton Legion, becoming its colonel. He succeeded J. E. B. Stuart as commander of the Army of Northern Virginia's cavalry corps after Stuart's death at Yellow Tavern. Hampton was effective in keeping the Union cavalry at bay around Richmond and Petersburg until the winter of 1864 (Warner, *Generals in Gray* 122).

53. The attack by the Alabama brigade under Col. J. C. C. Sanders at the Battle of the Crater began at 11 a.m. on July 30, 1864, with 628 men attacking from a ravine northeast of the crater. By 3:25 p.m. the crater was resecured (Trudeau 122–24). The Alabama brigade was in Mahone's Division of A. P. Hill's corps and had been just north of the mine when it exploded before sunrise on July 30 (*OR* 42.2:1212–17). See Nicholas J. Floyd's article "Concerning the Battle of the Crater," *Confederate Veteran* 16 (1908): 159; also B. F. Phillips's article, "Wilcox's Alabamians in Virginia," *Confederate Veteran* 15 (1907): 490. According to Capt. John C. Featherston of the 9th Alabama, Sanders's Alabama brigade took 89 casualties and Mahone's Division took 498 (John C. Featherston, "The Battle of the Crater as I Saw It," *Confederate Veteran* 14 [1906]: 24, 108).

54. Brig. Gen. William Francis Bartlett had lost a leg at Yorktown in 1862 while captain of the 20th Massachusetts (Sears, *To the Gates of Richmond* 50). During the Battle of the Crater, a shell had smashed his cork leg, making it impossible for him to move; and thus he was captured (Trudeau 123–24). Bartlett was the commander of the 1st Brigade of Gen. James Ledlie's 1st Division of Burnside's 9th Corps (*OR* 40:536–37). The 51st regiment mentioned may refer to the 51st Pennsylvania.

55. Brig. Gen. Victor Jean Baptiste Girardy was born in France on June 26, 1837; and he immigrated to Georgia in his youth. He was on the division staff of General Mahone in May 1864 and was promoted to brigadier general for his outstanding

performance during the Battle of the Crater. He was killed at the Battle of Fussell's Mill on August 16, 1864, while leading his troops (Warner, *Generals in Gray* 105–6).

56. Lt. Richard B. Fuller of Company H enlisted on June 10, 1861, and was wounded at Frayser's Farm. He took twenty-five men of the 9th Alabama Regiment with him when he deserted (CSR, Richard B. Fuller).

57. On August 15, the 9th Alabama Regiment was moved by train from Petersburg toward Richmond. The regiment disembarked and marched across the James River on a pontoon bridge near Drewry's Bluff. They went into position east of the Darbytown Road. The 9th stayed at or near this position until November 1, when they were sent a half-mile toward the rear for a few days (diary of William Eppa Fielding in Axford, *To Lochaber* 127, 131).

58. Trudeau 68–80. The Weldon Railroad linked Richmond with the Deep South, and it was a key transportation route with connections to the other Southern railroads. Grant was attempting to envelop Petersburg and to cut off the city from its last southern railroad connection. Grant had spent the entire summer forcing Lee further back toward Richmond and Petersburg, and he planned to turn that line by the fall (Hattaway and Jones 332). Mahone's and Wilcox's divisions halted and drove back Maj. Gen. John Gibbon's 2nd Corps along the Jerusalem Plank Road on June 22 (Trudeau 79–80).

59. On August 13, Federal forces crossed the James River in a demonstration that lasted through August 20. The Federals were probing Confederate positions and at the same time diverting attention away from Petersburg. The fighting William is describing took place at Deep Bottom and Fussell's Mill on August 17–18 (Trudeau 158–60).

60. William Eppa Fielding of the 9th Alabama identified the ten men from Company F as Pvt. Thomas W. Adkins, who was wounded at Salem Church (CSR, Thomas W. Adkins); Augustus T. Wooley, an eighteen-year-old farm laborer from Athens (Limestone County, Alabama, 1860 Census 39); Pvt. William S. Andrews, a twenty-seven-year-old farmer who was wounded at Sharpsburg and Salem Church (CSR, William S. Andrews); Pvt. E. H. Hughey, a thirty-two-year-old farmer from Athens, who deserted August 10, 1864 (ADAH, E. H. Hughey); Pvt. B. Rufus Hughey, a twenty-one-year-old farmer from Athens, who deserted August 10, 1864 (ADAH, B. Rufus Hughey); Pvt. Thomas L. Greeson, who was wounded at Frayser's Farm, (CSR, Thomas L. Greeson); Pvt. Joseph Evans, a twenty-four-year-old single farmer from Athens (CSR, Joseph Evans); Pvt. J. E. Johnson, who was captured at Gaines's Mill, deserted August 10, 1864, and was recaptured September 21, 1864, in Knoxville, Tennessee (CSR, J. E. Johnson); Pvt. R. Johnson (not identified); and Pvt. James M. Horn, a twenty-one-year-old farmer who was wounded at Frayser's Farm (CSR and ADAH, James M. Horn). See Axford, *To Lochaber* 127). The August 12 desertion of Lieutenant Fuller and the twenty-five men of the 9th Alabama Regiment was brought to the attention of the secretary of war, James A. Seddon, by Robert E. Lee on August 14: "General [A. P.] Hill reports, on the 12th instant, the

desertion of a lieutenant and twenty-four men from the 9th Alabama Regiment . . . the troops are suffering much discomfort in the trenches, which may in part account for these desertions . . . In the Ninth Alabama from which there have been numerous desertions, it is said that the dismissal, last winter, of a favorite officer [Maj. Jeremiah Henry Johnston Williams] gave great dissatisfaction. The deserters are supposed to be making their way home with the intention of joining some cavalry commands that are being organized in Alabama, as I am informed" (*OR* 42.2:1175–76).

61. A "freebooter" was a person who pillaged and plundered (*The American Heritage Dictionary* s.v. "freebooter"). A "jayhawker" was a free-soil guerrilla in Kansas and Missouri during the border conflicts of 1857–59 (*The American Heritage Dictionary* s.v. "jayhawker").

62. Mahone's Division had 360 officers and 4,120 men present for duty on September 10, 1864, out of 15,258 aggregate present and absent (*OR* 42.2:1243). The division was positioned near the center of the Confederate line.

63. J. C. C. Sanders was killed on August 21, 1864, in one of the engagements on the Weldon Railroad. He was shot through both thighs and bled to death (Warner, *Generals in Gray* 268).

64. George McClellan ran unsuccessfully as a Democrat in attempting to unseat the incumbent, Abraham Lincoln. Democrats and Southerners had hoped that the popularity of the former general and the discontent of the war would give them the victory. The Copperheads influenced Democrats to adapt a platform for immediate cessation of hostilities and the restoration of peace. The Copperheads were a group of mostly Northern Democrats who turned against the North (like the snake that strikes without warning). The Secret Order of the Golden Circle was largely composed of Peace Democrats such as Clement L. Vallandigham (Johnson 212).

65. William Joseph Hardee was born in Camden County, Georgia, in 1815. He graduated from West Point in 1838 and was breveted for gallantry in the Mexican War. He served as commandant of cadets at West Point and wrote the standard book on military tactics, *Rifle and Light Infantry Tactics.* Hardee served as a lieutenant general commanding a corps at Chattanooga, and he served under Johnston at Atlanta. Toward the end of the war, he opposed Sherman's forces in Georgia and South Carolina (Warner, *Generals in Gray* 124).

66. Federal cavalry under Gen. George Stoneman conducted a raid from Atlanta toward Macon, Georgia, on July 26–27. Stoneman was captured along with 950 of his men (OR 38.3:632–33).

67. A deserter from the 9th Alabama Regiment interrogated at Union army headquarters in late 1864 reported that there were only eighty-seven muskets in the regiment, and not more than six hundred in Sanders's brigade, with an average of no more than eight hundred per brigade (*OR* 42.2:683–84).

68. Andrew McWilliams was a private in Company F and was slightly wounded at Salem Church. He was later killed at the Battle of the Crater on July 30, 1864 (CSR, Andrew McWilliams). Tandy W. Lewis enlisted on June 4, 1861, and became

a wagon master in February 1863. He was killed in front of Petersburg in July 1864 (CSR, Tandy W. Lewis). William Pink Neal died from disease at Petersburg on June 24, 1864 (CSR, William Pink Neal).

69. On September 19, Union general Philip Sheridan opened the Battle of Winchester (Opequon Creek) with an attack on Jubal Early's main line. The Confederates were outnumbered 38,000 to 17,000 (Livermore 127) and, despite a stubborn resistance, were driven from the field and south to Fisher's Hill, about twenty miles away near Strasburg, Virginia. On September 22, Sheridan's forces drove Early from Fisher's Hill southward and almost out of the Shenandoah Valley. Union casualties were more than 5,000, but Confederate casualties were proportionally higher with 3,600 killed, wounded, and missing (*OR* 43.1:554–55).

70. These were all members of the 4th Alabama Regiment. Pvt. Robert D. Tribble of Company F enlisted as a nineteen-year-old farmer, was wounded at Gettysburg and at the Wilderness, and was paroled at Appomattox (CSR, Robert D. Tribble). Lt. Robert N. Hughes of Company F enlisted as a twenty-four-year-old teacher and would be paroled at Appomattox (CSR, Robert N. Hughes). Sgt. Allen V. Walls enlisted in Company F as a twenty-four-year-old salesman and was paroled at Appomattox (CSR, Allen V. Walls). Pvt. John R. Hawkins of Company I was wounded in the shoulder at the First Battle of Manassas and served with the provost guard after June 12, 1863 (CSR, John R. Hawkins). Dock White may be Pvt. Sandy White of Company F, who was an eighteen-year-old student and was wounded at Gettysburg. Pvt. James G. Cochran of Company H was a lawyer, who was hospitalized with typhoid fever early in the war but returned to the company and was paroled at Appomattox (CSR, James G. Cochran). "Wilson" could be Pvt. John Wilson of Company E, who was wounded in Richmond on March 5, 1865, and was paroled at Appomattox (CSR, John Wilson).

71. This was only a camp rumor.

72. Gen. Joseph Wheeler conducted a cavalry raid between August 10 and September 9 on the Federal rail and communications lines in north Georgia and east Tennessee (Dunnavant, *The Railroad War* 31; *OR* 44: 408–12). Wheeler also pursued William Tecumseh Sherman's forces on their march to the sea. There was little chance that Wheeler could have done much damage to Sherman's troops, especially as those forces were screened by Brig. Gen. Hugh Judson Kilptrick's cavalry (Warner, *Generals in Blue* 296).

73. Gen. Nathan Bedford Forrest was in northern Alabama heading for Tennessee on September 20. His forces skirmished with Union troops on September 23 and he captured the town the next day. On September 25 Forrest took the Sulphur Branch Trestle north of Athens (Dunnavant, *Historic Limestone County* 87).

74. On October 19, Jubal Early struck the Federal encampment at Cedar Creek, Virginia, near Belle Grove; captured the Union position; and then attacked the 6th Corps commanded by Gen. Horatio Wright. Gen. Philip Sheridan had been in Washington and had arrived in Winchester in time to hear of the disaster. He ar-

rived on the battlefield in time to rally the Union forces and to drive Early back with nearly three thousand casualties (Hattaway and Jones 619–20; Livermore 130). Union losses were 5,665 (*OR* 43.1:137).

75. After the capture of Athens, and the battle at Sulphur Branch Trestle, Forrest moved northward toward Pulaski, Tennessee, and raided in Lincoln, Giles, and Moore counties before returning south (*OR* 39.1:542–49; Dunnavant, *The Railroad War* 121–34).

Chapter 11

1. *OR* 46.1:384.

2. Trudeau 420. Much of the change in Lee's army was due to desertion. Confederate reports for a ten-day period ending March 8, 1865, show that A. P. Hill's 3rd Corps lost 337 men to desertion—96 of those from Mahone's Division (*OR* 46.21:1292). The month before, Hill's corps had lost 586 to desertion with 83 from Mahone's Division (*OR* 46.2:1265). While most historians agree that the Army of Northern Virginia was suffering from a decreasing supply of manpower that eventually led to the army's demise, Steven H. Newton's *Lost for the Cause: The Confederate Army in 1864* refutes this premise.

3. Union assistant surgeon Samuel Adams placed Confederate casualties at 2,149 (*OR* 46:321). Confederate losses have been estimated by others at 4,000 (Trudeau 353).

4. See the chapter "I Have Ordered a General Assault along the Lines" in Trudeau's *The Last Citadel.*

5. Diary of Mary Fielding in Axford, *To Lochaber* 152.

6. McMillan 404–7.

7. Robert Anderson McClellan to Thomas Joyce McClellan, 15 March 1865. McClellan, Robert A. Papers.

8. Black 227–28, 282–85.

9. Glanders is a contagious and destructive disease in horses caused by bacteria. Horses exhibit lesions which later become ulcers (G. C. Ulett, A. Leakey, N. Ketheesan, and R. G. Hirst. "The Role of Macrophages in the Pathogenesis of Melioidosis," presented at the Australian Immunology Society Conference, Perth, 1997, http://www.capsid.jou.edu.clu/micro/publicatlconfpres/uleasi97.htm).

10. These papers were not found.

11. This is the last-known letter written by William Cowan McClellan during the war. In just over a week, Richmond would fall and Gen. Robert E. Lee's army would begin its march to Appomattox Court House.

12. Calkins, *The Appomattox Campaign* 97–111, 202.

13. Calkins, *The Appomattox Campaign* 116–17.

14. *Compiled Service Records of Confederate Soldiers Who Served in Organizations from the State of Alabama,* 9th Infantry, (National Archives Microfilm Publication M311FC 29–7, roll 187). According to Col. Hilary Abner Herbert of the 8th Ala-

bama, two companies of the 9th Alabama were posted at High Bridge with orders to burn it after the Confederate retreat (Fortin 186–87).

15. *Selected Records of the War Department Related to Prisoners of War, 1861–1865* (National Archives Microfilm Publication M598, 10–31–8, roll 115, 481).

16. *Compiled Records Showing Service of Military Units in Confederate Organizations*, 9th Alabama (National Archives Microfilm Publication M861, 10–31–5).

17. Seven of the men died while in prison at Point Lookout in Maryland: John Yeldell of Company G, who was wounded at Fraser's Farm and captured at Gettysburg (CSR, John Yeldell); Thomas Rambo of Company H, who was wounded at Gaines's Mill and Salem Church and captured at Gettysburg (CSR, Thomas Rambo); J. G. Harmond of Company F who was captured at Gettysburg (CSR, J. G. Harmond); Bertrand (Black Jack) Eagin of Company F, captured at Gettysburg (CSR, Bertrand Eagin); C. J. Fuller of Company C who was captured at Gettysburg; D. Bullock of Company G who was wounded at Gaines's Mill (CSR, D. Bullock); and Sgt. Sam Booth of Company H who was captured at Gettysburg (CSR, Sam Booth) (Edwin W. Beitzel, *Point Lookout Prison Camp for Confederates* [St. Mary's, MD: St. Mary's County Historical Society, 1972], 123–75).

18. Christopher M. Calkins, *The Final Bivouac: The Surrender Parade at Appomattox and the Disbanding of the Armies, April 10–May 20, 1865* (Lynchburg, VA: H. E. Howard, 1988), 71.

19. Beitzel 19.

20. Diary of Luther Hopkins in Beitzel 89.

21. Beitzel 122.

Epilogue

1. Qtd. in Walker 129.

Bibliography

Unpublished Sources

Manuscript Collections

Alabama Department of Archives and History. Alabama Civil War Service Cards File in the Alabama Civil War Service Database. Montgomery, AL.

Buchanan-McClellan Papers, 1816–1917. Accession #1850. Manuscript Department. Southern Historical Collection. Library of the University of North Carolina at Chapel Hill.

Compiled Records Showing Service of Military Units in Confederate Organizations. Alabama, roll 2. War Department Collection of Confederate Records. Record Group 109. National Archives Building. Washington, D.C.

Compiled Service Records of Confederate Soldiers Who Served in Organizations from the State of Alabama. War Department Collection of Confederate Records. Record Group 109, M311. National Archives Building. Washington, D.C.

Confederate States Army Casualties: List and Narrative Reports 1861–1865. War Department Collection of Confederate Records. Record Group 109. National Archives Building. Washington, D.C.

Herbert, Hilary A. Papers. Southern Historical Collection. Library of the University of North Carolina at Chapel Hill.

Letters Received by the Confederate Adjutant and Inspector General, 1861–1865. War Department Collection of Confederate Records. Record Group 109. National Archives Building. Washington, D.C.

Letters Received by the Secretary of War, 1861–1865. War Department Collection of Confederate Records. Record Group 109. National Archives Building. Washington, D.C.

Mahone, William. Papers. Library of Virginia, Richmond, Virginia.

McClellan. Family Letters. Carter family. Tullahoma, Tennessee.

McClellan. Family Papers. George Smith Houston House and Library. Athens, Alabama.

McClellan. Family Papers. Limestone County Archives. Athens, Alabama.

McClellan, Robert Anderson. Papers. Special Collections. Duke University Library. Durham, North Carolina.

McClellan, Thomas Joyce. Papers. Alabama Department of Archives and History. Montgomery, Alabama.

Selected Records of the War Department Related to Confederate Prisoners of War 1861–1865. M598. War Department Collection of Confederate Records, Record Group 109. National Archives Building, Washington, D.C.

Wilcox, Cadmus. Papers. Manuscript Division. Library of Congress. Washington, D.C.

Published Sources

Books, Articles, Pamphlets

Adams, Michael C. C. *Our Masters the Rebels: A Speculation on Union Military Failure in the East, 1861–1865.* Cambridge, MA: Harvard University Press, 1978.

Allan, William. *Stonewall Jackson, Robert E. Lee, and the Army of Northern Virginia, 1862.* 2 vols. 1880 and 1892. Reprint in 1 vol., New York: Da Capo Press, 1995.

Andrews, J. Cutler. *The South Reports the Civil War.* 1970. Reprint, Pittsburgh: University of Pittsburgh Press, 1985.

Ash, Stephen V. *When the Yankees Came: Conflict and Chaos in the Occupied South, 1861–1865.* Chapel Hill: University of North Carolina Press, 1995.

Axford, Faye Acton, ed. *The Journals of Thomas Hubbard Hobbs.* Tuscaloosa: University of Alabama Press, 1976.

———. *To Lochaber Na Mair: Southerners View the Civil War.* Athens, AL: Athens Publishing Company, 1986.

Barrett, John G., ed. *Yankee Rebel: The Civil War Journal of Edmund DeWitt Patterson.* Chapel Hill: University of North Carolina Press, 1966.

Beitzell, Edwin W. *Point Lookout Prison Camp for Confederates.* St. Mary's, MD: St Mary's County Historical Society, 1972.

Beringer, Richard E., Herman Hattaway, Archer Jones, and William N. Still Jr. *Why the South Lost the Civil War.* Athens, GA: University of Georgia Press, 1986.

Black, Robert C., III. *The Railroads of the Confederacy.* 1952. Reprint, Chapel Hill: University of North Carolina Press, 1998.

Blair, William A. "Maryland, Our Maryland." *The Antietam Campaign.* Ed. Gary W. Gallagher. Chapel Hill: University of North Carolina Press, 1999. 74–100.

Boatner, Mark Mayo, III. *The Civil War Dictionary.* 1959. Reprint, New York: David McKay Company, 1961.

Bollet, Alfred Jay. *Civil War Medicine: Challenges and Triumphs.* Tucson, AZ: Galen Press, 2002.

Bright, Eric W. "Nothing to Fear from the Influence of Foreigners: The Patriotism of Richmond's German-Americans during the Civil War." Master's thesis, Virginia Polytechnic Institute and State University, 1999.

Brock, R. A. *The Appomattox Roster: A List of the Paroles of the Army of Northern Virginia issued at Appomattox Court House on April 9, 1865.* 1887. Reprint, New York: Antiquarian Press, 1962.

Busey, John W., and David G. Martin. *Regimental Strengths at Gettysburg.* Baltimore: Gateway Press, 1982.

Calkins, Christopher M. *The Appomattox Campaign: March 29–April 9, 1865.* Conshohocken, PA: Combined Books, 1997.

———. *The Final Bivouac: The Surrender Parade at Appomattox and the Disbanding of the Armies, April 10–May 20, 1865.* Lynchburg, VA: H. E. Howard, 1988.

———. *From Petersburg to Appomattox: A Tour Guide of the Routes of Lee's Withdrawal and Grant's Pursuit.* Farmville, VA: *Farmville Herald,* 1993.

Civil War Centennial Commission. *Tennesseans in the Civil War: A Military History of Confederate and Union Units with Available Rosters of Personnel.* Vol. 1. Nashville, TN: Civil War Centennial Commission, 1964.

Clark, George. "Chancellorsville and Salem Church." *Confederate Veteran* 18 (1910).

Clinton, Catherine, and Nina Silber, eds. *Divided Houses: Gender and the Civil War.* New York: Oxford University Press, 1992.

Coco, Gregory A. *The Civil War Infantryman: In Camp, on the March, and in Battle.* Gettysburg, PA: Thomas Publications, 1996.

Coddington, Edwin B. *The Gettysburg Campaign: A Study in Command.* 1968. Reprint, New York: Charles Scribner's Sons, 1984.

Concise Dictionary of American Biography. Ed. Joseph G. E. Hopkins. New York: Charles Scribner's Sons, 1964.

Coulter, E. Merton. *The Confederate States of America.* Vol. 7 of *A History of the South.* Ed. Wendell Holmes Stephenson and E. Merton Coulter. Baton Rouge: Louisiana State University Press, 1950.

Crofts, Daniel W. *Reluctant Confederates: Upper South Unionists in the Secession Crisis.* Chapel Hill: University of North Carolina Press, 1989.

Cunningham, H. H. *Doctors in Gray: The Confederate Medical Service.* 1958. Reprint, Baton Rouge: Louisiana State University Press, 1993.

Davis, Burke. *To Appomattox: Nine April Days, 1865.* New York: Rinehart and Company, 1959.

Davis, George B., Leslie J. Perry, and Joseph W. Kirkley. *The Official Military Atlas of the Civil War.* New York: Gramercy Books, 1983.

Davis, Jefferson. *The Rise and Fall of the Confederate Government.* 2 vols. 1938. New York: Garrett and Massie. Reprint, New York: Da Capo Press, 1990.

Davis, William C. *Battle at Bull Run: A History of the First Major Campaign of the Civil War.* New York: Doubleday and Company, 1977.

———. *A Government of Our Own: The Making of the Confederacy.* 1994. Reprint, Baton Rouge: Louisiana State University Press, 1997.

———. *Jefferson Davis: The Man and His Hour.* 1991. Reprint, Baton Rouge: Louisiana State University Press, 1996.

Denman, Clarence Phillips. *The Secession Movement in Alabama.* Montgomery: Alabama State Department of Archives and History, 1933.

Dunnavant, Robert, Jr. *Historic Limestone County Alabama.* Athens, AL: Pea Ridge Press, 1995.

———. *The Railroad War: N. B. Forrest's 1864 Raid through Northern Alabama and Middle Tennessee.* Athens, AL: Pea Ridge Press, 1994.

Dupre, Daniel S. *Transforming the Cotton Frontier: Madison County, Alabama, 1800–1840.* Baton Rouge: Louisiana State University Press, 1997.

Eaton, Clement. *A History of the Southern Confederacy.* New York: Free Press / MacMillan Company, 1954.

———. *The Mind of the Old South.* 1964. Reprint, Baton Rouge: Louisiana State University Press, 1991.

Edwards, Chris, and Faye Acton Axford. *The Lure and Lore of Limestone County.* Tuscaloosa, AL: Portals Press, 1978.

Evans, Clement A., ed. *Alabama and Mississippi.* Vol. 12 of *Confederate Military History.* 1899. Reprint, The Blue and Gray Press, n.d.

Faust, Drew Gilpin. "Confederate Women and Narratives of War." *Divided Houses, Gender and the Civil War.* Ed. Catherine Clinton and Nina Silber. New York: Oxford University Press, 1992.

———. *Mothers of Invention: Women of the Slaveholding South in the American Civil War.* New York: Vintage Books, 1997.

Featherston, John C. "The Battle of the Crater as I Saw It." *Confederate Veteran* 14 (1906).

Fischer, David Hackett. *Liberty and Freedom: A Visual History of America's Founding Ideas.* New York: Oxford University Press, 2005.

Fisher, Noel C. *War at Every Door: Partisan Politics and Guerilla Violence in East Tennessee, 1860–1869.* Chapel Hill: University of North Carolina Press, 1997.

Fleming, Walter L. *Civil War and Reconstruction in Alabama.* 1905. Reprint, Gloucester, MA: Peter Smith, 1949.

Floyd, Nicholas J. "Concerning the Battle of the Crater." *Confederate Veteran* 16 (1908).

Ford, Lacy K., Jr. *Origins of Southern Radicalism: The South Carolina Upcountry, 1800–1860.* 1988. Reprint, New York: Oxford University Press, 1991.

Fortin, Maurice S., ed. "Colonel Hilary A. Herbert's 'History of the Eighth Alabama Volunteer Regiment, C.S.A.'" *Alabama Historical Quarterly* 39.5 (1977).

Frank, Joseph Allan. *With Ballot and Bayonet: The Political Socialization of American Civil War Soldiers.* Athens, GA: University of Georgia Press, 1998.

Freedman, Carol (Historic Centreville Society). Interview by John C. Carter. 10 September 1999.

Freeman, Douglas Southall. *Lee's Lieutenants: A Study in Command.* 3 vols. 1942. Reprint, New York: Charles Scribner's Sons, 1944.

———, ed. *Lee's Dispatches: Unpublished Letters of General Robert E. Lee, C.S.A., to Jefferson Davis and the War Department of the Confederate States of America, 1862–65.* Baton Rouge: Louisiana State University Press, 1994.

Gallagher, Gary W. *The Confederate War: How Popular Will, Nationalism, and Military Strategy Could Not Stave Off Defeat.* Cambridge, MA: Harvard University Press, 1997.

———. "Confederates Evaluate the Battle." *The Fredericksburg Campaign, Decision on the Rappahannock.* Ed. Gary W. Gallagher. Chapel Hill: University of North Carolina Press, 1995.

——. Introduction. *Chancellorsville: The Battle and Its Aftermath.* Ed. Gary W. Gallagher. Chapel Hill: University of North Carolina Press, 1996.

——. "The Net Result of the Campaign Was in Our Favor: Confederate Reaction to the Maryland Campaign." *The Antietam Campaign.* Ed. Gary W. Gallagher. Chapel Hill: University of North Carolina Press, 1999.

——. "Our Hearts Are Full of Hope: The Army of Northern Virginia in the Spring of 1864." *The Wilderness Campaign.* Ed. Gary W. Gallagher. Chapel Hill: University of North Carolina Press, 1997.

——. "The Yanks Have Had a Terrible Whipping, Confederates Evaluate the Battle." *The Fredericksburg Campaign, Decision on the Rappahannock.* Ed. Gary W. Gallagher. Chapel Hill: University of North Carolina Press, 1995. 113–41.

——, ed. *The Antietam Campaign.* Chapel Hill: University of North Carolina Press, 1999.

——, ed. *Chancellorsville: The Battle and Its Aftermath.* Chapel Hill: University of North Carolina Press, 1996.

——, ed. *Fighting for the Confederacy: The Personal Recollections of General Edward Porter Alexander.* Chapel Hill: University of North Carolina Press, 1989.

——, ed. *The Fredericksburg Campaign: Decision on the Rappahannock.* Chapel Hill: University of North Carolina Press, 1995.

——, ed. *The Third Day at Gettysburg and Beyond.* Chapel Hill: University of North Carolina Press, 1994.

——, ed. *The Wilderness Campaign.* Chapel Hill: University of North Carolina Press, 1997.

Gilham, William. *Manual of Instruction for the Volunteers and Militia of the Confederate States.* Baltimore: Cushings and Bailey, 1861.

Gracie, Archibald. "Gracie's Battalion at Williamsburg in 1862." *Confederate Veteran* 19 (1911).

Greene, A. Wilson. "From Gettysburg to Falling Waters: Meade's Pursuit of Lee." *The Third Day at Gettysburg and Beyond.* Ed. Gary W. Gallagher. Chapel Hill: University of North Carolina Press, 1994.

Griffith, Paddy. *Battle Tactics of the Civil War.* 1989. Reprint, New Haven: Yale University Press, 2001.

Grimsley, Mark. *The Hard Hand of War: Union Military Policy toward Southern Civilians, 1861–1865.* Cambridge: Cambridge University Press, 1995.

Hanson, Joseph Mills. *Bull Run Remembers . . . The History, Traditions, and Landmarks of the Manassas (Bull Run) Campaigns before Washington, 1861–1862.* 1951. Reprint, Prince William, VA: Prince William County Historical Commission, 1991.

Harsh, Joseph L. *Confederate Tide Rising: Robert E. Lee and the Making of Southern Strategy, 1861–1862.* Kent, OH: Kent State University Press, 1998.

Hastings, Earl C., Jr., and David S. Hastings. *A Pitiless Rain: The Battle of Williamsburg, 1862.* Shippensburg, PA: White Mane Publishing Company, 1997.

Hattaway, Herman, and Archer Jones. *How the North Won: A Military History of the Civil War.* Urbana: University of Illinois Press, 1983.

Hennessy, John J. *Return to Bull Run: The Campaign and Battle of Second Manassas.* 1993. Reprint, New York: Simon and Schuster, 1994.

Hewett, Janet B., ed. *The Roster of Confederate Soldiers, 1861–1865.* Wilmington, NC: Broadfoot Publishing Company, 1996.

Historical Times Illustrated Encyclopedia of the Civil War. Ed. Patricia L. Faust. New York: Harper Perennial, 1991.

Hogan, N. B. "The Virginia Campaign: A Touching Incident." *Confederate Veteran* 21 (1894).

Holien, Kim Bernard. *Battle at Ball's Bluff: Leesburg, Virginia October 21, 1861.* 1985. Reprint, Rapidan Press, 1989.

Houck, Peter W., ed. *Confederate Surgeon: The Personal Recollections of E. A. Craighill.* 2nd ed. Lynchburg, VA: H. E. Howard and Company, 1989.

Jimerson, Randall C. *The Private Civil War: Popular Thought during the Sectional Conflict.* 1988. Reprint, Baton Rouge: Louisiana State University Press, 1994.

Johnson, Robert Underwood, and Clarence Clough Buel, eds. *Battles and Leaders of the Civil War.* 4 vols. Seacacus, NJ: Castle, n.d.

Johnson, Thomas H., ed. *The Oxford Companion to American History.* New York: Oxford University Press, 1966.

Johnston, Joseph E. *Narrative of Military Operations during the Civil War.* 1874. Reprint, New York: Da Capo Press, 1990.

Jordan, Donaldson, and Edwin J. Pratt. *Europe and the American Civil War.* New York: Octagon Books, 1969.

Katcher, Philip. *The Army of Robert E. Lee.* London: Arms and Armour, 1994.

Kelbaugh, Ross G. *Introduction to Civil War Photography.* Gettysburg, PA: Thomas Publishing Company, 1991.

Krick, Robert K. *Lee's Colonels: A Biographical Register of the Field Officers of the Army of Northern Virginia.* Dayton, OH: Morningside, 1992.

———. *Stonewall Jackson at Cedar Mountain.* Chapel Hill: University of North Carolina Press, 1990.

Leech, Margaret. *Reveille in Washington, 1860–1865.* Garden City, NY: Garden City Publishing Company, 1941.

Limestone County, Alabama, 1850 U.S. Census

Limestone County, Alabama, 1860 Census.

Linderman, Gerald F. *Embattled Courage: The Experience of Combat in the American Civil War.* New York: Free Press, 1987.

Livermore, Thomas L. *Numbers and Losses in the Civil War in America, 1861–65.* 1900. Reprint, Civil War Centennial Series no. 10. Dayton, OH: Morningside, 1986.

Madison County, Alabama, 1860 Census.

McCarthy, Carlton. *Detailed Minutiae of Soldier Life in the Army of Northern Virginia, 1861–1865.* 1882. Reprint, Lincoln: University of Nebraska Press, 1993.

McClellan, Robert Anderson. "Early History of Limestone County." Published in *Athens Post* (June 1881).

McDonald, Archie P., ed. *Make Me a Map of the Valley: The Civil War Journal of Stonewall Jackson's Topographer.* By Jedediah Hotchkiss. Dallas: Southern Methodist University Press, 1989.

McMillan, Malcolm C., ed. *The Alabama Confederate Reader.* 1963. Reprint, Tuscaloosa: University of Alabama Press, 1992.

McPherson, James M. *For Cause and Comrades: Why Men Fought in the Civil War.* New York: Oxford University Press, 1997.

———. *Ordeal by Fire: The Civil War and Reconstruction.* New York: Alfred A. Knopf, 1982.

———. *What They Fought For, 1861–1865.* Baton Rouge: Louisiana State University Press, 1994.

Miller, Virginia J. "The Diary of Miss Virginia J. Miller, November 15, 1861–April 17, 1862." The Miles/LeHane Group, http://www.mileslehane.com/diary.html (accessed December 2001).

Mitchell, Reid. *Civil War Soldiers: Their Expectations and Experiences.* New York: Viking Penguin, 1988.

Netherton, Nan, Donald Sweig, Janice Artemel, Patricia Hickin, and Patrick Reed. *Fairfax County, Virginia: A History.* 1978. Reprint, Fairfax, VA: Fairfax County Board of Supervisors, 1992.

Newton, Steven H. *Lost for the Cause: The Confederate Army in 1864.* Mason City, IA: Savas Publishing Company, 2000.

Odom, A. P. "The Battle of Salem Church." *Confederate Veteran* 16 (1908): 61.

Owen, Thomas McAdory. *History of Alabama and Dictionary of Alabama Biography.* 4 vols. 1921. Reprint, Spartanburg, SC: The Reprint Company Publishers, 1978.

Palmer, Michael A. *Lee Moves North: Robert E. Lee on the Offensive.* New York: John Wiley and Sons, 1998.

Parker, Price. *From Alabama to Appomattox: History of the Ninth Infantry.* Athens, AL: Athens News Courier, 1970.

Patterson, Gerard A. *From Blue to Gray: The Life of Confederate General Cadmus M. Wilcox.* Mechanicsburg, PA: Stackpole Books, 2001.

Pfanz, Harry W. *Gettysburg, the Second Day.* Chapel Hill: University of North Carolina Press, 1987.

Phillips, B. F. "Wilcox's Alabamians in Virginia." *Confederate Veteran* 15 (1907).

Power, J. Tracy. *Lee's Miserables: Life in the Army of Northern Virginia from the Wilderness to Appomattox.* Chapel Hill: University of North Carolina Press, 1998.

Priest, John M. *Antietam: The Soldiers' Battle.* Shippensburg, PA: White Mane Publishing Company, 1989.

Radley, Kenneth. *Rebel Watchdog: The Confederate States Army Provost Guard.* Baton Rouge: Louisiana State University Press, 1997.

Reyer, Philip. *The Heritage of Limestone County, Alabama.* Clanton, AL: Heritage Publishing Consultants, 1998.

Robertson, James I., Jr. *Stonewall Jackson: The Man, the Soldier, the Legend.* New York: Macmillan Press, 1997.

Roman, Alfred. *The Military Operations of General Beauregard in the War between the States, 1861 to 1865.* 2 vols. 1884. Reprint, New York: Da Capo Press, 1994.

Saunders, Col. James Edmonds. *Early Settlers of Alabama.* 1899. Reprint, Baltimore: Genealogical Publishing Company, 1969.

Sears, Stephen W. *Chancellorsville.* Boston: Houghton-Mifflin Company, 1996.

———. *Landscape Turned Red: The Battle of Antietam.* New Haven: Ticknor and Fields, 1983.

———. *To the Gates of Richmond: The Peninsula Campaign.* New York: Ticknor and Fields, 1992.

Sibley, F. Ray, Jr. *The Confederate Order of Battle: The Army of Northern Virginia.* Vol. 1. Shippensburg, PA: White Mane Publishing Company, 1996.

Sifakis, Stewart. *Compendium of the Confederate Armies—Alabama.* New York: Facts on File, 1992.

Smith, B. Eugenia. *Centreville Virginia: Its History and Architecture.* Fairfax, VA: Fairfax County Office of Planning, 1973.

Snow, William P. *Lee and His Generals.* 1867. Reprint, New York: Fairfax Press, 1982.

Stackpole, Edward J. *Chancellorsville: Lee's Greatest Battle.* Harrisburg, PA: Stackpole Company, 1958.

Stocker, Jeffrey D., ed. *From Huntsville to Appomattox: R. T. Coles's History of 4th Regiment, Alabama Volunteer Infantry, C.S.A., Army of Northern Virginia.* Knoxville: University of Tennessee Press, 1996.

Storey, Margaret M. *Loyalty and Loss: Alabama's Unionists in the Civil War and Reconstruction.* Baton Rouge: Louisiana State University Press, 2004.

Stowe, Steven M. *Intimacy and Power in the Old South: Ritual in the Lives of the Planters.* Baltimore: Johns Hopkins University Press, 1987.

Supplement to the Official Records of the Union and Confederate Armies, Part II, *Record of Events.* Vol. 1, Alabama. Ed. Janet B. Hewett. Wilmington, NC: Broadfoot Publishing Company, 1994.

Sutherland, Daniel E. *Seasons of War: The Ordeal of a Confederate Community, 1861–1865.* New York: Free Press, 1995.

Tatum, Georgia Lee. *Disloyalty in the Confederacy.* Lincoln: University of Nebraska Press, 2000.

Templeman, Eleanor Lee. *Arlington Heritage: Vignettes of a Virginia County.* Arlington: privately published, 1959.

Thomas, Emory M. *Bold Dragoon: The Life of J. E. B. Stuart.* New York: Harper and Row 1986.

———. *The Confederate Nation, 1861–1865.* New York: Harper Torchbooks, 1979.

———. *The Confederate State of Richmond: A Biography of the Capital.* 1971. Reprint, Baton Rouge: Louisiana State University Press, 1998.

Thornton, J. Mills, III. *Politics and Power in a Slave Society: Alabama, 1800–1860.* Baton Rouge: Louisiana State University Press, 1978.

Tolley, Capt. W. P. "Mrs. F. G. Buchanan." *Confederate Veteran* [1894].

Trudeau, Noah Andre. *The Last Citadel: Petersburg, Virginia, June 1864–April 1865.* 1991. Reprint, Baton Rouge: Louisiana State University Press, 1993.

Turner, George Edgar. *Victory Rode the Rails: The Strategic Place of the Railroads in the Civil War.* 1953. Reprint, Lincoln: University of Nebraska Press, 1992.

Ulett, G. C., A. Leakey, N. Ketheesan, and R. G. Hirst. "The Role of Macrophages in the Pathogenesis of Melioidosis." Presented at the Australian Immunology Society Conference, Perth, 1997. http://www.capsid.jou.edu.clu/micro/publicatlconfpres/uleasi97.htm.

Wagner, Margaret E., Gary W. Gallagher, and Paul Finkelman, eds. *The Library of Congress Civil War Desk Reference.* New York: Simon and Schuster, 2002.

Walker, Robert Henry. *A History of Limestone County.* Athens, AL: Limestone County Commission, 1973.

———. *Legendary Limestone: Its Colorful Character and Events.* Athens, AL: Limestone County Commission, 1966.

The War of the Rebellion: A Compilation of the Official Records of the Union and Confederate Armies. Ed. Col. Robert N. Scott. 128 vols. 1880–1901. Reprint, Ann Arbor, MI: Historical Times, 1985.

Warner, Ezra J. *Generals in Blue: Lives of the Union Commanders.* 1964. Reprint, Baton Rouge: Louisiana State University Press, 1992.

———. *Generals in Gray: Lives of the Confederate Commanders.* 1959. Reprint, Baton Rouge: Louisiana State University Press, 1997.

Wayland, John W. *Twenty-five Chapters on the Shenandoah Valley.* 1957. Reprint, Harrisonburg, VA: C. J. Carrier, 1989.

Wert, Jeffry D. *General James Longstreet, The Confederacy's Most Controversial Soldier: A Biography.* New York: Simon and Schuster, 1993.

Wiley, Bell Irvin. *The Life of Johnny Reb, The Common Soldier of the Confederacy.* Indianapolis: Bobbs-Merrill Company, 1943.

———. *The Road to Appomattox.* 1956. Reprint in paperback, Baton Rouge: Louisiana State University Press, 1994.

Wills, Mary Alice. *The Confederate Blockade of Washington, D.C., 1861–1862.* 1975. Shippensburg, PA: Burd Street Press, 1998.

Wright, R. W. "Richmond since the War." *Scribner's Monthly Magazine* 14.3 (July 1877).

Index

www.ingramcontent.com/pod-product-compliance
Lightning Source LLC
LaVergne TN
LVHW050555110926
847619LV00018B/63